MAP OF PROPOSED YOSEMITE
NATIONAL PARK REGION

By John Muir, 1890

{green} Yosemite Grant.

{pink}   Watershed of the Yosemite streams.

{blue}   Desirable limits of the National Park.

JOHN MUIR AND THE SIERRA CLUB

JOHN MUIR
and the
SIERRA CLUB

The Battle for Yosemite

By HOLWAY R. JONES

SIERRA CLUB   *San Francisco*

Publisher's Note: The book is set in Benedictine Book, Garamond and Caslon by Kingsport Press Inc., Kingsport, Tennessee. It is printed on Warren's Olde style and Mead's White Printflex Offset Enamel and bound in Holliston Roxite by Kingsport Press. The design is by Gary Gore.

The Sierra Club, founded in 1892 by John Muir, has devoted itself to the study and protection of national scenic resources, particularly those of mountain regions. All Sierra Club publications are part of the nonprofit effort the club carries on as a public trust. The club is affiliated with the International Union for Conservation, the Natural Resources Council of America, and the Federation of Western Outdoor Clubs. There are chapters in California, the Pacific Northwest, the Great Basin, the Rocky Mountains, the Southwest, the Great Lakes region, and on the Atlantic seaboard. Participation is invited in the program to enjoy and preserve wilderness, wildlife, forests, and streams. *Address: Mills Tower, San Francisco; 25 West 45 Street, New York; 712 Dupont Circle Building, Washington, D.C.*

TO WILLIAM E. COLBY

(1875–1964)

*—and to all others who believe
enough in natural beauty and the
wilderness experience to work
devotedly toward their preservation.*

Contents

APPENDICES

MAPS

ILLUSTRATIONS

Foreword

WHAT WAS most significant about the fight for Yosemite National Park was that it occurred at all and, in the climatic Hetch Hetchy controversy of 1913, that it became a major national issue. One hundred or even fifty years before, a similar proposal to build a dam in a wilderness valley would not have occasioned the slightest ripple of public protest. Traditional American assumptions about the role of wild country did not include reserving it in national parks for its recreational, esthetic, and inspirational values. The emphasis was all the other way, on civilizing wilderness in the name of prosperity and progress.

Beneath this dominant attitude, however, a contrary set of ideas slowly gained prominence. So far as it offered solitude, mystery, and a chance to escape the boredom of civilized life, wilderness—or more exactly the idea of wilderness—appealed to romantics. Primitivists went a step further and asserted that life was best and man noblest apart from civilization. Exponents of natural theology, notably the transcendentalists Ralph Waldo Emerson and Henry David Thoreau, maintained that wild country, as "pure" nature, most perfectly manifested the existence and the excellencies of God. In addition, cultural nationalists contended that wilderness constituted a distinctive and valuable characteristic of the new nation, which artists and writers would do well to take as their subject if they wished to portray the true American spirit. The impact of these ideas was to begin to raise the national estimation of wilderness.

In the closing decades of the nineteenth century the appreciation of wilderness, which previously had been confined to a small group of intellectuals, broadened to include increasing numbers of the American people. As a master publicist, who reached a nationwide audience through his numerous writings in popular magazines, John Muir did much to strengthen and promote this sentiment. Giving Muir important support was an end-of-the-century feeling that conditions of American life were changing and not entirely for the better. For more than half of American history wilderness dominated the map and posed the biggest obstacle for civilization and its cutting edge, the pioneer, to overcome. But by the end of the 1800's what remained of the primitive continent was rapidly disappearing under the pressure of an expanding population. More and more Americans lived in urban environments, where there was no necessity to struggle with wild country for existence. From the perspective of a sidewalk, wilderness lost most of the sinister connotations that had seemed so formidable in a pioneer's clearing. In fact, the elements of risk, hardship, and self-dependence that had intimidated frontiersmen became magnetic to their city-dwelling grandchildren. Moreover, it was clear in retrospect that wilderness had played one of the most important roles in shaping national character. As America's foremost historian, Frederick Jackson Turner attracted considerable attention in 1893 when he dramatized the ending of the frontier as a major factor in the nation's development. Along with many of his contemporaries, Turner wondered about his country's future without the wilderness contact that had fostered and nourished individualism and democracy. Likewise, Theodore Roosevelt expressed concern that the end of pioneering threatened to undermine the courage and manliness essential to national greatness. In a host of ways, an urban-industrial way of life seemed to stifle the individual's happiness while endangering his mental and physical well-being. These circumstances encouraged Americans, both as individuals and in organizations such as the Sierra Club of 1892, to seek wilderness for recreation, relief, and reinvigoration. The same rise to dominance of civilization increased the urgency to preserve some of the remaining American wilderness.

The Hetch Hetchy controversy occurred at a time when Americans as a people were becoming conscious of wilderness in other ways than as undeveloped natural resources. The reason John Muir, Robert Underwood Johnson, and the Sierra Club were successful in arousing a widespread national protest against plans to use the valley as a reservoir was that many of their contemporaries were ready to be aroused. Concern was not limited to destruction of wilderness and national parks. The struggle over Hetch Hetchy seemed to many at the time to be symbolic of a larger conflict between beauty and materialism, sentiment and the utilitarian viewpoint, morality and irreligion. At stake, it appeared, was not just a wild valley but whether Americans would ever be able to place the finer things of life above pursuit of the main chance.

The campaign literature that the wilderness preservationists produced in defense of Hetch Hetchy stressed these larger questions. The public responded, and beginning in 1907, but especially in the fall of 1913, Hetch Hetchy became a *cause célèbre.* Hundreds of newspapers throughout the country published editorials on the subject, most of which took the side of preservation. Leading magazines carried articles protesting the reservoir. The United States Congress conducted two sets of hearings and debated the issue on the floor for the better part of two weeks. Key Congressmen received thousands of letters. Women's groups, outing clubs, scientific societies, and the faculties of colleges and universities passed resolutions. Wilderness had never been so popular before.

In the fight for Yosemite the wilderness preservation movement was born. For the first time the claims of wilderness and civilization received a thorough hearing before the American people. The account that follows documents the way in which this examination took place. The maneuverings both in politics and out, the hopes, fears, and doubts of the men who fill its pages must be seen in a broad context as part of a continuing debate in American culture on whether it is justifiable to maintain wilderness in the face of pressure to use it to satisfy material demands. Broader still is the question of the value of wilderness to civilization.

RODERICK NASH
Madison, Wisconsin
April 20, 1965

Preface

FROM ITS very beginning the Sierra Club had an intimate relationship with Yosemite; the goal of its preservation took precedence over all other early objectives.

The club earned the respect of the early Army administrators in Yosemite National Park, some of whom were members, and although it was not successful in preventing the boundary changes of 1905 and 1906, its advice was sought by the federal commission appointed to examine private land claims inside the reserve. With the establishment of the National Park Service in 1916, Stephen Mather, its Director, an enthusiastic member of the Sierra Club since 1904, prepared special reports on Yosemite and other parks for the club's Board of Directors and was constantly in touch with its officers until his death in January 1930.

Throughout this love story between a magnificent park and its devoted friends runs the persistant theme of the basic conflict in values between the utilitarian and the preservationist breeds of conservationists. This conflict involves Yosemite, first as a "state park" under commissioners who began their difficult task in high purpose, headed by Frederick Law Olmsted, whose name is legendary in urban park development, and second, as a *national* park plagued with enemies from within and without who did not understand why their pioneer privileges of settlement and use could not continue unhampered. Two names stand out above all others—John Muir, founder of the club, and Will Colby, its secretary and a lawyer, whose steady hand and practical mind laid the foundation that survived the dissentions spawned by the Hetch Hetchy controversy.

This book begins by tracing the early development of Yosemite as background for the founding of the Sierra Club two years after the establishment of the national park. It ends with the unsuccessful fight for Hetch Hetchy's preservation, the death of John Muir, and the establishment of a new federal agency to protect the nation's wilderness parks.

Although a number of prominent people enter this story at various times, I have chosen not to emphasize personal roles, but rather to relate the relevant political and economic actions of city, state, and federal bodies to the corporate personality of the young conservation club in San Francisco. This is not, therefore, a biography of Muir or Colby or of any of the other actors on stage.

My interest in this subject was prompted by a trip which my wife-to-be and I made with the club on the Yampa and Green rivers at the height of the Echo Park controversy. As a student at the University of California I had earlier become acquainted with the Sierra Club and had participated as a guest on a number of its local outings in the Bay Area. But the trip through Dinosaur National Monument piqued my curiosity about this California-based group. What was it doing in Utah? Why this almost fanatic desire to save wilderness America? What *really* was its beginning? I had read the early *Sierra Club Bulletins,* good source materials as far as they went, but were there first-hand documents that would substantiate the bare skeleton outline revealed in the *Bulletins* and a few secondary sources?

I soon discovered that there were, indeed, documents—primarily letters—which when carefully pieced together could put flesh on the bones. The Bancroft Library had recently acquired the *Robert Underwood Johnson Papers* and these formed the basis for my Master's thesis on "The History of the Sierra Club."

In this early phase of my work Francis Farquhar was my godfather and adviser, as he has been for so many aspiring scholars at the University. He generously opened his private library to me, particularly his notable collection of correspondence relating to the national parks of California (most of which has now been deposited in the Bancroft Library). Without his assistance the project could never have gotten off the ground. I was also extremely fortunate in the members of my thesis committee. Seminars with John D. Hicks and Lawrence Kinnaird had imbued me with a critical approach to sources and awakened an intense interest in natural-resource history. The third member of this committee, A Starker Leopold, was himself a Director of the Sierra Club, and his understanding of the ecological problems in which the club has always been interested proved immensely helpful to one without training in the life sciences.

Subsequently, through the encouragement of Richard Leonard, then President, and David Brower, Executive Director of the Sierra Club, I was urged to revise and expand my thesis for possible publication. I realized, of course, that much additional material must be available and that the story was far from complete. The club provided a grant enabling me to take a partial leave of absence from my library position with the

Department of City and Regional Planning at the University to devote myself to research and writing. I was also able, through the generosity of past Director Walter A. Starr (now Honorary President), to spend several weeks at the National Archives in Washington to search for certain essential records dealing with the California parks.

The greater part of the Sierra Club Archives, which I had the privilege of using, had never previously been placed in any order. In the preparation of this book, boxes of letters and other memorabilia that were unknown or forgotten were rescued from oblivion and put in at least rudimentary order for future scholars. Whatever else is accomplished by this book, perhaps this alone has justified the effort.

The number of people who have contributed to this work are legion. In addition to those already mentioned, William E. Colby, to whom I gratefully dedicate this volume, was a source of never-failing inspiration. My debt to him can never be measured. The hours of recording time we spent together will always remain one of the highlights of my research, and I shall not forget the warm hospitality he and his wife, Helen, offered me in their beautiful Big Sur home. I entered the Sierra Club scene late in its history, of course, but I had the good fortune to talk with the three then remaining Charter members: James S. Hutchinson, Louis Bartlett, and William Denman.

As a librarian myself, this time in the role of researcher instead of professional reference guide and curator, I came to appreciate more than ever the dedicated work of my colleagues. There are so many of these unsung heroes that to name them all would fill several pages. The staffs of the Bancroft Library, Documents Department, Institute of Governmental Studies, Water Resources Center, Archives, and the Forestry Library at the University of California, Berkeley, were especially helpful. At Stanford University, Ruth Scibird, now retired from her position as Curator of the Stanford Collection, proved an invaluable source of information about early Club members on the faculty, many of whom she had known personally. Other California librarians to whom I am particularly indebted are: Allan Ottley, State Library; James de T. Abajian, California Historical Society; William Davis, Jr., State Archives; and Herbert G. Shultz, Huntington Library and Art Gallery, San Marino.

In Washington, D.C., I was guided through the intricacies of its two major repositories by a number of people, but especially by David C. Mearns, Manuscript Division, Library of Congress, and Oliver W. Holmes, then with the National Archives and Records Service, who introduced me to Eivind T. Scoyen, Associate Director of the National Park Service, now retired.

Either directly or through correspondence, I used the resources of the following organizations: Special Collections at the Universities of Arizona, Oregon, and California at Los Angeles; Appalachian Mountain Club, Boston; Western History Department, Denver Public Library; Division of Public Records, Pennsylvania Historical and Museum Commission, Harrisburg, Pennsylvania; Harriet Monroe Modern Poetry Collection, University of Chicago; and the Geographic Society of Chicago.

I wish to thank two people who corresponded with me in some detail, Laura Wood Roper, who is writing a biography of Frederick Olmsted and who was able to describe the contents of pertinent papers of his in the Library of Congress, and Arthur H. Carhart, Director of the Conservation Library Center, who furnished information on several collections.

Among those who read parts of the manuscript and offered valuable criticism were Francis Farquhar and William Colby; Carl P. Russell, historian, and former Superintendent of Yosemite National Park; John A. Hussey, Chief, Division of History and Archaeology, Western Regional Office, National Park Service; Charles W. Snell, Regional Chief, Branch of Historic Sites, National Park Service; and two on-the-scene Yosemite historians, Mary V. Hood and Shirley Sargent. Finally, I would be remiss in my acknowledgments if I did not mention the editorial assistance of Anne Brower, who has the knack of knowing when a phrase is too cumbersome and a word too stilted.

Whatever photographic merit this book possesses is owed to a host of people who dug into musty corners and old files in response to my urgent requests. I should like especially to thank John Barr Tompkins, who has a phenomenal memory of the Bancroft sources; Coyt Hackett and William Jones of the Yosemite Museum naturalist staff; Carroll D. Hall, Curator, Sutter's Fort, Sacramento; J. H. Morrison, Curator, Ventura County Pioneer Museum; C. Raymond Clar, California State Division of Forestry; Richard Pitman, whose Oakland home is a treasure house of stereoscopic pictures taken by the early Yosemite photographers; Hans Huth, who graciously loaned his magnificent portrait of Olmsted; Hank Johnston, author of two fascinating railroad histories of the Yosemite region; Mrs. William F. Badè, wife of the former President of the Club; A. William Hood, who made available to me some "before" and "after" photographs of the Valley. I should like to acknowledge, also, important help from the Stanford University Press and the family and friends of William Dudley, John C. Branner, and Elliott McAllister.

The delightful Muir sketch map, reproduced in color as end papers for this book, was provided through the kind permission of George P. Hammond, Director, Bancroft Library, and the color transparency personally made by William Hawken. My gratitude to both these gentlemen for their part in enhancing this publication.

I am indebted to Keith Newsom, a graduate student in the University of Washington cartography program, for the excellent maps, without which the complicated boundary disputes and land-use conflicts in the park would be virtually incomprehensible. In this regard, I am deeply grateful also to Mary and Bill Hood for permission to publish, in advance of their own work on this subject, research on certain man-made disfigurements in Yosemite Valley which illustrate one part of this story.

An author's wife plays a very special role in the incubation of any manuscript. Frances Doreen Jones not only contributed inspiration at critical times, but also aided me immeasurably with her editorial and secretarial skills.

So many individuals assisted me in the long process of research and writing that someone may easily have been overlooked. If so, I hope they will forgive me.

This book is, of course, incomplete and perhaps can never really be finished. Historians will criticize, and add details, and reinterpret. Certain aspects of the story are insufficiently documented and must await the opening or the discovery of new archival materials. The story is also incomplete in that it covers a relatively short span of time. I am presently working on a sequel to this volume to cover the political history of Sequoia and Kings Canyon national parks in relation to the central viewpoint of the Sierra Club; it is hoped that this will add depth to the beginnings made here.

HOLWAY R. JONES
Eugene, Oregon
May 1965

1

THE FOUNDING
OF THE
SIERRA CLUB

*". . . Hoping that we will be able to
do something for wildness and
make the mountains glad, . . ."*
—John Muir

THE 1890's mark a fundamental turning point in American political and social philosophy. Historians have labeled this era Progressive—not without reason. In the preceding decades the frontier had virtually disappeared and with it good, cheap farm land. Empty ruts in the landscape were all that attested to the "hoof and saddle" monarchies that herded cattle into the heartland of America along the Chisholm and Goodnight trails. Fences now marched across the hills and plains and farm buildings began to dot the western countryside. Railroads already crisscrossed the land, and were sending out feeder lines to invite settlement and industry. The decision for an urban America had been made, the seeds already planted for the great metropolitan cities whose exploding populations in the mid-twentieth century would exert undreamed of pressures on remaining wilderness pockets.

The release of human energy for the final assault on the western wilderness following the Civil War led to almost unchecked exploitation. Corporate monopolies were formed that exercised absentee-landlordism to a degree that would have made the New England colonists shudder and their grievances against England pale in comparison. Virgin timber, east of the great plains, was rapidly becoming a memory. The rush for mineral wealth, precipitated by the widely publicized discovery of gold at Coloma, hastened the scientific exploration of the West and brought statehood to California possibly thirty years prior to its natural evolution. Mining activities in California were so intensive that although it was in 1884 that federal circuit court judge Lorenzo Sawyer delivered the "fatal blow to the hydraulic mining industry," forever stopping the mountain-eroding placer techniques the farmers hated, the scars were already so deep and the debris so high that eighty years later these giant disfigurements can easily be identified.[1]

As the Progressive Era approached there were signs of change in America. Men of intellectual status and scientific attainment—George P. Marsh, Franklin B. Hough, Charles S. Sargent, Asa Gray, and others—were joined by men of practical politics, such as Carl Schurz and Senator George Boutwell of Massachusetts, in urging new laws for the protection of the

[1] Robert L. Kelley, *Gold vs. Grain; the Hydraulic Mining Controversy in California's Sacramento Valley—A Chapter in the Decline of Laissez Faire* (Glendale, Calif., The Arthur H. Clark Co., 1959), p. 243.

forests and the creation of government reserves. Most of these men were protagonists for what is today the popular image of the main stream of conservation—the preservation of commodity resources or those resources with high economic value which, because of their relative scarcity and importance to society, no man or corporation should pre-empt for private gain. It was this group of learned and farsighted individuals who largely controlled the American Association for the Advancement of Science, particularly after its incorporation in 1874, and who through it and the American Forestry Association founded the next year, promoted the ideas that led ultimately to the establishment of the Division of Forestry in the United States Department of Agriculture. The essential notion that laissez faire methods in acquiring and utilizing natural resources must be modified to permit government interference—specifically by withdrawal of public lands from private exploitation and the wise management of these lands for the optimum economic and social benefit of the people as a whole—was a disturbing concept in the free-wheeling economic world of that day. It tended to overshadow the equally important but generally less recognized philosophical and esthetic implications of what these enlightened scientists and politicians were proposing.

Only slowly did these implications begin to be understood. The idea that lands should be preserved solely for their esthetic qualities and enduring value as places of "natural" re-creation of body and soul found translation in organized programs of exploration and fellowship. Among the earliest of such groups in America was the Williamstown Alpine Club founded in 1863.[2] Particularly responsive to local sympathies and enthusiasms, these associations or clubs usually centered around a particular mountain chain or region. A decade after the Williamstown Club, three more regional organizations became active—the White Mountain Club (Portland, Maine) in 1873, the Rocky Mountain Club (Colorado Springs) in 1875, and the influential Appalachian Mountain Club (Boston) a year later.[3] The first three of these four clubs existed primarily for the sport of mountain climbing and hiking, but the Appalachian Mountain Club, perhaps unconsciously, was a response to the disappearance of the New England frontier and a reaction against the squalor and slums beginning, like measles, to dot the face of many Eastern cities. In the 1880's two organizations with somewhat different orientations were formed; the American Ornithological Union, in 1883, and the first Audubon Society, in 1886, came into existence primarily to study bird migrations and to publicize the necessity for bird preservation. Still another group, again with a very different purpose, was the Boone and

[2] Samuel H. Scudder, "The Alpine Club of Williamstown, Mass.," *Appalachia*, IV (December, 1884), pp. 45–54.
For an interesting resumé of early alpine and exploring groups in America, see Allen H. Bent, "The Mountaineering Clubs of America," *Appalachia*, XIV (December, 1916), pp. 5–18.
[3] According to Bent, *op. cit.*, p. 8, the White Mountain Club lasted only about ten years, but at least two local groups were later formed to improve the trails in the White Mountains—the Waterville Athletic and Improvement Association (1888) and the Wonalancet Outdoor Club (1898). A. J. Mackintosh, *Mountaineering Clubs, 1857–1900* (London, Spottiswoode & Co., 1907), p. 25, lists the Rocky Mountain Club with a founding date of April 15, 1876.
[4] George Bird Grinnell, a charter member of the Boone and Crockett Club and for many years editor of *Forest and Stream*, wrote in 1910 what appears almost as an apology for the organization's emphasis in its constitution on big game destruction and recreation of riflemen. He goes to some pains to detail the Club's part in the preservation of Yellowstone National Park and its influence on the creation of the first forest reserves. See his *Brief History of the Boone and Crockett Club with Officers, Constitution and List of Members for the Year 1910* (New York, Forest and Stream Pub. Co., n. d.), particularly pp. 10–31 and 58.
[5] The Sierra Club soon had considerable company in the promotion of scenic preservation, conservation, and wildlife protection. Most of these organizations were specialized in their interests, but all, at one time or another, supported the new conservation and occasionally cooperated with one another. These groups and their dates of founding are: Cooper Ornithological Society (1893); Mazamas (1894); New York Zoological Society (1895); American Scenic and Historic Preservation Society (1895); American Park and Outdoor Art Society (1897); League of North American Sportsmen (1898); North American Fish and Game

Protective Association (1900); Association for the Protection of the Adirondacks (1900); Society for the Preservation of Historical and Scenic Spots (1900); Society of American Foresters (1900); American League for Civic Improvement (1901); American Alpine Club (1902); American Civic Association (1904)—a merger of the American Park and Outdoor Art Society and the American League for Civic Improvement; National Association of Audubon Societies (1905); American Bison Society (1905); National Conference on City Planning (1905); Seattle Mountaineers (1906); National Conservation Association (1909); Wildlife Protective Association (1910); American Game Protective and Propagation Association (1911); Garden Club of America (1913); Permanent Wildlife Protection Fund (1914); Ecological Society of America (1915); Associated Mountaineering Clubs of North America (1916); National Parks Association (1919); Isaak Walton League of America (1922); American Nature Association (1922); National Committee on Wildlife Federation (1928); Federation of Western Outdoor Clubs (1931); and Wilderness Society (1935). In addition to these, the *Bulletin of the Associated Mountaineering Clubs of North America* for May 1926 lists seventy-one "clubs and societies, having in addition to outdoor and mountaineering activities, a common interest in the creation, development and protection of National Parks and Forests" (pp. 2–3).

[6] If climbing qualifications are considered essential to the concept of a true alpine club, the Mazamas (1894) were the first such group in America. But the earliest Pacific Coast mountaineering association without climbing qualifications was the Oregon Alpine Club founded in Portland in 1887 with a former U.S. Senator, Henry W. Corbett, as president and W. G. Steel, the father of Crater Lake National Park, as head of the Department of Exploration. The organization lasted only until 1890. (See William G. Steel,

Crockett Club, organized by Theodore Roosevelt and others in 1887. Its objects were primarily "to promote manly sport with the rifle" and "to work for the preservation of the large game of this country," but nevertheless it was one of the first sportsmen's organizations to promote the preservation of scenic lands.[4]

On the west coast, where nature had been lavish in creating spectacular scenery, there assembled in San Francisco a group of men who were to play a leading role in the new conservation. On June 4, 1892, twenty-seven men signed the Articles of Incorporation of the Sierra Club.[5] Although this was not the first mountain society on the Pacific Coast,[6] it was the first organization formed specifically in response to a public need to guard against depredation of scenic lands. The drama of the early years of this organized human effort, which occupies center stage throughout this book, brings life to the phrase, "Progressive Era."

II

Two events helped prepare the soil in which the Sierra Club eventually took root; one was the discovery of Yosemite, the other the pilgrimage of a man who was to devote himself to scientific exploration and a crusading career in nature preservation.

There is no longer major disagreement about who first sighted the great valley of the central Sierra Nevada. Careful analysis of the route used by Joseph R. Walker, American fur trader and explorer, indicates that he, or some of his scouts, actually viewed Yosemite Valley in 1833.[7] The effective discovery, however, came on March 25, 1851, when the men who made up the Mariposa Battalion, determined to end the Indian raids on their properties in the Sierra foothills, rode into the Indian "fortress" and were astonished to discover its beauty and grandeur. News of the discovery was published in the leading newspaper of the day, the *Daily Alta California*, but it commanded little attention outside the state.[8]

After the abatement of gold discoveries and the gradual subsidence of the gold fever, more and more explorers began to penetrate the Yosemite area. Prompted by publicity in the San Francisco press, publisher James Mason Hutchings gathered together a small band of tourists whom he led into the Valley in 1855. The account of this excursion appears in the *Mariposa Gazette* of July 12, 1855. Accompanying Hutchings was Thomas A. Ayres, a pioneer artist, whose first sketches of Yosemite Falls and the massive granite walls excited public imagination when they were later lithographed "and spread widely over the East."[9] The following year Hutchings began publication of his *California Magazine* and in 1859 he introduced the first photographers to the wonders of the Valley.[10] There was a gradual increase in the number of people making the arduous trip by horseback and foot over the often hot and dusty foothills into the unique valley that was Yosemite; one source gives the figure as 653 visitors for the first nine years after Hutchings' tour.[11]

As California entered its second decade of statehood, certain citizens, prodded by the eulogies of world-famous travelers and appreciative guests from a more settled Eastern Seaboard, began to realize that in this Valley they had one of the truly great scenic marvels of the earth.[12] Appreciation of the Valley's unique beauty may have been responsible in part for the Whitney Geological Survey of 1860–1864; it is possible that Starr King, who visited Yosemite in 1860, communicated his enthusiasm to his good friend Judge Stephen Field, and it was Field who was influential in bringing Whitney to California to begin the Survey.[13] The growing awareness of the value of Yosemite was the impetus for a movement to reserve the Valley and the Mariposa Big Trees, "that they may be exposed to public view, . . . used and preserved for the benefit of mankind."[14] This statement, remarkable in an era of civil strife and heedless opening of the public domain, came from Senator John Conness, who, in March 1864, introduced in the United States Senate a bill to grant to the State of California tracts of land embracing the entire Valley and the Big Trees.[15] Debated, but passed by both houses of Congress with ease, the measure was signed by President Lincoln on June 30, 1864 and officially accepted by the state two years later. This significant episode in American efforts to preserve its natural heritage was the first instance of Congressional action for scenic preservation, preceding by eight years the creation of the first national park at Yellowstone.[16]

The second important event which would affect the course of the Sierra Club occurred toward the end of the 1860's. A thirty-year-old wandering Scot, a naturalized citizen named John Muir, stepped ashore for the first time on California soil on a San Francisco wharf March 27, 1868.[17] The year before he had completed a journey on foot from Indiana to Florida, sharpening his already acutely developed habits of observation and deepening his sensitive love for nature. He was at home in the wilds of swamp or forest, but man's "ugly commercialism" was a sight to which he would never become reconciled. No sooner had he landed in San Francisco, he later related to his friends, than he stopped a carpenter on Market Street to ask the quickest way out of town. " 'But where do you want to go?' asked the astonished

The Mountains of Oregon, Portland: David Steel, 1890, pp. 67–84, and Steel, "Preliminary History of the Mazamas," *Mazama*, I (May 1896), pp. 12–14. For a brief account of the organization of the Mazamas on top of Mount Hood, July 19, 1894, when 193 persons attended the ceremonies, see E. Fay Fuller, "Historian's Report for 1894," *Mazama*, I (May 1896), pp. 15–20. The Sierra Club may actually be the first organization in America founded to protect a governmental reserve, although two eastern groups with similar purposes were formed just prior to the Sierra Club: The Adirondack Park Association in New York (1890) and Trustees for Public Reservations in Massachusetts (1891). For more information on the history of the Adirondack Forest Preserve, see Roger C. Thompson, *The Doctrine of Wilderness: A Study of the Policy and Politics of the Adirondack Preserve-Park* (Ph.D. dissertation, State University of New York, College of Forestry, Syracuse, N.Y., 1962) to be published by Syracuse University Press; also Thompson's article, "Politics in the Wilderness: New York's Adirondack Forest Preserve," *Forest History*, VI (Winter 1963), pp. 14–23.

[7] Francis P. Farquhar, "Exploration of the Sierra Nevada," *California Historical Society Quarterly*, IV (March 1925), pp. 6–7; F. P. Farquhar, "Walker's Discovery of Yosemite," *Sierra Club Bulletin* (hereafter referred to as *SCB*), XXVII (August 1942), pp. 35–49; and Carl P. Russell, *One Hundred Years in Yosemite: The Romantic Story of Early Human Affairs in the Central Sierra Nevada* (Stanford, Stanford University Press, 1931), later revised as *One Hundred Years in Yosemite: The Story of a Great Park and Its Friends* (Berkeley and Los Angeles, University of California Press, 1947), pp. 5 and 7. For the account by the clerk of Walker's expedition, see John C. Ewers, editor, *Adventures of Zenas Leonard, Fur Trader* (Norman, University of Oklahoma Press, 1959).

The Yosemite is rich in litera-

6

man. 'Anywhere that is wild,' said Muir. 'He seemed to fear that I might be crazy, and that . . . the sooner I got out of town the better, so he directed me to the Oakland ferry.' "[18]

Muir and a young English shipboard companion who had agreed to accompany him to Yosemite crossed the Bay and walked south through the Santa Clara Valley, climbed Pacheco Pass, and waded "knee-deep" through the spring wild-flower beds of the San Joaquin Valley, to Yosemite. Muir remained there for the next five years, except for brief intervals. This Yosemite period proved highly fruitful for the forces of the new conservation. From it stem Muir's first influential writings, beginning with the publication of his "Yosemite Glaciers" in the *New York Tribune* of December 5, 1871. In the twenty-one years that preceded the formation of the Sierra Club, more than sixty-five separate magazine and newspaper articles by Muir appeared, some of them scientific but most devoted to popularizing the mountains and forests, in such widely read journals as *Scribner's Monthly, Overland, Century, Atlantic, Harper's Weekly*, the *New York Tribune*, and the *San Francisco Bulletin*.[19] What began for Muir as the simple pilgrimage of a devout nature lover ended in his bringing the Yosemite story to the common man all over the continent; certainly Muir awakened a new enthusiasm for the preservation of natural wonders for their own sake.

III

Thus, in an awakening of public consciousness of the natural scene, stimulated by the gifted pen of the Scottish naturalist, and in a growing scientific curiosity about Yosemite and the great "Range of Light," the Sierra Club had its birth. Suggestions that an alpine club be formed came from two sources, one local and one outside the state. According to Joseph N. LeConte (whose father had joined the University of California faculty in 1868 as its first professor of geology, botany, and natural history), the local idea grew out of a letter from one of his faculty colleagues, J. Henry Senger, to Walter E. Dennison, then state guardian of Yosemite Valley.[20] Senger's 1886 letter expressed the hope that a mountaineering library could be established in the Valley as a gathering place for anyone interested in exploring the heart of the Sierra. There is no evidence that the guardian or his employers, the California Commissioners to Manage Yosemite Valley, responded to this idea, but in University of California circles Senger's proposal soon expanded into the formation of a

ture. An excellent general listing is *A Bibliography of National Parks and Monuments West of the Mississippi River* (Berkeley, U.S. National Park Service, 1941), I, pp. 1–134. For additional Yosemite references, see Carl P. Russell, *op. cit.*, pp. 197–213. A highly selective, carefully annotated and informative bibliography is Francis P. Farquhar, *Yosemite, the Big Trees and the High Sierra; a Selective Bibliography* (Berkeley and Los Angeles: University of California Press, 1948). Many numbers of the *SCB* and of the *Yosemite Nature Notes* contain historical material on Yosemite.

[8] So preoccupied was Captain John Boling with his pursuit of the Yosemites that his letter published in the *Alta*, June 12, 1851, does not mention the magnificent scenery surrounding the soldiers' camp near the present Sentinel Bridge. A possible earlier description of the Valley, from the vicinity of Inspiration Point, by William Penn Abrams in October 1849 is described by Neil R. Bassett, "The Discoverers of Yosemite," *Yosemite Nature Notes*, XXXVI (April 1957), pp. 32–34.

[9] Hans Huth, "Yosemite: The Story of an Idea," *SCB*, XXXIII (March 1948), p. 64.

[10] The trip is described in "The Great Yo-Semite Valley," *Hutchings' California Magazine*, IV (October 1859), pp. 145–160, and is reprinted in R. R. Olmsted, editor, *Scenes of Wonder and Curiosity from Hutchings' California Magazine, 1856–1861* (Berkeley, Howell-North, 1962), pp. 271–288. This was one of five articles on Yosemite that appeared in publicist Hutchings' periodical from the lead piece, "The Yo-ham-i-te Valley," in volume I, no. 1, pp. 2–8, July, 1856, to the demise of the magazine in 1861. The first photographs of the Valley were taken by C. L. Weed and R. H. Vance and placed on display in Sacramento at the Fifth Annual Fair of the State Agricultural Society. See Mary V. Hood, "Charles L. Weed, Yosemite's First Photographer," *Yosemite Nature Notes*, XXXVIII (June 1959), pp. 76–87.

club or association. John Muir, who had married into a wealthy landed family and settled in the Alhambra Valley, some thirty miles northeast of Berkeley, had many friends among the faculty and must have listened with delight to the discussions of a possible mountain club. Doubtless, too, he contributed ideas of his own.

Local interest was shared by an Eastern editor with considerable political influence who was shrewd enough to see that Muir's views needed a nationwide forum. Robert Underwood Johnson, Associate Editor of *Century Magazine* opened its pages to Muir, and, primarily through the influence of these two men, the government set aside a large area as a "federal forest reserve" surrounding the state-controlled Yosemite Valley. The creation of Yosemite National Park, as the reserve was soon called, gave added incentive to the men desiring a mountain club.

Johnson knew that the Yosemite reserve would need protection from commercial pressures. In 1891 he wrote to several friends interested in the outdoors about the formation of a Yellowstone and Yosemite Defense Association. One of these friends suggested that the Boone and Crockett Club might be a vehicle for the kind of "defense" Johnson had in mind.[21] However, Arnold Hague, an officer of the Club, felt that his organization, with its headquarters in New York City, should restrict its attention to the Rockies. He wrote, "Those especially interested in the Yosemite Park could form an association having for its object the maintenance of the California parks. When necessary this latter association could unite with the Boone and Crockett Club in any work in which they were both interested. Many members might belong to both clubs."[22] Johnson also wrote to Muir about his ideas, and the enthusiastic naturalist replied: "Count me in the Defense Association. Armes will start a branch here."[23] The Armes referred to by Muir was William ("Billy") Dallam Armes, a lecturer in English at Berkeley, who had first met Muir in September 1890. Johnson's farsighted interest in a "defense association" and the university community's desire to explore and enjoy the Sierra happily coincided in the informal discussions of Muir, Armes, Senger, one or two Stanford University professors, and a few business associates. A letter from Armes to Muir in May 1891 indicates that these discussions had begun earlier in the year, possibly late in 1890, and that the name "Sierra Club" was proposed for the new association.[24] Armes told Muir that he felt sure, if dues were not made too high, the club could expect a charter membership of twenty or twenty-five. He asked Muir's advice on calling the organizational meeting—whether to meet "at once" or after the summer vacation. These two forces, then, the one inspired in the intel-

[11] California. Commissioners to Manage the Yosemite Valley and the Mariposa Big Trees. *Biennial Report . . . for the Years 1887-88* (Sacramento, 1888), p. 9. Also in Calif. Leg. *Appendix to Journals of the Senate and Assembly*, 28th Sess., vol. 2.

[12] See, for example, "The Yo-hem-i-ty Valley and Falls," *Country Gentleman*, VIII (1856), p. 243; T. Addison Richards, *Illustrated Handbook of American Travel* (New York, Appleton, 1857), p. 377; "Yosemite," *Ballou's Pictorial Drawing-Room Companion*, XVI (May 21, 1859), p. 325; Horace Greeley, *An Overland Journey* (New York, 1860), pp. 307, 313, and 381; articles by Starr King in *Boston Evening Transcript*, December 1, 15, 31, 1860; January 12, 19, 26, and February 2, 9, 1861; editorial by Oliver W. Holmes, *Atlantic Monthly*, XII (July, 1863), p. 8, which compares the Yosemite photographs of Carlton E. Watkins "with the finest European work"; and Fitz-Hugh Ludlow, "Seven Weeks in the Great Yo-Semite," *Atlantic Monthly*, XIII (June, 1864), pp. 739-754. These are all cited by Huth, *op. cit.*, p. 78, and are cited also in his *Nature and the American; Three Centuries of Changing Attitudes* (Berkeley and Los Angeles, University of California Press, 1957), pp. 222-223.

[13] See Huth, *SCB*, XXXIII (March 1948), p. 66.

[14] *Congressional Globe*, 38th Cong., 1st Sess. (May 17, 1864), p. 2301.

[15] *Ibid.*, (March 28, 1864), p. 1310.

[16] *Infra.*, p. 26. Albert Matthews was perhaps the first author to recognize the importance of Yosemite's precedence over Yellowstone National Park in the national park idea. See his "The Word Park in the United States," *Publications of the Colonial Society of Massachusetts*, transactions, 1902-1904, VIII (Boston, published by the Society, 1906), pp. 373-399. More recently the point has been thoroughly documented by Hans Huth, *SCB*, XXXIII (March 1948), pp. 47-78. Huth traces the historic origins of the idea of preserving lands for

1. "JOHN MUIR AMONG THE PINES."

2. WILLIAM E. COLBY, by Ansel Adams.

3. WILLIAM DALLAM ARMES, lecturer in
English at the University of California and a prime
mover in the establishment of the Sierra Club. He
was a signer of the Articles of Incorporation,
a first Director, and the first Recording Secretary,
1892–1893.

4. JOACHIM HENRY SENGER, eminent
philologist and Professor of German at the
University of California, who brought together
Muir, Armes, Olney, and other signers of the
Articles of Incorporation. He served as a Director
and as Corresponding Secretary and Treasurer.

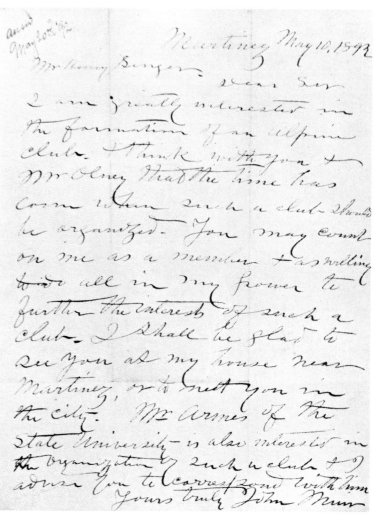

5. JOHN MUIR'S LETTER of May 10, 1892, expressing his willingness to participate in the founding and life of an alpine club.

6. ROBERT MARTIN PRICE, charter member of the Sierra Club and the only student among the first Directors; he subsequently served for many years on the Board.

7. CORNELIUS BEACH BRADLEY, a Professor of Rhetoric at the University of California, who was one of the signers of the Articles of Incorporation, and who served as a Director and Treasurer. He was the father of Harold C. Bradley, President of the Sierra Club from 1957 to 1959.

8. DAVID STARR JORDAN, President of Stanford University and a charter member of the Sierra Club. He served as Chairman of the editorial committee for the *Bulletin* and was a Director for eleven years. In 1905 he was made an Honorary Vice-President.

their scenic values alone. In general, the article is a refutation of the myth that Yellowstone was the birthplace of the national park idea. See also Carl P. Russell, "The National Park Idea, 1833–1872," from the *Museum Prospectus for the Yellowstone History Museum,* prepared in 1960 and his more recent, "Birth of the National Park Idea," *Yosemite, Saga of a Century, 1864–1964* (Oakhurst, Calif., Sierra Star Press, 1964), pp. 4–7.

[17] Badè gives the date as March 27 in *The Life and Letters of John Muir* (Boston and New York, Houghton Mifflin Co., 1923), I, p. 177. Wolfe uses the date March 28 in her *Son of the Wilderness; the Life of John Muir* (New York, Knopf, 1945), p. 116.

[18] Wolfe, *loc. cit.*

[19] A somewhat incomplete bibliography of Muir writings appears in the Muir Memorial Number of the *SCB:* Jennie Elliot Doran, "A Bibliography of John Muir," *SCB,* X (January 1916), pp. 41–54. See also Cornelius Beach Bradley, "A Reference List of John Muir's Newspaper Articles," *SCB,* X (January 1916), pp. 55–59, and William B. Rice, "A Synthesis of Muir Criticism," *SCB,* XXVIII (June 1943), pp. 79–95. See also the bibliography in Edith Jane Hadley, *John Muir's Views of Nature and Their Consequences* (Ph.D. dissertation, University of Wisconsin, 1956).

[20] Joseph N. LeConte, "The Sierra Club," *SCB,* X (January 1917), p. 136.

[21] Grinnell, New York, to Johnson, New York, May 6, 1891, *Robert Underwood Johnson Papers* (hereafter referred to as *Johnson Papers*), CB-385, box 4, folder no. 219, Bancroft Library, University of California, Berkeley.

[22] Hague, Washington, D.C., to Johnson, New York, June 5, 1891, *Johnson Papers,* box 4, folder no. 232.

[23] Muir, Martinez, to Johnson, New York, May 13, 1891, *Johnson Papers,* box 7, folder no. 362.

[24] Armes, Berkeley, to Muir, Martinez, May 15, 1891, *Johnson Papers,* box 1, folder no. 38.

lectual community of the Bay Area by faculty and students interested in an alpine club, and the other inspired by Johnson for the formation of an association to protect Yosemite, gave rise to the Sierra Club as a citizen guardian of California's largest federal park.

Several months went by, however, before formal steps were taken. On New Year's Day, 1892, Senger wrote to Frank W. Freeborn, Secretary of the Rocky Mountain Club, requesting a copy of that organization's constitution and bylaws.[25] A few days later he wrote to his friend, Warren Olney, a San Francisco attorney whom he had met in the Sierra, asking his help in establishing a Sierra Club. Olney replied two days later: "I should be pleased to confer with you in regard to the forming of a Sierra Club. Don't know that I could take an active part, but should be pleased to be present at the birth of the Club."[26] On January 16 the first of several informal meetings was held between Olney and Senger. At one of these it was decided to call together all interested persons and write articles of incorporation. In response to this invitation, Muir wrote to Senger from his Alhambra Valley home: "I am greatly interested in the formation of an Alpine Club. I think with you and Mr. Olney that the time has come when such a club should be organized. You may count on me as a member and as willing to do all in my power to further the interests of such a Club. . . . Mr. Armes of the State University is also interested in the organization of such a club and I advise you to correspond with him."[27] A second letter was received by Senger indicating Muir's intention to attend the organizational meeting on Saturday, May 28, at Olney's San Francisco office, 101 Sansome Street. It ended with this characteristic Muir flourish "Hoping that we will be able to do something for wildness and make the mountains glad."[28]

By June 4, 1892, the Saturday following the first meeting, the articles of incorporation, prepared by Olney, were ready for signing by the twenty-seven men present.[29] Six leaders were selected by the twenty-seven, constituting in part the first board of directors of the newborn Club: John Muir, president; Warren Olney and John C. Branner (Stanford University's first professor of geology), first and second vice-presidents; William Armes and Henry Senger, both faculty members at the University of California, secretary and corresponding secretary; and Mark B. Kerr, U.S. Geological Survey, treasurer.

Muir was the logical and unanimous choice for president. In a sense his fifty-four years had been a preparation for this role. The uniqueness of this preparation, his sometimes gentle, often puckish, occasionally blazing denunciation of intolerance and

9

bigotry, his gift of phrase-making, and his enthusiastic devotion to nature were factors in molding together the heterogeneous group the charter members of the Sierra Club comprised. It was fortunate, also, that men like Senger, Armes, and Branner, who had strong academic ties and were able to interest students and colleagues, and Olney, who supplied the necessary legal advice and had a wide acquaintance among lawyers and business people throughout the Bay Area, were also fervent believers in the Club and readily joined their talents with Muir's. Joseph LeConte's son, like his father a charter member, felt that the two men who contributed most to the wording of Section III of the articles of incorporation were Olney and Senger. Senger's original idea of making the Sierra Nevada more accessible is embodied in the beginning of this section and Olney's contribution is seen in the phrase, "enlisting the support . . . of the people and the government."[30]

In addition to the six officers there were three other members of the board of directors: David Starr Jordan, president of Stanford University; William Johnson, U.S. Geological Survey; and Robert Martin Price, a candidate for the Ph.B. degree at the University of California. These nine men, elected for one year, formed the central governing body of the young club. Three standing committees were appointed, of which the most important at first was admissions. The thirteen men of this committee were responsible for passing upon new members as well as seeking prospective ones. The roll of charter members was kept open through October so that those who had expressed an interest in the Club but who could not attend the organizational meeting might become associated. The leadership of the Sierra Club, from the very first, fell to men who were already well known, or were to become leaders, in their respective fields. This fact and the realization that this was the first alpine club in California gave the responsible leadership unusual prestige in the conservation controversies the Club faced at the turn of the century.

The original bylaws provided for two meetings each year. On September 16, 1892, "about two hundred and fifty members and friends" met at the California Academy of Sciences, 809 Market Street. Armes, who had written Muir earlier in the week that "a meeting . . . without John Muir would be like Hamlet with Hamlet left out," presented a brief account of the objectives of the Sierra Club and the methods to be used in achieving them.[31] A verbatim record of Armes's remarks would be of interest to members today, but probably no written record ever existed. Muir was unable to attend the first meeting to deliver the "introductory remarks" as planned and Armes apparently filled in for him at the last moment. Three other members spoke about

[25] Senger, Berkeley, to Freeborn, Colorado Springs, January 1, 1892, Sierra Club Archives, San Francisco (hereafter referred to as SCA).

[26] Olney, San Francisco, to Senger, Berkeley, January 14, 1892, reprinted in LeConte, *op. cit.,* p. 138.

[27] Muir, Martinez, to Senger, Berkeley, May 10, 1892, copy in *William E. Colby Papers* (hereafter referred to as *Colby Papers*), CB-519, Bancroft Library, University of California, Berkeley. See also LeConte, *op. cit.,* p. 138.

[28] Muir, Martinez, to Senger, Berkeley, May 22, 1892, copy in *Colby Papers.* See also LeConte, *op. cit.,* p. 138.

[29] See Appendix A, *Articles of Incorporation.*

[30] LeConte, *op. cit.,* p. 141. See Section III, *Articles of Incorporation.*

[31] Armes, Berkeley, to Muir, Martinez, September 13, 1892, author copy.

10

their respective trips into wilderness areas of Alaska and the Sierra. Although Armes had worried that Muir's absence would be detrimental and that the program would be "unfortunately short," he wrote Muir after the meeting that it "was very successful . . . and made a very favorable impression. Several members joined that night and several more since then so that today we have one-hundred-and-sixty-two names on our roll."[32]

In fact, enthusiasm ran so high after the first general meeting that two more meetings were called that fall. "Between five and six hundred persons" assembled on October 14 to hear Major John Wesley Powell, director of the U.S. Geological Survey, tell of his explorations of the Grand Canyon.[33] At the November 5 meeting the following ten prominent men were elected to honorary membership in the Club: Professor John Tyndall, British natural philosopher and author of *Glaciers of the Alps;* Edward Whymper, British mountaineer who made the first ascent of the Matterhorn in 1865; John W. Noble, Secretary of the Interior, 1889–1893; Senator Paddock of Nebraska, who had introduced a bill providing for the protection of the forest reserves (see page 15); B. E. Fernow, chief of the forestry division in the Department of Agriculture; J. W. Greeley, Arctic explorer; Professor J. D. Whitney, former head of the California Geological Survey; Clarence King, author of the classic *Mountaineering in the Sierra Nevada* and the first director of the U.S. Geological Survey; Major Powell; and Robert Underwood Johnson, already referred to.[34] The determination of this policy of honorary membership at an early date in the Club's history—a policy that has continued on a limited scale to the present day—proved to be important in building the reputation of the young organization.

IV

The Sierra Club was founded as a guardian for the Yosemite reservation, and it was not long before the Club found itself in the role of active defender. In the late spring months of 1892 it was brought to the directors' attention that Representative Anthony Caminetti, a lawyer from Jackson and a former California Assemblyman, had introduced a bill to eliminate a large number of townships on the west, north, and east sides of Yosemite.

Muir and two other charter members were quick to protest Caminetti's bill, but it was several months before the directors acted. On the first of October 1892, a meeting was held in War-

[32] Armes, Berkeley, to Muir, Martinez [September 18, 1892 (?)] (letter not dated), author copy. A brief account of the meeting appears in the *San Francisco Call,* September 17, 1892, p. 7. Note that the charter membership roll had not yet been closed.

[33] "Proceedings of the Sierra Club," *SCB,* I (January 1893), p. 23.

[34] *San Francisco Call,* November 20, 1892, p. 2.

ren Olney's office to discuss this bill and to prepare public action against it. At the general meeting two weeks later, the meeting at which Powell was the speaker, Senger explained the provisions of the bill. It was not until the November 5 meeting, however, that the Club passed a resolution "directing the Board of Directors . . . to prepare a memorial to Congress against the bill and to use every effort to defeat it."[35]

The Caminetti bill had had its origins some time earlier. Since the creation of the federal reserve around Yosemite Valley, many citizens in the counties of Mariposa, Tuolumne, Mono, and Fresno—those counties from which the park had been carved—felt that they were losing an important source of tax revenue. Other settlers, who had been free to run their cattle and sheep on the upland Sierra pastures, also objected to a sudden closing of the public domain. Local opposition, fanned by newspaper editorials, meetings of stockmen's and lumbermen's associations, resulted in petitions to Congress and a demand for government redress or reduction in the size of the park.[36]

Caminetti was the logical person to introduce a bill to settle these differences between the government and his constituents. He was not an enemy of the Yosemite reserve, however, and in common with many other citizens of California he looked upon the park as an important means of conserving the upper watershed areas of the Merced, the Tuolumne, and other streams flowing out of the region. Thus, at one point during debate on the Sundry Civil Appropriation bill (H. R. 7520) he attempted to call for an amendment asking $10,000 for the improvement and protection of Yosemite.[37] The amendment was denied. Even his own bill to reduce the reserve included a section empowering and directing the Secretary of Agriculture to furnish suitable varieties of fish for propagation in the lakes and streams of the park. Nevertheless Caminetti was not going to neglect the needs of his friends in California's second Congressional district. On February 10, 1892 he introduced H. R. 5764, which William F. Badè, the literary executor of the Muir estate, has called "a loosely drawn measure" which had "the object of altering the boundaries . . . in such a way as to eliminate about three hundred mining claims, and other large areas desired by stockmen and lumbermen."[38] The bill was referred to the Committee on Agriculture,[39] and although it never came up for debate a clue to Caminetti's thoughts on altering the boundaries is found in his reply to Representative Otis of Kansas, in which Caminetti spoke of the grievances of settlers on the public domain, using Yosemite as an example.[40] Otis, an avowed enemy of the forest reserves, had himself introduced a bill (H. R. 8445) that apparently Sierra Club leaders were not aware of. This bill

[35] "Proceedings of the Sierra Club," *op. cit.,* p. 24.
[36] For expressions of local opinion, see *Reservation of Certain Lands in California,* U.S. 55th Cong., 3rd Sess., S. Doc. 48 (January 5, 1898), serial no. 3592 (24 pp.); also U.S. 52nd Cong., 2nd Sess., S. Report 1248 (February 2, 1893), serial no. 3072 (82 pp.). A typical petition is that of John Conway, Cold Springs, Mariposa County dated January 29, 1891, 3 p., R. G. 79, National Archives, Records of the National Park Service.
[37] *Congressional Record,* 52nd Cong., 1st Sess., vol. 23, pt. 5 (May 26, 1892), p. 4726.
[38] Badè, *op. cit.,* II, p. 257.
[39] *Congressional Record,* 52nd Cong., 1st Sess., vol. 23, pt. 2 (February 10, 1892), p. 1042.
[40] *Ibid.,* vol. 23, pt. 8 (Appendix), p. 620.

went much further than Caminetti's and would have repealed the 1890 California reserves.[41] Neither of these bills was acted upon at either session of Congress. Although the Caminetti bill has been erroneously described as being "rushed through the House by a large vote,"[42] and as "passed easily by the House,"[43] as a matter of record it never got to first base.

The Congressman himself was to have appeared at the Club's November 5, 1892 meeting to debate his bill with Olney, but illness in his family prevented his attendance. Olney, however, according to the story in the *San Francisco Call,* "by the aid of a large map of the National Park explained what the Caminetti bill proposed to do" and led the discussion which ended in the formal resolution against the bill referred to earlier.

This resolution and the accompanying memorial is the first official conservation pronouncement of the still infant organization; it may be interesting to quote the reasons given by the directors in opposing the elimination of certain townships:

First: Endanger, in T-4-S, R-25-E and R-26-E, and T-3-S, R-25-E, the headwaters of the San Joaquin River, a river on whose water the irrigation of the whole San Joaquin Valley is dependent.

Second: In T-1-S, T-2-S, R-19-E and T-1-S, R-20-E, it will denude the watersheds between the branches of the Tuolumne River of the most valuable timber, destroy forests which in their magnificent growth form an attraction to visitors not only from the State of California but from all over the United States and from abroad, and, although provision is made in said Bill to reserve a tract one mile square containing the Tuolumne Big Tree Grove and also a similar tract about the Merced Grove, the destruction of the surrounding forest will necessarily cause a great danger from forest fires to these two groves of Sequoia Gigantea which ought to be and have heretofore been protected by the United States government with singular interest.

Third: The taking out of the Reservation of T-2-N and T-1-N, R-19-E will hand over to private ownership most valuable reservoir sites which ought to be zealously guarded for the benefit of the State at large.

Fourth: The exemption of ½ T-2-N, R-20-E, of T-2-N, R-21-E, T-2-N and ½ T-1-N, R-22-E, of T-2-N and ½ T-1-N, R-23-E, of T-2-N, and ¾ T-1-N, R-24-E, and of T-1-S, R-25-E will endanger the watershed of the tributaries of the Tuolumne River as it passes through the Grand Cañon of the Tuolumne River and finally through the Hetch Hetchy, a valley which in grandeur and uniqueness is in many respects the peer of Yosemite, and will in the future form one of the principal attractions of the Sierra Nevada of California.

If the territory of the National Park should be reduced . . . the dangers, to guard against which the Park was originally set aside, would again arise, the herds of sheep which now for two seasons have successfully been kept out of the reservation would denude the water-sheds of their vegetations, the forest fires following in the wake of the herds would destroy the magnificent forests and threaten the reservation itself and the timber of priceless value to the prosperity of the State would become the prey of the speculator.[44]

In the handwritten draft of the resolution this section is followed by a paragraph that apparently was the cause of some

[41] *Ibid.,* vol. 23, pt. 4 (April 28, 1892), p. 3762.
[42] Wolfe, *op. cit.,* p. 255.
[43] Robert Shankland, *Steve Mather of the National Parks* (New York, Knopf, 1951), p. 46.
[44] A handwritten draft of the memorial is in the SCA.

disagreement among the framers of the memorial. This short paragraph, which never appeared in the formally passed resolution sent to the Chairman of the House Committee on Agriculture, would have approved the removal of certain townships recommended for elimination by Secretary of the Interior John W. Noble in his 1891 Annual Report.[45] Since no directors' minutes survived the fire of 1906, there is no way of knowing today what faction of the Board won the day on this question. In the spring, before the formation of the Sierra Club, Muir had written to Secretary Noble expressing his agreement with that official that certain townships should be eliminated,[46] but either his stand on the question changed during the summer or he was overruled by his colleagues. At any rate, the resolution calling for *no* changes in boundaries was sent to Washington. Taking no chances, however, Muir wrote Johnson in New York: "Caminetti's bill . . . needs watching."[47] In February 1893, Johnson evidently heard from Capitol Hill that action was expected on the Caminetti measure because he wired Muir to have the Club send protests to the Committee. Muir immediately telegraphed the Chairman: "The Caminetti bill is in favor of sheepmen & timbermen chiefly the latter. We urge delay until the light shines."[48] Whatever action Johnson expected never materialized. Near the end of the session, Muir again wrote to Johnson verifying that the danger was over, "at least for this time."[49]

With the Caminetti and Otis bills dead in committee, nothing was accomplished by the fifty-second Congress toward settling the grievances of California citizens. In the fifty-third Congress, Caminetti introduced another bill (H. R. 7872) which left it open to the Secretary of the Interior to reduce the area of the Park.[50] This bill met considerable opposition and did not come to a vote, although it was reported out of the Committee on Public Lands with the recommendation that it be passed with the boundary changes suggested by Captain A. E. Wood, Acting Superintendent of the Park.[51] Muir was furious that Secretary of the Interior Smith (who had replaced Noble in 1893) also favored the elimination of certain sections of the Park.[52] He arranged for "an expression of opinion of the Sierra Club on the bill to be sent to the Secretary."[53] Elliot McAllister, recording secretary of the Club and at this time a California legislator, aided the cause by introducing Senate Joint Resolution 4 on January 15, 1895, calling for the defeat of Caminetti's bill.[54] The Resolution passed both houses of the Legislature and was forwarded to Washington. The state Legislature had its wish; the bill died with the end of the fifty-third Congress on March 2, 1895. Caminetti was defeated in his second bid for re-election to Congress, and the matter of Yosemite boundary revisions did

[45] U.S. 52nd Cong., 1st Sess., *House Executive Doc.* 1, pt. 5 (vol. 14), p. cxli. Noble wrote: "Cap. Wood [Acting Superintendent of the Park] makes in his report a recommendation for diminished boundaries of the Park; but it is deemed not best to follow this; although it is presented by him upon very good reasons. It is believed that it will be sufficient to relieve a great majority of those having claims within the present boundaries, if T-3 and 4, Range-19-East, and west half of T-3 and 4, R-20-E are excluded. This is recommended."

[46] Muir agreed that T-3 and 4-S, R-19-E and the west one-half of T-3 and 4-S, R-20-E should be eliminated from the park. See Muir, Martinez, to Noble, Washington, D.C., March 24, 1892, R. G. 79, National Archives. It is interesting to note that Muir was thus more aware of possible legitimate reasons for eliminating certain portions of the Yosemite reserve than were his Sierra Club colleagues John T. McLean and James Hutchings, who also wrote to Noble vigorously protesting *any* elimination. In fact, Hutchings wanted T-1-N, R-25-E added to the park so as to embrace Mt. Dana and Mt. Warren. See McLean, Alameda, to Noble, Washington, D.C., March 25, 1892, and Hutchings, San Francisco, to Noble, Washington, D.C., March 26, 1892, R. G. 79, National Archives.

[47] Muir, Martinez, to Johnson, New York, November 20, 1892, *Johnson Papers,* box 7, folder no. 371.

[48] Muir, Martinez, to Johnson, New York, February 26, 1893, *Johnson Papers,* box 7, folder no. 377. Muir and the Club were supported by the California Academy of Sciences, which passed a resolution protesting Caminetti's measure on February 6, 1893. (See J. R. Scupham, San Francisco, Secretary, to Noble, Washington, D.C., February 9, 1893, R. G. 79, National Archives.)

[49] Muir, Martinez, to Johnson, New York, March 21, 1893, *Johnson Papers,* box 7, folder no. 380.

[50] *Congressional Record,* 53rd Cong., 2nd Sess., vol. 26, pt. 8

not disturb the Club again until 1898 (see p. 49). The Sierra Club thus won its first test as an organized conservation association—defeating one of several attempts to reopen to public entry the reserved lands of the federal government.

V

Another conservation topic discussed at the November 5, 1892 meeting of the Club was the Forestry Bill (S. 3235) introduced by Senator Paddock of Nebraska, "To provide for the establishment, protection, and administration of public forest reservations."[55] Following Secretary Armes' analysis of the bill, the directors were authorized to memorialize Congress in favor of it.

The Club was not alone, of course, in urging amendments to the 1891 Forest Reserve Act in which Congress had so unfortunately failed to provide the necessary protection for timberlands reserved by presidential proclamation. The American Forestry Association, the American Association for the Advancement of Science, Secretary of Interior Noble, Congressmen Paddock, McRae, Holman, and Townsend, as well as many eminent scientists, spoke out strongly in favor of protection. The McRae bill, H. R. 119 (53rd, 1st), of several introduced in the fifty-second and fifty-third Congresses, aroused the greatest debate. Eventually two bills radically different from either the Paddock or the McRae bill passed the House and Senate. John Ise in *The United States Forest Policy* writes, "perhaps fortunately the House never had an opportunity to vote on the substitute."[56]

The Sierra Club had a special interest in the various forest reserve protection bills before the creation of the California reserves, but by the spring of 1893, the urgency of such legislation became more apparent with the creation by President Harrison of four large reserves in California. One of these was the Sierra Forest Reserve surrounding Yosemite National Park—the second largest reserve in the United States, estimated to be 4,096,000 acres.[57] Although the Paddock bill failed to come to a vote and the McRae bill did not succeed, the Sierra Club, in common with other groups oriented toward forest protection, continued to work for this goal. The Club's annual meeting of November 24, 1894, was devoted, in part, to discussion of forest reserve problems, resolutions being offered that the parks and reserves should be placed under the War Department.[58]

A year later the Club felt the problem had grown acute and responded by devoting an entire public meeting to the subject.[59] President Muir and William Dudley, a professor of botany at

(August 1, 1894), p. 8103.

[51] *Ibid.*, 53rd Cong., 3rd Sess., vol. 27, pt. 1 (December 10, 1894), p. 170. See also *House Report* 1485 to accompany H. R. 7872 (serial no. 3345). For Wood's proposals, see "Report of the Acting Superintendent of the Yosemite National Park," in U.S. Cong., 1st Sess., *House Executive Doc.* no. 1, vol. 16, pp. 659–666 (serial no. 2935).

[52] See Muir, Martinez, letters to Johnson, New York, of December 6, 1894 (box 7, folder no. 392) and December 7, 1894 (box 7, folder no. 393) in *Johnson Papers.*

[53] Muir, Martinez, to Johnson, New York, December 13, 1894, *Johnson Papers*, box 7, folder no. 394.

[54] *Journal of the Senate*, California Legislature, 31st Sess. (1895), p. 90. Copy also in *Johnson Papers*, box 11, folder no. 853.

[55] *Congressional Record*, June 1, 1892, p. 4887. See also U.S. 52nd Cong., 1st Sess., *S. Report* 1002, July 20, 1892 (12 pp.), serial no. 2915, and John Ise, *The United States Forest Policy* (New Haven: Yale University Press, 1924), p. 122.

[56] *Op. cit.*, p. 128.

[57] Established by Presidential proclamation of February 14, 1893, and enlarged twice by President Roosevelt, on July 25, 1905 and April 20, 1908. On July 2, 1908, Sequoia, Inyo, Mono, and Stanislaus national forests were established from parts of the Sierra reserve.

[58] *San Francisco Call*, November 25, 1894, p. 9.

[59] The topic as officially announced was "The National Parks and Forest Reservations." "Proceedings of the Sierra Club," *SCB*, I (January 1896), p. 286. For a news account of this meeting, see *San Francisco Call*, November 24, 1895, p. 8.

Stanford University, were the principal speakers. Dudley gave a report on his personal observations of the southern portion of the Sierra Forest Reserve and outlined briefly a plan for selection and sale of timber to settlers. He concluded his remarks with a strong plea for action in setting aside state groves of redwoods, referring particularly to the magnificent trees in the Big Basin area south of San Francisco.[60] The meeting was adjourned without the Club's taking any significant action, but on February 26, 1896, a circular sent to all Club members urged them to assure wide distribution of one thousand copies of the *Bulletin* containing the proceedings of the forest reservation meeting by "distributing them where they will do the most good."[61]

The Club directors met on March 14, 1896, after receiving news from Robert Underwood Johnson concerning the establishment of a forestry commission and newspaper clippings suggesting the reduction of the Cascade Range Forest Reserve in Oregon. The Mazamas, too, asked the Sierra Club to "take every possible means to defeat any measure which . . . might [subject the Reserve] to encroachment or diminution"[62] Sierra Club resolutions were passed and wired to the Secretary of the Interior favoring the proposed commission and strongly opposed ". . . to the reduction of the area of any forest reservation. We believe that the interests of the people require that these reservations be extended rather than diminished even to the extent of prohibiting the sale to private parties of any portion of forest land included in the public domain."[63]

In the same year the Club aided forest preservation policy by giving a dinner in San Francisco for the members of the National Academy of Science's Forestry Commission.[64] Under the Act of June 11, 1896, Congress had appropriated $25,000 to meet the expenses of this Commission to investigate and submit recommendations on a national forestry policy for the United States. The Commission was composed of several outstanding forest conservationists: Charles Sargent (chairman), a Harvard botanist; William Brewer of Yale University, a former member of Whitney's California Geological Survey team; Alexander Agassiz, Harvard zoologist; General H. L. Abbot, engineer; Arnold Hague of the U.S. Geological Survey; and Gifford Pinchot. John Muir became a kind of ex-officio member, accompanying the Commission on its tour of the western forest states.[65]

Prior to the public release of the Commission's report, Sargent wrote a letter to President Gibbs of the National Academy in which he recommended the creation of thirteen forest reservations, including two additional ones in California.[66] Subsequent events proved Sargent's letter of February 1897 to be an error in judgment, but there can be no doubt that it made conservation

[60] See William Dudley, "Forest Reservations: With a Report on the Sierra Reservation, California," *SCB*, I (January 1896), pp. 254–267.

[61] *Circular* of February 26, 1896, p. 2.

[62] Printed resolution, Mazamas, Portland, Oregon, 1896. Copy in Sierra Club Archives. Also T. Brook White, Historian, Mazamas, Portland, to Muir, Martinez, April 2, 1896, author copy.

[63] Copy in *Johnson Papers*, box 9, folder no. 744. It was enclosed in a letter from McAllister to Johnson, April 6, 1896, in box 5, folder no. 318.

[64] McAllister, San Francisco, to Senger, Berkeley, November 28, 1896, SCA. See also "Secretary's Report," *SCB*, II (May 1897), p. 120.

[65] Muir's journal of the Oregon-California phase of the trip has been edited by Linnie Marsh Wolfe, *John of the Mountains, the Unpublished Journals of John Muir* (Boston, Houghton-Mifflin, 1938), pp. 356–364.

[66] Ise, *op. cit.*, p. 129.

9. GEORGE DAVIDSON, charter member and a Director of the Sierra Club until 1910; he shared Muir's adventures in Alaska.

10. WARREN OLNEY, in whose law office twenty-seven mountaineers signed the Articles of Incorporation on June 4, 1892. Elected first Vice-President and a Director, Olney served on the Board until 1909

11. FIRST NATIONAL BANK BUILDING, northwest corner of Bush and Sansome streets, San Francisco, where the Sierra Club had its first headquarters.

12. CALIFORNIA ACADEMY OF SCIENCES BUILDING, 809 Market Street, in which the Sierra Club had its headquarters from 1893 to 1898.

13. MERCHANTS EXCHANGE
BUILDING, 475 California Street,
headquarters from 1898 to 1903.

14. MILLS BUILDING,
after the earthquake and
fire of April 18–19, 1906.
In 1903, the Sierra Club
moved into this steel and
concrete structure designed
by Burnham ("make no small
plans . . ."); the new
headquarters burned in the
fire following the
earthquake. After the fire
headquarters were
reëstablished on the third
floor and have remained
in the Mills Building and
Mills Tower ever since.

15. ELLIOTT McALLISTER, a charter member, was useful to the Club as a member of the State Legislature; he also served as a Director, Recording Secretary, Vice-President, and Editor of the *Bulletin*.

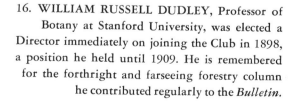

16. WILLIAM RUSSELL DUDLEY, Professor of Botany at Stanford University, was elected a Director immediately on joining the Club in 1898, a position he held until 1909. He is remembered for the forthright and farseeing forestry column he contributed regularly to the *Bulletin*.

an issue of national prominence for the first time. On Washington's Birthday President Cleveland proclaimed the thirteen reservations. Congress let out a roar. In less than a week after Cleveland's proclamation the opposition senators had passed an amendment to the Sundry Civil Appropriation bill, restoring to the public domain all the Cleveland reservations except the ones in California, "which were allowed to stand at the suggestion, it is understood, of the senators from that state."[67] The exception thus made of California was most gratifying to the Club directors and they responded with the adoption of the following resolution on March 30, 1897:

> . . . RESOLVED that the Sierra Club heartily endorses the action of the Senators and Representatives of California in Congress in their support of forest reservations.
>
> In our opinion their action is in the line of a wise public policy.
>
> As a club we are heartily in favor of a general scheme for the management of our forest, and believe that the wisdom of such a plan has already been demonstrated by experience.[68]

When the rider to the Sundry Civil Bill came over to the House, Representative Lacey of Iowa offered a substitute amendment "giving the President authority to modify or vacate altogether any executive order creating forest reserves."[69] The Lacey substitute was accepted by the Senate, but President Cleveland subverted the opposition by a pocket veto of the Sundry Civil Bill. The new president, McKinley, called a special session of Congress immediately after his inauguration and not until the passage of the compromise act of June 4, 1897 did Western hostility subside. The 1897 Act suspended the Cleveland proclamations for nine months, enabling speculators and mining companies to file entry, but it also firmly established the principle of sale of timber but not of the land, set forth a statement of purpose for the reserves, and authorized the Secretary of the Interior to provide protective measures.

The Forestry Commission's report was finally made public on May 1—"an important paper," noted Dudley in the *Sierra Club Bulletin*.[70] The Club could take pride in its small but effective part in that report, particularly the addition of Stanislaus Forest Reserve, which was prompted by the proposals of several Club members.

The Sierra Club continued to enjoy an advisory role in the formulation of forestry policy following the 1897 Act. Gifford Pinchot, a young and energetic thirty-two, was on the eve of his most spectacular achievements in building the administrative machinery of the U.S. Bureau of Forestry (later the Forest Service)—achievements that would win lasting fame in the annals of commodity conservation, but that would also lead him

[67] Dudley, "Forestry Notes," *SCB*, II (January, 1898), p. 202. California's two senators at this time were George C. Perkins, a charter member of the Sierra Club, and Stephen M. White. Dudley may not have been accurately apprised of White's position on the Cleveland proclamations; at any rate, White's remarks in Congress do not indicate a favorable attitude toward the reservations (see Ise, *op. cit.*, p. 134).

[68] *Circular* no. 14, Sierra Club, March 27, 1897, p. 1.

[69] Ise, *op. cit.*, p. 131.

[70] Dudley, "Forestry Notes," *SCB*, II (January 1898), p. 203. Muir received frequent communications from members of the Commission during their deliberations. Arnold Hague's request is typical: "I write now to ask if there is any additional matter or information you can give us in regard to this country lying between Yosemite Park and Lake Tahoe that would in your judgment make a good reserve, and also, if you can give us any points not already before this Commission that will aid us in drawing our conclusions. . . ." (Hague, Washington, D.C., to Muir, Martinez, December 15, 1896, author copy). See also U.S. National Forestry Commission, *Letter of the Secretary of the Interior of the President Transmitting a Report of the . . . to the National Academy of Sciences, Recommending the Establishment of Additional Forest Reservations* (Washington, D.C., February 6, 1897), 12 pp.

into a major clash with Muir and the leaders of the Sierra Club in the first decade of the new century. Although there was disagreement between the two men over military supervision of the reserves, Pinchot wrote to Muir toward the end of 1897 asking the Club's assistance in his work. Pinchot was ready to ask for the general withdrawal of all timber lands, but realizing the necessity of a less ambitious alternative plan should the President not accept his first choice, he proposed to Muir that he mark on a copy of the General Land Office Map of California "any areas of government forest land, not yet reserved, which should be included." Pinchot specifically asked Muir to include devastated forest lands "because the government alone can protect them and secure their return to usefulness."[71] Muir and the Club thus assisted materially in the delineation of boundary lines for the new California reserves created by President Theodore Roosevelt in his first term in office.

VI

Among the important recommendations of the Sargent report were those on the establishment of Grand Canyon and Mount Rainier National Parks. The latter is particularly interesting because it is an early example of cooperation among preservation organizations. On December 30, 1893, the Sierra Club Directors appointed a committee consisting of John Muir, David Starr Jordan, R. M. Johnson, George B. Bayley, and P. B. Van Trump—the latter had made the first ascent of Mt. Rainier in 1870—to assist the National Geographic Society, the American Association for the Advancement of Science, the Geological Society of America, and the Appalachian Mountain Club in the preparation of a memorial urging park status for Rainier.[72] Senator Squire and Representative Doolittle of Washington introduced bills for this purpose, but they failed of passage. The next Congress, the fifty-fourth, actually passed the bill that would have created the park, but President Cleveland pocket-vetoed it because of its objectionable feature granting valuable privileges to the Northern Pacific Railroad. Finally, on March 2, 1899, a similar measure moved through Congress and was signed by President McKinley—unfortunately with most generous "lieu land" provisions for the Northern Pacific.[73]

In the summer of 1905 the Sierra Club conducted its first out-of-state outing on Mt. Rainier in conjunction with the Mazamas. On July 25 sixty Sierrans (fifteen were women) stood on top of the Northwest's most magnificent glacier-bound peak, having ascended almost 5,000 feet from Camp Muir in five

[71] Pinchot, Washington, D.C., to Muir, Martinez, December 15, 1897, author copy. Less than a month after Pinchot's request, a national magazine published Muir's article in which he attacked the young forester's utilitarian concept of conservation ("The Wild Parks and Forest Reservations of the West," *Atlantic Monthly*, LXXXI [January, 1898], pp. 15–28). Angry words had been exchanged between the two men during the previous summer when Muir accused Pinchot of reversing his position on sheep grazing in the forest reserves. For further discussion of this, see Lawrence Rakestraw, "Sheep Grazing in the Cascade Range: John Minto *vs.* John Muir," *Pacific Historical Review*, XXVII (November, 1958), pp. 371–382.

[72] U.S. 53rd Cong., 2nd Sess., *S. Misc. Doc.* 247 (serial no. 3171), 6 pp.

[73] Ise, *op. cit.*, pp. 120–121, and Bailey Willis, "The Mt. Rainier National Park," *Forester*, V (May 1899), pp. 97–103.

hours. The Mazamas placed forty of its members on the summit the following day—probably the greatest mass ascent of a major snow peak since the memorable founding of the Mazamas on Mt. Hood near Portland in 1894.[74]

The most important result of the excursion, however, was a joint report of the two clubs on Mt. Rainier National Park, to which representatives of the Appalachian Mountain Club and the American Alpine Club also added their names. The memorial was submitted to President Roosevelt and Secretary of Interior Hitchcock. It recommended that the U.S. Department of Agriculture investigate the rapidly dying subalpine fir and alpine hemlock, construct access roads and trails to favorable points (including a circuit trail), and extinguish title to privately held mineral springs in the Park.[75]

VII

The Sierra Club was reaching a certain maturity. In less than five years' experience it had aided in preventing the proposed disruption of Yosemite Park and had brought to the attention of the public the important question of forest reservation and protection. Public meetings proved essential means of spreading the Club message, but also important was the *Bulletin*, the Club's general contact with its members and subscribers. The first issue appeared in January 1893 and contained twenty-four pages. By the turn of the century fourteen issues of the *Bulletin* had appeared, and the number of pages had increased to about one hundred and twenty each. One of the most valuable features of the early numbers was the column contributed by William Dudley. His "Forestry Notes" were printed for the first time in the January 1898 *Bulletin*. Dudley was a strong advocate of government control and protection of forest lands and urged, more than once, that the Sierra Club "throw the weight of its little influence in favor of reserving all the forest land surrounding the great valleys of California and retaining it forever in the hands of the United States government."[76]

The *Bulletin* was the major vehicle for articles on Sierra exploration, wildlife, and flora, but from time to time the Club issued special publications, too. These were included in a numbered series along with the *Bulletin*. No. 1 (1892) was the *Articles of Association, By-Laws, and List of Members*. Nos. 4 and 5 (1893) were maps of the Sierra Nevada adjacent to Yosemite and to Kings River drawn by Joseph N. LeConte; no. 12 (1896) was a "Map of the Sierra Region" by Theodore Solomons. In 1892 Mark B. Kerr and R. H. Chapman began work

[74] "Report of Outing Committee," *SCB*, VI (January 1906), pp. 50–51.

[75] *Report of the Joint Committee of the Mazama Club and the Sierra Club on the Mt. Rainier National Park* (San Francisco, 1905?), 15 pp. The copies mailed to government officials contained several photographs of the mountain and its climbers and an article by Alden Sampson, Game Preserve Expert of the U.S. Biological Survey, on "Wild Animals of the Park." The report is available in *SCB*, VI (January 1906), pp. 44–50.

[76] Dudley, "Forestry Notes," *SCB*, III (January 1900), p. 117.

on a *Table of Elevations within the Pacific Coast;* this was published as no. 8 in 1895. No. 21, *Ramblings through the High Sierra,* Joseph LeConte's account of his first trip into the "Range of Light" in 1870 with Professor Frank Soule, Jr. and eight University of California students, was printed in the *Bulletin* and issued later in 1900 as a separate. In 1902 the Club published Alice Eastwood's *A Flora of the South Fork of King's River from Millwood to the Head-Waters of Bubb's Creek.*[77] These contributions to scientific and topographic knowledge brought added stature to the young organization.

Another means of reaching the Sierra Club membership was the *Circulars,* edited at irregular intervals and at first unnumbered. These usually alerted the members to a specific conservation problem or announced a special meeting. By 1900 the Club evidently felt that it had done its work so well that its membership needed reminding that it could not rest on its laurels. William E. Colby, the new recording secretary, wrote to the members on November 12, 1900: "Unless we are careful, our Club will lose some of its usefulness now that our work of aiding in National Forest Reservations is nearly completed. This threatened void can doubtless be filled by creating amongst our members a spirit of good fellowship, by conferring often together, and there planning and making suggestions for Club work and exchanging our experiences and knowledge of routes, trails, outfitting, etc., gained on our mountain trips."[78]

Membership by May 5, 1900, stood at 480.[79] In eight years the membership had more than doubled, bringing forth this optimistic statement on the part of the secretary: "Never before in the history of the Club has its outlook for the future been more promising. . . . We no longer have to solicit for members, . . . they are unsought, and the persons in joining do so because they are in sympathy with the Club's work and appreciate the advantages they receive from such membership. . . . the Club is entirely out of debt."[80]

The first directors' meetings had been held in Warren Olney's Sansome Street office, but on May 22, 1893, Secretary Elliott McAllister announced to the members that the new headquarters, Room 51-A in the California Academy of Sciences Building on Market Street, would be opened "in a few days."[81] For five years this room proved very convenient because of its proximity to the Academy's facilities for large public gatherings; however, the Club was forced by its growth and the prior tenant's need for additional space to make arrangements in 1898 to share space with the Geographical Society of the Pacific in the Merchants Exchange Building.[82] Still another move was necessary by 1903, this time into the Burnham-designed "skyscraper" just off Mar-

[77] "King's" is incorrect according to the rules of the U.S. Geographic Board; the apostrophe is not used since the name is the shortened English version of *Rio de los Santos Reyes,* or "River of the Holy Kings," a reference to the three magi who visited the infant Jesus. See Francis P. Farquhar, "Place Names of the High Sierra," *SCB,* XII (1924), p. 51.

[78] *Circular* no. 21, Sierra Club, November 12, 1900.

[79] *Record of Proposals for Membership to the Sierra Club Opened May 29, 1893,* p. 51, in SCA, San Francisco.

[80] "Secretary's Report," *SCB,* III (June 1901), p. 330.

[81] *Circular,* May 22, 1893, SCA.

[82] George Davidson, a charter member of the Sierra Club, was president of the Geographical Society from March 2, 1881 until his death three decades later. His biographer, Oscar Lewis, reports Joseph N. LeConte's recollection that Davidson and Muir would sometimes "fall into reminiscences of their experiences on the Alaska mainland and in the Aleutians." These "discussions frequently proved so fascinating to the others that the purposes for which the [Sierra Club] Board had assembled were completely forgotten and the meetings adjourned without transacting any business at all." See *George Davidson; Pioneer West Coast Scientist* (Berkeley and Los Angeles, University of California Press, 1954), p. 123.

ket Street in what was to become the heart of the West Coast's "Wall Street." On the third floor of the Mills Building, the Club found, at last, appropriate quarters for its growing collections of maps and mountaineering journals. From that day to the present the Club office has been either in the Mills Building or the Mills Tower—sharing space with prominent attorney members or occupying its own quarters near by—except for a brief period following the earthquake and fire of April 1906, when Colby used his home in Berkeley as official headquarters.

VIII

Certainly the Club was widely recognized and also had many enthusiastic supporters among its rank and file, of whom perhaps none was more boundless in his energy than the young William Colby, who replaced Robert Price as recording secretary on May 5, 1900.

The Club's role was praised by President Roosevelt in an address delivered at Stanford University on May 12, 1903, "California has for years . . . taken a more sensible, a more intelligent interest in forest preservation than any other state. It early appointed a Forest Commission; later on some of the functions of that Commission were replaced by the Sierra Club, a club which has done much on the Pacific Coast to perpetuate the spirit of the explorer and pioneer."[83] When Colby reported this to the members, his own enthusiasm was clearly evident, "The Club is honored by this recognition, and should enter upon the work of the future with redoubled zeal. There is not the slightest question but that the Sierra Club is destined to be one of the greatest clubs of its kind, for where else, in the civilized world at least, has a club such magnificent opportunities as are presented at our very door for the enjoyment and study of the mountains, with the majestic range of the Sierra stretching from one end of the state to the other, clothed with matchless forests, abounding in marvelous scenery, and crowned with eternal snows?"[84]

Colby's devoted service to the Sierra Club was unique and extended over more than sixty years.[85] His father, Gilbert Colby, arrived in San Francisco on September 1, 1849, and his mother, Caroline (Smith) came to California a few years later. They were married in December 1866, and William, one of five children, was born on May 28, 1875 in Benecia. The death of both his mother and father left him an orphan at the age of six. A legal-minded aunt saw to his education, and Colby, who had once expressed a wish to be a naturalist like Muir, took an early interest in the law. He eventually entered the University of Cali-

[83] Theodore Roosevelt, *California Addresses* (San Francisco: The California Promotion Committee, 1903), pp. 69–70. The address is given in full.
[84] "Communication from the Secretary," *SCB*, V (January 1904), pp. 72–73.
[85] William E. Colby, *Reminiscences; Tape Recorded Interviews for the Bancroft Library, October-November, 1953*, by Corinne L. Gilb. Manuscript in Bancroft Library.

21

fornia where, after two years of study, financial problems forced him to drop out of school to teach in an Oakland preparatory school. The ambitious Colby was not to be denied his goal, however; he made two round-trips daily across the Bay, one to attend an early-morning class at Hastings Law School, and then another Bay crossing in the afternoon to attend more classes at Hastings. Under this strict routine, Colby managed to graduate with the class of '98. Fatigued with the grueling efforts of acquiring his law degree, Colby was more than ready for a change of scenery when the Sierra Club offered him the post of Club representative in Yosemite Valley the summer following his graduation.

The directors had discussed the possibility of a Yosemite headquarters in 1892, but decided that a city location was more appropriate in furthering the broad objectives of the organization. Now, through the suggestion of Abbott Kinney, from 1886 to 1889 chairman of the State Board of Forestry and after 1897 a member of the State Board of Yosemite Commissioners, the Club and the Commissioners agreed to the use of the Sinning Cottage as a public reading room and information center for tourists. The Club in the spring of 1898 furnished the cottage with appropriate maps and publications, and it was agreed that the Club would hire an attendant for the summer with salary shared equally by the Club and the State Board. In addition to acting as caretaker for the Club property, the attendant was to assist the Guardian of the Valley—a paid official appointed by the Commissioners—"by directing campers to their grounds, and giving general information concerning the Valley to visitors."[86]

Undoubtedly Colby's enthusiasm for the mountains and the many Club friends he had made on his first trip into the Sierra won this appointment for him. Four years previously, between his freshman and sophomore years at the University of California, Colby has been introduced to Muir's "Range of Light" accompanied by two fellow students whom he had met while working on the staff of the *Occident,* then a weekly student literary publication. Both these students, Ernest C. Bonner and Leon Solomons, had become members of the Club, but the younger Colby did not have the money to join. On the trip from Calaveras Big Trees to Lake Eleanor, Hetch Hetchy, and Yosemite Valley, Colby met charter members Henry Senger, chairman of the Club committee on publications and communications; Jacob Reinstein, a San Francisco attorney and president of the University of California Alumni Association; Joseph LeConte, vice-president; Robert M. Price, a director; and Leon's brother, Theodore Solomons, who was engaged in photograph-

[86] "Notes and Correspondence," *SCB,* II (June 1898), pp. 239–240. See also LeConte, *op. cit.,* p. 143. Shirley Sargent notes correctly that Galen Clark was in charge of the Club's first *informal* headquarters in the Valley in 1893, but is in error in stating that he was not a charter member. Sargent, *Galen Clark; Yosemite Guardian* (San Francisco, Sierra Club, 1964), p. 139.

[87] Statement made to the author by Colby, May 20, 1955, in recorded interview.

ing the Grand Canyon of the Tuolumne for the first time.[87] These fortuitous meetings proved happy events for the Sierra Club. Robert Price sponsored Colby's application, and on May 14, 1898, the directors officially brought into the inner councils of the association a man who was to serve as secretary from 1900 to 1946—an indefatigable leader who was to carry on his shoulders the burden of many conservation battles.[88]

[88] In 1917–1919 there was a two-year break in Colby's service as secretary, when he served as president. In 1949 he was made honorary chairman of the Board of Directors and in 1950, upon the death of Joseph N. LeConte, honorary president.

2

YOSEMITE

". . . As I have urged
over and over again,
the Yosemite Reservation
ought to include
all the Yosemite fountains."
—John Muir

I

IF COLBY felt that the Sierra Club would "lose some of its use-fulness" owing to the successful completion of its work for na-tional forest reservations, he did not count on the tenacity with which vested interests would oppose the government in its res-ervations of any but the wildest and most "useless" lands. Yo-semite, of course, was the scenic lodestone. Unfortunately, it was also attractive to a variety of economically and politically ambitious entrepreneurs.

As we have seen, the Sierra Club was created partly as an ex-pression of the comradeship and exploratory interests of men who had tramped the Sierra and found their challenge and beauty unique in the mountain world. In addition, the twenty-seven signers of the Articles of Incorporation, cast themselves in a pioneer drama of another sort. Their chief role would be as defender of the new conservation—a dedication to preservation of scenic lands for the enjoyment and esthetic enrichment of all the people.

To understand the principle which the Club tried to embrace during its first decade one must know the story of Yosemite. The land reservations in the central Sierra region in 1893, less than a year after the Club's organizational meeting in Warren Olney's office, were complex. First, the heart and center of the reserve was Yosemite Valley itself, a reservation granted to the State of California by the United States Congress in 1864. Sur-rounding this center, after 1890, was the protective shell of Yosemite National Park, a federal reservation under the super-vision of the Secretary of the Interior and strictly patrolled by U.S. Army officers. Then, in 1893, as a result of the Congres-sional Act of March 3, 1891, the President proclaimed the vast Sierra Forest Reserve, which surrounded the Valley and the outer ring of the Yosemite National Park. Like the Park, the Sierra Forest Reserve, also under the administration of the Inte-rior Department, was withdrawn from sale and entry, but, un-like the Park, its lands were not at first protected from fire, timber thieves, and sheep herders any more than was the nonreserved public domain. This was the situation in the Yosemite region as the leaders of the Sierra Club prepared to defend the federal park from attacks by persons and corporations who hoped to penetrate the protective reserves and who, according to some were slowly damaging the inner core of the Valley itself.

What were these vested interests?

They may be grouped in two categories. First, there were the "public" interests in Yosemite Valley, represented by the State Commissioners, whose management policies seemed designed for self-aggrandizement. Second, there were the "private" interests of many different types, little interested in a Park that denied financial rewards from the rich bounties of the land. The latter group ultimately forced a reduction of Yosemite National Park, and the former lost administrative control through recession of the Valley to the federal government. Of course, these "public" and "private" interests are closely interrelated and cannot be separated, but the reservation of the Valley has precedent in time and should be dealt with first.

II

Abraham Lincoln's signing of the Congressional Act granting Yosemite Valley and the Mariposa Big Trees to California, on June 30, 1864, although little publicized probably represented the most significant episode in America's efforts to preserve its natural heritage up to the time of the Civil War. The later recession of these lands to the federal government through the back-stage maneuvers of a powerful railroad lobby and the direct testimony of many individuals and organizations in Sacramento only serves to underscore the importance of the early grant—an importance overlooked by most writers, as Hans Huth and Yosemite historian, Carl P. Russell, have pointed out.[1] In fact, the erroneous conception that the Yellowstone National Park act was the first to express the idea that "there were places of transcendent beauty, or scientific importance that no individuals had a right to grab,"[2] has been perpetuated by the most prominent historians and interpreters of the national parks.[3] Undoubtedly these authors are influenced by the failure of most of the leading participants in the Yellowstone exploration and park establishment to give any hint in their published accounts "that their National Park Idea may have grown out of an earlier identical idea."[4] Russell believes that David Folsom and Charles Cook, who explored the Yellowstone area in 1869, and the group of Montana pioneers who persuaded Lieutenant Doane and an escort of soldiers to accompany them in a survey of the region in 1870, were "intelligent, sensitive men with time to read the journals of their day, and it is reasonable to believe that they did know something of the Yosemite reserve."[5] The one contemporary

[1] Hans Huth, "Yosemite: The Story of an Idea," *SCB*, XXXIII (March, 1948), pp. 47–48; Carl P. Russell, "The National Park Idea, 1833–1872," *Museum Prospectus for the Yellowstone History Museum* (1960), 4 pp. I am indebted to Mr. Russell for permission to use this document. See also his "Birth of the National Park Idea," in *Yosemite; Saga of a Century, 1864–1964* (Oakhurst, Calif., Sierra Star Press, 1964), pp. 4–7.

[2] Russell, *Museum Prospectus,* p. 1.

[3] See, for example, John Ise, *Our National Park Policy; a Critical History* (Baltimore, Published for Resources for the Future, Inc. by the Johns Hopkins Press, 1961), pp. 53–54; Freeman Tilden, "The National Park Concept," *National Parks Magazine,* XXXIII (May, 1959), p. 4; W. Turrentine Jackson, "The Creation of Yellowstone National Park," *Mississippi Valley Historical Review,* XXIX (September 1942), p. 196; Louis C. Cramton, *Early History of Yellowstone National Park and Its Relation to National Park Policy* (Washington, D.C., G. P. O., 1932), p. 30; Jenks Cameron, *The National Park Service; Its History, Activities, and Organization,* Institute for Government Research Service Monographs of the United States Government no. 11 (New York, D. Appleton & Co., 1922), pp. 1–7; and Hiram M. Chittenden, *The Yellowstone National Park* (Cincinnati, Ohio, Stewart & Kidd, 1895), p. 30.

[4] Russell, *Museum Prospectus,* p. 1.

[5] *Ibid.*, p. 2.

among the explorers who acknowledged the precedent of Yosemite was U.S. Geologist F. V. Hayden. At the time of Congressional consideration of the Yellowstone bills, Hayden wrote, "We have as a precedent, a similar action with regard to the Yosemite Valley, and this noble act has met with the hearty approval of the people."[6] And before the introduction of these bills, he had said, "Why will not Congress at once pass a law setting the Yellowstone apart as a great public park for all time to come, as has been done with that not more remarkable wonder, Yosemite Valley?"[7] Nathaniel Langford, one of the most persistent advocates of federal preservation of Yellowstone, is reported as having referred to Yosemite.[8] During debate on the Yellowstone bills (H. R. 764 and S. 392) Senator Lyman Trumbull of Illinois and Congressman Henry L. Dawes of Massachusetts also recognized the Yosemite Act of 1864. After California's Senator Cole had voiced opposition to S. 392 in language "typical of the land-looting spirit of the time,"[9] Trumbull replied: "I think our experience with the wonderful natural curiosity, if I may so call it, in the Senator's own state should admonish us of the propriety of passing such a bill as this. There is the wonderful Yosemite Valley, which one or two persons are now claiming by virtue of preemption. . . . We did set apart the region of country on which the mammoth trees grow in California, and the Yosemite valley also we have undertaken to reserve."[10] In the House Representative Dawes spoke of Yosemite in these terms: "[H. R. 764] follows the analogy of the bill passed by Congress six or eight years ago, setting apart the Yosemite Valley and the 'big tree country' for the public park, with this difference: that the bill granted to the State of California the jurisdiction over that land beyond the control of the United States. This bill reserves the control over the land, . . . it will infringe upon no vested rights, the title to it will still remain in the United States, different from the case of the Yosemite Valley, where it now requires the coordinate legislative action of Congress and the State of California to interfere with the title."[11]

Perhaps the pre-emption rights to which Trumbull refers were a factor in influencing these congressmen to create a *federal* preserve rather than to grant control to Wyoming Territory. The private land claims of James M. Hutchings and J. C Lamon in Yosemite had been disposed of by the previous Congress, partly through the alertness of Dawes himself—an action that certainly marks him as one of the early conservationists in Washington.

Congressman Clagett of Montana, who introduced the Yellowstone legislation in the House, was a freshman legislator with

[6] F. V. Hayden, "The Hot Springs and Geysers of the Yellowstone and Firehold Rivers," *American Journal of Science and Arts*, third series, III (March 1872), p. 176.

[7] F. V. Hayden, "The Wonders of the West, II: More About the Yellowstone," *Scribner's Monthly*, III (February 1872), p. 396.

[8] Report of lecture delivered by Nathaniel Langford, *New York Tribune*, January 23, 1871, quoted in Chittenden, *op. cit.*, 1911 edition, p. 91. But in this connection, see Albert Matthews, "The Word Park in the United States," *Publications of the Colonial Society of Massachusetts*, Transactions, 1902–1904, VIII (Boston, Published by the Society, 1906), pp. 378–380.

[9] John Ise, *op. cit.*, p. 16.

[10] *Congressional Globe*, 42nd Cong., 2nd Sess., vol. 45:1 (January 30, 1872), p. 697.

[11] *Congressional Globe*, 42nd Cong., 2nd Sess., vol. 45:2 (February 27, 1872), p. 1243.

only two weeks' experience in Congress. It is reasonable to suppose that he, or Henry Dawes, who probably assisted him in the drafting of the bill, would have used the prior Yosemite legislation as inspiration and guidance. Carl Russell points out that although the federal responsibility for management was new, "neither the choice of words nor the concept, 'set apart as a public park or pleasuring ground for the benefit and enjoyment of the people' was new."[12] One has only to compare the language of the two acts to discover that there are definite overtones of similarity.[13] Even the idea of a *national* public park predated the Yellowstone act as is evident in the thinking of J. D. Whitney, chief of the California Geological Survey, ". . . the Yosemite Valley is a unique and wonderful locality; it is an exceptional creation, and as such has been exceptionally provided for jointly by the Nation and the State—it has been made a National public park and placed under the charge of the State of California."[14]

"With the evidence at hand," Russell observes "it is hardly reasonable to assume that either the Yosemite Act of 1864 or the Yellowstone Act of 1872 sprang into existence full-blown and without some prior cerebration on the parts of members of an earlier generation."[15] This is precisely why Albert Matthews' early investigation of the park idea and Hans Huth's later researches are so important to our understanding of how it was that a few farsighted citizens and legislators, in a period of assault on the public lands, could dare talk preservation and act on their convictions.[16]

III

Let us now examine more closely the events surrounding the Yosemite grant. The credit for this momentous, if imperfectly drawn, legislation apparently belongs to Israel Ward Raymond, the California representative of the Central American Steamship Transit Company of New York, and Senator John Conness —after whom a prominent peak on the eastern boundary of Yosemite Park is named—who sponsored the bill at Raymond's urging. It seems likely that certain wording was suggested to Raymond by some of the men later appointed as Commissioners to Manage Yosemite Valley, including Frederick Law Olmsted, who arrived in the state in September 1863.[17] At any rate, the concepts, if not the exact words, are to be found in a letter which Captain Raymond addressed to Senator John Conness on February 20, 1864. Following the description of the "cleft or gorge," Raymond uses this significant language: "The above are granted for public use, resort and recreation and are

[12] Russell, *Museum Prospectus,* p. 2.

[13] Section 1 of the 1864 Act reads: ". . . that the said State shall accept this grant upon the express conditions that the premises shall be held for public use, resort and recreation; shall be inalienable for all time, but leases not exceeding ten years may be granted for portions of said premises. All incomes derived from leases of privileges to be expended in the preservation and improvement of the property, or the roads leading thereto. . . ." (13 *U.S. Stat. at L.,* 1864, 325). The 1872 Yellowstone Act reads: ". . . is withdrawn from settlement, occupancy, or sale under the laws of the United States, and dedicated and set apart as a public park or pleasuring-ground for the benefit and enjoyment of the people. . . . The Secretary may, in his discretion, grant leases for building purposes, for terms not exceeding ten years, of small parcels of ground, at such places in the park as may require the erection of buildings for the accommodation of visitors; all of the proceeds of such leases, and all other revenues that may be derived from any source connected with the park, to be expended under his direction in the management of the same, and the construction of roads and bridle paths therein" (17 *U.S. Stat. at L.,* 1872, 32).

[14] J. D. Whitney, *The Yosemite Book; A Description of the Yosemite Valley and the Adjacent Region of the Sierra Nevada, and of the Big Trees of California,* Geological Survey of California (New York, Published by authority of the Legislature, 1868), p. 22. See also other references in Matthews, *op. cit.,* pp. 384–385.

[15] Russell, *Museum Prospectus,* p. 2.

[16] Albert Matthews, *op. cit.,* pp. 373–399 (see footnote 4, p. 383, for Yosemite citations); the paper was presented before the Colonial Society on April 28, 1904. See also Hans Huth, *op. cit.,* pp. 47–78, and his *Nature and the American; Three Centuries of Changing Attitudes* (Berkeley and Los Angeles, University of California Press, 1957).

[17] Galen Clark told an employee of Hubert Howe Bancroft that "Jessie Benton Fremont, together with I. W. Raymond, were, to his knowledge, 'the most active workers on the Yosemite park proposal.'" (Russell, "Birth of the National Park Idea," in *Yosemite, Saga, of a Century*, p. 5).

[18] Letters Sent Concerning Private Land Claims, Records of the General Land Office, vol. 25 (1862–65), National Archives, Washington, D.C. Quoted in Huth, "Yosemite; the Story of an Idea," *SCB*, XXXIII (March 1948), pp. 66–67.

[19] Miscellaneous Letters Received 033572, Records of the General Land Office, National Archives, Washington, D.C. Quoted in Huth, *SCB*, XXXIII (March 1948), p. 68. For discussion of bill in Congress, see John Ise, *op. cit.*, p. 53.

[20] *California Statutes*, 16th. Session, 1865–66, Chapter DXXXVI, pp. 710–711.

[21] According to a notation found among the Commissioners' miscellaneous records all the Letter Books and Minute Books were shipped via Wells Fargo to the Governor for deposit in the Archives following the closing of the San Francisco office in 1906; that the materials arrived in Sacramento seems evident from the long list of documents, prepared by the outgoing Secretary for the shipment, which is extant. No minutes of the Executive Committee exist prior to 1881, although there are minutes for the Board itself, with gaps, from 1867. One Letter Book remains, that for 1902–03.

[22] 13 *U.S. Stat. at L.* (1864), 325.

[23] Huth, *SCB*, XXXIII (March 1948), p. 66. For more information on Olmsted as the first administrator of Yosemite, see C. Frank Brockman, "Principal Administrative Officers of Yosemite: Frederick Law Olmsted," *Yosemite Nature Notes*, XXV (September 1946), pp. 106–110.

[24] William H. Brewer, *Up and Down California in 1860–1864; The Journal of William H. Brewer*, edited by Francis P. Farquhar (New Haven, Yale University Press, 1930) and another

inalienable forever. . . ."[18] Conness sent Raymond's letter to the Commissioner of the General Land Office requesting that he prepare a bill "and send it to the committee of the Senate or to myself."[19] Significantly he repeated, "Let the grant be inalienable."

Following approval of the Act in June 1864, Governor Frederick F. Low issued a proclamation naming the Commissioners and forbidding trespassing, settlement in the Valley, and the cutting of timber. The state act of 1866 accepting the Grant, one of the conditions of the federal law, provided that the Commissioners should serve without compensation, but that they might appoint a resident Guardian at a sum not to exceed $500 a year.[20]

For forty-two years the Yosemite Valley was managed by a board of eight commissioners, the Governor serving as a ninth member and ex-officio president. The period of state control was marked, first, by an era of consolidation in which private claims to the Valley, after long litigation, were extinguished, and, second, by an interval of increasing commercial pressures upon the Valley, cutbacks in state appropriations, and appointment of commissioners more for their political and business acumen than for their dedication to scenic preservation. The full story of these commissioners, maligned and discredited in the popular view, has never been told and, unfortunately, may never be known in its entirety because of the careless way in which the state cared for its archives prior to the 1940's.[21]

The first appointees, however, augured well for the preservation of the " 'cleft' in the Granite Peak of the Sierra Nevada," as the 1864 Act described the Yosemite Valley.[22] For once, "the right man [was] in the right spot at the right time."[23] The right man in this case was Frederick Law Olmsted, whose chief monument was to be New York's Central Park. Forty-two years old and manager of the mining estate at Bear Valley near Mariposa formerly owned by John C. Frémont, Olmsted had the previous year left his work with the U.S. Sanitary Commission to accept the new responsibility in California. His family soon followed him. In August 1864, he and his family camped in the Valley most of the month, Olmsted spending a week with William H. Brewer of the Geological Survey party, whom he had met at Galen Clark's ranch at Wawona.[24] "The Yosemite offered [Olmstead] a great experience and a great opportunity" to deepen his concern and his knowledge about landscape "and its potentialities for advancing human morality and happiness."[25] Keenly observant of nature, its forms, and its relation to man, Olmsted was aware of the unique opportunity the Commissioners would have to establish criteria and a philosophic rationale for the "public use, resort, and recreation" of a reservation "to be inalienable for all time."[26] Although never officially designated as chairman of the Commissioners, Olmsted's name led the list of appointees; furthermore, he was singled out by the Governor as the one to whom "all propositions for the improvement of the aforesaid tracts of land" should go.[27]

It was evident to Olmsted that two steps were immediately necessary in the organization of the state's trust. Paying all expenses himself, he entrusted two members of Whitney's Geological Survey, Clarence King and James T. Gardner, with the survey of the grant and publication of a scale map. These were completed in 1865.[28]

The second duty fell to Olmsted himself—the preparation of a report to the California Legislature defining the policy that should govern the management of the grant and making specific recommendations for its effectuation. Olmsted was engaged nearly a year in consulting people whose opinions he valued highly and in writing the report, which he read in person before a meeting of the Commissioners held in the Valley on August 8, 1865.[29]

It is an extraordinary document. Not only does it reveal Olmsted's philosophic basis for the practice of landscape architecture, as others have pointed out, but it also anticipated by some six years the principles underlying the Yellowstone National Park legislation, which in turn may have influenced the men who drafted the 1916 act creating the National Park Service.[30] Since Olmsted's statement is important in understanding the motivations behind the idealism of the new conservation and in explaining the actions of Muir and the Sierra Club in opposing the Yosemite Commissioners, it is worth careful analysis.

"Two classes of considerations may be assumed to have influenced the action of Congress [in passing the 1864 Bill]," said Olmsted. "The first and less important is the direct and obvious pecuniary advantage which comes to a commonwealth from the fact that it possesses objects which cannot be taken out of its domain." Then, laying much greater stress on the second reason, he wrote: "It is the main duty of government, if it is not the sole duty of government, to provide means of protection for all its citizens in the pursuit of happiness against the obstacles, otherwise insurmountable, which the selfishness of individuals or combinations of individuals is liable to interpose to that pursuit."[31]

There followed a long passage on the effect of nature contemplation on the health and vigor of man. He named several factors that contribute to the "severe and excessive exercise of the mind," such as concern over family income, the wearing down of

edition published by University of California Press (Berkeley and Los Angeles, 1949), p. 547.

[25] Laura Wood Roper, "Introductory Note," published as a preface to Olmsted's "The Yosemite Valley and the Mariposa Big Tree Grove," *Landscape Architecture*, XLIII (October 1952), p. 12.

[26] 13 *U.S. Stat. at L.* (1864), p. 325.

[27] "Proclamation" of Governor F. F. Low, September 28, 1864, reprinted in "Report of the Commissioners to Manage the Yosemite Valley and the Mariposa Big Tree Grove," *Appendix to Journals of Senate and Assembly of the 17th Session of the Legislature of the State of California* (hereafter cited C.Y.V. . . . . A.J. S.A. . . .), doc. 40 (Sacramento, 1868), II, p. 22.

[28] Roper, *op. cit.*, p. 12. The map is reproduced in the article. The original is in the Yosemite Museum, Yosemite National Park, and has been reproduced in J. D. Whitney's *Yosemite Book* (1868) and his *Yosemite Guide Book* (1870).

[29] Roper, *op. cit.*, p. 13.

[30] Diane Kosteial McGuire, "Frederick Law Olmsted in California; An Analysis of His Contributions to Landscape Architecture and City Planning" (M. S. thesis in Landscape Architecture, University of California, 1954), pp. 37–38. See also Jenks Cameron, *op. cit.*, pp. 1–4.

[31] F. L. Olmsted, "The Yosemite Valley and the Mariposa Big Tree Grove," *Landscape Architecture*, XLIII (October 1952), p. 17.

the "whole constitution" by political and personal persuasion, and especially the small and uninteresting details of life necessary for some future goal. But "in the interest which natural scenery inspires there is the strongest contrast to this. It is for itself and at the moment it is enjoyed. . . . It employs the mind without fatigue and yet exercises it; tranquillizes it and yet enlivens it; and thus, through the influence of the mind over the body, gives the effect of refreshing rest and reinvigoration of the whole system."[32]

Olmsted's distress at the historic pattern of Europe's private hunting grounds and recreation parks for the wealthy led him to reflect that unless "means are taken by government to withhold" scenic areas "from the grasp of individuals, all places favorable in scenery to the recreation of the mind and body will be closed against the great body of the people." He felt that the reasons that applied to the guarding and care of natural scenery were the same as those that applied to government protection against private appropriation and use of navigable waters. To simply reserve such areas from monopoly by individuals was not enough, however; "they should," he said, "be laid open to the use" of the people.[33]

He then turned his attention to the immediate task at hand. It was his feeling that after suggesting the proper legislative action in carrying out the terms of the grant, the Commissioners should resign in order to give the Governor and Legislature a free hand in implementing the policies which only they could officially determine. He recommended their appointment on an annual basis and desired that four of the eight be "students of natural science or landscape artists."[34]

The final sections of the nearly 8,000-word paper outlined Olmsted's conceptions of the Commissioners' responsibilities —principles which today shape National Park Service policy. He said: "The main duty with which the Commissioners should be charged should be to give every advantage practicable to the mass of the people to benefit by that which is peculiar to this ground and which has caused Congress to treat it differently from other parts of the public domain. This peculiarity consists wholly in its natural scenery. The first point to be kept in mind then is the preservation and maintenance as exactly as is possible of the natural scenery; the restriction, that is to say, within the narrowest limits consistent with the necessary accommodations of visitors, of all artificial constructions and the prevention of all constructions markedly inharmonious with the scenery or which would unnecessarily obscure, distort, or detract from the dignity of the scenery."[35]

Two other considerations seemed uppermost to Olmsted:

[32] *Ibid.*, pp. 20–21.
[33] *Loc. cit.*
[34] *Ibid.*, p. 25.
[35] *Ibid.*, p. 22.

31

"First: the value of the district in its present condition as a museum of natural science and the danger, indeed the certainty, that without care many of the species of plants now flourishing upon it will be lost and many interesting objects be defaced or obscured if not destroyed. Second: . . . in permitting the sacrifice of anything that would be of the slightest value to future visitors to the convenience, bad taste, playfulness, carelessness, or wanton destructiveness of present visitors, we probably yield in each case the interest of uncounted millions to the selfishness of a few individuals. It should, then, be made the duty of the Commission to prevent a wanton or careless disregard on the part of anyone entering the Yosemite or the Grove, of the rights of posterity as well as of contemporary visitors, and the Commission should be clothed with the proper authority and given the necessary means for this purpose. This duty of preservation is the first which falls upon the state under the Act of Congress, because the millions who are hereafter to benefit by the Act have the largest interest in it, and the largest interest should be first and most strenuously guarded. Next to this, and for a similar reason preceding all other duties of the state in regard to this trust, is that of aiding to make this appropriation of Congress available as soon and as generously as may be economically practicable to those whom it is designed to benefit."[36]

Olmsted recommended the construction of "double trail and foot paths" to accommodate the future travel of carriages, a few small bridges, and five cabins strategically placed at points of interest throughout the Valley. Most important, he saw the immediate necessity for an access road into the Valley and to Mariposa Grove where he wisely recommended carrying the road "completely around it" as a fire break. "For these and other purposes," he wrote, "the Commissioners ask" that $37,000 be appropriated. More than two thirds of this amount was to be used for the 100-mile-long access road.

The large appropriation that Olmsted desired proved the undoing of his plan. His report was withheld from the Legislature by three of his fellow Commissioners, two of whom were then involved in an all-out struggle to get more money for the languishing State Geological Survey. At an informal meeting held in November 1865, J. D. Whitney and William Ashburner, a mining engineer who had associated himself with Whitney's staff in 1860, were joined by Israel Raymond himself in the unfortunate decision to suppress the Olmsted document.[37] Surely this is a major and tragic turning point in Yosemite's history! Meanwhile, with the Bear Valley estate moving toward bankruptcy—a financial condition Olmsted was powerless to prevent—he decided to accept a new position in the East. He

[36] *Ibid.*, pp. 22–23.
[37] I am indebted to Mrs. Roper for this information (letter to the author, July 4, 1962).

32

17. CAPTAIN ISRAEL WARD RAYMOND, a forty-niner and California Representative of the Central American Steamship Transit Company of New York, phrased the significant concept of Yosemite Valley as "inalienable forever" and as a place of "public use, resort, and recreation"—terms used in the Conness bill to preserve the Valley and the Mariposa Big Trees.

18. SENATOR JOHN CONNESS introduced the Congressional bill on February 20, 1864, granting Yosemite Valley and the Mariposa Big Trees to the State of California. It passed a few months later. The prominent peak north of Tioga Pass in Yosemite National Park bears his name.

19. JAMES M. HUTCHINGS, a charter member of
the Sierra Club and creator of *California Magazine*
as well as author of two important guidebooks to
the Yosemite region; he was the first to recognize
the tourist possibilities of Yosemite.

20. FREDERICK LAW OLMSTED,
about four years prior to his
appointment to the Board of Yosemite
Commissioners. The famous landscape
architect's report on Yosemite Valley
was suppressed and not made known
for almost ninety years. Constant
attention to its precepts could have
made the history of Yosemite's
preservation quite different.

21. WILLIAM HARRISON MILLS, member of the Yosemite Commission and a Southern Pacific land agent, assisted the Sierra Club's secretary in drafting the recession bill.

22. GALEN CLARK, a charter member of the Sierra Club, was Guardian of Yosemite for many years; his Wawona Station was the center of hospitality for travelers approaching the Valley from the south.

23. CHARLES D. ROBINSON, painter and eccentric, who almost single-handedly spearheaded the Legislative investigation of the Yosemite Commissioners in 1889.

24. "YOSEMITE FALLS," painting by Charles D. Robinson, probably completed about 1886 and reproduced in John Muir's *Picturesque California.*

arrived in New York with his family on November 22 and officially resigned from the Commission October 10, 1866.[38] How different the development of Yosemite might have been had his report received the serious consideration of the State Legislature for whom it was intended and if he himself had remained at his Commission post!

There were other sincere and able members among the first Commissioners, although it is doubtful if any of them regarded their responsibilities in the same light as did Olmsted. Certainly the appropriations recommended in the first Commissioners' report to the Governor were trifling compared to Olmsted's proposal.[39] This is the only report signed by Whitney, and it may be that his influence over the Board diminished after 1868. The reports from 1869 to 1879 were signed by William Ashburner. In 1875 he asked the Legislature to appropriate $26,500 for trails and bridges, including $10,000 for the services of a landscape engineer.[40] Again in 1877 he renewed his plea for a larger appropriation for the same purposes.[41] Perhaps he regretted the suppression of Olmsted's report and salved his conscience by including in his recommendations some of the ideas expressed by his former colleague. It is known that Ashburner had a fierce pride in his membership on the Board, so much so that he contested both Governor George C. Perkins' right to appoint new Commissioners after the Constitutional Act of 1879 and a new law which limited the terms of office to four years. Ashburner took the case all the way to the Supreme Court of the United States, refusing to give up the books of the Commission until ordered to do so by the Court.[42] From September 1880 until March 1881, there were two sets of Commissioners and two Guardians, an absurd situation which destroyed what little prestige the Commissioners may have had with the Legislature. From this point forward the Commissioners were in the direct line of political fire—subject to the whim and fancy of any governor who might thereafter choose to exercise the spoils of his office.

The record of the Legislature indicates that it did not understand the needs in Yosemite. Except for some $2,000 appropriated for the survey of the grant, in part to repay Olmsted, and $10,000 granted in 1878 for the "improvement and preservation of the Valley and Big Trees," all other monies until 1881 were spent for the expenses of the Commissioners and to pay the salary of the Guardian.[43] The most notorious Legislative action had come in 1868, however, when the 17th Session approved Assembly Bill 238 in both houses, a proposition to give J. M. Hutchings and J. C. Lamon full possession of their 160-acre claims in the Valley upon ratification by the Congress of the

[38] McGuire, *op. cit.*, p. 115.

[39] "Report C.Y.V.," *A.J.S.A.*, 17th Sess., Doc. 40 (Sacramento, 1868), II, p. 11. Whitney asked for $5,000.

[40] "Biennial Report C.Y.V. . . . 1874 and 1875," *A.J.S.A.*, 21st Sess., Doc. no. 36 (Sacramento, 1876), V, p. 17.

[41] "Biennial Report C.Y.V. . . ." *A.J.S.A.*, 22nd Sess., Doc. no. 7 (Sacramento, 1878), III, p. 16.

[42] *Ashburner v. California* (Oct. 1880), 103 U.S. 575–579. The decision is partly reprinted in "Report C.Y.V., 1883–84," *A.J.S.A.*, 26th Sess., Doc. no. 6 (Sacramento, 1885), V, pp. 31–32.

[43] "Biennial Report C.Y.V. for the Years 1893–94," *A.J.S.A.*, 31st Sess., doc. 5 (Sacramento, 1894), VI, pp. 7–8. According to Galen Clark, Guardian from 1866–1880 and again from 1889–1896, James Hutchings "and his friends were so successful as Lobbyists in the State Legislature that they defeated appropriation Bills for Yosemite and for four years there was not a dollar approximated for the incidental expenses of the commission or for the pay of the Guardian." Clark MS. in Yosemite Museum dated February 18, 1894 and intended for publication in the *San Francisco Examiner;* quoted in Shirley Sargent, *Galen Clark; Yosemite Guardian* (San Francisco, Sierra Club, 1964), p. 148.

United States.[44] Governor Haight vetoed the bill, stating, ". . . it is in effect a repudiation by the state of a trust deliberately accepted for public purposes, and an appropriation of the whole Yosemite Valley to private ownership."[45] The Legislature passed the bill over the governor's veto. The appropriate bill was then introduced in the U.S. Congress, but the Senate failed to go along with the House measure passed on June 3, 1868.[46] Meanwhile, the Yosemite Commissioners took the case to a district court, where the decision was favorable to the land claimants. When notice of appeal to the State Supreme Court was filed, Hutchings decided to make the long train trip to Washington to lobby on the settlers' behalf. A new measure was introduced in the new Congress by George W. Julian of Indiana, Chairman of the House Committee on Public Lands, who championed Hutchings' cause; the bill, however, was reported adversely in the Senate and tabled in the lower chamber.[47] If Hutchings' hopes had not been dashed by an intransigent Senate, they certainly were delivered a final legal blow when the State Supreme Court reversed the decision of the lower court in 1871, and the U.S. Supreme Court in December 1872, sustained the decision on the grounds that pre-emption claims established on unsurveyed lands were not valid.[48] A sympathetic Legislature in 1874 finally granted indemnity payments of $24,000 to Hutchings and lesser amounts to three other claimants.[49] Hutchings appears to have accepted his defeat in a public-spirited manner, although he continued his attempts to win special concessions in the Valley.[50] As late as 1895 he was influential enough with the Legislature to obtain the use of a cabin and five acres of orchard for ten years.[51]

When we consider on what a thin margin decisions of this sort were won by the advocates of preservation for "public use, resort and recreation"—the Senate adverse ruling in the Hutchings case was secured by only one vote according to the claimant—we realize how fortunate it is that there were a few statesmen in Congress who could understand the implications of private ownership in areas of superlative scenery. Although Representative Julian went to considerable length to prove that the Hutchings and Lamon claims were only a tiny part of the floor's acreage and although neither of these gentlemen would have been likely to take advantage of his valuable ownership rights, the possible sale of these lands to less principled individuals might have prevented the public's enjoyment and free access to portions of the upper Valley. If this early recognition that private ownership is completely incompatible with public use in a park had been more carefully followed as a principle by later Congresses, the National Park Service would not be handicapped by some of

[44] *Journal of the Assembly,* California Legislature, 17th Sess. 1867–68, pp. 304, 321, and 338.

[45] "Veto Message of the Governor in Relation to Assembly Bill no. 238, an Act Granting Lands in Yosemite Valley," February 4, 1868, *A.J.S.A.,* 17th Sess. (Sacramento, 1868), II, 4 pp.

[46] *Journal of the Senate,* California Legislature, 17th Sess., 1867–68, pp. 417–418 (February 20, 1868); *Congressional Globe,* 40th Cong., 2nd Sess., vol. 39, pt. 3 (June 3, 1868), p. 2817.

[47] *Congressional Globe,* 41st Cong., 2nd Sess., vol. 42 (June 3, 1870), p. 4043, and (July 2, 1870), p. 5132. Julian's long report in defense of Hutchings and the U.S. pre-emption laws is printed in the *Globe,* pp. 5132–5134. Following defeat of these bills in Congress, the Pre-emptors' Union issued a pamphlet reprinting Julian's arguments in the hope of securing public sympathy (see *The Rights of Settlers Voted Down in Congress,* n. d. 8 pp., bound in *Pamphlets on Yosemite* in Bancroft Library, University of California, Berkeley).

[48] 41 *California Reports* (July 1871), 658–9; *The Yosemite Valley Case* [*Hutchings v. Low*] (December, 1872), 82 U.S. 77–94.

[49] *California Statutes,* 20th Sess., 1873–74, Chapter CCCLXII, pp. 523–524.

[50] See Hutchings *In the Heart of the Sierras; The Yosemite Valley, Both Historical and Descriptive and Scenes by the Way* (Yosemite Valley and Oakland, Pacific Press Publishing House, 1886), pp. 153–162. Also his earlier *Scenes of Grandeur and Curiosity in California* (San Francisco, 1871), pp. 61–171. Much less kind is the interpretation of Hutchings in Sargent, *op. cit.,* pp. 68–69, 73–75, 124–125, 136, and 146–148.

[51] Senate Concurrent Resolution no. 18, *Journal of the Senate,* California Legislature, 31st Sess., 1895, p. 1125.

the grievous problems it faces today in Yosemite and elsewhere.

There were also attempts by the California Legislature to repudiate the Congressional grant. The same year that a generous Legislature appropriated $60,000 to extinguish squatters' rights, Senator Dyer attempted to repeal the 1866 Act of Acceptance, which would have nullified the original Congressional grant.[52] According to C. Raymond Clar, in his account of the State government and forestry, there were also two attempts to pass resolutions urging Congress to open the area to private entry, but fortunately all these attacks failed.[53]

A new regime took over on April 19, 1880, although the Commission's books were not made available until some months later. The only hold-over members were I. W. Raymond and William G. Priest, who had taken Whitney's place upon the latter's return to the East.

There is some evidence that the new Board of Commissioners was dominated by men favorable to the Southern Pacific Railroad. One of its agents, William H. Mills, was an influential member of the Executive Committee of the Board during most of the 1880's. From time to time the Commissioners depended upon the advice of the Railroad's structural engineers—particularly in regard to bridge design in the Valley.[54] Furthermore, the Board appears to have enjoyed rather good relations with the railroad-dominated State Legislature. In contrast to its appropriation record during the incumbency of the first Commissioners, the Legislature during the 1880's appropriated $169,000 for purchase, construction, and improvement of trails and bridges, erection of a major hotel, water supply works, underbrushing, and other improvement projects suggested by the Commissioners.

The Commissioners met once each June in the Valley and occasionally at other times throughout the year. Much of the routine business, however, was conducted by the Executive Committee. An office was maintained in San Francisco, and informal meetings were held as frequently as two or three times a month. Although there were many problems to be dealt with, none proved more vexing than the proper management of the Valley floor.

To assist them in this, the Commissioners asked William Ham Hall, State Engineer, to conduct a survey of the grant and to recommend policies to guide future action. Hall's document, "To Preserve from Defacement and Promote the Use of Yosemite Valley," was presented to the Commissioners on May 20, 1882.[55] The report lacks the sensitive insights shown by Olmsted; clearly, it is an engineer speaking and not a landscape

[52] Senate bill no. 338, *Journal of the Senate,* California Legislature, 20th Sess., 1873–74, p. 500.

[53] C. Raymond Clar, *California Government and Forestry from Spanish Days until the Creation of the Department of Natural Resources in 1927.* (Sacramento, Division of Forestry, Department of Natural Resources, 1959), p. 31.

[54] Colonel George E. Gray, Chief Engineer, for example, advised the Commissioners in 1879 on where to cross the Merced River. "Biennial Report C.Y.V.," *A.J.S.A.,* 23rd Sess., doc. 14 (Sacramento, 1879), I, p. 4.

[55] William Ham Hall, "Report of the State Engineer to Preserve from Defacement and Promote the Use of the Yosemite Valley," appended to "Report C.Y.V.," *A.J.S.A.,* 27th Sess., doc. no. 15 (Sacramento, 1887), I, pp. 13–31.

architect. Nevertheless, the report had two important effects. It strengthened the hand of the Commissioners in asking for an enlargement of the Yosemite grant, and its suggestions for management of the Valley floor, when carried out later under the Board's orders, subjected the Commissioners to increasing attack from sincere advocates of differing preservation ideas and from malcontents whose privileges were abridged or denied.

Two management policies were particularly offensive to preservationists. In regard to tree cutting, Hall had said: ". . . certainly you should be safe from censure if, in opening out the views, caring for the full development of the timber, and clearing up the more unsightly parts of the Valley lands of the Yosemite, you apply the axe right freely."[56] Unlike some of his purist friends, John Muir was not disturbed by tree-cutting, for he recognized the importance of a landscape plan that included "the thinning and clearing of undergrowth jungles."[57] It was Hall's second management policy that was really repugnant to the future Sierra Club's president. Hall had emphasized that about 1,000 acres would be needed to grow hay for the accommodation of tourists bringing in horses. The result of carrying out this policy was that the hotel and saddle concessionaires plowed under grassy meadows and enclosed their furrows with barbed-wire fences.

For a variety of reasons, then, complaints against the Commissioners' policies were heard, but most of these were brushed aside as coming from dissatisfied and unsuccessful bidders for Valley privileges. There were, however, two particularly vocal critics who made their views known to the press. One was George G. Mackenzie, about whom little is known except that he published a guide to Yosemite under the pseudonym Lewis Stornoway in 1888.[58] The other was Charles D. Robinson, an artist who spent a part of each year from 1880 to 1890 in the Valley.

Robinson was a colorful individual, of medium height, square-shouldered, muscular, with piercing blue eyes. In spite of what some of his critics have said, he was a man of considerable artistic talent although unquestionably not the equal of his contemporaries, William Keith and Albert Bierstadt. He painted more than ninety canvases of Yosemite during his ten years of Valley residence, many of which were sold to visiting Englishmen (one now hangs in Buckingham Palace). Something of the esteem with which his fellow artists held Robinson is indicated by his election as President of the Palette Club, a group of independent painters who opposed the more socially elite San Francisco Art Association.[59] Brother Cornelius speaks of Robinson in his biography of William Keith as a colleague who admired the older man's work.[60] In contrast to Keith's, Robinson's associa-

[56] *Ibid.*, p. 27.

[57] Quoted by William E. Colby, in "Yosemite's Fatal Beauty," *SCB*, XXXIII (March 1948), p. 86. This is a quote from a document that is described as available in Muir's own handwriting in the Sierra Club office; I have not been able to find it, however.

[58] *Yosemite: Where to Go and What to Do; A Plain Guide to the Yosemite Valley* (San Francisco, C. A. Murdock & Co., 1888), 98 pp.

[59] "Charles Dorman Robinson, 1847–1933; Biography and Works," *California Art Research*, abstract of Project no. 2874, Op. 65-3-3632 (San Francisco, Works Progress Administration, December, 1936), III, pp. 81–82.

[60] Brother Fidelis Cornelius, *Keith, Old Master of California* (New York, G. P. Putnam's Sons, 1942), pp. 221–222, 245.

[61] *Picturesque California: The Rocky Mountains and the Pacific Slope: California, Oregon, Nevada, Washington, Alaska, Montana, Idaho, Arizona, Colorado, Utah, Wyoming, etc.* (N.Y. and San Francisco, J. Dewing Publishing Co., 1887), 5 vols. Other editions in 1888 and 1894. "A Rival of the Yosemite; the Canyon of the South Fork of King's River, California," *Century Magazine*, XLIII (November, 1891), pp. 77–97.

[62] Elizabeth H. Godfrey, "Thumbnail Sketches of Yosemite Artists: C. D. Robinson," *Yosemite Nature Notes*, XXIII (April, 1944), p. 39.

[63] Muir, Martinez, to Johnson, New York, September 13, 1889, reprinted in "The Creation of Yosemite National Park," *SCB*, XXIX (October, 1944), p. 50.

[64] See for example Stuart Daggett, *Chapters on the History of the Southern Pacific* (New York, Ronald Press, 1922), particularly Chapter XII, "The Southern Pacific and Politics," pp. 199–221; Oscar Lewis, *The Big Four; The Story of Huntington, Stanford, Hopkins, and Crocker, and of the Central Pacific* (New York, Alfred A. Knopf, 1938; reprinted 1959), pp. 354–412; and George E. Mowry, *The California Progressives* (Berkeley and Los Angeles, University of California Press, 1951), particularly Chapter I, "The Southern Pacific's California," pp. 1–22; also p. 57 ff. For briefer analysis, see John Walton Caughey, *California*, 2nd edition (Englewood Cliffs, N.J., Prentice-Hall, Inc., 1953), pp. 381–383, 399–402; Robert Glass Cleland, *From Wilderness to Empire; a History of California*, edited and brought up to date by Glenn S. Dumke (New York, Alfred A. Knopf, 1959), pp. 235–236 ff; and Carey McWilliams, *California; the Great Exception* (New York, A. A. Wyn, 1949), pp. 178–180.

[65] In doing research on a bribery scandal that broke in 1896 over contracts for advertising in the *Examiner*, Robert H. Becker made a check through the files of the paper for its attitude toward the Railroad. He discovered that sporadic attacks were made from

tion with Muir was rather superficial; he did, however contribute several illustrations for Muir's *Picturesque California* and for his *Century Magazine* article on Kings Canyon.[61] The artist is reported to have said, "It takes a crank to move the world, and I would rather be a crank than a nonentity."[62]

This self-characterization would seem to be accurate and is supported by a letter of Muir's to Robert Underwood Johnson giving Muir's impression of the man upon meeting him on a San Francisco street one afternoon: "Robinson held me with his glittering eye on Davis Street and held forth on the wickedness and woe of the Yo. and its affairs in grand devil may care right or wrong style and denounced my poor peeping letter on the valley with great vigor but with fine fatherly regard withal. I quoted your favorite saying on the power of understatement in contentions of this sort, but he would have none of it. He modestly declared that the cure for all the Yo. woes was a band of lovely disinterested Commissioners made up of He, Me, and Hutch[ings]. He, the artist with the eye, Hutch with the long love, and me the poetico-trampo-geologist-bot. and ornithnatural, etc., etc. !-!-! I told him that you mentioned the possibility of a short paper on Kings River and he said he wanted to write it, or if I was going to do it, then he wished to illustrate it and help to write it. His illustrations I have not yet seen but feel sure they are very good."[63]

Robinson was one of the twenty-seven signers of the Articles of Incorporation and therefore a charter member of the Sierra Club. He is important to its history, however, more for his catalytic action in hastening the downfall of the Commissioners and recession of the Valley than for any positive contribution to its annals.

In 1885 the Commissioners granted Robinson the right to build and lease a small studio in Yosemite Valley. This privilege was later revoked, and, according to Robinson, his studio forcibly broken into by Guardian Dennison. Robinson's ire was now thoroughly aroused, and he brought public charges against the Commissioners.

These charges must be assessed against a background of two important facts. One was the effective control of the Legislature by senators and assemblymen sympathetic to the powerful Southern Pacific Railroad—a political fact that several historians have recognized.[64] The other was the role of the *San Francisco Examiner* under the muck-raking zeal of William Randolph Hearst. Throughout the period of active efforts to consummate recession of the Valley, the city's Democratic daily remained an implacable enemy of the Railroad.[65] The switch of this paper from support for Robinson's charges against the

Commissioners to extreme opposition to Muir and the Sierra Club fifteen years later is best explained in the changing attitudes of the Southern Pacific. When the Railroad publicly favored the Commissioners, the *Examiner* was opposed; when the Railroad later supported recession "behind the scenes," the Examiner reversed its position.

At intervals throughout the year 1888 the *Examiner* printed articles and editorials derogatory to the Commissioners and their policies.[66] Apparently most of this material was fed to the newspaper by Robinson, although Hutchings (remember that he, too, had good reason to oppose the Commissioners) sent a long letter to the *Examiner* that it published with sketches showing the stumps of felled pines and fenced pastures.[67]

Shortly after the 28th Session of the California Legislature opened in January 1889, Assemblyman E. C. Tully from San Benito County introduced the twenty-two sworn charges of Robinson.[68] Both the Senate and the Assembly appointed committees to investigate the charges with the stipulation that they were to report back to the Legislature before the end of the session. Testimony began on February 4, 1889.

Robinson's charges ranged from the specific to the general and covered practically all the criticisms heard against the Commissioners in the Valley—from "squandering and misapplying appropriations and public moneys" to "employment of state labor upon work for private parties." Several of the charges were not supported by the evidence and were indeed thrown out by the investigators. The hearings dragged on through the first two weeks of February and may be said, in effect, to have resulted in a hung jury.

The report of the Senate committee, as the *Examiner* had predicted it would be, was a whitewash of the Commissioners: ". . . we find that nothing more . . . than a difference of opinion existed between some witnesses and the Yosemite Commissioners, as to the best method of management of the affairs of the Valley."[69] The president, *pro tem,* of the Senate, Stephen M. White, later United States Senator, felt compelled to submit a "Special Report" to the Senate. His remarks imply criticism of the Senate investigation and regret on his part that illness and the pressure of public business prevented him from making "any report such as I would care to present to the public."[70] When the Senate hearings were later published, it was discovered that important testimony had been left out, corroborating White's criticisms.

Majority and minority reports were submitted by the Assembly investigating team. In light of railroad dominance in the Legislature, the resentment felt by many Legislators over being

January 1891 through late June 1894, and that from July 1894 through December 1896, all but one of the 64 sample issues in which the *Examiner* mentioned the Southern Pacific Railroad were definitely adverse. ("The San Francisco Examiner and the Southern Pacific," a paper presented to the Library School, University of California, Berkeley, MS., 6 pages and appendices, copy in Bancroft Library.)

[66] *San Francisco Examiner,* May 21, 1888 (p. 1), June 13 (p. 4), June 17 (p. 8), June 20 (p. 8), June 25 (p. 4, editorial), July 29 (p. 9), Dec. 9 (p. 8), Dec. 22 (p. 8, interview with Olmsted), and Dec. 23 (p. 4, editorial).

[67] *Ibid.,* July 29, 1888, p. 9.

[68] *Journal of the Assembly,* California Legislature, 28th Sess., 1889, p. 942. The twenty-two charges are listed in full.

[69] "Report of the Senate Committee on Yosemite Valley" (March 16, 1889), Journal of the Senate, California Legislature, 28th Sess., 1889, p. 1056.

[70] "Special Report," *Ibid.,* p. 1056.

made to dance to the *Examiner's* tune (comments were made that this was the paper's investigation, not the government's), and statements in the anti-*Examiner* press calling the investigation a "screaming farce" and a "miserable fizzle," it is remarkable that the majority report signed by William Rundell, L. R. Tulloch, and E. C. Tully was as honest and as objective a report as it was.[71] Nevertheless, the fact that two of these signers represented the people of counties in which the Yosemite region was located may very well have prejudiced their minds against the Commissioners.

The majority report absolved the Commissioners of several of the Robinson charges, called specific attention to several others, and suggested a number of remedies which, as it proved, were not calculated to receive the serious support of the Legislature and certainly not the favor of the existing Yosemite Board. These recommendations included the building and furnishing of a new hotel, like the Leidig Hotel, which the Commissioners had ordered torn down, to cater to middle-class tourists and to allow "a reasonable latitude for competition"; the immediate abolition of all "barbed-wire fences and other unsightly enclosures, except as are necessary to protect the orchards and gardens and to keep the milch cows required for the hotels"; the construction of barns to store hay; the reconstruction of some of the Valley roads and their watering down during the summer months to settle dust; the bidding for concessions on a fair basis with the "most open competition" and "no privileges of an exclusive character . . . save such regulations as may be deemed necessary for the general good"; an appropriation of "not less" than $10,000 per annum to be at the disposal of the Commissioners; the clearance of debris in the Big Tree Grove to pervent fire; the control of the Yosmite watershed through appropriate action of Congress; and, finally, a radical reorganization of the Board itself.

Regarding the latter recommendation, the authors of the majority report felt it necessary to preface their remarks with a careful statement designed to allay suspicion of their motives: "We are fully aware of the fact that we are treading upon delicate, if not holy ground. Yet we feel it our duty to speak our convictions freely and candidly, and assure you that in doing so we are not actuated by any motives of a personal character. We have endeavored throughout this entire investigation to confine our inquiry strictly to the management . . . avoiding, as far as possible consistent with the discharge of our duties, to leave out of sight persons or individual members of the Commission."[72]

The authors felt the Commission was too large and cumbersome. Noting that much of the business had in the past been done by the three-member Executive Committee, they recommended

[71] "Report of Committee on Yosemite Valley and Mariposa Grove of Big Trees" (March 14, 1889), *Journal of the Assembly,* California Legislature, 28th Sess., 1889, pp. 944–949. A "minority report" was signed by three other members of the Committee: C. M. Crawford (Lake County), John Gardner (Calaveras County), and Henry Hock (Contra Costa County), *ibid.,* pp. 949–950. (For comments by the other San Francisco newspapers, see the *Chronicle,* February 5, 6, 7, 8, 12, 13, 14, and 21, 1889; and *Call,* February 5, 7, 12, 14, and 21, 1889.)

[72] *Ibid.,* p. 948.

a three-man Commission, to be salaried by the State, whose members should be required to live, at least a part of each year, in the Valley. There should also be a nonmember Secretary with "a handsome salary—one that would secure talent of the highest order, coupled with unquestioned integrity," who also should be required to live in the Valley. The members "should be selected for their peculiar fitness for these delicate duties . . . they should not only be intelligent but they should possess those high natural qualities or gifts of nature which alone will fit them for the proper discharge of these duties"—apparently an oblique reference to the suggestions by Muir and others that a landscape architect ought to be placed in charge of the Valley.[73]

Two of the majority-report recommendations were embodied in a relatively harmless resolution passed by both houses and transmitted to Congress. Assembly Concurrent Resolution no. 16 called for a grant to the state of the public lands comprising the watershed of the streams flowing into the Valley and a request to Congress to amend the Act of 1864 so that the Legislature could elect three Commissioners to be paid by the State and required to reside in the Valley during the season it was accessible to visitors.[74] As we shall see, Congress chose to react quite differently.

One more point should be mentioned here. It may seem curious that Muir was not called as a witness in the state investigation. His views, of course, were already well known—and certainly not favorable to the Commissioners. As early as 1872 he had addressed a letter to the *New York Tribune* in which he charged the Commissioners with "vulgar, mercenary improvement" of the Valley.[75] As a frequent visitor and resident in the Valley he was, of course, well acquainted with what the Commissioners were doing as well as the criticisms raised by others. Muir would never condone any policy that allowed the injudicious cutting of trees, plowing of meadows, and fencing of large areas of Valley bottomland.

Hutchings, and Muir too—perhaps others—were aware of Olmsted's 1865 report. Hutchings apparently had a copy of at least parts of the document, which he made available to the *Examiner*.[76] The legacy that Olmsted left in California was nurtured by men who agreed with his ideas and who felt that the only solution for the Valley was the employment of someone as gifted as he in his judgments about nature and its preservation. Indeed, attempts were made by Robert Underwood Johnson, Associate Editor of *Century Magazine*, to interest Olmsted in returning to California to investigate conditions, a suggestion he felt obliged to decline because of an "existing professional engagement."[77]

[73] *Loc. cit.*

[74] *Journal of the Assembly,* California Legislature, 28th Sess., 1889, p. 787. (Also *Journal . . . Senate,* 1889, p. 1046.)

[75] Quoted in Linnie Marsh Wolfe, *Son of the Wilderness; the Life of John Muir* (New York, Alfred Knopf, 1945), p. 157. Article, "Yosemite in Winter" appeared in *New York Tribune.* Muir dated article or letter January 1, 1872, but I was not able to locate it in subsequent issues of the *Tribune.* Another article, "Yosemite in Spring," datelined May 7, 1872, was not printed by the *Tribune* until July 11 (p. 2). Having just experienced a severe earthquake in the Valley, Muir commented: "But the billed laws of Sacramento, and paper compulsions and prohibitions of our managing Commissioners, do us little harm or good. . . . We make laws for the mountains—make Commissioners to Manage Yosemite Valley. As well make Commissioners for the management of the moon."

[76] *San Francisco Examiner,* February 12, 1889, p. 2, an article which discusses the Senate investigation.

[77] Frederick Law Olmsted, *Governmental Preservation of Natural Scenery* (Brookline, Mass., privately printed, 1890), p. 1. Report is dated March 8, 1890. Reprinted in *SCB,* XXIX (October 1944), pp. 61–66. The unsigned article by Johnson in which he refers to "a competent judge" and quotes from Olmsted without naming him appears in *Century Magazine,* XXXIX (January 1890), pp. 474–475.

25. SINNING COTTAGE, which became the Club's Yosemite headquarters in 1898.
Probably built before 1875, it derived its name from Adolph Sinning, who acquired
the building in 1877 and conducted a woodworking and curio shop there.
(Photograph by J. N. LeConte.)

26. INTERIOR VIEW of
Sinning Cottage remodeled to
serve as the Club's Yosemite
headquarters, with a meeting
room and a public display
area containing a small
mountaineering library.
(Photograph by J. N. LeConte.)

27. HAYSTACK in Sentinel
Meadow, illustrating the type of
destruction of the natural scene
that angered Muir. This
photograph was taken in 1867 by
Eadweard Muybridge {Edward
Muggeridge} on his first
photographic trip to the Valley.
(See (5), map on p. 190.)

28. ALMOST A HUNDRED
YEARS LATER. William Hood's
photograph from the same
vantage point shows the major
change in tree growth and
recovery of the foreground
vegetation.

29. A STEREO, taken in 1867 or 1872 by Muybridge, showing the type of fencing that replaced barbed wire in some areas.

30. "A VALLEY IMPROVEMENT," another Muybridge photograph taken in either 1867 or 1872, showing another type of fencing around the meadows. (See (3), map on p. 188.)

31. "CATHEDRAL ROCKS AND REFLECTIONS" Identified as a Houseworth
{no. 43}, but believed to be a Muybridge; date unknown. (See (2), map on
p. 186.)

32. VALLEY VIEW POINT on the
trail to Yosemite Falls, taken by
George Fiske, probably in 1890.
The Sentinel Hotel is in the lower
right-hand corner and fences
criss-cross the meadows. (See (4),
map on p. 189.)

IV

In effect the state investigation of 1889 vindicated the Yosemite Commissioners. It should also have warned them that the public interest demanded reconsideration of management policies. The policy of active promotion to enlarge the state grant—a recommendation that had been made by Hall in his report to the Board—at first drew the support of the new conservationists, but later, when the effects of Valley management became all too evident, they turned against *state* administration for an enlarged reserve.

Efforts for enlargement of the grant had begun long before the investigation of 1889. When the new commissioners appointed by Governor Perkins met in San Francisco on March 22, 1881 they unanimously adopted a resolution that "it is the deliberate judgment of the undersigned Commissioners and other citizens, that important purposes of Health, Pleasure, Education and Science would be subserved by . . . an extension of the Yosemite Valley and Mariposa Big Tree Grants."[78] One of the Commissioners, William H. Mills, assisted in securing signatures favorable to enlargement. This petition, as well as some letters, were left by Secretary Briggs in Washington when he visited the Capitol in June; he also had an interview with President Garfield on the subject just three days before the latter's assassination.[79]

There is some evidence that Muir, in spite of his criticism of the Commissioners, cooperated with them in the framing of a bill which was passed along to U.S. Senator Miller.[80] In December 1881, Miller introduced S. 393 to create an enlarged grant, but an apathetic Congress took no action when local opposition, castigated later by the Commissioners in their *Biennial Report,* suddenly became aware of what was happening.[81] The editorial that appeared in the *San Francisco Chronicle* after public submission of William Ham Hall's recommendations is typical of this opposition:

It is a good time to repeat here the arguments often urged . . . that in accepting this Yosemite grant from the Federal Government, on the condition that the State shall improve and beautify it at its own expense, we got a white elephant. No doubt Yosemite is one of the wonders of the world. It would be the same, and retain all its beauties, if the U.S. had surveyed and sold the Valley to settlers and cultivators. It would be better, in fact, to have two or three small villages there and fifty small farmhouses, inhabited by fifty industrious and thriving farmers with their wives and children, than that the whole thing should be monopolized by the State, with one or two hotels, run at the expense of the taxpayers, and a corps of landscape gardeners and surveyors to keep it in

[78] "Minutes of a Meeting . . . Called by the Executive Committee in the Office of the Secretary, San Francisco, March 22, 1881," C.Y.V., *Minute Book,* California State Archives, p. 24.

[79] "Biennial Report C.Y.V., so Extended as to Include All Transactions of the Commission from April 19, 1880, to December 18, 1882," *A.J.S.A.,* 25th Sess. (Sacramento, 1882), doc. 6, IV, pp. 10–12.

[80] Linnie Marsh Wolfe, *op. cit.,* p. 227.

[81] *Congressional Record,* 47th Cong., 1st Sess., vol. 13, pt. 1 (Dec. 12, 1881), p. 68. Miller also introduced S. 463 the following day "for setting apart a certain tract of land in the State of California as a public park" (p. 78). The success of this bill would have created a Sequoia-Kings Canyon reserve and completely changed the long drawn-out history to establish these two parks, which culminated only as recently as 1940—almost sixty years later! Petitions for and against both Miller bills were presented in Congress and referred to the Committee on Public Lands. George G. Mackenzie, in one of his many letters to the editor of the *New York Times,* refers to the Miller bill and a petition against it which he says "he never saw . . . or learned who the men were who signed it." (Letter dated Wawona, January 18, 1890, in *Times,* January 26, 1890, p. 10.)

order. We do not believe that Lake Como or Lake Leman would be as attractive as private enterprise has made them if the respective governments in which they lie held them in fee and exercised full control over their surroundings. But this is not all. Places like Yosemite and Yellowstone Park in the Rocky Mountains are seldom visited by the common people, and never from any distance by the poor. The rich—foreign and native—enjoy a monopoly of these pleasure grounds. It is wrong in principle and oppressive in practice for any government to tax the common people and the poor for the exclusive benefit of the rich. We long ago pointed out that if the State carries out the intention of the conditions of this Yosemite grant, it will be at the cost of many thousands of dollars in the shape of taxes on the property of the great masses of the people who never can and never expect to see that Valley or derive the slightest benefit from its beauty and sublimity.[82]

Such editorial notice in the press did not prevent similar bills from being thrown into the hopper in the next two Congresses, although also without success.[83] The Commissioners were not discouraged, however. The report of the committee on legislation, adopted June 2, 1887, sets forth the Board's convictions:

. . . A considerable extension of the limits of the Yosemite Grant to the eastward is essential to the preservation of the water supply in the streams meeting in the Valley. In our judgment the territory embraced in the watershed of the Valley proper, or in other words the entire basin of every stream leading into the Valley should be under the control of the Commissioners to the end that the timber, shrubbery and grasses thereon may be preserved to retain the snow and rain upon which the grandeur and beauty of all Yosemite streams depend.

. . . We recommend that the Executive Committee be instructed to prepare a bill to be introduced in the next Congress having for its object the extension of the Yosemite Grant in accordance with the foregoing suggestions, that said Committee also cause to be prepared and mailed to every Representative and Senator in Congress a memorial address setting forth the necessities of the proposed extension; and that said Committee . . . take such further steps as may seem likely to secure the passage of said measure.[84]

Again, in 1888, the report of the Committee on Preservation of the Valley, Grove, Morals, and Good Order favored "the most active efforts to secure an early and material extension of the boundaries of the Yosemite Grant so as to place the watershed of the Valley within the control of the Commissioners."[85] We have seen, finally, that the Legislature itself, following its investigation into the affairs of the Commissioners, asked Congress to extend the Grant.[86]

Congress acted, but not in the way the Commissioners or the Legislature hoped it would. On September 22, 1890, Senator Plumb, Chairman of the Public Lands Committee, called for an investigation into the charges of maladministration in the Valley, and, in separate action a few days later, Congress passed the Yosemite bill creating a *federal* reserve around the state grant.[87]

[82] *San Francisco Chronicle*, June 26, 1882, p. 2.

[83] S. 2454, by Senator Miller, *Congressional Record*, 48th Cong., 2nd Sess., vol. 16, pt. 1 (Dec. 15, 1884), p. 230. Also H. R. 5568, by James A. Louttit, *Congressional Record*, 49th Cong., 1st Sess., vol. 17, pt. 2 (Feb. 15, 1886), p. 1443. No further action was taken on either bill.

[84] "Report, Committee on Legislation," C.Y.V. *Minutes of the Board*, Exhibit K, Book 3053, California State Archives, pp. 214–215.

[85] "Report," Committee on Preservation . . . , Exhibit D., *ibid.*, p. 300.

[86] *Supra.*, p. 40.

[87] *Congressional Record*, 51st Cong., 1st Sess., vol. 21, pt. 10 (Sept. 22, 1890), p. 10297. Also *ibid.*, vol. 21, pt. 11 (Sept. 30, 1890), pp. 10740 and 10752.

What happened? Does part of the answer lie in Muir's long opposition to the Commissioners, the effective promotion of his good friend and Washington lobbyist, Robert Underwood Johnson, and perhaps the secret support of the Southern Pacific Railroad?

v

Johnson first met Muir in San Francisco's Palace Hotel and traveled with him in June 1889 to the Yosemite Valley.[88] Out of this well-known journey the idea was born of establishing a magnificent new national park of the high mountain country about Yosemite. Johnson asked Muir to write two articles on the proposed park, and in the spring of 1890 Muir did so.[89]

On March 4, 1890, Muir wrote to Johnson discussing "the extension of the grant," which he felt should "at least comprehend all the basins of the streams pouring into the Valley."[90] Enclosing a map in his own hand, marking in detail the boundaries he proposed for the new park, he commented further: "A yet greater extension I have marked on the same map, extending north and south between lat. 38° and 37° 30' and from the axis of the range westward about thirty-six or forty miles. This would include three groves of Big Trees, the Tuolumne Cañon, Tuolumne Meadows, and Hetch Hetchy Valley. So large an extension would, of course, meet more opposition. Its boundary lines would not be nearly so natural, while to the westward many claims would be encountered; a few also about Mounts Dana and Warren, where mines have been opened."[91]

Two weeks after Muir wrote this letter to Johnson a Yosemite Park bill (H. R. 8350) was introduced by Representative William Vandever.[92] The Vandever bill, however, did not create the park envisioned by Muir. It did not include the Soda Springs campsite nor did it include any of the Tuolumne River watershed. In fact, it omitted a good deal of the north portion of the Merced drainage—Lake Tenaya, for example. H. R. 8350 asked that Congress set aside "for the purpose of preserving the forest, and as a recreation ground for the people as a public park," a block of eight townships surrounding and including the state-controlled Yosemite Valley grant, an area of approximately 288 square miles.

After the introduction of Vandever's bill, Johnson worked hard to convince the House Committee on Public Lands that it did not go far enough. He wrote to Muir twice in April 1890, asking him to write an "emphatic" letter supporting the suggestion to extend the Vandever limits so that Johnson could present

[88] See Robert U. Johnson, "Personal Impressions of John Muir," *The Outlook*, LXXX (June 3, 1905), pp. 303–306; also his *Remembered Yesterdays* (Boston, Little, Brown and Company, 1923), pp. 279–280; and Wolfe, *op. cit.*, p. 244.

[89] "Treasures of the Yosemite," *Century Magazine*, XL (August 1890), pp. 483–500; and "Features of the Proposed Yosemite National Park," *Century Magazine*, XL (September 1890), pp. 656–667.

[90] Muir, Martinez, to Johnson, New York, March 4, 1890, reprinted in *SCB*, XXIX (October 1944), pp. 51–54. Also reprinted in part in William F. Badè, *The Life and Letters of John Muir* (Boston and New York, Houghton Mifflin Co., 1924), II, pp. 237–240. The map enclosed with this letter was copied by the *Century* engraver to illustrate Muir's articles cited above. It is now in the Bancroft Library, University of California.

[91] Badè, *op. cit.*, II, pp. 239–240.

[92] *Congressional Record*, 51st Cong., 1st Sess., vol. 21, pt. 3 (March 18, 1890), p. 2372.

this evidence to the Committee.[93] On April 20, 1890 Muir wrote Johnson: ". . . As for the reservation being controlled by the Federal Government, this is of all things what the present management most dread. . . . Stand up for the Vandever Bill and on no account let the extension be under state control if it can possibly be avoided."[94]

And again on May 8: ". . . As I have urged over and over again, the Yosemite Reservation ought to include all the Yosemite fountains. They all lie in a compact mass of mountains that are glorious scenery, easily accessible from the grand Yosemite centre, and are not valuable for any other use than the use of beauty. No other interests would suffer by this extension of the boundary. Only the summit peaks along the axis of the range are possibly gold bearing, and not a single valuable mine has yet been discovered in them. Most of the basin is a mass of solid granite that will never be available for agriculture—while its forests ought to be preserved. The Big Tuolumne Meadows should also be included since it forms the central camping ground for the High Sierra adjacent to the Valley. The Tuolumne Cañon is so closely related to the Yosemite region it should also be included, but whether it is or not will not matter much since it lies in rugged rocky security as one of Nature's own reservations. As to the lower boundary, it should, I think, be extended so far as to include the Big Tree Groves below the Valley, thus bringing under Government protection a section of the forest containing specimens of all the principal trees of the Sierra, and which, if left unprotected, will vanish like snow in summer."[95]

Armed with these statements, Johnson appeared before the Committee on Public Lands on June 2, 1890.[96] (This was slightly less than two weeks before Muir sailed for Alaska, to return in September.) Johnson urged the Committee to extend the limits set forth in the Vandever Bill to include the Tuolumne River watershed and the Ritter Range on the east. That Johnson seemed satisfied with the Committee intentions is indicated by the footnote he appended to the Muir map reproduced in the September 1890 issue of *Century*: "As we go to press, the Committee seems disposed to extend the north and south limits eastward to the Nevada line."[97]

Johnson's efforts to demonstrate the inadequacies of the Vandever bill, however, proved unnecessary. A second Yosemite bill (H. R. 12187) was substituted for H. R. 8350 and passed through both houses of Congress on September 30, the last day of the first session, without the customary bill printing. This new bill provided for a park that was, almost township for township, like the one Muir had sketched for Johnson in the

[93] Johnson, New York, to Muir, Martinez, April 25 and 29, 1890, Author copies.

[94] Muir, Martinez, to Johnson, New York, April 20, 1890, reprinted in *SCB*, XXIX (October 1944), pp. 55–57.

[95] Muir, Martinez, to Johnson, New York, May 8, 1890, reprinted in *ibid.*, pp. 57–58.

[96] U.S. Congress. House Committee on Public Lands. *Minute Book*, June 2, 1890, National Archives, Legislative Division.

[97] Editor's footnote in Muir, "Features of the Proposed Yosemite National Park," *Century Magazine*, XL (September 1890), p. 666.

33. "LEIDIG MEADOWS," plowed in October 1888 for hay. (Probably one of the photographs supplied by Charles D. Robinson to Robert Underwood Johnson during the Senate investigation of conditions in Yosemite Valley; it accompanied Muir's article, "Treasures of the Yosemite.") (See (1), map on p. 185.)

34. STUMP FOREST in "State Pasture." (This picture and legend from an 1890 *Century Magazine* indicate that some eight acres were cut over in June 1887, about 2,000 trees being felled.)

35. SPECIMEN TREE TRIMMING, 1887–1888. Some preservationists were alarmed at the amount of trimming and cutting resulting from the Commissioners' order to clear away undergrowth and to open up views of the canyon walls. Muir advocated judicious trimming and "the thinning and clearing of undergrowth jungles."

36. WILLIAM VANDEVER, Congressional representative from Ventura County, introduced a Yosemite National Park bill in 1890, in which year he also introduced two bills to establish Sequoia National Park.

37. CURTIN'S "COW CAMP" in Yosemite National Park, typical, isolated, private landholding within the Park boundaries. Failure of cattle owners to fence their property adequately led to friction between them and the Army administrators.

38. COLONEL HARRY C. BENSON, assigned to Yosemite in 1895 and Acting Superintendent, 1905–1908, was uncompromising in his enforcement of regulations for park protection.

39. **ON THE WAY TO THE YOSEMITE VALLEY.** For twenty-three years,
following the discovery of Yosemite, tourists could visit the Valley only by foot
or on horseback.

40. "YOSEMITE STAGE AND TURNPIKE COMPANY COACH going downgrade into the Valley," a photograph by George Fiske of the stage on the Wawona road. When the Coulterville and Big Oak Flat roads reached the Valley in 1874, the stage coach was the chief means of access.

41. THE FIRST AUTOMOBILE in Yosemite, which entered in July 1900, was a Stanley Steamer driven by Mr. A. E. Holmes of San Francisco.

42. TRAIN TERMINAL AT EL PORTAL. Beginning construction in September 1905, the Yosemite Valley Railroad ran its first train along the Merced River to El Portal on May 15, 1907. There were twelve passengers. From that time on, it dominated the tourist passenger service to the Valley until a severe flood in 1937 wiped out a considerable part of the track. Although rebuilt, it finally went out of service in 1944.

Joseph LeConte (signature)

43. JOSEPH LECONTE was one of the first appointees to the new University of California faculty in 1869, where he was Professor of Geology, Botany, and Natural History. He was a charter member of the Club, a Director until 1898, and served a term as Vice-President.

44. J. N. LECONTE, Joseph LeConte's son, was affectionately called "Little Joe" by his friends. He continued the long family association with the University and the Sierra Club, serving as a Director for forty-two years (1898–1940) and as Treasurer from 1899 to 1915, when he succeeded Muir as President. In 1931 he was elected the first Honorary President, serving until his death in 1950.

45. LECONTE MEMORIAL LODGE was completed in 1904 in time
for the summer season, three years after Joseph LeConte's death. It
was moved in 1919 from its original site near what is now Camp
Curry to the south side of the Valley.

46. SHEEP NEAR YOSEMITE. A Herbert Gleason photograph of sheep near Alger Lake, from which they could easily wander into the park. Colonel Benson discouraged such infractions by removing the sheepherders to the opposite side of the park and leaving the sheep.

47. CHARLES M. BELSHAW, Senator for California, introduced the recession bill which Colby and Mills had prepared and led the recession fight in the Senate. The photograph in Yosemite was taken three years after the passage of the bill.

map he had enclosed in his March 4 letter to his friend.[98] The substitute bill, which became law on October 1, created a park more than five times the size of the one described by Vandever—a huge district of 1,512 square miles. John Ise, in his book, *Our National Park Policy,* neglects to mention the significant difference in size proposed by each of the two bills; he wonders how the substitute bill could have passed so quickly and goes on to suggest that the commercial interests may have been taken by surprise and that Congress may have confused the new park with the Valley.[99] A curious point is that H. R. 12187 used the phrase, "Yosemite forest reservation," rather than "Yosemite National Park" as in the Vandever bill. Did the promoters of the park purposely change the name to confuse their opponents?

The circumstances surrounding the introduction and passage of these bills to establish Yosemite Park are lost in the passage of time and insufficient documentation. Vandever himself denied that *Century Magazine* had anything to do with this bill.[100] The California Commissioners, perhaps anxious to appropriate to themselves the honor of having succeeded in enlarging the reservation, even if not under their jurisdiction, make it appear that they were responsible for Vandever's bill. This is possible, of course, especially in the light of their unanimous resolution of March 1881, the Hall recommendations of May 1882, and the report of the committee of legislation of June 1887, but it is by no means clear from the evidence.

It is known that the Commissioners discussed the Vandever bill at their June 4, 1890, meeting in the Valley and that John P. Irish, Secretary and Treasurer, reported that he had visited the Assistant U.S. Land Commissioner in Washington, William M. Stone, who promised to inspect the Yosemite "this summer 'with a view to reporting such administrative and legislative action as he would deem necessary to protect the surrounding forests and the water courses which supply the falls of the Valley.' "[101] In their *Biennial Report* of 1889–1890 the Commissioners state that Representative Vandever and Holman of Indiana "collaborated in a bill" to save the Yosemite watershed from deforestation.[102] Three years later in a letter from the Executive Committee addressed to the Secretary of the Interior, the flat statement is made that the Commissioners "moved first in the matter of requesting Federal Reservation of the watershed of the Yosemite Valley" and that the bill was introduced "at our request."[103]

Should the Commissioners' statements be taken at their face value? From what we know of the controversy between some of the Commissioners and John Muir; from an assumption that the

[98] *Congressional Record,* 51st Cong., 1st. Sess., vol. 21, pt. 11 (Sept. 30, 1890), p. 10752.

[99] Ise, *op. cit.,* pp. 57–58.

[100] William Vandever to John P. Irish, September 9, 1890, reprinted in *Biennial Report C.Y.V. for the Years 1889–90* (Sacramento, 1890), pp. 7–8.

[101] Remarks of John P. Irish quoted by George G. Mackenzie in the latter's letter to the editor dated July 13, 1890, *New York Times,* July 20, 1890, p. 3.

[102] *Biennial Report C.Y.V. for the Years 1889–90* (Sacramento, 1890), p. 7.

[103] Executive Committee of the C.Y.V., San Francisco, to the Secretary of the Interior, Washington, D.C., June 15, 1893, Records of the Interior Department, National Archives, R.G. 79.

commissioners must have been acquainted with Muir's desire to have a federal reserve surrounding the Valley; and from the absence of any corroborative evidence in support of the Executive Committee's statement to the Secretary of the Interior, it seems improbable, on the one hand, that the Commissioners could have asked Vandever to introduce a bill that in its second section placed the proposed park under the "exclusive control of the Secretary of the Interior," thus denying to the commissioners authority over an extended land area and management of the Merced watershed.

On the other hand, the role of the preservationists is equally unclear; the disparity between Vandever's boundary description and the ideas of Muir for the park would seem to suggest that neither Muir nor Johnson asked Vandever to introduce the bill. Who did, then? Was it the Commissioner of the General Land Office or Secretary of Interior Noble? Could the Southern Pacific Railroad possibly have had a hand in the introduction of this bill?

The role of the Southern Pacific in the establishment of the California parks is one of the most provocative conservation questions yet to be explored by the historian. Did this powerful transportation monopoly support the state Commissioners in its public pronouncements only to lobby secretly in Washington for federal control of the Yosemite area? One indefatigable critic of the commissioners' management policies, George G. Mackenzie, whose well-phrased letters to the editor were published in the *New York Times,* believed that if any opposition developed to the proposed enlargement of Yosemite such opposition would be "likely to crystallize into a cry that [it] is a scheme in the interest of the Southern Pacific Company and of a monopoly said to exist in the business of accommodating travelers."[104] Mackenzie felt there was no basis for such objections—"If the Southern Pacific has any improper designs in this direction, they are altogether too remote and mysterious for ordinary comprehension."[105] Living near the Valley a part of each year, Mackenzie knew the hotel and transportation concessionaires; he believed that they were not in favor of enlarging the grant under state administration. If this is so, perhaps they took this view because they felt their leases might be protected better if the jurisdiction in the Yosemite region were divided between the federal government and the state.

Muir himself believed that the "soulless Southern Pacific R.R. Co., never counted on for anything good, helped nobly in pushing the bill for this park through Congress."[106] Ten days after the creation of the park, the *San Francisco Bulletin* published the first news of the new reservation, reporting, "The Southern

[104] *New York Times,* January 26, 1890, p. 10.
[105] *Loc. cit.*
[106] "Proceedings of the Meeting of the Sierra Club Held November 23, 1895," *SCB,* I (January 1896), p. 275.

Pacific people, who are much interested in the project, [are] taking steps already to make these reservations known as attractive resorts for tourists.''[107]

Only ten days after the President signed the Yosemite Act, Southern Pacific Company stationery displayed a map of Sequoia National Park's extension—an extension incorporated in the third section of the substitute Yosemite bill (H. R. 12187). Subsequently alluring railroad tourist folders on Yosemite, Sequoia, and the Big Trees were issued; and *Sunset Magazine* appeared, first published in 1898 by the Southern Pacific to publicize California's attractions. All this is concrete evidence that the railroad took a prompt interest in the parks and their promotion as soon as the legislation creating them had been signed into law.[108]

There is no question that the Southern Pacific was strongly motivated by the potential of tourist traffic to the Sierra parks. Very early in Yosemite's transportation history the railroad had built a spur line to Raymond, in Madera County, to connect with the Wawona Road, which opened in 1875. According to popular opinion of the time—as witness Mackenzie's comment—the Southern Pacific had succeeded in capturing much of the tourist trade to the Valley prior to the opening of the Yosemite Valley Railroad's more direct line up the Merced River Canyon to El Portal in 1907. In fact, when its business was threatened by the El Portal line, the Southern Pacific succeeded in convincing Congress that boundary alterations in the park should be made to accommodate its proposed electric line from Fresno.

It is known that the railroad had representatives in Washington, and it seems entirely plausible that they may indeed have aided Johnson and the Committee on Public Lands in securing the much enlarged park so similar to Muir's ideas but so unlike Vandever's bill.[109]

VI

The Sierra Club, established as a defender of the newly created federal reserve, faced two vital problems: the boundary disputes that arose over the federal park and, later, the recession of the Valley to the federal government. It must be remembered that there were two groups of vested interests in the Yosemite region, the State Commissioners, who had exercised the prerogatives of the "public interests" since 1864, and the commercial or private interests.

It is obvious that the legislation setting up the new federal

---

[107] *San Francisco Bulletin*, October 11, 1890, p. 3. It is interesting that the *Mariposa Gazette,* the only newspaper which could be called a "hometown" paper for the Valley, carried no mention of the Congressional action until its issue of October 25, and then it was a reprint of the *Bulletin* story. Even less notice was taken in the nation's great dailies of the day; the *New York Times* and the *New York Daily Tribune* did not report on the Yosemite Act, although the former had published editorials in favor of the park and a number of letters from Johnson, Mackenzie, and others.

[108] The original of the Southern Pacific Company map of Sequoia National Park is in the National Archives, Records of the Interior Department, R.G. 79; it is reproduced in Oscar Berland, "Giant Forest's Reservation: The Legend and the Mystery," *SCB*, XLVII (December 1962), p. 79. Berland is unable to account for the Giant Forest's addition to Sequoia National Park through the enactment of Section III of the Yosemite bill of September 30.

[109] In an attempt to discover if any Southern Pacific records survived the 1906 fire, I wrote to the railroad's Public Relations Department and received this frustrating reply: "We think there must be some validity to your belief because we did turn up a file index with notations referring to files 'covering correspondence and agreements on the establishment of Yosemite Park.' When we checked, though, the files had been destroyed in 1938 . . ." (letter from William Phelps, San Francisco, to author, Oakland, June 21, 1962). For additional information on the Yosemite bills, see my "Mysterious Origin of the Yosemite Park Bill," *SCB*, XLVIII (December 1963), pp. 69–79.

park took little account of the existing patented lands within its boundaries. Not long after the Park had been created, Captain Wood, military superintendent from 1891 to 1893, estimated that there were "more than 65,000 acres in homestead, pre-emption, and timber claims" and perhaps as many as three hundred mining claims.[110] In fairness to the promoters of the enlarged Park, however, it should be noted that they recognized its boundaries included private lands that would have to be purchased by the government. "The cost will not be great," said Muir, who honestly believed the government would buy these lands.[111] Fourteen years later, however, the Yosemite Park Commission estimated that it would cost the government more than four million dollars to extinguish all private claims.[112]

What were these private interests that claimed such a significant amount of land in the new reserve? They were those of the miners, in whom hope always springs eternal no matter how barren the pay dirt, who had staked claims principally in the Mt. Dana–Minarets area in the east and in the Chowchilla region in the west. They were those of the lumber companies, which needed only better access to small private holdings and further consolidation of them in order to begin logging operations. (Indeed, it was rumored that a major lumber company would soon buy out its rivals, thus monopolizing the magnificent sugar pine forests near the Merced and Tuolumne groves of Big Trees.) They were the rival interests of the Southern Pacific and the Yosemite Valley Railroad Company, which threatened to alienate certain lands in the west. They were the interests of the hunters, whose sport would be multiplied if park lands could be transferred to the Sierra Forest Reserve, where game was not preserved. Finally, they were the interests of the sheep and cattle ranchers—of people like John Curtin, whose voluminous correspondence with the acting superintendents of Yosemite National Park, particularly with Major Harry C. Benson, is a classic expression of the rugged individualism exhibited by western pioneers in resisting the slightest government control.[113] Many of even those people who believed firmly in the reservation of the forests did so only because they desired government protection of watershed and reservoir sites until the ultimate development by private initiative of water storage, irrigation works, power projects, and associated rights of way. These were the groups who desired to push the Park boundaries eastward into higher mountains or to eliminate the Park altogether.

Curtin's vindication in the Supreme Court of the United States indicates that not all justice favored the federal government.[114] Curtin had legally acquired title to several hundred acres

[110] "Report of the Acting Superintendent of the Yosemite National Park," July 15, 1893, *Report of the Secretary of the Interior*, U.S. 53rd Cong., 2nd Sess., vol. III (House Ex. Doc., 1893–94, vol. XIV), p. 651.

[111] Muir, Martinez, to Johnson, New York, May 8, 1890, reprinted in Badè, *op. cit.*, II, p. 245.

[112] *Report of the Yosemite Park Commission*, U.S. 58th Cong. 3rd Sess., S. Doc. 34 (1904), p. 7. Although these lands had been sold by the government at $2.50 an acre under the homestead, timber, and pre-emption laws, by the time a federal Commission investigated conditions, fourteen years after the formation of the enlarged Park, values had so risen that some land was appraised at $30 or more an acre. Nevertheless, in relation to the more than six millions paid in the 1930's, $5,000,000 would have been cheap. In terms of relative cost, then, Muir was right; that is, the cost would probably not have exceeded half the amount later estimated by the Chittenden Commission, if Congress had been willing to appropriate the money in the 1890's.

[113] H. C. Benson to Secretary of the Interior, Washington, D.C., May 28, 1906, 41 pp., presents the Acting Superintendent's side of the story and quotes from several letters to and from Curtin. This report and many of the letters themselves are in the Records of the National Park Service, R. G. 79, National Archives.

[114] *Curtin v. Benson* (Oct. 1911), 222 U.S. 78.

of private land at Gin, Crane, and Tamarack flats within the Park. Much of this land was used as summer grazing grounds for his cattle herds. Typically, these meadows were not fenced, or at least not completely enclosed, so that cattle frequently trespassed upon Park lands. There were regulations against this sort of encroachment, of course, and Curtin's disregard of Park rules appeared so flagrant to the Acting Superintendents that he was prevented from driving his animals along the private toll roads through the Park to his property. Curtin brought suit against Benson and at first lost the decision in the Circuit Court for the Northern District of California, only to be upheld by the court of highest appeal.[115]

There were a number of obviously legitimate private holdings within the boundary lines of the new Park. Ise has chronicled in some detail the various bills introduced in Congress during the 1890's to "ascertain damage to persons," to cut out certain parts of the Park, and to apply "the 'lieu-scrip' provisions already applicable to the forest reserves."[116] The most serious of these "reduction" measures in the 1890's was the Caminetti Bill, the defeat of which, as noted in the first chapter, was the first important conservation work of the Sierra Club.

Suspecting that more serious problems with inholdings lay ahead, Elliott McAllister, then secretary of the Sierra Club, searched the records of the General Land Office in Stockton. McAllister then wrote a long letter to the Secretary of the Interior listing patented lands within the park "with a view of showing that there is little real merit in the legislation; and with a view of having the material at hand should it become necessary to show just what interests are affected and to show where any alterations should be made."[117] Although McAllister's work was not entirely accurate, his premonition proved more than correct. Between 1898 and 1904 no fewer than nine bills were introduced by Senator Perkins and California Representatives De Vries and Gillett to restore valuable park timber lands to the public domain.[118] It was also in this critical period that Congressman De Vries succeeded in pushing through his notorious Right of Way Act of 1901—a law that was to prove particularly damaging to the Park.[119]

Matters came to a head in 1903 when a lumber company began cutting trees on its properties within the Park.[120] Finally, in 1904, Congress, having turned a deaf ear to the numerous bills to cut out parts of the Park, granted $3,000 in the Sundry Civil Appropriation Act for an examination in the field.[121] To undertake this investigation Secretary Hitchcock in June appointed Hiram M. Chittenden, an Army Engineer who had had charge of the road-building in Yellowstone National Park since

[115] For an interesting account of Curtin's Yosemite problems, see Irene D. Paden and Margaret E. Schlichtmann, *Big Oak Flat Road; An Account of Freighting from Stockton to Yosemite Valley* (San Francisco, Lawton Kennedy, 1955).

[116] Ise, *op. cit.*, pp. 65 ff.

[117] McAllister, Sierra Club, to Secretary of the Interior, Washington, D.C., June 12, 1896, R. G. 79, National Archives. A complete listing of the private lands for Mariposa and Tuolumne counties up to 1904, both within the then existing Park boundaries and within the proposed Park boundaries, appears in *Report of the Yosemite Park Commission*, U.S. 58th Cong., 3rd Sess., S. Doc. 34 (1904), pp. 31–39. A fold-out map in color pinpoints the exact location of the various holdings by their method of acquisition—homestead, pre-emption, etc.

[118] *Infra.*, pp. 74 ff.

[119] *Infra.*, pp. 89 ff.

[120] Edith Germain Kettlewell, "Yosemite: The Discovery of Yosemite Valley and the Creation and Realignment of Yosemite National Park" (M. A. thesis in history, University of California, 1930), p. 57.

[121] 33 *U.S. Stat. at L.* (1904), 487.

49

1899; Robert Marshall, a topographer with the U.S. Geological Survey engaged in the first surveys for the Yosemite, Dardanelles, and Mount Lyell map sheets; and Frank Bond, chief of the drafting division, General Land Office. The Chittenden Commission met at Wawona near the end of the month. On July 2, Muir received a communication from Chittenden asking for an interview and assuring him that "we should feel greatly disappointed unless we can see you and obtain a full expression of your views."[122]

The Sierra Club, of course, had a vital interest in the boundary question, and shortly after the appointment of the commission the directors appointed their own committee to make recommendations to Chittenden. These recommendations were prepared during the summer and submitted to the Commission on August 23, 1904. The committee, composed of Muir, LeConte, and Colby, felt that the needs of the large number of private land owners "regretfully" necessitated the removal from the Park of Townships 2, 3, and 4 South, Range 19 East on the southwest corner; but "to withdraw any larger area either to the east or north of the three townships mentioned would, we believe, be too great an encroachment upon the wonderful scenic features."[123] On the northern and southern boundaries the committee not only felt that no land should be eliminated, but also . . . expressed a favorable attitude toward the extension of these boundaries. The recommendation of the Club committee concerning the eastern boundary urged the *addition* to the park of the following lands: "The west one half (½) of Township 1 North, Range 25 East; all of Township 2 South, Range 26 East; and the west one half (½) of Township 4 South, Range 27 East."[124]

The additional eastern townships suggested by the committee included what is now the popular resort areas around June Lake. The recommendation for their inclusion was made because the Club felt that the Park was insufficiently protected along its eastern border from the scourge of sheep invasions and because it contained scenic features "of so remarkable a nature that they should be made a part of the National Park."[125] The committee's thinking was perhaps conditioned by the numerous violations of the park boundary detected during the Club's outing to Tuolumne Meadows in the summer of 1904.[126]

The Commission, however, was strongly of the opinion that a natural boundary line would be "far easier to protect than that proposed by the Club," and added: "Valuable mineral lands will be excluded, the scenery will not be injured, for it is on too large a scale, and the forests will be protected in a forest reserve. The extension of the boundaries, as proposed by the Sierra Club,

[122] Chittenden, Yosemite Valley, to Muir, Martinez, July 2, 1904. Author copy. For an interesting characterization of the Commission's chief, see *H. M. Chittenden: a Western Epic; Being a Selection from His Unpublished Journals, Diaries, and Reports* (Tacoma, Washington State Historical Society, 1961), 136 pp.

[123] "To the Honorable Board of Commissioners Appointed to Investigate and Report on the Boundaries of the Yosemite National Park," *SCB*, V (January 1905), p. 250. See also *Report of the Yosemite Park Commission*, p. 51.

[124] *Loc. cit.*

[125] *Ibid.*, p. 251.

[126] William Colby, San Francisco, to Chittenden, August 28 1904, reprinted in *SCB*, V (January 1905), pp. 251–252.

would include the Tioga mines, a large number of private holdings, and the mining town of Mammoth, and would create new complications in the east of the park like those which it is sought to get rid of in the west."[127]

The Club, of course, recognized the validity of the mining claims, but Colby—a specialist in mining law—met the question in this fashion: "While there are many claims, yet they can only cover a small area of the territory,—and would it not be possible to allow their owners to retain and work them, under restrictions, of course? Would it not be better to suffer some small detraction of this nature than to cut off the area contemplated and the magnificent scenery it embraces, and thus lose it to the park entirely? Having had a large experience with mines and mining . . . I feel that very few of these claims will ever be exploited to any extent."[128]

Perhaps the Sierra Club realized it was asking more than it could reasonably expect the Commission to favor. At any rate, after the Club was informed that the Commission would recommend that the eastern boundary be changed to conform to the crest of the Sierra, Colby again wrote to Chittenden saying that the Club would not object to this decision if "at least one tier of townships fronting all along on this proposed eastern boundary be included in an extension of the forest reserve" to act as a buffer against invasion.[129]

The Act of February 7, 1905, redrew the map of Yosemite National Park.[130] It eliminated a number of townships on the four corners of the park—including all the Chowchilla mining claims in the southwestern section—and established as the eastern boundary the present Foerster–Isberg–Triple Divide Peak crest, thus eliminating the beautiful country of the upper San Joaquin River, the Minarets, Mount Ritter Range, and the Devil's Postpile. Altogether, some 542 square miles were excluded and 113 square miles added—mostly on the north to conform to natural terrain.

A few years later *Collier's*, under the by-line of Agnes C. Laut, published an article criticizing preservationists and referring to the slicing off of the corners of the Park in 1905 without "a word of protest from a living soul in the United States."[131] In reply, Colby cited the Commission's official report, indignantly remarking: "We protested vigorously against the elimination of Mt. Ritter region, and if you had heard our arguments before the Commission, you would not have thought it was any perfunctory protest. We never came into 'hearty accord' . . . on this change of boundaries and we still differ with them though overruled."[132]

With better protection of park boundaries today and the

[127] *Report of the Yosemite Park Commission*, p. 51.

[128] Colby, San Francisco, to Chittenden, August 28, 1904, reprinted in *SCB*, V (January 1905), p. 252.

[129] Colby, San Francisco, to Chittenden, September 7, 1904, reprinted in *SCB*, V (January 1905), p. 253.

[130] 33 *U.S. Stat. at L.* (1905), 702–703. This Act officially changed the name of the Yosemite Forest Reserve to Yosemite National Park. Unfortunately for the new conservationists, Congress failed to heed one important recommendation of the Chittenden Commission—the repeal of the 1901 Right-of-Way Act.

[131] Agnes C. Laut, "The Fight for Water in the West," part III, *Collier's*, XLIV (November 20, 1909), p. 15.

[132] Colby, San Francisco, to Laut, Wassaic, New York, December 17, 1909, copy, SCA. See also Colby, San Francisco, to Norman Hapgood, New York, November 26, 1909, copy, SCA.

abortion of most of the mining claims in the east (as Colby had predicted), the Club has regretted that a stronger position on this point was not maintained.[133] From that day to this the region has been a part of the national forest, although the Club did successfully persuade President Taft to proclaim the Devil's Postpile–Rainbow Falls section a national monument on July 11, 1910.[134]

The Yosemite boundary decision was accepted only with great reluctance by the Sierra Club. The keen disappointment that Club leaders must have felt was soon to be tempered, however, by the dramatic conclusion of the recession fight—a controversy that provided Muir and Colby valuable lessons in political expediency.

[133] The problem of the return of the Minarets—Reds Meadow region to national park status, or, more recently, to the status of a Wilderness Area under U.S. Forest Service jurisdiction, has been the subject of much discussion at Directors' meetings of the Sierra Club. See the memo prepared by the Club on August 2, 1926 (copy in Farquhar's private library) and the more recent action of February 4, 1950, May 6, 1950, January 19, 1957, June 8, 1957, and May 6, 1961. The latest action was the Club's reaffirmation of its opposition to any trans-Sierra road in the vicinity of Mammoth Pass, which would necessarily pass through or very close to Reds Meadow. This stand was taken when an official of the Curry Company suggested that an arrangement be worked out whereby the Club would support a new cross-Sierra road in return for Forest Service support of park status for this country. Although the Club continues to support wilderness status for the North Fork San Joaquin River Basin, it does not believe in compromising one principle to buy another.

[134] Richard J. Hartesveldt, "Historical Events at the Devil's Postpile," *Yosemite Nature Notes,* XXXIII (January 1954), p. 8. The draft of the proclamation and a map of the area were prepared by Walter Huber, then District Engineer with the U.S. Forest Service and later president of the Sierra Club (1925–1927), after Colby and LeConte had conferred with Henry S. Graves, Chief Forester, who had come to San Francisco on business. (Walter Huber to John C. Preston, Superintendent of Yosemite National Park, n.d., reprinted in the *SCB,* XXXIX (June 1954), pp. 80–81). See also file of correspondence relating to establishment of the Monument in *Water Resources Reports by Walter L. Huber,* Water Resources Center Archives, University of California, Berkeley.

3
RECESSION

". . . sound the loud timbrel and let every
Yosemite tree and stream rejoice . . ."
—John Muir

IT TOOK more than fifteen years of public education, thousands of words of news print, and a determined campaign on the part of Muir and the Sierra Club before victory was won in the fight for the recession of Yosemite Valley to the federal government.

And, at first, not all the new conservationists were convinced that the battle was an important one. In 1890 Muir complained to his friend Johnson: "The love of Nature among Californians is desperately moderate; consuming enthusiasm almost wholly unknown. . . .

"As to the management [of Yosemite Valley], it should, I think, be taken wholly out of the Governor's hands. The office changes too often and must always be more or less mixed with politics in its bearing upon appointments for the Valley. A commission consisting of the President of the University, the President of the State Board of Agriculture, and the President of the Mechanics Institute would, I think, be a vast improvement on the present commission. . . . Such changes would not be likely, as far as I can see, to provoke any formidable opposition on the part of Californians in general. Taking back the Valley on the part of the Government would probably be a troublesome job. . . . Everybody to whom I have spoken on the subject sees the necessity of a change, however, in the management, and would favor such a commission as I have suggested. For my part, I should rather see the Valley in the hands of the Federal Government. But how glorious a storm of growls and howls would rend our sunny skies, bursting forth from every paper in the state, at the outrage of the 'Century' Editor snatching with unholy hands, etc., the diadem from California's brow! . . . These Californians now sleeping in apathy, caring only for what 'pays,' would then blaze up as did the Devil when touched by Ithuriel's spear. A man may not appreciate his wife, but let her daddie try to take her back!"[1]

Johnson, perhaps doubtful that Californians would ever initiate recession of the Valley, continued to explore ways of bringing about action by the federal government. The legal difficulties seemed insurmountable, and in November 1893 the discouraging prospects were confirmed by a letter to Johnson from Richard Olney, Attorney General of the United States, enclosing

[1] Muir, Martinez, to Johnson, New York, March 4, 1890, reprinted in William Frederic Badè, *The Life and Letters of John Muir* (Boston, Houghton Mifflin Co., 1924), II, pp. 237–238. Also reprinted in *SCB*, XXIX (October, 1944), pp. 50–51.

the form letter applicable to such cases; Olney wrote: "You will observe that the Secretary of the Interior recommends that the State of California be applied to for a reconveyance of the territory to the United States. In my judgment the rights of the United States and of the public it represents in the territory can only be availed of either in the manner recommended by the Secretary of the Interior, or by other legislation looking to such legal proceedings as may be necessary to re-vest the land in the United States."[2] Shorn of its legal verbiage, this simply meant that the federal government was reluctant to act in such a touchy matter without express approval from California.

Nevertheless, officials of the Interior Department were well aware of the controversy over Valley management. The printed hearings of the California Legislative investigations were available to Secretary of the Interior John Noble. Following Senator Plumb's resolution in Congress calling for further investigations by the Secretary of the Interior, Noble received a number of letters from his Special Land Inspectors in the field which detailed conditions in the Valley.[3] It is apparent that some of the opinions of these inspectors were formed from information received from biased sources—particularly Charles D. Robinson, George Mackenzie, and J. M. Hutchings; Major Eugene F. Weigel's report, however, was largely based on interviews with Galen Clark, then Guardian and an employee of the State Commissioners, and this report expresses some of the same complaints and indicates that "a large majority of the people" living in and near the Valley "would be in favor of letting the government of the Yosemite Valley revert to the national government."[4] Robinson and Mackenzie not only kept Johnson informed, but also wrote several letters to the Secretary directly.[5]

Robinson supplied photographs and maps of the Valley conditions to Johnson and to Noble, which the Secretary appended to the report of his special inspectors when he reported to the Senate Public Lands Committee as a result of Plumb's resolution. Apparently Congress, like the executive branch of government, did not feel it had jurisdiction, or perhaps was not sufficiently impressed by the evidence, to advance its case in revoking the 1864 Act. In any case, no action was taken on the Secretary's report.

It was now obvious to Johnson that the first step must be taken by California if the anomaly of a state-administered territory surrounded by a federal-administered area was to be removed. Johnson believed that the Sierra Club was the best vehicle for this job. The Club, however, as we shall see, was slow to take up this particular responsibility for a number of reasons, partly personal, partly political.

[2] Richard Olney, Washington, D.C., to Johnson, New York, November 2, 1893, *Johnson Papers,* CB-385, box 6, folder no. 560, in Bancroft Library, University of California, Berkeley, hereafter cited as *Johnson Papers.*

[3] Thomas J. Newsham, San Francisco, to Noble, Washington, D.C., November 24, December 6, 7, 8, and 17, 1890, R. G. 79, National Archives. Also A. G. Speer, San Francisco, to Noble, Washington, March 2, 1892; and John S. Stidger, San Francisco, to Noble, Washington, May 18 and November 15, 1892, R. G. 79.

[4] "Report of Inspection from Major Eugene F. Weigel, Special Land Inspector," October 3, 1892, in *Report of the Secretary of the Interior,* U.S. 52nd Cong., 2nd Sess., House Executive doc. 1, pt. 5 (Washington, D.C., G.P.O., 1893), p. cxxxiv.

[5] C. D. Robinson, San Francisco, to Noble, Washington, D.C., October 23, December 8, 1890; January 20, 26, February 4, 15, July 15, October 18, 1891; and July 14, 1892. Also Robinson, San Francisco, to Hoke Smith, Washington, D.C., May 12, 1893. Mackenzie, Raymond, to Noble, Washington, D.C., November 1, 1890 and March, 1891 (n. d.). Robinson, San Francisco, to Johnson, New York, January 20, March 13, and April 12, 1891; and Robinson, San Francisco, to R. W. Gilder (editor of *Century,* New York), July 11, 1892. Mackenzie, Raymond, to Johnson, New York, February 7, March 20, and March 26, 1891. Also Johnson, New York, to Noble, Washington, October 20, 1890, in which he enclosed Robinson's photographs and gives this impression of the artist: "Mr. Robinson has been subjected to much persecution because of his opposition to Yosemite authorities, and consequently writes with heat, but so far as my observation goes, with accuracy." Also Johnson, New York, to Noble, Washington, D.C., May 5, 1891, September 11, 1891, and August 19, 1892, all in R. G. 79, National Archives. There are also Robinson and Mackenzie letters in the *Johnson Papers,* Bancroft Library.

II

A short time after the Sierra Club's organization in Olney's office in June 1892 William Armes received a letter from Charles D. Robinson urging that the Club take action against the Commissioners' management policies. Armes immediately asked Muir to come to San Francisco to discuss these problems, but evidently a quorum could not be mustered during the summer months.[6] A man of little patience, Robinson vented his anger against the Club in several letters to Johnson. In October 1892, he wrote: "The Sierra Club . . . has a mere existence for its own pleasure—that is all. I have preferred one serious complaint to it of a fire in the Valley timber which was neglected for two days by the Valley management, but no Club or official action was taken upon it. In short the Club, like the state, is nerveless and dead regarding Yosemite, as I see things."[7]

The following spring, his patience strained to the breaking point, Robinson grew even more scornful in his denunciation of the Club:

I think you entirely overestimate my power to urge legislation. I am entirely without power in political circles. In the Sierra Club I imagine I am regarded with the same sort of distrust that a giant powder cartridge would excite in a pan of ashes. The members of that association I think are inclined to regard me as a sort of interloper in public affairs, who had no business to know anything regarding Yosemite matters. . . .

I am sure that you will only receive from the Sierra Club courteous but evasive or ambiguous answers to your endeavors to stir up an active interest in Yosemite Valley. At the last meeting of the Club in Pioneer Hall some three months ago [November 5, 1892] enthusiastic resolutions were passed against any cutting down of the Yosemite National Park. Eulogies and praises without number were lavished upon the Park, . . . but not one word was uttered condemnatory of the conditions let alone the management of the Park's crown jewel, the Yosemite Valley.

Warren Olney came to me & whispered if I would say a few words *if it became necessary.* I said yes. It did *not* become necessary & I still have the words. Professor John [sic.] LeConte was very & ably eloquent & interesting about the Park, but not a word about the Valley. I asked him if he wouldn't say something regarding the Valley & its needs & condition before he left his seat & he said he couldn't because he didn't know anything about it. Is it possible that these parties sing one song in your ears & another in mine?[8]

The tone of Robinson's letter continues in this vein with charges that the Southern Pacific was so influential among Club members that it was obstructing its potential good work: "See the number of names among the charter members of the Club from 4th. and Townsend Streets [the offices of the Southern Pacific] and then make up your mind whether any ardent opposition to so much wealth & absolute power in California as is

[6] Armes, Oakland, to Muir, Martinez, July 22, 1892, Author copy.
[7] Robinson to Johnson, New York, October 28, 1892, *Johnson Papers,* box 9, folder no. 672.
[8] Robinson, San Francisco, to Johnson, New York, February 11, 1893, *Johnson Papers,* box 9, folder no. 674.

57

represented by these people can be expected from a Club of which they are charter members.''[9]

There were five "4th and Townsend" members among the charter group, including first vice-president of the Southern Pacific, C. H. Crocker, and the general ticket agent, T. H. Goodman. According to Louis Bartlett, one of the charter members, and William Colby, later secretary, none of these men played an important role in decisions of the Club.[10] They were not among the organizers and did not serve on the board of directors.

Johnson never wavered in his friendship for Muir or in his faith that the Sierra Club would eventually live up to his expectations concerning the Valley recession. He does not seem to have taken Robinson's criticisms very seriously, although he continued to forward the artist's impressions to Secretary Noble.

There is no question, however, that President Muir was having difficulty in swinging the Club behind him in action against the Commissioners. February 14, 1893, he wrote to Johnson: "At a meeting of the Directors . . . last Saturday I urged your views as to the advantages of pushing the Yosemite recession question to a vote in our legislature. All were opposed or doubtful as to the wisdom of doing so, though recognizing the value of keeping the matter alive by agitation in the papers and by attacking the annual appropriations for Yosemite when it comes up in the Legislature. All seem to think that at present the question of mismanagement should be held in abeyance, but that we cannot be wrong in requesting our legislature to voluntarily give back the Valley to the general government and to urge economy and the natural fitness of things in placing the Valley and the surrounding Park under one management, inasmuch as the Valley and the National Park are in fact one and inseparable. I met our Senator, McAllister, after the meeting and discussed Yosemite matters with him. . . . I advised . . . him to go ahead and make a name for himself on park and valley affairs. One of our members, a lawyer, will probably draft a bill or resolution of some sort or other to guide the Senator who unfortunately is young and inexperienced.''[11]

A few days later another Muir letter arrived in Johnson's New York office: "Our Sierra Club altogether refuses to make a fight at present on account of mismanagement, but the enclosed resolution was forwarded to Senator McAllister a few days ago. What its fate or effect may be I don't know.''[12]

This resolution, which was never introduced in the Legislature, was the first protest of the Club against the management of the Valley, although couched in such mild language that one could scarcely take it as a rebuke. It asked that the California

[9] *Loc. cit.*

[10] Author interviews with Colby, May 20, 1955, and Louis Bartlett, November 11, 1956. Bartlett, a former mayor of Berkeley, said: "No connection; I don't think I ever heard the name Southern Pacific mentioned; I would have known it because at that time . . . they were anything but popular. If you were connected with the Southern Pacific, in some quarters you were [persona] non grata."

[11] Muir, Martinez, to Johnson, New York, February 14, 1893, *Johnson Papers,* box 7, folder no. 375. Muir's reference to having "one of our members, a lawyer" draft a bill is curious, since McAllister himself was a lawyer and member of the Club. Perhaps Muir referred to Warren Olney.

[12] Muir, Martinez, to Johnson, New York, February 19, 1893, *Johnson Papers,* box 7, folder no. 376.

Legislature request Congress to appoint a commission "to make an examination into the propriety of including all [the Yosemite Reservation] under one management . . . and to report to Congress and to the State of California the result of their investigations."[13] It also asked that the Governor appoint a group of three California citizens to meet with the federal commission.

Quite independently, Senator Goucher, a former Commissioner himself and one of the star witnesses in the 1889 Legislative investigation, introduced Senate Joint Resolution no. 21 on February 3, 1893, "relative to making Yosemite Valley a National Park."[14] No further action was taken either in the Legislature or by the Club during that spring or summer, which caused Robinson to warn Johnson that "The S. C. has . . . split into factions. Armes has been put aside as Secretary & Elliot McAllister, Lawyer and ex-state Senator, has succeeded him. Mr. Olney, Mr. Bailey, and Mr. McAllister are now running the Club. . . . Unless the Club takes action at once on Yosemite affairs, I shall retire from it."[15]

There is no record of whether Robinson carried out his threat, but meanwhile the Club contented itself with committee investigations into "Yosemite matters, tree-cutting, the accounts of the Commissioners, etc." but made no serious effort to disrupt the hold of the state.[16]

In fact, a spirit of cooperation between the Club and the Commissioners manifested itself during the mid-90's. In their *Biennial Report* for 1893–1894, the Commissioners stated that a consultation between themselves and a committee of the Club appointed to consider "reports relating to the injury and defacement of natural objects in Yosemite Valley" developed "an active sympathy on the part of the Club with this Commission and its work."[17] As a result of this conference the Commissioners drew up "Rules and Regulations for the Convenience and Safety of Campers and Tourists and the Preservation of the Valley" and submitted them to the Club committee for approval. On May 5, 1894, the Sierra Club committee replied that it thought the rules "reasonable, judicious, and well calculated to accomplish their object," but added that enforcement would be almost impossible unless "two or more" guards and a "resident magistrate . . . before whom . . . offenders . . . could be promptly arraigned" were placed in the Valley, at least during the summer.[18] Eight months later, however, Elliott McAllister communicated the Club's regrets that the Commissioners had not complied with its recommendations, again urging them to do so.[19] The result of this was a meeting on February 19, 1895, at which several of the Commissioners and Professor George Davidson and McAllister were present. Muir himself was not at

[13] Typed copy of unnumbered Senate Joint Resolution offered by the Sierra Club (McAllister) for introduction in the California legislature, *Johnson Papers*, box 9, folder no. 850. Johnson scribbled note along margin, "Probably never offered."

[14] *Journal of the Senate*, California Legislature, 30th Session, 1893, p. 308.

[15] Robinson, San Francisco, to Johnson, New York, June 11, 1893, *Johnson Papers*, box 9, folder no. 679. This is a particularly angry letter. McAllister, the new recording secretary, he says, "could not have been elected Senator if the S. P. opposed him and altogether I begin to suspect that as usual the fine underground hand of the S.P. is successfully working its way into the Club."

[16] Muir, Martinez, to Johnson, New York, December 20, 1893, *Johnson Papers*, box 7, folder no. 383.

[17] *Biennial Report C.Y.V. . . . 1893–1894* (Sacramento, 1894), p. 11.

[18] George Davidson, *et al.* (Sierra Club Committee), to Secretary of the Commissioners, May 5, 1894, reprinted in *Biennial Report C.Y.V. . . . 1893–1894*, p. 12. Members of the Sierra Club committee were Professor George Davidson, Judge M. H. Myrick, Thomas Magee, James E. Runcie, and Elliott McAllister.

[19] Resolution of the Sierra Club, December 1, 1894, submitted by McAllister to Henry K. Field, January 3, 1895, reproduced in *Annual Report of the Executive Committee, C.Y.V., for the 46th Fiscal Year, July 1, 1894 to June 30, 1895* (July, 1895), p. 5, California State Archives.

the meeting, but according to the report of the Executive Committee of the state Commissioners "a full and frank discussion" resulted in "the gentlemen" expressing "themselves as entirely satisfied with the management of the affairs of Yosemite Valley."[20] The camper's code formulated at this meeting became the core of the administrative regulations for the operation of the park up to its recession.[21]

There is also other evidence that the Club worked with the Commissioners. When Governor Budd threatened to reduce the appropriations for care of the Valley, the Commissioners appealed to the Club for help. Muir, who was never convinced of the good faith of the Commissioners, saw in this an opportunity to make the state promise to employ a "competent landscape engineer of the highest skill and repute obtainable, to map out a systematic plan of forestry" for the "care, protection, and preservation" of the Valley before the Club would assist them.[22]

In April 1894 McAllister informed the Commissioners of the Club's plan to erect a monument at Glacier Point as an index to the panoramic view from that famous vantage point.[23] This was followed by a letter in May detailing the work so far accomplished by Joseph N. LeConte.[24] The Executive Committee was gratified by "this evidence of interest," and expressed its hope "that when the tablet is erected its suggestion may influence other interested and public spirited citizens of the State to contribute in similar ways to the enhancement of the pleasures of the Valley."[25] Toward the end of the century, too, there were negotiations through Abbott Kinney, who was one of the Commissioners and also a Club member, over the housing of an alpine library and the employment of a Club representative in the Valley during the summer months—a position, as we have seen, that went to William Colby.[26] Kinney reported to the Commissioners: "The Sierra Club Building is a complete success, and should bring the Commission into sympathetic touch with the lovers of nature in California. Among these are our most prominent and influential men. Science, literature, sport, outdoor life and the general healthy heart renewal coming from contact with nature are all served in the Yosemite, and can be and must be still more so in the grand and almost unknown scenery of the High Sierra. This is at the very gates of the Yosemite. The Sierra Club will be a center of information for travel into the wonders of these peaks, volcanoes of the past, glaciers, rivers, and lakes."[27]

In June 1899 Charles A. Bailey of the Sierra Club's Committee on Parks and Reservations addressed the Commission on the advantages of a trail to Sierra Point, which he and others had named in honor of the Club the previous summer.[28] After Joseph LeConte's untimely death in Yosemite Valley in 1901, the Club

[20] *Ibid.*, p. 7.

[21] Edith Germain Kettlewell, "Yosemite: The Discovery of Yosemite Valley and the Creation and Realignment of Yosemite National Park" (M.A. thesis in history, University of California, 1930), p. 74.

[22] Resolution of the Sierra Club, December 1, 1894, submitted by McAllister to Henry K. Field, January 3, 1895, reproduced in *Annual Report of the Executive Committee, C.Y.V., ibid.*, p. 6, California State Archives. Muir, Martinez, to Johnson, New York, April 11, 1895, *Johnson Papers*, box 7, folder no. 401.

[23] McAllister, San Francisco, to Executive Committee, C.Y.V., San Francisco, April 21, 1894, reproduced in *Annual Report of the Executive Committee to the Commission at Its Annual Meeting, June 6, 1894*, p. 21, California State Archives.

[24] McAllister, San Francisco, to John P. Irish, San Francisco, May 8, 1894, reproduced in *Ibid.*, p. 22.

[25] *Ibid.*, p. 23.

[26] *Supra.*, p. 22.

[27] Abbott Kinney, *Report of Work Accomplished and with Recommendations of Further Improvement of Yosemite Valley*, June 1, 1898, p. 2, in Records of the C.Y.V., California State Archives.

[28] *Proceedings of the Annual Meeting, C.Y.V.*, June 7, 1899, p. 6, in Records of the C.Y.V., California State Archives. See also Charles A. Bailey, "A Yosemite Discovery," *SCB*, II (June, 1898), pp. 216–221, and Bailey, "The Vantage Point of Yosemite," *Sunset*, II (April, 1899), pp. 121–123.

arranged with the Commissioners to erect a permanent stone building to replace the Sinning Cottage, which the Club had used as summer headquarters since 1898. The Commissioners approved the plans in November 1902, and assisted in the costs of utility connections upon the opening of the memorial to LeConte in the following year.[29] Although Henry Field's vice-presidential report to the Commissioners is obviously self-laudatory, the general tone of his remarks that the former feelings of hostility toward the Commissioners had largely disappeared rings true, at least for a short period during the mid-90's. He included the Sierra Club as a "friend and supporter" whereas "only a short time ago," it was one of the "most aggressive enemies of the Commission."[30]

Undoubtedly there were some members of the Sierra Club who honestly believed the state would lose prestige if it suffered the recession of the Valley to the federal government. Others, of course, did not, and in 1895, the *San Francisco Call* editorialized: "It is an interesting coincidence that just as the Fruit-Growers' Convention in Sacramento is passing resolutions for the better regulation and protection of the mountain forest, the Sierra Club is moving in the same direction and with the same end in view—the guarding of the water supply of the valleys. The Sierra Club's activity was inspired by a knowledge of the woeful conditions of affairs in Yosemite Valley, and from a determination to bring about the better management of that matchless natural wonder. . . . John Muir and Prof. Dudley . . . are leading the movement. . . . The Club is discussing the advisability of beginning an agitation for the transfer of the Valley to the U.S. . . ."[31] The *Call* then hints that there is not unanimity of opinion among Sierra Club members: "It is respectfully suggested to the Sierra Club that if any of its members are lacking in an understanding of the great value of these forests to the welfare of the State, and for that reason are hesitating to enter the fight for preserving the forests on wise and patriotic principles, they are alluring objects of missionary labor."[32]

Johnson and Muir would certainly have met the *Call's* standards for missionary zeal. During a lull in the attacks on Yosemite Park, Johnson addressed an open letter to the board of directors of the Club asking "whether the Sierra Club might not now profitably set on foot a campaign [to procure the recession of the Valley] at the next session of the Legislature." Johnson offered to submit further suggestions "which might be of use in such a movement [if the directors decided to take up the cause] which I believe to be the cause of California and of the general public."[33] Secretary McAllister had Johnson's letter cop-

ABBOTT KINNEY, Chairman of the Yosemite Commissioners, from a *San Francisco Post* cartoon. He helped organize the California Society for Conserving Waters and Protecting Forests.

[29] J. J. Lerman, San Francisco, to Colby, San Francisco, November 22, 1902, and J. J. Lerman, San Francisco, to McAllister, San Francisco, July 30, 1903, in *Letter Book, C.Y.V.,* covering January 30, 1902 to August 31, 1903, California State Archives.

[30] *Report of the Vice-President, Yosemite Commission,* n.d., p. 2, in Records of C.Y.V., California State Archives. Internal evidence indicates a date after the occupation of the Sinning Cottage by the Sierra Club.

[31] *San Francisco Call,* November 11, 1895, p. 6. (In the November 20 issue there is a long article by Muir in which he describes Valley conditions and suggests remedies. He remarks, "Nearly all the members of the Sierra Club with whom I have talked favor putting an end to this political management," (p. 10).

[32] *Loc. cit.*

[33] Johnson, New York, to Sierra Club Board of Directors, San Francisco, n.d., SCA.

ied and referred to each director for a personal expression of opinion.[34] No record is preserved of these individual opinions, but it is obvious that Johnson's entreaty fell on deaf ears.

At least one member of the Board of Directors had a personal reason for this. Vice President Warren Olney was a warm friend of John P. Irish, secretary and treasurer of the Commissioners from 1889 to 1893. Irish was an outspoken advocate of state control of the Valley whose public statements criticizing Muir must have caused Olney much uneasiness.[35] But Muir was slowly bringing Olney around to his way of thinking, and on January 14, 1896, he was able to write Johnson that Olney favored the move at last and that he expected the directors to take positive action soon.[36] However, another whole year went by and still there were directors who were not solidly behind the recession idea. In January 1897 Muir addressed Olney, who had finally offered a resolution favoring recession: "I think with you that a resolution like the one you offered the other day should be thoroughly studied and discussed before final action is taken and a close approximation made to unanimity, if possible. Still, I don't see that one or two objectors should have the right to kill all action of the Club in this or any other matter rightly belonging to it. Professor Davidson's objection is also held by Professor LeConte, or was, but how they can consistently sing praise to the federal government in the management of the National Parks, and at the same time regard the same management of Yosemite as degrading to the State, I can't see. For my part, I'm proud of California and prouder of Uncle Sam, for the U.S. is all of California and more. And as to our Secretary's objection, it seemed to me merely political, and if the Sierra Club is to be run by politicians, the sooner mountaineers get out of it the better. . . . I shall insist on getting it squarely before the Club. I had given up the question as a bad job, but so many of our members have urged it lately I now regard its discussion as a duty of the Club."[37]

It is certain that spirited discussion took place at the directors' meetings concerning the appropriate role of the Club in recession; unfortunately no record survives. Although by the end of the month a resolution was offered in the California Assembly by W. S. Melick of Pasadena granting Governor Budd authority to take whatever action he felt necessary to secure the addition of the Valley to the surrounding federal park, Muir was forced to say to Johnson: "No thanks to the Sierra Club in this, but I still hope to get a resolution favoring recession at our next Directors' meeting. . . ."[38] As Elmo R. Richardson notes, the failure of the 1897 recession movement in the legislature was due "to the belated endorsement of the Sierra Club, the absence of spokes-

[34] McAllister, San Francisco, to members of the Board of Directors, June 2, 1894, SCA. McAllister indicates that the Johnson letter referred to in the preceding footnote was received by him on May 22, which would date Johnson's letter some time in May 1894.

[35] Irish wrote a letter to the *Oakland Tribune* published September 8, 1890, in response to Muir's article favoring the return of the Valley to the federal government, which had appeared two days previously. Irish called Muir a "pseudo-naturalist" who "cut

Colonel John P. Irish, Yosemite Commissioner.

and logged and sawed the trees of the Valley with as willing a hand as any lumberman in the Sierras." This outburst infuriated William D. Armes, who only a few days earlier had met Muir for the first time, and he immediately penned a letter to the editor, which appeared in the September 12 issue. Muir replied, too (*Tribune*, September 16, 1890) and then wrote his friend Johnson (October 24, 1890, *Johnson Papers*, box 7, folder no. 360) a very humble statement of the affair. The *Tribune*, incidentally, editorialized in favor of recession on September 6, 1890. The specter of Irish's charge followed Muir the rest of his life. In 1905 when the California legislature was considering the recession bill, his opponents circulated the rumor once again. His artist friend, William Keith, found it necessary to defend Muir in the *San Francisco Chronicle* (letter dated January 27, 1905, reprinted in Cornelius, *op. cit.,* I,

p. 287). For Irish's point of view on this personal controversy as well as interesting comments on Gifford Pinchot's "support" of Muir "to employ an expert forester as landscape engineer," see Irish letter to George F. Parker, January 9, 1893, reprinted in *Iowa Journal of History and Politics* (July, 1933), pp. 435–438, and Irish, to J. Wilson, March 24, 1910, *John P. Irish Papers*, Stanford University, California. A recent interpretation is given by historian Elmo R. Richardson who believes that Muir held the notion that an aim or objective—in this case the appointment of a trained landscape architect or forester who would be sensitive to the ecological relationships in Yosemite Valley—was "far more important . . . than the probability of ruining the reputations of men who were not directly culpable." His reference is to Irish, who, Richardson states, "was sincerely interested in preserving the Yosemite forests, but [who] entertained opinions about resource use which were unscientific and often superficial." Richardson, *The Politics of Conservation; Crusades and Controversies, 1897–1913*, University of California Publications in History, vol. 70 (Berkeley and Los Angeles, University of California Press, 1962), p. 13. Irish was assailed by the "crusaders" at home and in the columns of *Century Magazine* and perhaps cannot be blamed for his own bitter attacks on Muir.

[36] Muir, Martinez, to Johnson, New York, January 14, 1896, *Johnson Papers*, box 7, folder no. 407.

[37] Muir, Martinez, to Warren Olney, San Francisco, January 18, 1897, reprinted in Badè, *op. cit.*, II, p. 303.

[38] Muir, Martinez, to Johnson, New York, February 4, 1897, *Johnson Papers*, box 7, folder no. 418. Melick's Assembly Concurrent Resolution no. 2 was enclosed in this letter. The full text is available in *Journal of the Assembly*, California Legislature, 32nd Session, 1897, p. 267.

[39] This comment appears in Richardson's "The Politics of the Conservation Issue in the Far West, 1896–1913" (Ph.D. disser-

men for it, and to the legislature's admitted lack of understanding of the matter."[39]

The Melick resolution was largely the result of the prodding of one man, Theodore P. Lukens, a southern California pioneer in forestry protection, real estate promoter, and bank executive, who had enjoyed a "mountain friendship" with Muir near Hetch Hetchy in 1895.[40] Lukens had joined the Club in 1894 and subsequently participated as a member of the Committee on Publications and Communications. Perhaps discouraged over the slowness with which the Sierra Club was acting on Yosemite problems, Muir asked Lukens to start a new club in Southern California. "The more clubs, the better," wrote Muir.[41]

Muir was not alone in his concern for more public education and action on the problems of Yosemite, for effective forest protection, and for the conservation of water in the state. Many other resource-minded persons and organizations, such as the State Board of Trade, were promoting the formation of citizen groups to advance "the leadership which government declined to exert."[42] Associations developed in both Southern and Northern California. In the South, Lukens, Abbott Kinney, and others formed the Forest and Water Society of Southern California in March, 1899.[43] The Sierra Club itself was prominent in assisting the formation in San Francisco of the California Society for Conserving Waters and Protecting Forests on January 21, 1899, and when this organization failed to persuade the State Legislature to pass a bill setting up a forestry commission, it appointed its own commission composed almost wholly of Sierra Club members, including Professors E. W. Hilgard and William Dudley, Abbott Kinney, and Warren Olney, Sr.[44] Perhaps the strongest and most influential of all these groups was the California Water and Forest Association, which eventually had more than 5,000 members and issued an important monthly periodical called *Water and Forest*.[45]

III

After the turn of the century conservation-minded leaders held high offices in state and national government, and the climate of public opinion in the state concerning Yosemite's management began to crystalize after 1902. An increasing number of newspapers editorialized on Yosemite conditions. State pride began to give way to a realization that dual administration in the Yosemite region was hampering the purposes for which the reserves had been made. Perhaps most convincing of all was the claim of economy-conscious legislators that Yosemite was costing the state too much money.

Several specific events now hastened the movement for recession. In the spring of 1903, President Theodore Roosevelt made a swing through the West, spending a number of days in California. Muir was persuaded by Benjamin Ide Wheeler, president of the state university, Chester Rowell, and others that he should forego a forest inspection trip to Asia, which Muir had already arranged with Professor Sargent of Harvard, in order to accompany Roosevelt to Yosemite. Muir agreed and succeeded in confirming the President's convictions about recession which, as early as 1894, when he was Governor of New York, he had expressed in a letter to the Secretary of the Interior.[46] The Presidential party included Governor George Pardee, who had taken office in January 1903, so Muir had an opportunity to impress both leaders with the necessity of returning the Valley to the national government. According to Colby, Governor Pardee told Muir that he would sign a recession measure if it could be pushed through the state legislature.[47]

Part of the groundwork for the next legislative session in 1905 was laid at a conference held in Sacramento in July 1904, approximately a year after the President's visit to Yosemite. The members of the Yosemite Boundary Commission, Major Chittenden, Robert Marshall, and Frank Bond, met with State Senators Chester Rowell and Frank R. Devlin, ex-Congressman James A. Loutitt from Stockton, and members of the Governor's staff. Lieutenant Governor Aldin Anderson asked Muir to attend the conference, and when Muir found he was unable to go he expressed his views in a long letter.[48] Muir's suggestions "were very well received" and played a part in further convincing the state administration that California should give up its trusteeship.

To Muir, however, the most heartening action toward his long cherished goal was the unified and positive action of the Sierra Club. Colby prepared a strong statement with Muir's help and this was later unanimously endorsed by the entire Board of Directors.

The Club's arguments were typical of those publicized by other California groups supporting recession, such as the California Water and Forest Association, the Native Sons of the Golden West, and the State Board of Trade. In essence these reasons were:

1) Overlap of authority and divided jurisdiction. The Valley formed the natural base of operations for the Yosemite region; this was denied to the federal administrators. There was conflict of authority in fighting forest fires, dealing with range trespassers, and posting regulations for the use of camp sites, and the like.

tation in history, University of California, Los Angeles, 1957) but the reference to the Sierra Club is deleted in the book based on his dissertation (Richardson op. cit., p. 15.)

[40] Badè, op. cit., II, p. 290.

[41] Muir, Martinez, to Lukens, Pasadena, December 28, 1898 and January 10, 1899, Theodore P. Lukens Papers, Henry E. Huntington Library, San Marino, California. Muir may or may not have had the establishment of a Southern California chapter of the Sierra Club in mind in making this suggestion to Lukens. In 1905 the Directors amended the By-Laws to authorize a Southern California chapter and in 1911 the Angeles Chapter was formed on a permanent and active basis.

[42] C. Raymond Clar, California Government and Forestry from Spanish Days until the Creation of the Department of Natural Resources in 1927 (Sacramento, Division of Forestry, Department of Natural Resources, 1959), p. 167.

[43] Richardson, The Politics of Conservation: Crusades and Controversies, 1897–1913, pp. 15–61.

[44] Clar, op. cit., pp. 169–172, presents the best discussion of this.

[45] Ibid., pp. 173–176. See also Samuel P. Hays, Conservation and the Gospel of Efficiency; the Progressive Conservation Movement, 1890–1920 (Cambridge, Harvard University Press, 1959), p. 24.

[46] Roosevelt to H. Smith, April 7, 1894, Theodore Roosevelt Papers, Library of Congress, Washington, D.C.

[47] Author interview with Colby, May 20, 1955. See also Colby, "Yosemite and the Sierra Club," SCB, XXIII (April 1938), p. 13 and "The Recession of Yosemite Valley," SCB, XLVII (December 1962), p. 24. The importance of this meeting of Muir, Pardee, and Roosevelt has been stressed by several authors. The most vivid account is given in Linnie Marsh Wolfe, Son of the Wilderness; the Life of John Muir (New York, Alfred Knopf, 1945), pp. 289–294; but see also Badè, op. cit., II, pp. 408–413; Richard Hartesveldt, "Roosevelt and Muir—Conservationists," Yosemite Nature

48. LOGGING DESTRUCTION between Hazel Green and Crane Flat on Yosemite
Lumber Company Lands. The building of the Yosemite Valley Railroad and, later,
the railroad to Hetch Hetchy Valley opened up richly timbered, privately owned
lands for logging.

49. LOGGING NEAR PARK, 1913. A typical operation in the area above
the first incline.

50. GEORGE C. PERKINS, Governor of California, 1879–1883, U.S. Senator, 1893–1915, was influential in shepherding the recession bill through Congress. He was a charter member of the Sierra Club.

51. WILLIAM FRANKLIN HERRIN, Chief Counsel for the Southern Pacific Company, by political manipulation in Sacramento materially aided the preservationists who wished to end state control in Yosemite.

52. JAMES D. PHELAN, Mayor of San Francisco during the Hetch Hetchy controversy. Phelan made the first filings on the mountain reservoir sites and later transferred his rights to San Francisco.

53. PERCY V. LONG, City Attorney during the Phelan administration, which strongly advocated the Hetch Hetchy project.

54. MARSDEN MANSON, a Sierra Club member and mountain enthusiast, but also a persistent advocate of Hetch Hetchy water development; as City Engineer he drew up the first plans.

55. M. M. O'SHAUGHNESSY replaced Manson as City Engineer of San Francisco; owing largely to his careful planning, the city was able to carry out the Hetch Hetchy project.

56. PRESIDENT ROOSEVELT AND JOHN MUIR at Glacier Point,
1903. On the week-end of May 16–17, the two took the Eleven-Mile
Train down to the Valley, camping out one night. This meeting brought
a promise from Roosevelt that he would support a recession bill.

Notes, XXXIV (November 1955), pp. 133–136; and William E. Colby, "John Muir and Theodore Roosevelt in Yosemite," *Yosemite Nature Notes,* XXXVII (July 1959), pp. 90–97.

[48] Muir, Martinez, to Lt. Gov. Anderson, Sacramento, July 13, 1904, *Pardee Papers,* Bancroft Library, University of California, Berkeley, folder no. 2744.

2) Insufficient appropriations and care by the state. Roads were few and in poor condition. There were not sufficient accommodations to take care of the increasing numbers of tourists.

3) The state had been granted only a legal trust in the Valley. To recede the Valley was to bring this trust to an end. The United States would not close the Valley or prevent the public from enjoying its superlative scenery, but would open it to greater use. The Club's statement concluded:

. . . the past has demonstrated that the Yosemite Valley is of a national character, and every citizen of the United States is vitally interested in its welfare. The State assumed the burden of caring for it, and has expended its money for the benefit of every citizen of the United States. Forty years has proven that the State cannot afford to appropriate out of the funds at its disposal a sufficient amount to adequately care for this National Park. . . .

But the United States is amply able to do this, and will, if given the opportunity. . . . The result would be the improvement of the valley and National Park by the construction of the best of roads, bridges, and trails. Ample hotel accommodations of the best quality would be provided. A telephone system for the entire park to guard against forest fires would be inaugurated. The patrol system of the National Park would be rendered far more effective and the valley itself placed under the same system, so that perfect order would prevail, no matter how great the number of visitors. The toll-road system would be abolished, and in all probability a splendid boulevard constructed up the Merced Canyon, which would reduce the time and expense of travel one half and greatly increase the comfort. . . .[49]

And then a prophetic note:

Each of these tourists would not only learn something of our great State, but would spend money in it. Few of us even begin to dream of the wealth that will some day be poured into California by the multitude of travelers who will annually come to enjoy our unparalleled scenic attractions. We want to hasten that day, and we trust that the members of the State Legislature will do their part in aiding to bring about this result by receding the Yosemite Valley and Mariposa Grove of Big Trees to the National Government.[50]

[49] "Statement Concerning the Proposed Recession of Yosemite Valley and Mariposa Big Tree Grove by the State of California to the United States," *SCB,* V (January 1905), p. 246. Original is in R. G. 79, National Archives.

[50] *Ibid.,* p. 247.

[51] William E. Colby, *Reminiscences; Tape Recorded Interviews for the Bancroft Library, October-November, 1953,* Bancroft Library, University of California, Berkeley, p. 34, hereafter cited as *Reminiscences.*

The Sierra Club statement was printed as a separate leaflet and distributed to members of the Legislature before the January 1905, session. "I got it out none too soon," Colby commented later, "In fact, the Speaker of the Assembly, William Waste . . . told me that he received my little leaflet in the mail just before he left Berkeley to attend a Masonic meeting in Oakland one evening. He read it on the way over . . . and became thoroughly convinced that our cause was just. During the Masonic meeting, he was called out by an *Examiner* reporter and asked what he thought about this proposition. . . . He was able to tell him without any question."[51]

This was a mid-December evening. On the morning of December 17, 1904, the *San Francisco Examiner,* in the three right-hand columns of the first page, ran a picture of Yosemite

Falls with the headline: "California Must Retain Control of the Yosemite." In a long article it set forth its opposition to recession and quoted at length from several legislators—all opposed to recession. No mention was made of the Sierra Club or any other groups favoring recession.[52]

This, of course, was a complete about-face for the large San Francisco daily, which had so tenaciously goaded the Legislature into an investigation of the Yosemite Commissioners in 1888–1889. Did the *Examiner's* reporters perhaps have wind of the Southern Pacific's inquiry to the Secretary of the Interior for all back annual reports and other data relating to the California parks?[53] Did the *Examiner* guess that the Railroad's interest in tourist promotion was swinging it behind support for the recession movement which public opinion in the state now seemed to favor? Although the *Examiner* did not once mention the Southern Pacific during its campaign against recession, it seems likely that it may have suspected the Railroad's position. Colby, however, believes that the newspaper's opposition is explained primarily by the fact that the *Examiner's* chief legal counsel, J. J. Lerman, was also Secretary of the Commissioners at that time.[54] His office was paid for by the state and if recession took place, his position would naturally be abolished.

The following day, December 18, the *Examiner* again played up its opposition to recession, this time by running a headline across the top of the first page of the second section, reading, "State Board of Agriculture Rejects Scheme to Take Yosemite Away from California."[55] The accompanying article briefly set forth the position of the Board of Agriculture, and presented the arguments against recession of Colonel Benson's old Yosemite opponent, now Senator John Curtin.[56] A picture of Vernal Falls accompanied the article, which announced a petition:

"SIGN THIS"
To the honorable, the Legislature of the State of California:

We respectfully petition your honorable body to oppose any movement for the purpose of receding the Yosemite Valley to the Federal Government.

The Yosemite Valley is California's greatest pride. It should be cared for by California in a manner reflecting glory upon the state.

There is no legitimate reason for placing the management of this marvel of natural beauty in the hands of the Federal Government.
NAME............
ADDRESS...........

Sign this, cut it out and mail it to the Yosemite Editor, Examiner Office, San Francisco.

This sudden publicity on the part of the *Examiner* aroused its rival, the *San Francisco Chronicle* to editorialize on December 20:

[52] *San Francisco Examiner*, December 17, 1904, pp. 1–2.

[53] D. A. Chambers, Washington, D.C., to Secretary of the Interior, April 6, 1904, R. G. 79, National Archives. Chambers, a Washington attorney acting on behalf of the Southern Pacific Company, received a letter from T. H. Goodman dated San Francisco, March 23, 1904, asking him to secure material relative to Yosemite National Park because "large numbers of people in California" want the Valley returned to the federal government. Chambers transmitted the reports to Goodman on April 12, 1904. It would appear from this that Herrin, the Southern Pacific's legal counsel and close associate of Goodman's, was familiar with Yosemite problems—probably a good deal more familiar than Colby knew—*before* Muir appealed to Harriman to prompt his lieutenant in San Francisco to action favorable to the recession forces in the California Legislature. (*Infra.*, pp. 71–72.)

[54] Colby, *Reminiscences*, pp. 35–36.

[55] *San Francisco Examiner*, December 18, 1904, p. 29.

[56] First elected to the California Senate in 1898 and reelected three times, Curtin was a stubborn orator of real talent whose frequent refuge in the U.S. Constitution during debate earned him the nickname, "Constitutional John."

The attempt of one of our city contemporaries to stir up a sensation over the question of receding the Yosemite Park to the federal government has a very queer look. Its fundamental statement is that the proposal is a "scheme of the politicians," and it supports its contention with letters from politicians and from nobody else. The fact is that nobody in the State who is well informed, and who is not in some way connected with the Yosemite Commission or a beneficiary of its management has any desire whatever to prevent the recession. At least, if they have such desire, they say nothing about it.

Our management of the Park has been distinctly discreditable. In the nature of things it will remain so. Membership in the Commission is as much a "political plum" as membership in the Harbor Commission. It is assumed to be a position of peculiar honor, with no emolument except very large personal expenses, and has usually, we presume, been bestowed as wisely as political exigencies have permitted. The virtually unanimous testimony of intelligent visitors is that the result has been very bad. The fertile valley lands, constituting one of the most attractive features in their natural conditions are turned into grain fields. The management of the wooded areas is severely criticized. There is no continuity of purpose and never will be. And the state has not the money to spare to properly care for the Park, even if competent and continuous direction were possible under our system. If the Federal Government assumes charge, the guardianship of the Park will be placed in competent hands and kept there.[57]

The battle was on. From the date of the opening attack the *Examiner* published pictures of Yosemite Valley, numerous columns of material—mostly quoting persons objecting to recession—and reprinted its petition from December 19, 1904 through January 9, 1905.

In January the battle of the printed column moved into the California Legislature for oral debate. The Sierra Club had laid its groundwork carefully. It had issued its leaflet and distributed this to newspapers, prominent individuals, and organizations likely to be sympathetic to its case. It had strong support from the Native Sons of the Golden West and the State Board of Trade, which in August 1904 had adopted a resolution favoring recession and had published a thirty-three page booklet for distribution to the Legislature.[58]

The recession bill itself was drafted by Colby with the assistance of William H. Mills, head of the Southern Pacific Land Department.[59] This was an astounding reversal for a former Yosemite Commissioner; Mills had occupied a strategic position of influence on the executive committee of the Commission in the 1880's. He had strongly favored enlargement of the Yosemite grant under *state* control. Finally, he was the Commissioner in charge of the questioning of witnesses on behalf of the state Board during the 1889 legislative investigation. Perhaps some of his disenchantment at state management policies began during the investigation when Governor Waterman replaced him by Irish, but the real explanation of his change in attitude lies in the opportune decision of his employer, the Southern Pacific, to seek

[57] *San Francisco Chronicle*, December 20, 1904, p. 6.
[58] *Yosemite Valley: History, Description and Statement of Conditions Relative to the Proposed Recession to the National Government* Circular no. 13. (Sacramento, California State Board of Trade, 1904?).
[59] Author's interview with Colby, May 20, 1955.

67

advantage for itself through quiet support of recession while continuing to wield influence over Board appointments. Thus, the Sierra Club was brought into "partnership" with the Railroad over recession. Colby and Muir were political realists who knew that this was the only effective way to break the back of the opposition in a Legislature dominated by a virtual transportation monopoly, called the "Octopus" by crusading novelist Frank Norris.[60] Having made this decision, then, Colby acted quickly, brought in Mills to assist him, and transmitted the completed draft via William Waste to Assemblyman Miguel Estudillo from Riverside and Senator C. M. Belshaw from Antioch; both these legislators held key positions on the committees that would consider the bills.

On January 11, 1905, Estudillo introduced the recession bill (Assembly bill no. 248) and at the same time Belshaw introduced Senate bill no. 170 for the same purpose. Both bills were sent to the appropriate committees for reports. For a number of days comparative silence was maintained by both camps—even the *Examiner* remaining strangely silent—but on January 18th the Assembly Committee on Public Lands and Forestry and the Senate Committee on Forestry and Water Preservation scheduled a joint hearing in Sacramento and invited a number of interested people to participate. Arthur Briggs, Secretary of the State Board of Trade, had arranged for a number of speakers to represent the cause of recession. These included R. H. McNoble, former president of the Native Sons of the Golden West; John G. North, president of the California Water and Forest Association; A. S. Knapp, an attorney from San Francisco; Mrs. Mary Fairweather, president of the California Club; and four Sierra Club members—President Muir, Secretary Colby, Joseph N. LeConte, and Warren Olney, at that time Mayor of Oakland.[61]

Chief, and certainly most vocal supporter for the opposition to recession was Senator Curtin, who had already been a thorn in the side of the Sierra Club over the Yosemite boundary question. Oddly enough, however, Curtin had expressed himself somewhat differently in correspondence with Governor Pardee, who had vetoed the Senator's bill (no. 152) to appropriate $150,000 for construction of a Yosemite Valley Hotel. Curtin had been conciliatory toward the Governor and took the trouble to express himself on the recession question: ". . . but I certainly feel that at the next session of the Legislature, if it is determined that the State cannot afford to build a hotel in the Valley, which will be in keeping with the Valley, *then a bill ought to and likely will be introduced by myself*, repealing the act accepting the grant from Congress, and let the Valley go back under the jurisdiction

[60] *The Octopus, a Story of California* (New York, Doubleday, Page and Co., 1901). 652 pp. (The Epic of the Wheat, no. 1.)

[61] Newspaper accounts of the hearing appear in the *Sacramento Evening Bee*, January 18, 1905 (p. 5) and January 19 (p. 2); *San Francisco Chronicle*, January 19, 1905 (p. 4); and *San Francisco Examiner*, January 19, 1905 (p. 4 first section).

of the federal government, and then there will be no question but what appropriations will be made liberally for the support of that Valley."[62] [Emphasis supplied.]

This did not sound like the same Curtin who addressed the joint legislative committee meeting on January 18, 1905. The *Sacramento Evening Bee* reported:

> Poverty had been pleaded in connection with recession arguments, but such a cry had not gone up when the Big Basin property was purchased.[63]
>
> California owns Yosemite . . . and California is able to take care of it.
>
> Superintendent after Superintendent of the National Yosemite Park had pleaded for the purchase of roads, but without results. The Federal Government . . . will not buy a road, will not build one, and will not build a bridge. He [Curtin] would not vote to give up Yosemite Valley to be guarded by soldiers.
>
> [Curtin] was quoted as saying: "You can buy plenty of redwood parks, . . . but I assure you that you can never buy another Yosemite Valley."
>
> He [Curtin] said he did not want a government in control in Yosemite which would confiscate guns. Now Yosemite is open and free through all seasons, but Yellowstone National Park is closed. . . . No man in California would begrudge a tax of fifty cents to build a hotel in Yosemite.[64]

This obviously was a Curtin who was approaching the recession question with rancor engendered by past animosities toward Acting Superintendent Benson, the army regulations, and Pardee's veto.

The *Examiner*, as might be expected, reported fully on Curtin's "straight from the shoulder" speech, but made a mockery of the side favoring recession. When Colby got up to speak (the *Examiner* reported):

> Mr. Colby, the earnest and perhaps excitable secretary of the Sierra Club . . . quoted President Roosevelt as saying he desired the recession of the Yosemite, and insisted that the *Examiner* and *Lodi Sentinel* are the only papers in the State that oppose recession. I do not recall the editor of the *Lodi Sentinel,* but it's a safe bet he does not ride on a railroad pass and that he has a mind of his own. I'd like to meet that man. But the "Hotel Gazette" favors recession and that ought to give almost anybody pause.
>
> Mr. Colby got on more rational ground when he said that Congress gave nearly $500,000 to the Yellowstone in two years, while California hasn't given much more in forty years. That's sense, but why not make California do better instead of saying to the world that she is a miserly slattern, incapable of caring for her own, and that the children of which she should be proudest must be placed in a public institution?
>
> Assemblyman Gans got tired at this juncture and went away. Whether Colby's speech tired him or he feared to face the rigors of Warren Olney's oratory, I cannot say, but he excused himself and then, Olney, Mayor of Oakland, came on. I couldn't excuse myself. Happy Assemblyman Gans.[65]

The article goes on in this vein.

After the various speakers on each side had presented their

[62] John Curtin, Sonora, to Governor Pardee, April 7, 1903, *Pardee Papers,* Bancroft Library, University of California, folder no. 89.

[63] A reference to the California Redwood State Park, proposed by the Sierra Club in 1896, and the purchase of lands in the Big Basin, Santa Cruz County for this purpose.

[64] *Sacramento Evening Bee,* January 18, 1905, p. 2.

[65] *San Francisco Examiner,* January 19, p. 4.

views to the joint committee, the Assembly group voted 6 to 1 to report favorably on recession at the next day's session of the Legislature.[66] On January 19, 1905 the majority report, as signed by Assemblyman Fayette Mitcheltree, recommended to the Senate that the bill pass, but gave no reasons. A minority report was signed by C. V. Jones from Sonora. Again, no reasons were given.[67]

During the next few days, the battle scene shifted from the legislative halls back to the public press. On the 20th the *Examiner* carried a story about its petition and printed a picture of a man rolling it up for presentation to the California Legislature. A total of 62,890 names were claimed by the *Examiner* against the recession of the Valley.[68] Two days later, in the *Examiner's* rival, the *Chronicle*, there appeared an interview with John Muir, his picture, and quotations from him in favor of recession.[69]

Belshaw's bill was scheduled for floor debate on the 24th. According to the *Sacramento Bee*, "The Senate galleries were crowded with spectators as Senator Belshaw's recession bill came up for final decision."[70] Belshaw opened debate by speaking in behalf of his own bill. His chief arguments were that California had the right to recede the Valley since the state had never really owned the land, which was only leased to it by the Congressional Act of 1864. Belshaw further felt that appropriations would be increased under federal jurisdiction, as witness the Yellowstone example.

Senator Ralston presented the *Examiner's* petition and stated that he was against recession not only because it was a matter of prestige to keep Yosemite Valley, but also because California would lose some of its federal rivers and harbors appropriations to the Valley if it came under federal financing. Charles Shortridge, Senator from Santa Clara County, spoke against the bill, but specifically mentioned David Starr Jordan's letter favoring recession. Shortridge was obviously baffled by Jordan's stand, but had not yet felt the brunt of his constituents' letters and petitions. (Shortridge later switched his stand on the floor of the Senate.)

Curtin talked for two hours against recession, and with such effectiveness that Edward Hamilton, reporter for the *Examiner*, headlined his story, "Recession is Beaten in Senate."

. . . Curtin's effort belongs in a place by itself. It took the debate into the domain of statesmanship.

I am free to say that he went into Constitutional depths, where I could not follow him, . . . but he spoke "as one having authority and not as the scribes and pharasees." And when he was in the domain of facts and figures he was singularly the master of conciseness, of dramatic presentation, and, at least once,

[66] *San Francisco Chronicle*, January 19, p. 4.
[67] *Journal of the Assembly*, California Legislature, 36th Session, 1905, p. 202.
[68] *San Francisco Examiner*, January 20, 1905, p. 4. Was it mere coincidence that there was a remarkable similarity in the number of names that appeared on this petition and the same newspaper's petition to the U.S. Congress during debate over House Joint Resolution no. 118 to accept the recession of the Valley from California (*infra.*, p. 77)?
[69] *San Francisco Chronicle*, January 22, 1905, p. 40.
[70] *Sacramento Evening Bee*, January 25, 1905, p. 5.

of inspired oratory. It was far and away, the best thing I have heard Curtin do. . . .

. . . It would take some pages of print to set out all he told. I have notes of his speech that would fill three or four columns and I cannot boil the thing down intelligently.

He told of personal experiences under military rule in the Yosemite National Park, and thrilled his hearers with his vivid story of individual wrongs and Czar-like disregard of personal rights. It was a tale of confiscation and abuse that stirred the blood.

Next he showed how the Congress had refused to appropriate money for other Federal parks, and how the Yellowstone went six years without a dollar. "Do you want Yosemite to stand six years without a dollar?" he asked and the crowd could scarce forebear a cheer. . . . And then he burst into a genuinely thrilling apostrophe to feeling that started tears in some eyes that do not often cry.[71]

After Curtin's long speech, Senator Coggins made a motion that the bill be postponed until February 2nd. Belshaw seconded this and it carried the Senate by a large majority. Belshaw knew that the power of Curtin's talk, emotional as it may have been, had swayed opinion, and that to risk a vote at this time would mean probable defeat for his bill. The *Sacramento Bee* quoted "a well-known politician" (the name is not given) as saying, "The object of postponement was to devise some other plan for carrying the recession proposition. The probabilities are that a constitutional amendment will be offered to submit the matter to the people, to be voted upon at the next general election."[72]

Meanwhile, in the lower house, Estudillo's companion recession bill weathered the dilatory tactics of the opponents on February 1st and was quietly placed on special order for the following day. On the 2nd, Assembly Bill no. 248 passed by an overwhelming vote: 46 ayes to 19 noes.[73] The final decision now rested with the Senate.

The Sierra Club kept in the background in the legislative fight. Muir and Colby made nine trips to Sacramento during the period of debate to confer with committee members and legislators. Colby remarks that he was greatly discouraged with his first day of lobbying "realizing that the merits of the bill would have little to do with the outcome."[74] Probably this political venture on the floor of a public policy-making body was not altogether successful.

The real turning point in persuasion came in quite a different manner. In 1899 Muir had accompanied the Edward Harriman expedition to Alaska. Harriman and Muir had developed a strong liking for each other. Now Harriman, who had taken over the presidency of the Southern Pacific in 1900 upon the death of Collis P. Huntington, was in a position to help his friend.[75] Colby urged Muir to write Harriman in New York,

[71] *San Francisco Examiner,* January 25, 1905, pp. 1 and 3. The complete text of Curtin's speech (35 pp.) is available in *Pardee Scrapbook* no. 58, "Yosemite" in Bancroft Library, University of California, Berkeley.

[72] *Sacramento Evening Bee,* January 25, 1905, p. 2.

[73] *Journal of the Assembly,* California Legislature, 36th Sess., 1905, p. 549.

[74] Colby, "The Recession of Yosemite Valley," SCB, XLVII (December 1962), p. 26.

[75] For a sympathetic view of the Southern Pacific and Harriman's control over the railroad, see Neill C. Wilson and Frank J. Taylor, *Southern Pacific; the Roaring Story of a Fighting Railroad* (New York, McGraw-Hill, 1952), pp. 107–115.

which he did in January, probably before the recession bills were introduced. Johnson, also in New York, was informed of Muir's action, and he, too, got in touch with Harriman, reporting to Muir on January 17 that Harriman's secretary "phoned me that he has instructed his men to do what can be done to further our wishes."[76]

Harriman was as good as his word. William Herrin, the Railroad's chief counsel in California, called Colby to his San Francisco office and the strategy was laid. Colby was to continue the distribution of Sierra Club material in favor of recession; Herrin would alert "his men" in the Legislature. Herrin made it clear, however, that the Railroad could not openly attack the antirecession forces, but that when the showdown vote came, he felt there would be a sufficient number of votes to swing the bill.[77]

In the end it appeared that Herrin's influence was considerable. The canvas of potential votes, however, was close—so close, in fact, that on one occasion Colby made a special trip to see Herrin to report to him that Senator Shortridge was causing trouble. (This was after Shortridge's January 24th speech against recession mentioned above.) Herrin suggested that Colby write David Starr Jordan and other influential persons in the Senator's district to get them to write to Sacramento and tell him how they felt about this matter. Herrin added that Shortridge was a man who could be persuaded rather easily. The idea worked. The *Sacramento Evening Bee* reported Shortridge's change of heart:

> Shortridge read a letter from the San Jose Chamber of Commerce signed by a dozen or so prominent individuals from whom he had borrowed money; the letter urged him to face about and support recession.
>
> Shortridge humourously said he would give as graceful an exhibition as possible of a statesman doing a flip-flop. While he had previously opposed recession, he would, in deference to his constituency, support it.[78]

There seems to have been some confusion as to the final floor vote. Colby recalls that it was Shortridge's switch which made the difference whereas the *San Francisco Chronicle* states: "Pendleton, Senator from Los Angeles, avoided voting when the roll was called, but when a motion was made for a call of the Senate, he asked that he be recorded as voting in the affirmative. His vote was the one needed to pass the bill."[79] The official records indicate, however, that the recession bill passed by a vote of 21 to 13.[80]

A comparison of the senators who finally voted "yes" with the names of those the *Examiner* claimed as against recession nearly two months earlier shows that at least nine men changed their opinions in this interval.[81] Herrin had planned his strategy well. Certain senators "who were notoriously controlled by the

[76] Johnson, New York, to Muir, Martinez, January 17, 1905, Author copy.

[77] The San Francisco press of the day gives considerable space to William Herrin's influence in the California Legislature. See, for example, the article, "Candidates Wooing the Herrin Smile," *San Francisco Chronicle,* January 10, 1905, p. 4.

[78] *Sacramento Evening Bee,* February 23, 1905, p. 5.

[79] *San Francisco Chronicle,* February 24, 1905, p. 3.

[80] *Journal of the Senate,* California Legislature, 36th Sess., 1905, p. 924. Colby explains the apparent discrepancy in the vote by reference to a Senate rule which required a majority vote of the entire Senate, not merely a majority vote of those Senators present on the floor and voting.

[81] *San Francisco Examiner,* January 3, 4, and 5, 1905. The nine Senators were: Anderson, Bauer, Broughton, Greenwell, Hahn, Haskins, Rowell, Savage, and Shortridge.

57. **THEODORE ROOSEVELT PARTY** at Mariposa Grove. Right to left:
Benjamin Ide Wheeler (President of the University of California), Private Secretary
Loeb, Nicholas Murray Butler (President of Columbia University), John Muir,
Dr. Rixey, President Roosevelt, Governor Pardee, Secretary of the Navy Moody, and
Secret Service men. (Photograph by J. N. LeConte.)

58. **PRESIDENT TAFT** at Mariposa Grove. Once again John Muir became a special
nature guide for a busy President. Muir is on Taft's immediate left and the
Governor of California (Gillett) on his right.

59. ROBERT UNDERWOOD JOHNSON, Editor-in-Chief of *Century Magazine* and chairman of the National Committee for Preservation of Yosemite National Park.

60. HARRIET MONROE, founder and for many years editor of *Poetry Magazine,* was an active mountaineer and member of the Sierra Club from Chicago and one of the leading supporters of Hetch Hetchy Valley.

61. HERBERT W. GLEASON, Boston lecturer and member of the Appalachian Mountain Club, assisted the Sierra Club in its Hetch Hetchy campaign by accompanying one of its trips to that region and preparing extensive slide programs.

62. WILLIAM F. BADÈ, literary executor of the Muir estate and Professor of Old Testament Literature and Semitic Languages at Pacific Theological Seminary (now Pacific School of Religion). He wrote the first biographies of Muir, was an enthusiastic mountaineer, and served eleven years as editor of the *Sierra Club Bulletin.* He crossed the Atlantic to testify at a Hetch Hetchy hearing in Washington.

63. THE MUIRS AND PARSONS AND HIS WIFE became fast friends in the cause
of Hetch Hetchy. This photograph was taken at the steps of South Hall, on the
University of California campus, shortly before 1914, the year both men died. Marion
Randall Parsons remained active in the Club, serving as a director from 1914 to
1938 and on the Editorial Board until her death in 1953.

64. EDWARD T. PARSONS became William
Colby's right-hand man in the planning
of Sierra Club High trips. He was an
accomplished writer and assisted Muir and Colby
in the long campaign to preserve Hetch Hetchy.
He was a club director, 1904–1914,
and a member of the Society for the
Preservation of National Parks.

railroad company were loud in their opposition to recession," yet voted *for* Belshaw's bill in the showdown. This game of "divide and conquer" played by the Southern Pacific was cleverly designed to keep the public and the press from guessing the real position of the Railroad. The company also put off a final vote on the recession bill until other issues in which the Railroad was interested had been settled so that no "severe repercussions and reprisals" might be visited on its legislative program.[82]

IV

The Sierra Club could pause for breath, but not for long. The intention of Colby and Mills in framing the original recession bill had been simply to "recede" the Valley to the federal government. In their eyes, the state had borrowed the land for public use, and now that it could no longer support the use of this land, the federal government should rightfully claim it back. As Colby had written to Secretary of the Interior Hitchcock when he referred the draft of the state recession bill asking for his suggestions, recession was made "operative upon the acceptance by the United States of such recession . . . to enable the federal government to take over the control of the Valley through its Executive Department."[83] When the Assembly bill passed on February 2, 1905, Colby sent Hitchcock a copy saying, "As I have previously written, I trust that the U.S. Government, through the President or other appropriate official, will be able to accept this grant without the necessity of Congressional action, as we had that idea when the bill was framed."[84] Hitchcock, however, apparently felt that Congressional approval was necessary. He asked Senator William B. Allison, Chairman of the Appropriations Committee, to incorporate a clause accepting recession in the Sundry Civil Bill (H. R. 18969).[85] This was subsequently done, acted upon favorably by the Senate, rejected in the House, sent to conference, and finally eliminated from the bill. With the failure of the Secretary's strategy and with adjournment of the 58th Congress only a day away, California's senior Senator, George Perkins, himself a charter member of the Sierra Club, introduced Senate Joint Resolution 115 on March 3, calling for acceptance of recession and appropriating $20,000 for administration.[86] It passed the Senate the same day. The House, however, struck out the recession section, leaving the title and appropriation unchanged![87] Perkins gave his approval to the revised House version of the Senate Resolution, apparently without realizing that it would be unacceptable to California. The resolution was signed by President Roosevelt on March 3,

[82] Colby, "Recession . . . ," *SCB*, XLVII (December 1962), p. 26.
[83] Colby, San Francisco, to Hitchcock, Washington, D.C., December 11, 1904, R. G. 79, National Archives.
[84] Colby, San Francisco, to Hitchcock, Washington, D.C., February 24, 1905; see also letter of February 5, 1905, R. G. 79.
[85] Hitchcock, Washington, D.C., to Allison, Washington, D.C., March 1, 1905, R. G. 79.
[86] *Congressional Record*, 58th Cong., 3rd Sess., vol. 39, pt. 4 (March 3, 1905), pp. 3962–3963.
[87] *Ibid.*, pp. 4018–4019.

1905—the same day that Governor Pardee signed the California law receding the grant.[88] The unfortunate action of the House in striking out the recession clause of Perkins' timely resolution delayed federal "occupation" of the Valley for another year and a half and gave the opponents an opportunity to regroup their forces for attack in the new Congress.

As it happened, the new attack was less an attempt to prevent recession—although some of the State Commissioners were adamant to the end—than it was an effort to combine acceptance of the Valley by Congress with yet another change in Yosemite National Park boundaries. This threat to the Park came from men who looked jealously at the Yosemite Valley Railroad Company, which had incorporated in December 1902 for the purpose of laying tracks up the Merced River Canyon—the natural gateway to Yosemite Valley and the only route open all year. Working from surveys and specifications drawn by N. C. Ray, the chief engineer whom Benson called "utterly unreliable and a teller of falsehoods," the company not only succeeded in convincing the Yosemite Park Commission that such a route was the only logical approach to the Valley, but also actually acquired the necessary rights-of-way, after the boundary act of February 7, 1905, to begin construction the following September.[89]

Meanwhile, a group of San Joaquin Valley businessmen, backed by the Southern Pacific Railroad (which saw its profitable Raymond approach about to be cut off), met and formed the Fresno Traction Company in September 1903 for the purpose of building a competing electric line from Fresno to Wawona and, they hoped, as far as Grouse Creek inside the Park.[90] The Southern Pacific anticipated congressional approval of the Yosemite Park Commission's recommendations, embodied in California Congressman Gillette's H. R. 17345, and, through the Railroad's representative in Washington, protested the passage of this bill, which would permit its rival to build up the Merced River Canyon. Their representative, in a letter to the Secretary of Interior, asserted that the proposed route would be "nearer to the Yosemite Valley grant that any other road, and thus drive all other transportation companies out of business."[91] The letter called attention to the plans of the Fresno Traction Company and urged that the Gillette bill be amended to authorize the Secretary of the Interior to grant rights-of-way *through Park lands,* thus equalizing the privileges that the Merced River railroad would gain with the exclusion of certain lands from the Park.

In February 1905, shortly after Congress had enacted the Gillette bill reducing the Park, Frank H. Short, the lawyer for

[88] 33 *U.S. Stat. at L.* (March 3, 1905), p. 1286, and *Calif. Stat.,* Chapter LX, 36th Session (1905), pp. 54–55.

[89] H. C. Benson, Wawona, to Secretary of the Interior, Wash., May 3, 1905, R. G. 79. An interesting aside in this connection is the letter from John P. Irish, Oakland, to W. S. Richards, Commissioner of the General Land Office, Wash., D.C., January 9, 1905, R. G. 79, urging the "public necessity" of the Gillette bill (H. R. 17345), which resulted in the reduction of the Park boundaries and enabled the Yosemite Valley Railroad to acquire the necessary rights-of-way to El Portal. Irish refers to the "monopolists" meaning the Southern Pacific and the Washburn Stage Company. For a readable account of this interesting railroad, see Hank Johnston, *Short Line to Paradise; the Story of the Yosemite Valley Railroad* (Long Beach, Calif., Johnston and Howe, 1962), 96 pp., and Hank Johnston, *Railroads of the Yosemite Valley* (Long Beach, Calif., Johnston & Howe, 1964), 208 pp.

[90] Articles of Incorporation, Fresno Traction Company, signed September 8, 1903, R. G. 79, filed in Secretary of State's Office, Sacramento, Sept. 22, 1903 (Record book 152, p. 330). The first five directors were William G. Kerckhoff and A. C. Balch from Los Angeles, and A. G. Wishon, H. P. Baumgartner, and W. E. Durfey from Fresno. Kerckhoff held 1,960 shares at par value of $100 each and all other directors held 10 shares each.

That there was some basis for concern on the part of the Southern Pacific Railroad is indicated by the Acting Superintendent's report of visitors for fiscal year 1907/08, the first year in which the Yosemite Valley Railroad carried tourists. 8,850 visitors were reported, of which all but 1,469 arrived via El Portal. ("Report of the Acting Superintendent of Yosemite National Park," *Reports of the Department of the Interior for the Fiscal Year Ended June 30, 1908* [Washington, D.C., 1908], I, 432).

the Fresno Traction Company, applied to Hitchcock for permission to make preliminary surveys in the Park with a view to extending the railroad to a point near Indian Creek. The Company promised to build the road within one year, to carry only passengers and baggage (by this it hoped to allay suspicion that it wanted to capitalize on logging operations), and to construct a wagon road from its terminus near the rim of the Valley to the floor.[92] Later in the spring Short addressed a petition to the Secretary asking permission to extend the surveys and enclosed a strong letter of support from Senators George Perkins and Frank Flint and Congressman J. C. Needham, who had been convinced for some time that a competing railroad would be good for the economy of the state.[93] Hitchcock referred this material to his representative in the Park, Benson, who was as steadfast in his opposition to the Fresno Traction Company as he had been earlier to the Yosemite Valley Railroad Company.[94] He recommended to his superior that the petition be denied, and this recommendation was upheld by Hitchcock, who so informed Short on July 12, 1905.[95] Short immediately responded with strong letters to both Benson and Hitchcock requesting reconsideration and stating, "so long as the present situation continues the matter amounts to an official discrimination in favor of one route and against all others to the Yosemite Valley."[96] Increasing pressures were brought to bear upon the California delegation in Congress, which as we shall see eventually forced an elimination of 10,480 acres on the southwest corner of the Park.

The railroad rivalry that led to a second reduction in Yosemite National Park, only a year and a half after a thorough examination in the field and careful analysis of all private and public factors by the Yosemite Park Commission, is best characterized by Chittenden, the chairman of that Federal Commission, in a communication to Congressman Needham. Commenting on the proposed route of the Fresno Traction Company, Chittenden urged that the boundary not be changed again to accommodate the desires of the Southern Pacific and suggested that the rival line from Fresno might better come down the South Fork of the Merced to join with the Yosemite Valley Railroad in a common terminus. He then stated:

. . . I would like to call your attention to the fact that your people do not seem to have reckoned with the government at all in this matter. They seemed to have overlooked the fact that they are completely dependent upon the national treasury for the success of their own scheme and they apparently entertain the idea that the generosity of Congress in the matter of appropriations is unlimited. . . . Is it the plan of the California delegation to ask funds from the next Congress to build roads to connect with both lines? If so they will meet with disappointment. If they ask for one only, which will it be, and what will the friends of the other have to say? . . . You *must* get to a common terminus

[91] W. S. Pladwell (c/o D. A. Chambers), Washington, D.C., to Secretary of the Interior, Washington, D.C., January 20, 1905, R. G. 79.

[92] Frank H. Short, Fresno, to Secretary of the Interior, Washington, D.C., February 23, 1905, R. G. 79.

[93] Frank H. Short, Fresno, to E. A. Hitchcock, Washington, D.C., May 9, 1905. The Congressman's letter was addressed to Hitchcock and dated May 1, 1905. R. G. 79. Senator Perkins and Congressman Needham had supported an earlier Gillette bill to cut out certain parts of the Park (H. R. 9310, 58th Cong., 2nd Session).

[94] Benson, Wawona, to Hitchcock, Washington, D.C., June 26, 1905, R. G. 79.

[95] F. L. Campbell, Acting Secretary of the Interior, Washington, D.C., to Frank H. Short, Fresno, July 12, 1905, R. G. 79.

[96] Frank H. Short, Fresno, to E. A. Hitchcock, Washington, D.C., July 24, 1905; also letter to Benson, Wawona, **same date**, R. G. 79.

with your lines in some way and go to Congress with a united front for an appropriation for one connecting road.[97]

Chittenden also told Needham that Speaker Cannon of the House of Representatives would support recession in Congress "if the improvement of the Park is planned on a rational and economical basis."

It seems to me, therefore, that you and your associates, who must look after these appropriations in the future, should view this subject from both sides—that of the government as well as that of your constituents. With reasonable concessions a vast amount of good will result to the Park in the next few years. But if the matter is dealt with on the basis of commercial rivalry only, without an effort to harmonize competing interests and bring them into cooperation, the development of proper facilities for visiting the Park may be set back indefinitely. It must be remembered that the people of the United States as a whole care nothing for these competing interests, but do care a great deal for the Yosemite, and they would rather see the development of the Park postponed indefinitely than to introduce conditions which will menace its integrity in the future.[98]

The Sierra Club was not yet aware of the plan to cut off the southwest corner of the Park, but it was determined that Sacramento's recession bill should not languish for want of Congressional acceptance. The directors prepared a new memorial to Congress and sent it with formally printed cover to the President and all members on Capitol Hill.[99] It cited the number of California organizations in favor of recession and asked that Congress accept the Yosemite Valley and Mariposa Big Tree Grove in accordance with the California act of the previous spring. Colby also addressed Hitchcock in October 1905, urging him to ask the President to include an acceptance recommendation in his annual message to Congress and warning the Secretary of possible lobby activities by certain Californians opposed to recession.[100]

Under the urging of the Sierra Club and others, Senator Perkins informed the Secretary of the Interior in December 1905, that he would introduce the necessary legislation in the new Congress if Hitchcock would prepare the bill for this purpose.[101] Neither the Secretary nor Perkins were party at this time to the amendment which the railroad interests sought, to eliminate lands between the South Fork of the Merced River and the Wawona Road—a ridge left inside the Park after the Act of February 7, 1905. On December 19, 1905, Perkins introduced Senate Resolution 14 as prepared by the Department of the Interior.[102] There was no mention of boundary changes in this document, but some time between December 19 and mid-January, Senator Perkins was evidently persuaded to amend his resolution. The amendment called for the elimination of ap-

[97] H. M. Chittenden, Yellowstone National Park, to J. C. Needham, Modesto, Calif., September 1, 1905, copy in R. G. 79.

[98] Ibid.

[99] Memorial of the Sierra Club of California to the President and Congress of the United States in Relation to the Recession of the "Yosemite Valley" and the "Mariposa Big Tree Grove" to the United States of America, R. G. 79.

[100] Colby, San Francisco, to E. A. Hitchcock, Washington, D.C., October 9, 1905, R. G. 79.

[101] Perkins, Washington, D.C., to Hitchcock, Washington, D.C., December 7, 1905, R. G. 79.

[102] Congressional Record, 59th Cong., 1st Sess., vol. 40, pt. 1 (December 19, 1905), p. 578.

proximately 23,000 acres from the Park. When the Secretary of the Interior referred Perkins' letter and amendment to W. A. Richards, Commissioner of the General Land Office, for a report, the latter recommended against any further reduction in the boundaries on the basis that the "construction of an unnecessary railroad along . . . the Wawona toll road, with all the customary evils in its wake," including "the removal of the forests by the lumbermen, a blasting of the flora and a drying up of the springs," was not commensurate with "public gain."[103] He also pointed out that the Perkins amendment would move the natural gateway to the Park several miles eastward to a point where the Merced's canyon walls are precipitous and no flat land available for a common railroad terminus. The Acting Superintendent of Yosemite, Benson, strongly opposed Perkins' amendment on the ground that its precedent might cause the removal of other parts of the Park for similar projects.[104] As soon as he was informed of the amendment, Colby wrote on behalf of the Sierra Club: "Understanding that there are private railroad, lumber, and cattle interests endeavoring to force an amendment . . . which would eliminate a large area from the western side of the Yosemite National Park, we wish you to be informed that the Sierra Club is unalterably opposed to any change of the present boundaries . . . , and we urge the immediate passage of the Bill accepting Yosemite Valley as originally introduced."[105]

The Perkins amendment obviously went much further than was necessary to accommodate the desires of the Fresno Traction Company, but it was Perkins' intention to eliminate as many private holdings within the Park as he could—particularly such areas as Wawona, Big Meadow, and Foresta—still major problems to National Park Service administrators. Congressman Gillette, who had already introduced resolutions similar to Perkins' Senate Resolution 14, now embodied in his final resolution, H. J. 118, a compromise as the result of a conference between the California delegation in Congress and the Department of the Interior.[106] The compromise resolution would remove from the Park somewhat less than half the acreage proposed for removal in the earlier Perkins amendment and would not move the western boundary eastward along the Merced River. The reasons given in the official Senate and House reports on H. J. Resolution 118 indicate that the Fresno Traction Company and the Southern Pacific had indeed convinced the government that a rival electric line deserved full and equal consideration with the already approved Yosemite Valley Railroad, which at that very moment was under construction in the Merced Canyon. The *Congressional Record* contains the Sierra Club memorial on recession and also the letter from Secretary Hitchcock of March 13,

[103] W. A. Richards, Washington, D.C., to Secretary of the Interior, Washington, D.C., January 27, 1906, R. G. 79.

[104] Benson, San Francisco, to Secretary of the Interior, Washington, D.C., February 13, 1906, R. G. 79. On March 17, 1906, Benson sent a telegram to his superior in Washington informing him that a surveying party for the Southern Pacific had completed a reconnaissance of the south bank of the Merced River, but that Ranger Leonard had prevented its advance into the Park. Benson favored this route for a rival line because it would not necessitate altering the Park boundary.

[105] Colby, San Francisco, to Hitchcock, Washington, D.C., March 6, 1906, R. G. 79.

[106] H. J. Resolution 77, *Congressional Record*, 59th Cong., 1st Sess., vol. 40, pt. 2 (January 15, 1906), p. 1111; H. J. Res. 114, *ibid.*, vol. 40, pt. 4 (March 8, 1906), p. 3562; H. J. Res. 116, *ibid.*, vol. 40, pt. 4 (March 9, 1906), p. 3655; and H. J. Res. 118, *ibid.*, vol. 40, pt. 4 (March 12, 1906), p. 3711. See also E. A. Hitchcock, Washington, D.C., to Allen Chamberlain, Appalachian Mountain Club, Boston, April 14, 1906, R. G. 48, Press copies of letters sent, Patents and Miscellaneous Division, 1902–1907, National Archives.

1906, in which he approves the elimination of land for an "electric road . . . to enable the people of southern California to have ready access to the Yosemite Valley."[107] It was not until May 7, 1906, that Gillette succeeded in obtaining the necessary recognition from Speaker Cannon, at which time his resolution passed on a voice vote without debate.[108]

The resolution moved into the Senate where it could be counted on for safe guidance by Senator Perkins, who, while sympathetic to the railroad interests, was also genuinely interested in recession. He met almost immediate opposition, however, from Senator Alfred B. Kittredge from South Dakota. Both Kittredge and Perkins were members of the Committee on Forest Reservations and the Protection of Game to which Gillette's resolution was referred. The California lobby against recession, which Colby had warned Hitchcock about, succeeded in buttonholing Kittredge and he refused to allow the committee to report the resolution. But Perkins was a powerful and well-liked man in the Senate, and he succeeded in obtaining the necessary two-thirds vote to bring the resolution to the floor. It passed the Senate on June 9, 1906, without substantial debate, although Kittredge tried to delay proceedings by presenting a letter from William H. Metson and C. S. Gidens, former state Yosemite Commissioners, objecting to recession on legal grounds.[109] President Roosevelt signed the bill on June 11, 1906, as he had promised Muir he would, and the long, often bitter, fight over recession was a closed chapter—almost.[110]

Colby was able to announce happily to his fellow members in the Sierra Club, after their high trip of that summer, that victory had been won: "The recession of Yosemite Valley to the Federal Government is an accomplished fact. . . . The Club is to be congratulated on this happy outcome of a bitter and protracted contest over the control of the Valley. Our President, Mr. Muir, has advocated this transfer for fifteen years, and it was largely due to his influence that it was brought about. The Club has never accomplished a more important work, and it is now duty bound to urge upon the next Congress the necessity of making a liberal appropriation for the improvement of the Valley."[111]

Muir, of course, was overjoyed and wrote Johnson: ". . . sound the loud timbrel and let every Yosemite tree and stream rejoice! You may be sure I knew when the big bill passed. Getting Congress to accept the Valley brought on, strange to say, a desperate fight both in the House and Senate. Sometime I'll tell you all the story. You don't know how accomplished a lobbyist I've become under your guidance. The fight you planned by that famous Tuolumne camp-fire seventeen years ago is at last fairly, gloriously won, every enemy down derry

[107] *Congressional Record*, 59th Cong., 1st Sess., vol. 40, pt. (June 9, 1906), p. 8143–8148 See also U.S. 59th Cong., 1st Sess. *S. Report 3623* (May 17, 1906) serial no. 4905 (4 pp.), and *H Report 2339* (March 16, 1906) serial no. 4906 (2 pp.).

[108] *Congressional Record*, 59th Cong., 1st Sess., vol. 40, pt. (May 7, 1906), p. 6487. Th full wording of the Resolution is given. Colby says that Gillett was successful in obtaining th Speaker's recognition because Ed ward Harriman was induced b Muir to intercede with Cannor (Colby, "The Recession of Yo semite Valley," *SCB*, XLVII (De cember, 1962), p. 27.)

[109] *Congressional Record*, 59th Cong., 1st Sess., vol. 40, pt. (June 9, 1906), pp. 8144–8145 The ex-Commissioners' letter wa dated April 10, 1906.

[110] 34 *U.S. Stat. at L.* (1906) 831–832.

[111] *Circular* no. 32, Sierra Club September 10, 1906, p. 2.

down. Write a good, long, strong, heart-warming letter to
Colby. He is the only one of all the Club who stood by me in
downright effective fighting.''[112]

A footnote to the recession fight was added some years later,
when there was agitation to bring Yosemite again under control
of the state. Senator Curtin was suspected of being behind this
movement, but the Sierra Club quickly scotched the plan. Colby
wrote Major William W. Forsyth, Acting Superintendent of
Yosemite, informing him of Curtin's intention to introduce such
a bill in the State Legislature, and asked Forsyth for a brief
statement "showing just what advantages have accrued by reason of Federal control of the Valley.''[113] Colby prepared a circular to be mailed to each member of the Legislature and to Club
members for their use in writing to their representatives. This
careful planning proved very effective. Not only was Curtin's
plan shelved, but the Legislature, through Assembly Joint Resolution no. 1, also urged the federal government to appropriate
$250,000 each year for four years, "such expenditure to be made
in pursuance of some comprehensive plan of development" for
Yosemite National Park.[114] The passage of this resolution in
December 1911 killed all further discussion of state control of
the Park.

V

In the winter of 1906, the Sierra Club leaders were naturally
triumphant over the recent successful fight for recession, but
sobered mightily by the shadow of a still greater controversy
that lay immediately ahead—as well as by the tragic loss in April
of that year of the Club's records, library, and memorabilia. In
December, Muir and Colby, from the Club's temporary headquarters in Berkeley, sent the following message to Secretary
Hitchcock: "We felt that the Nation was the proper custodian
of this world-famed Valley and would care for it better and
make more generous appropriation for it than could the State of
California. We advanced these as the reasons why the transfer
should be made and now that the Federal Government is in
control, we feel that we are under obligation to do our part in
seeing that our predictions are realized.''[115]

The two Club leaders urged that at least $100,000 be pro-
vided for improvement of the Valley and offered the assistance of
the Club in securing such an appropriation. Perhaps most important of all, Muir and Colby recommended that a general plan
of development be adopted and carried out in the years to come

[112] Muir, Adamana (Arizona),
to Johnson, New York, July 16,
1906, reprinted in Badè, op. cit.,
II, p. 357.
[113] Colby, San Francisco, to Forsyth, Presidio, San Francisco, January 27, 1910, copy, SCA.
[114] Calif. Stat. (1911), p. 253.
Copy also in SCA. For Colby's
statement supporting resolution,
see SCB, VIII (January, 1912),
pp. 229–230.
[115] Muir and Colby, Berkeley, to
E. A. Hitchcock, Washington,
D.C., December 4, 1906, R.G. 79.

"so that the work of each year would fit into and tend toward the fulfillment of the plan."[116]

Recession was an accomplished fact. Although other California organizations and individuals, supported by an overwhelming majority of the newspapers of the state, helped in educating the public on the advantages of a single administration in Yosemite, the Sierra Club played the key role. Its leaders were forced into the area of sophisticated political persuasion and planning by the predominant position of the Southern Pacific in California politics. The political knowledge that Muir and Colby gained in Sacramento and in more than a year of compromises in Washington was to be of inestimable value in the far more serious Hetch Hetchy campaign, which, whether the Club leaders realized it or not, had been well under way since 1901.

[116] *Loc. cit.*
A check of official Yosemite appropriations by Congress reveals that there was a sharp increase in funds designated for maintenance and improvement following acceptance of the Valley by the federal government. Prior to the special appropriation contained in Senator Perkins' Senate Joint Resolution 115 of March 3, 1905—the Resolution in which the House struck out recession but retained the $20,000!—annual appropriations for Yosemite National Park had fluctuated from zero to $6,000. Beginning in fiscal year 1907–08, however, $30,000 was funded each year, jumping to $62,000 in 1910–11, dropping to $50,000 in 1911–12, rising to $80,000 in 1912–13 and $125,000 in 1913–14, after which it fell back again during World War I.

The Yosemite Fall from the Geological Survey's *Yosemite Guide-Book*, 1870.

4

HETCH HETCHY
The Battle Within
the Battle

"... we have only begun our fight,
and we are not going to rest until
we have established the 'principle that
our National Parks shall be held
forever inviolate' ..."
—Will Colby

I

WHILE THE Sierra Club was engulfed in the recession campaign, almost under the windows of the Club offices in downtown San Francisco various city officials were quietly and efficiently planning how to obtain a water supply from the Yosemite National Park. They sought to make the municipality less dependent upon the privately owned Spring Valley Water Company—suppliers of this essential service since 1858.[1] The story of San Francisco's desire to make herself self-sufficient in this utility is marked by political maneuvering, steadfast devotion on the part of a handful of people, and coincidental circumstances which so often shape history. Although several writers have touched on the Hetch Hetchy narrative, and despite Ray W. Taylor's journalistic account and the excellent administrative study by Florence Monroy, no one has yet had the patience and the skill to sift through conflicting evidence, analyze the several technical engineering problems, and write the definitive history of the Tuolumne River water supply.[2] Nor is this attempted here. This account is concerned, rather, with how the Sierra Club was drawn into the conflict; how the Club influenced the course of events; and how it survived dissension among its members, while maintaining adherence to the original purposes of the founders.

[1] Ray W. Taylor, *Hetch Hetchy; the Story of San Francisco's Struggle to Provide a Water Supply for Her Future Needs* (San Francisco, Ricardo J. Orozco, 1926), pp. 15–16. For a brief story of the city's water supply, see Marsden Manson, "Outline of the History of the Water Supply of the City of San Francisco," reprinted from the *Journal of the Association of Engineering Societies*, XXXVIII, March 1907, pp. 109–124, and published as part of *Reports on the Water Supply of San Francisco, California, 1900 to 1908, Inclusive* (San Francisco, Board of Supervisors, 1908), pp. 3–13.

[2] *Ibid.* Taylor was a reporter for the *San Francisco Examiner.* Also Florence Riley Monroy, *Water and Power in San Francisco Since 1900; a Study in Municipal Government* (M.A. thesis in political science, University of California, 1944). See also Elmo R. Richardson, "The Struggle for the Valley: California's Hetch Hetchy Controversy, 1905–1913," *California Historical Society Quarterly*, XXXVIII (September, 1959), pp. 249–258; Judson King, *The Conservation Fight from Theodore Roosevelt to the Tennessee Valley Authority* (Washington, D.C., 1959), pp. 40 ff; John Ise, *Our National Park Policy: A Critical History* (Baltimore, Published for Resources for the Future, Inc., by Johns Hopkins Press, 1961), pp. 85–96; and references to recent unpublished dissertations in the "Bibliographical Note."

II

What was Hetch Hetchy? Was this Sierra valley worth the more than twelve years of political struggle that San Francisco officials waged? Was this remote mountain canyon and meadow truly "a wonderfully exact counterpart of the Merced Yosemite . . . one of nature's rarest and most precious mountain temples," as John Muir was to write during the heat of the campaign to obliterate the valley floor?[3] A fair appraisal of the scenic qualities and potential camping appeal of Hetch Hetchy is difficult for those who were emotionally involved on either side of the controversy, but reading some of the early descriptions of the valley, one is persuaded that it did possess special and unique charms and that it did, indeed, rival its famous neighbor fifteen miles to the southeast.

The earliest written descriptions of Hetch Hetchy were by members of the California Geological Survey. Whitney himself called the valley "almost an exact counterpart of the Yosemite," stating: "It is not on quite as grand a scale as that Valley; but if there were no Yosemite, the Hetch Hetchy would be fairly entitled to a world-wide fame; and, in spite of the superior attractions of the Yosemite, a visit to its counterpart may be recommended, if it be only to see how curiously nature has repeated herself."

Whitney's description of the Valley appears in the 1868 edition of *The Yosemite Book:* "The Hetch Hetchy is between 3,800 and 3,900 feet above the sea level, or nearly the same as the Yosemite; it is three miles long east and west; but it is divided into two parts by a spur of granite, which nearly closes it up in the centre. The portion of the Valley below this spur is a large open meadow, a mile in length and from an eighth to half a mile in width, with excellent grass, timbered along the edge. The meadow terminates below in an extremely narrow canon, through which the river has not sufficient room to flow at the time of the spring freshets, so that the Valley is then inundated, giving rise to a fine lake. The upper part of the Valley, east of the spur, is a mile and three quarters long, and from eighth to a third of a mile wide, well timbered and grassed. The walls of this Valley are not quite as high as those of the Yosemite; but, still, anywhere else than in California, they would be considered as wonderfully grand. On the north side of the Hetch Hetchy is a perpendicular bluff, the edge of which is 1,800 feet above the Valley, and having a remarkable resemblance to El Capitan. In the spring, when the snows are melting, a large stream is precipitated over this cliff, falling at least 1,000 feet perpendicular. The volume of water is very large, and the whole of the lower part of the Valley is said to be filled with its spray. A little farther east is the Hetch Hetchy Fall, the counterpart of the Yosemite. The height is 1,700 feet. It is not quite perpendicular; but it comes down in a series of beautiful cascades, over a steeply inclined face of rock. The volume of water is much larger than that of the Yosemite Fall, and, in the spring, its noise can be heard for miles. The position of this fall in relation to the Valley is exactly like that of the Yosemite Fall, in its Valley, and opposite to it is a rock much resembling the Cathedral Rock, and 2,270 feet high."[4]

Charles F. Hoffmann, Whitney's topographer, visited the valley in the summer when some of the falls were dry and reported briefly at the October 21, 1867, meeting of the California Academy of Natural Sciences. Less glowing than his chief, he nevertheless was impressed, particularly with the "singular fea-

[3] John Muir, *The Yosemite* (New York, The Century Co., 1912), pp. 249 and 255. Essentially the same material appears in the *SCB*, VI (January, 1908), pp. 211–220. See also other Muir descriptions of the Hetch Hetchy during San Francisco's campaign: "The Tuolumne Yosemite in Danger," *Outlook,* LXXXVII (November 2, 1907), pp. 486–489; "The Endangered Valley: the Hetch Hetchy Valley in the Yosemite National Park," *Century Magazine,* LXXVII (January, 1909), pp. 464–469; and "The Hetch Hetchy Valley; a National Question," *American Forestry,* XVI (May, 1910), pp. 263–269. Material appearing in "The Endangered Valley" was used in the pamphlets issued by the Society for the Preservation of National Parks in 1909.

[4] J. D. Whitney, *The Yosemite Book; a Description of the Yosemite Valley and the Adjacent Region of the Sierra Nevada, and of the Big Trees of California,* Geological Survey of California. (New York, Published by authority of the Legislature, 1868), pp. 98–99. As this account indicates Hetch Hetchy is smaller in size and lower in elevation than Yosemite; its summer climate is also somewhat warmer. The spring lake to which Whitney refers is interesting because the proponents of a reservoir argued that since the floor was subject to flooding and subsequent mosquito infestation, permanent flooding would enhance rather than detract from the Valley. When one realizes that the Yosemite Valley was originally subject to much more flooding than at present and for precisely the same reason as that described for Hetch Hetchy (that is, the narrow restriction of the canyon at the Valley's outlet)—a condition relieved only by blasting the Merced's channel during the term in office of Galen Clark as Guardian, at the instigation of the State Commissioners—one wonders what better fate Hetch Hetchy might have suffered had it been more easily accessible to tourists and had it, like Yosemite, been placed under the control of the state.

ture of . . . the total absence of talus or debris at the base of the bluffs."[5]

Although Muir's later impressions of the Hetch Hetchy may be colored by his impassioned advocacy of its preservation, his first observations, published in 1873, indicate that even then he considered the valley a noteworthy geologic exhibit. Remarking that about 10,000 persons had visited the Yosemite Valley up to the early 1870's, he said: "If this multitude could be set down suddenly in Hetch Hetchy, perhaps not one per cent of the number would entertain the slightest doubt of their being in Yosemite. They would find themselves among rocks, waterfalls, meadows, and groves, of Yosemite size and kind, grouped in Yosemite style; and, amid such a vast assemblage of sublime mountain forms, only acute observers, and those most familiar with the Yosemite Valley, would be able to note special differences. The only questions they would be likely to put would be, 'What part of the Valley is this? Where are the hotels?' "[6]

In 1878 and 1879 a federal survey party under the command of Lieutenant Montgomery M. Macomb, a part of the George M. Wheeler Geographical Surveys West of the 100th Meridian, completed reconnaisance for a large-scale topographic map of the Yosemite area. In a report to his superior, Macomb called Hetch Hetchy "worthy of especial remark as being perhaps the most remarkable feature of the great Tuolumne Canon. While it cannot be compared with the Yosemite in size or in grandeur, it perhaps more nearly resembles that Valley than any other known locality, and has at least sufficient beauty and individuality to produce an ineffaceable impression on the observer."[7]

Popular tourist guides to Yosemite and articles written for campers are either extravagant in their praise of Hetch Hetchy or ignore it altogether. Xenos Clark speaks of Hetch Hetchy as "superior" to Yosemite: "It is one perfectly-cut little gem. Yosemite is a long, strung-out cluster, too rambling and too extensive for a single sweep of the eye; moreover, the landscape-gardening of Yosemite is very rude, it is more like an area of enclosed country with its forests and its rough places, traversed by the Merced River. Hetch Hetchy, on the other hand, makes a picture."[8] Clark warns that a trip to the valley is only for "genuine out-door people. The skin must be a little toughened to the wilderness, and the heart must be entirely open on the nature side."[9]

The Southern Pacific publicist, Major Ben C. Truman, from 1887 to 1889 on the Yosemite Board, quotes T. P. Madden, a fellow Commissioner, as saying, "It is much smaller than the Yosemite and, therefore, many of its objects are grouped

[5] C. F. Hoffman, "Notes on Hetch-Hetchy Valley," *Proceedings of the California Academy of Natural Sciences*, III, October 21, 1867 (San Francisco, 1868), p. 369.
[6] John Muir, "Hetch Hetchy Valley; the Lower Tuolumne Yosemite," *Overland Monthly*, XI (July, 1873), p. 45.
[7] "Report of Lt. M. M. Macomb, 4th Artillery, in charge of Party 2, California Section, Field Seasons of 1878 and 1879," in *Annual Report of the Chief of Engineers to the Secretary of War for the Year 1879*, Part III, Appendix F, U.S. 46th Cong., 2nd Session, H.R. Ex. Doc. no. 1, pt. 2, vol. 2 (Washington, Government Printing Office, 1879), pp. 2237–2238.
[8] Xenos Clark, "The Hetch Hetchy Valley: A New Yosemite," *Outing; An Illustrated Monthly Magazine of Recreation*, VI (May, 1885), p. 151.
[9] *Ibid.*, p. 152.

together very grandly and very beautifully, and at once entrance the beholder; but Hetch Hetchy lacks many of the imposing features of the Yosemite. Still, if there had been no Yosemite, Hetch Hetchy would command the admiration of all who visit it, and would probably rank as the grandest and most beautiful aggregation of rock and water in the world—in fact, it would be Yosemite."[10]

Perhaps most extravagant of all the reporters was a correspondent of the *San Francisco Chronicle* (a Mr. W. P. B.), whom Truman quotes as follows: "Volumes have been written descriptive of Yosemite, but of her sister valley, equally beautiful, and in some respects even more remarkable, our public prints, our books of travel, and with one exception, even our guide-books are silent. Here is a valley, which, were it in Europe, Americans would cross the ocean by thousands to see. Yet, lying as it does, at our very doors, we doubt if one Californian in a hundred knows of its existence. From a rocky bluff, a half-mile down the cañon, Hetch Hetchy comes first into open view. It is a surprise. The panorama is a noble one, embracing in one vast amphitheatre all the most notable objects of interest of the Valley. Yosemite cannot produce its equal."[11]

In contrast, a number of other authors overlooked Hetch Hetchy or barely mentioned it in passing. John S. Hittell's *The Resources of California* has a single paragraph on Hetch Hetchy whereas it devotes eight full pages to Yosemite.[12] The best known of the Sierra boosters, James M. Hutchings, does not mention Hetch Hetchy in either of his major guidebooks, although one of these contains nearly 500 pages on the Yosemite region.[13] A number of other guidebooks are nearly as neglectful.[14] Hetch Hetchy, although fully appreciated by a few scientists and journalists, lacked wagon-road access and therefore had only a small complement of visitors; it never found favor with those who sought to capitalize on the beauty and grandeur of its more famous rival. So remote was Hetch Hetchy from the usual line of tourist travel that even Muir, when he proposed Yosemite park boundaries to Robert Underwood Johnson in 1890, wrote that although he believed the Tuolumne Canyon should be included in the reservation, "whether it is or not will not matter much since it lies in rugged rocky security as one of Nature's own reservations."[15]

III

Undeniably Hetch Hetchy possessed notable scenic attractions, but it was also precisely these same qualities—seen through the eyes of an engineer as steep rocky walls, narrow outlet, and large

[10] Major Ben C. Truman, *Tourists' Illustrated Guide to the Celebrated Summer and Winter Resorts of California Adjacent to and Upon the Lines of the Central and Southern Pacific Railroads* (San Francisco, H. S. Crocker and Co., 1883), pp. 34–35.

[11] *Ibid.*, p. 35.

[12] John S. Hittell, *The Resources of California Comprising the Society, Climate, Salubrity, Scenery, Commerce and Industry of the State*, 6th edition rewritten (San Francisco, A. Roman & Company; New York, W. J. Widdleton, 1874), p. 147.

[13] James M. Hutchings, *Scenes of Wonder and Curiosity in California* (San Francisco, 1862) and *In the Heart of the Sierras; the Yosemite Valley, Both Historical and Descriptive, and Scenes by the Way, Big Tree Groves, the High Sierra, with its Magnificent Scenery, Ancient and Modern Glaciers, and Other Objects of Interest; with Tables of distances and Altitudes, Maps, etc.* (Yosemite Valley and Oakland, Calif., Pacific Press Publishing House, 1886).

[14] See for example, John S. Hittell, *Yosemite: Its Wonders and Its Beauties* (San Francisco, H. H. Bancroft & Co., 1868), pp. 45–47; *Bancroft's Tourist Guide, Yosemite* (San Francisco, A. L. Bancroft & Co., 1871), no mention; John Erastus Lester, *The Yosemite; Its History, Its Scenery, Its Development* (Providence, 1873), no mention; Lewis Stornoway, *Yosemite: Where to Go and What To Do: A Plain Guide to the Yosemite Valley* (San Francisco, C. A. Murdock & Co., 1888), no mention; and D. J. Foley, *Yosemite Souvenir and Guide* (Yosemite Valley, 1902), pp. 85–86.

[15] John Muir, Martinez, to Johnson, New York, May 8, 1890, reprinted in *SCB*, XXIX (October, 1944), p. 58.

storage capacity—that lured San Francisco to this site for its long-sought independent water supply. Hetch Hetchy was a natural reservoir site. It was remote. It had a virtually level floor with a minimum of tree cover at its lower end. Most important, it had a narrow entrance where the granite walls rose perpendicularly for several hundred feet. A more suitable storage basin could scarcely be found anywhere in the Sierra, or so the city advocates believed. There was one major predicament—*this valley was inside a national park.*

San Francisco recognized the value of Hetch Hetchy as a dam site only after prolonged friction between the city and the Spring Valley Water Company "over the adequacy of rates, injunctions, dreary actions in the federal courts, the impounding of moneys," and "an occasional outburst from property owners . . . demanding water."[16] The city made several attempts to purchase the private company, but neither side could agree on a satisfactory price. On one particularly frustrating occasion the city attempted to purchase private rights in Calaveras Valley for a future water supply, only to have these rights snatched from it by an alert water company official. Following this affair the Board of Supervisors turned, for the third time in five years, to professional engineering assistance in making a new survey of possible sources of water. The Spring Valley Company once again offered its properties to the city, including the recently acquired Calaveras area, but the city refused as it so often had in the past, "on the ground that the price . . . is much in excess of the true costs of the works as shown by their own books."[17]

The new survey, conducted by George H. Mendell, a U.S. Army engineer, examined nine widely scattered sources in 1876–1877—including such important bodies as Lake Tahoe, Clear Lake, and the Mokelumne River—but, strangely, did not consider the Tuolumne River. Mendell's final report recommended the Blue Lakes scheme on the Mokelumne (now the source for the East Bay Municipal Utility District water supply). However, years of above-average rainfall, the completion of the Upper Crystal Springs dam by the local company, and an adverse opinion by the city's attorney limiting the right of San Francisco to construct water works, resulted in apathy among citizens and diverted the Board of Supervisors to more pressing problems. Exorbitant water rates charged by the monopolistic Spring Valley Company continued to irk city officials, however, and "finally in sheer desperation," says Taylor, the Board of Supervisors ordered an advertisement published in three San Francisco newspapers "for proposals from parties desiring to furnish water."[18] The city felt it might be able to force the hand of the private water works by inviting competition from a

[16] Taylor, *op. cit.,* p. 97.
[17] *Ibid.,* p. 22.
[18] *Ibid.,* p. 29.

87

new company or by buying out the rights of such a company and thus establishing a municipally owned rival. The city also hoped to bargain for time and leverage by which to force Spring Valley to a reasonable asking price on its properties.

Among the offers received by the Board of Supervisors was one from George M. Harris, dated May 11, 1894, in which he agreed to sell his acquired water rights in Hetch Hetchy and on the Tuolumne River for $200,000. His letter indicates that he had tendered these rights in 1888 to E. B. Pond, then Mayor of San Francisco, but official city records do not mention such an offer.[19] In 1894, then, there was the first official mention in the city records that the Hetch Hetchy was a definite possibility. Although this 1894 offer of Harris' was not accepted, the city was now aware of Hetch Hetchy as a possible source of municipal water, and later, during James D. Phelan's administration as mayor, the city's interest in this possibility was stimulated by two independent engineering reports.

In the same summer that the Yosemite Park bills were being considered, A. H. Thompson completed surveys of several Sierra reservoir sites including Hetch Hetchy. His report is the first federal mention of the Valley for this purpose, although William Ham Hall (who in his capacity as State Engineer had been employed a decade earlier by the Yosemite Commissioners to advise them in preservation policies) had earlier recognized the value of Hetch Hetchy and in 1889 had supervised the "segregation" of reservoir sites at Tenaya, Lake Eleanor, and Tuolumne Meadows.[20] A second U.S. Geological Survey report was issued in 1899 in which John Quinton concluded: "Another purpose which the dam and reservoir at Hetch Hetchy might be made to serve would be to furnish the City and County of San Francisco with an unfailing supply of pure water."[21] This statement was brought to the attention of Mayor James D. Phelan by C. E. Grunsky, City Engineer, who asked J. B. Lippincott—under whose authority the Quinton survey had been conducted—to effect personal filings in the name of the Mayor for rights of way and reservoir sites at Hetch Hetchy and Lake Eleanor. According to Marsden Manson, a member of the newly created Board of Works and later City Engineer, Hetch Hetchy was chosen over all other surveyed sources because of the following unrivaled advantages: "Absolute purity by reason of the uninhabitable character of the entire watershed tributary to the reservoirs and largely within a forest reservation; . . . abundance, far beyond possible future demands for all purposes; . . . largest and most numerous sites for storage; . . . freedom from complicating 'water rights'; and . . . power possibilities outside the reservation."[22]

[19] *Ibid.*, p. 30. The Harris letter is reproduced on this page and also as an appendix to Monroy's thesis. In 1882 Engineer J. P. Dart designed a piped system to bring water from the Tuolumne to the city, but his plan does not appear to have influenced San Francisco officials who chose to ignore it. (Taylor, *op. cit.*, p. 31.)

[20] A. H. Thompson, "Report Upon the Location and Survey of Reservoir Sites During the Fiscal Year Ended June 30, 1891," U.S. Geological Survey, *12th. Annual Report*, XII, part 2 (Washington, D.C., 1891), pp. 36–38.

[21] F. H. Newell, "Report of Progress of Stream Measurements for the Calendar Year, 1899," U.S. Geological Survey, *21st Annual Report*, XXI, part 4 (Washington, D.C., 1899–1900), p. 459. The section (pp. 450–465) on "Hetch Hetchy Reservoir" is by Quinton.

[22] Marsden Manson, *op. cit.*, p. 7. Note that Manson uses the language of the 1890 Act establishing Yosemite National Park, although it was popularly called "national park" from the very beginning, and was officially so designated in 1905.

The final reason given by Manson—power possibilities outside the reservation—was never fully developed either by C. E. Grunsky, or later by Manson himself during his term as City Engineer (but awaited the much more far-reaching insights of John R. Freeman in 1912). Although the arguments for cheap electric power were not stressed at this time, they appealed to Phelan and may have been decisive in convincing him that Hetch Hetchy, rather than one of the other possible sources, must be obtained by San Francisco at all costs. Hetch Hetchy, then, was a source with a double advantage: a continuous font of pure water in abundance unhindered by prior rights, and hydro-electric potential sufficient to reduce greatly the cost of the total project.

J. B. Lippincott, privately hired by Phelan's men, conducted his own surveys of the reservoir sites as quietly as possible, fearful lest unfavorable publicity cast an ill light on San Francisco, arouse the Acting Superintendent of Yosemite to unwelcome questioning, and awaken private parties to actual or fancied conflicts of interest in water rights on the Tuolumne.[23] From data supplied by Lippincott, Grunsky submitted a cost estimate for the Tuolumne system for $39,531,000, an estimate which included only the Hetch Hetchy reservoir and not Lake Eleanor.[24] Although Phelan left the mayor's chair in 1902, the personal investment which he and his engineers had committed to the Tuolumne water system made it absolutely mandatory that they press the pursuit of this particular source. In doing so, they turned their minds against other possible supplies, perhaps less desirable but fully adequate—sources that had received serious consideration from previous city administrations and were known to be available, though frequently encumbered with prior rights.

IV

While the engineering possibilities of Hetch Hetchy as a reservoir site were being investigated, Phelan and his friends in Washington were pursuing the legal possibilities of gaining entry into the Yosemite National Park to further San Francisco's interests. The Secretary of the Interior unwittingly came to the aid of the city in suggesting in his *Annual Report* that the confusion existing over the various Congressional acts concerning "rights of way" in national parks should be set straight by passing a new act. To accomplish this was the legislative intent of California Representative Marion DeVries of Stockton who introduced H. R. 11973 on May 29, 1900.[25] There is no proof that Phelan had anything to do with DeVries' bill, but there can be no doubt, in spite of assurances which William Colby said were made to him

[23] Marsden Manson, "Appendix B, In the Matter of the Application of the City and County of San Francisco for Reservoir Rights of Way in Hetch Hetchy Valley and Lake Eleanor, Within the Yosemite National Park; Reply to Objections of the Honorable Secretaries of the Interior and of Commerce and Labor; On Behalf of the City and County of San Francisco," in *Efforts to Obtain a Water Supply for San Francisco from Tuolumne River* (San Francisco, July 17, 1905), pp. 5–6. Manson addressed this brief to "The President;" it is an interesting exposition of San Francisco's case for Hetch Hetchy.

[24] C. E. Grunsky, San Francisco, to the Board of Public Works, San Francisco, July 28, 1902, reprinted in *Reports on the Water Supply of San Francisco, California, 1900 to 1908, Inclusive* (San Francisco, Board of Supervisors, 1908), p. 75.

[25] *Congressional Record*, 56th Cong., 1st Sess., vol. 37, pt. 7 (May 29, 1900), p. 6247. See U.S. 56th Cong., 1st Sess., *H. Rep.* 1850 (May 30, 1900), serial no. 4027, for remarks about legislative intent. The federal acts which needed clarification in the opinion of the Secretary of the Interior were: (a) Act of March 3, 1891 (26 *U.S. Stat. at L.,* 1101–1102, sec. 18–21), (b) Act of January 21, 1895 (28 *U.S. Stat. at L.,* 635), (c) Act of May 14, 1896 (29 *U.S. Stat. at L.,* 120), and (d) Act of May 11, 1898 (30 *U.S. Stat. at L.,* 404).

that H. R. 19973 did open the way to municipal use of Yosemite's Hetch Hetchy. In light of the subsequent events that led to the passage of the Raker Act in 1913, the Right of Way Act of February 15, 1901, was the turning point in a campaign of which the Sierra Club was not yet aware.

As John Ise has noted, "The act was in most respects perfectly tailored for looters of the parks, for it authorized the Secretary to grant rights of way through government reservations of all kinds," specifically including the three California parks, "for . . . canals, ditches, pipes and pipe lines, flumes, tunnels, or other water conduits, and for domestic, public, or other beneficial uses" provided the permit received approval from the chief administrative officer and was not "incompatible with the public interest."[26] The bill, although questioned, easily passed the House and was piloted through the Senate by Senator Perkins without a word being raised against it.

Mild objections were raised by the Commissioner of the General Land Office that DeVries' bill singled out the California parks for prejudicial action and hinted that all parks should be included, but the bill was given official administration sanction.[27] Neither the House nor the Senate objected to this feature, and no conservation group, including the Sierra Club, disputed this clause. This point was later discussed by Agnes Laut, in an article appearing in the November 20, 1909 issue of *Collier's Weekly*.[28] Colby, secretary of the Sierra Club, responding to Laut, wrote the editor of *Collier's* explaining why the Club had not protested the 1901 Act: "We, who were . . . trying to the best of our poor ability to save these great parks for the people, knew nothing of the bill until it was a law. We were probably not vigilant enough, but we certainly did not lack the desire to know of all that was going on. Be that as it may we later examined the Act and found that it was the intention of the Public Lands Committee which recommended its passage to still 'preserve and retain' the natural curiosities and wonders of the Park in their natural condition, and that such rights of way as were contemplated should not interfere with 'the attainment of the purposes for which the various reservations are established.' We felt that this apparently harmless act could not injuriously affect the park."[29]

The following lines from the same letter seem to indicate that the Sierra Club had been unaware, at the time of its passage, that this Act would play into the hands of persons friendly to the San Francisco position. Colby wrote: ". . . our confidence was of short duration when certain individuals in San Francisco conceived the idea that the Hetch Hetchy . . . should be flooded and destroyed as a camp ground. We protested vigorously. Secre-

[26] John Ise, *op. cit.*, p. 86. For the Act, see 31 *U.S. Stat. at L.* (1901), 790.

[27] Pinger Hermann, Washington, D.C., to Secretary of the Interior, Washington, D.C., February 11, 1901, R. G. 48, National Archives.

[28] Agnes Laut, "The Fight for Water in the West—Part III," *Collier's Weekly*, XLVI (November 20, 1909), p. 15.

[29] William E. Colby to Norman Hapgood, November 26, 1909, *The Johnson Papers*, CB-385, box 3, folder no. 140, Bancroft Library, University of California, Berkeley, hereafter referred to as *The Johnson Papers*.

tary Hitchcock relieved our apprehension and held that this act . . . did not authorize the destruction of one of the greatest wonders of the Park. It is a great misfortune to the American public that Secretary Garfield took a different view of the law."[30]

Exactly when Muir and other members of the Sierra Club sensed that something was in the wind is difficult to determine. The earliest reference I have been able to find to Hetch Hetchy's plight in Muir's correspondence is a letter addressed to Robert Underwood Johnson dated March 23, 1905—more than four years after passage of the Right of Way act.[31] Undoubtedly the DeVries bill slipped through Congress with very little fanfare. When one remembers that the Club had no established sources of information in Washington (as it did during the later phases of the Hetch Hetchy controversy), it is perhaps not surprising that the Club failed to notice the potential dangers in this bill. No statements appear in the *Sierra Club Bulletin* until the subject of Hetch Hetchy's preservation was thrown into public light by the newspapers of San Francisco and by public gatherings such as meetings of the Commonwealth Club of California.

As a result of the 1901 Act and the Lippincott surveys, Phelan, as we have seen, filed—or had filed in his name—an application with the Register of the Stockton Land Office for reservoir rights at Lake Eleanor and Hetch Hetchy on October 16, 1901.[32] Secretary of the Interior E. A. Hitchcock denied Phelan's application on January 20, 1903, and a month later Phelan formally transferred his "right, title, and interest" in the two reservoir sites to the city and county of San Francisco.[33] Subsequently a petition for rehearing was granted, and the application was again denied on December 22, 1903.[34] The City Attorney, Franklin K. Lane, later to become President Wilson's Secretary of the Interior, then directed a "Petition for Review" to Hitchcock who once again denied the city's application on February 20, 1905.[35]

Meanwhile the San Francisco political scene shifted. In 1902, the incumbent officials, who had been pushing for the Tuolumne water system, were swept out of office; a new mayor, E. E. Schmitz—later to be indicted for extortion—and a new group of supervisors took over. The water supply story now took on an official and an unofficial side, with the "outs," while waiting for the opportunity to return to office, spending much of the interim period in continuing their efforts for Hetch Hetchy.

During the first three years of the Schmitz administration, there was general agreement that the Tuolumne filings should be kept alive, and this was the aim of City Attorney Lane's formal request for a review of the original petition. After Hitchcock's

[30] *Loc. cit.*

[31] John Muir to Robert Underwood Johnson, March 23, 1905, *The Johnson Papers,* box 7, folder no. 455.

[32] *Reports on the Water Supply of San Francisco California, 1900 to 1908, Inclusive* (San Francisco, Board of Supervisors, 1908), p. 109.

[33] *Ibid.,* pp. 113–115.

[34] *Ibid.,* pp. 129–130.

[35] Lane's petition is reprinted in *Ibid.,* pp. 112–127; the Hitchcock denial, pp. 128–132.

denial of February 1905, however, the Schmitz administration lost interest in the Tuolumne supply. On February 3, 1906, the Board of Supervisors passed Resolution no. 6949, asking that the city abandon its attempts to enter Hetch Hetchy and that new investigations of other supplies be made.[36] On April 18, the earth heaved and split and a fire of destruction followed. No water system that could have been envisioned for the future could possibly have saved the city in that conflagration; nevertheless, the people were now more conscious than ever of the need for adequate water supplies.[37]

In the days following the earthquake citizen groups were formed to help in the rehabilitation of the city, among them the Federated Water Committee headed by Colonel W. H. Heuer. His group recommended purchase of the Spring Valley Water Company—certainly not a new idea. The Board of Supervisors, however, disregarded this advice, and asked that various individuals and companies submit offers of purchase for their respective water systems. Of the eleven proposals submitted, the Supervisors, following the recommendations of their special committee, selected the Bay Cities Water Company (operating on the South Fork of the American River and the North Fork of the Consumnes), and in December 1906 appointed City Engineer Woodward (who had replaced Grunsky in 1902) and Engineer J. R. Price to make a report.[38] No report was ever made. The graft prosecutions soon removed the corrupt Schmitz administration from office.

The Phelan group, meanwhile, was busy from 1903 to 1906 gaining the ears of President Roosevelt and Gifford Pinchot and resubmitting their application to Secretary Hitchcock. Manson talked with President Roosevelt in 1905, and, with the aid of Gifford Pinchot, Benjamin Ide Wheeler, and other close friends of the President favoring the San Francisco scheme, was able to win Roosevelt over. Early in 1905 Pinchot wrote Colby: "I have just received your confidential letter of February 10, and I want to reply in the same way because Congressman Needham has asked me not to make public my recommendations to the President. This letter is therefore strictly confidential. I reported to the President more than a week ago, recommending: first, the use of Lake Eleanor whenever the city shall make the necessary application and acquire the necessary rights. Second, the reservation of the Hetch Hetchy and Big Tuolumne Meadows reservoir sites for the eventual use of San Francisco and the other adjacent cities, provided a time comes when they need them. This recommendation seems to me to fit almost exactly with that expressed in your letter. I feel very strongly that San Francisco must have an adequate water supply, and it has seemed to me that the action

[36] Taylor, *op. cit.*, p. 61. The resolution is reproduced in full on p. 60.

[37] After the earthquake and fire, Phelan charged in public that Secretary Hitchcock's denial of his application for reservoir sites directly contributed to San Francisco's disaster. W. B. Acker, Chief of the Patents and Miscellaneous Division of the Interior Department, prepared a memorandum for the Secretary that clearly established that the Tuolumne water system could not have been completed until at least two years *after* the 1906 earthquake and that the loss of water with which to fight the fire following the shake was due to structural damage to the distribution pipes and not to insufficient water in storage reservoirs *outside* the city. Acker, Washington, D.C. to Hitchcock, Monadnock, N.H., September 28, 1906, and "Memorandum for the Secretary . . . ," September 27, 1906 (12 pp.), R. G. 79, National Archives.

[38] Taylor, *op. cit.*, p. 66.

of the Secretary of the Interior was based purely on a technicality and entirely failed to meet the needs of the situation. On the other hand, I agree with you fully as to the extreme desirability of preserving the Hetch Hetchy in its original beauty, just as long as that can be done without serious interference with a matter of such large importance as the water supply of a great group of communities. From what I can gather, it will be not less than 50 years before any supply further than that which can be derived from Lake Eleanor is required, and perhaps twice as long. In the meantime, it would be unwise to allow rights to accrue which would eventually prevent the use of the other reservoir sites by the city, or make that use possible only after extremely expensive condemnation proceedings."[39]

As a result of the encouragement received from administration officials, Manson renewed the city's application for Hetch Hetchy and Lake Eleanor on July 27, 1905.[40] Roosevelt asked Attorney General Purdy for an opinion on the reopening of the city's rights. Purdy's decision was that the Secretary had the power to grant the right if he desired. Although this decision was rendered in October 1905, for some reason it was not made known to San Francisco officials until the following year—in the same month that the earthquake and fire struck.

Buttressed by Purdy's opinion and the support of Gifford Pinchot, who on May 18, 1906 wrote Manson that "I will stand ready to render any assistance which lies in my power,"[41] the San Francisco Board of Supervisors in 1907 determined to fight for the Tuolumne supply and not to honor the Schmitz decision, which in effect had been discredited as a result of the graft trials. Circumstances in Washington conspired at the same time to help the city's case. Secretary Hitchcock, who had steadfastly refused to grant the city's application, resigned, and James R. Garfield was appointed Secretary in his place. Anticipating Garfield's appointment, Pinchot wrote Manson again suggesting that he assume the new Secretary's attitude would be favorable and that he set the case before him.[42] Later in the year Garfield, on a tour of the West Coast, met with officials of the city and set a date for a rehearing of the San Francisco application. As a result of the testimony brought forth at this hearing (July 27, 1907) and the official support of the administration, Garfield decided in favor of the city on May 11, 1908.[43]

For the first time, the way now seemed open for the city to get the kind of water supply it felt it should have. The administration was favorable to its cause; the Attorney General had delivered a favorable opinion, and, finally, the Secretary himself, in whose hands the law had placed the decision, had granted his official approval.

[39] Gifford Pinchot to William Colby, February 17, 1905, *The Johnson Papers,* box 8, folder no. 621.

[40] Marsden Manson, "Appendix B, In the Matter of the Application of the City and County of San Francisco for Reservoir Rights of Way in Hetch Hetchy Valley and Lake Eleanor, Within the Yosemite National Park; Reply to Objections of the Honorable Secretaries of the Interior and of Commerce and Labor; On Behalf of the City and County of San Francisco," in *Efforts to Obtain a Water Supply for San Francisco from Tuolumne River* (San Francisco, 1907), pp. 1–30.

[41] Commonwealth Club of California, "Water Supply for San Francisco," *Transactions,* II (June, 1907), p. 340. Also reprinted in Robert U. Johnson, *Remembered Yesterdays* (Boston, Little, Brown, and Co., 1923), pp. 307–308. Letter is dated May 28 by Johnson.

[42] *Loc. cit.* Pinchot's letter is dated November 15, 1908.

[43] "Hearing on the Application of the City of San Francisco for Reservoir Sites and Rights of Way in the Yosemite National Park for Domestic Water Supply Source . . . ," in *Reports on the Water Supply of San Francisco, California, 1900 to 1908, Inclusive,* pp. 148–168. The Garfield decision is reprinted in the *Reports,* pp. 217–222. It may also be found in the *SCB,* VI (June, 1908), pp. 321–327.

V

What was the Sierra Club doing about this, the most serious attack yet to be made on Yosemite National Park? The Club had been deeply involved in the recession campaign, which, as we have seen, was not resolved until early 1905 in Sacramento and not until mid-1906 in Washington. The energies of Muir and Colby during this period were largely devoted to the successful completion of recession and to the urging of larger appropriations for Yosemite. Muir and Colby evidently became aware of the city's filings at Hetch Hetchy early in 1905, but little action seemed necessary at this time, since Secretary Hitchcock had denied the San Francisco application. Reassured by the fact that the Phelan administration, the original and most persistent advocates of a Tuolumne water system, was out of office at this time, the Sierra Club probably was not aware of the activities of Manson, City Attorney Percy V. Long, and others in Washington during 1905. The Club was further thrown off guard by the apparently sincere desire of the Schmitz administration, after February 1906, to rescind the actions of Phelan's Board of Supervisors and to look elsewhere for an independent water supply. However, evidence indicates that, as late as mid-1907, Manson, who had joined the Sierra Club in 1895 and had been an active contributor to its *Bulletin,* still hoped to convince Muir that a reservoir in Hetch Hetchy would not interfere with any of the grand features of the park and that such a lake would break up "the great breeding spots of the mosquito."[44]

Furthermore, the Club was not aware until Gifford Pinchot's letter to Colby in February 1905 that Pinchot would support San Francisco's desire to obtain water rights in Hetch Hetchy. Pinchot's position was probably the decisive element in the administration's support of San Francisco. He had examined Phelan's application for reservoir sites in 1903 and after consultation with James C. Needham, the California Congressman in whose district Hetch Hetchy lay, apparently was convinced that no serious injury to Yosemite National Park would occur and that San Francisco's water needs were paramount. Samuel P. Hays, in a monograph on the Progressive Movement, writes that Theodore Roosevelt, also a political realist, supported Pinchot "with indecision." Although Muir tried to convince his friend of the 1903 camping trip, Roosevelt appears to have sided with San Francisco early in the controversy, and his later letters to Muir, Johnson, Hitchcock, and Garfield indicate his abandonment in this instance of the preservationist viewpoint.[45]

[44] Marsden Manson, San Francisco, to Muir, Martinez, July 29 and August 9, 1907. Author copies. His contributions to the *SCB* were on the effects of partial suppression of annual forest fires and a remedy for denudation of vegetation (*SCB*, II, June 1899, pp. 295–311, and VI, January, 1906, pp. 22–24). He remained a member of the Club until April 1913. (See Manson, San Francisco, to Sierra Club, April 2, 1913, Sierra Club Archives, hereafter referred to as SCA.)

[45] Gifford Pinchot, Washington, D.C., to W. Bertrand Acker, Chief, Patents and Miscellaneous Divison, Interior Department, December 12, 1903, R. G. 79, National Archives; T. Roosevelt, Washington, D.C., to Secretary of the Interior, February 8, 1905, R. G. 79, N.A.; Roosevelt to John Muir, September 16, 1907, *Theodore Roosevelt Papers,* Library of Congress, hereafter referred to as *T. R. Papers;* Roosevelt to Garfield, April 27, 1908, *T. R. Papers;* Muir to Roosevelt, April 21, 1908, reprinted in Badè, *The Life and Letters of John Muir* (Boston and N.Y., Houghton Mifflin Co., 1924), II, pp. 417–420; Roosevelt to Muir, April 27, 1908, *T. R. Papers;* and Roosevelt to Johnson, December 17, 1908, *T. R. Papers.*

[46] Elmo Richardson, *The Politics of Conservation, Crusades and Controversies, 1897–1913,* University of California Publications in History, vol. 70 (Berkeley and Los Angeles, University of California Press, 1962), p. 44. Samuel P. Hays, *Conservation and the Gospel of Efficiency; the Progressive Movement, 1890–1920,* Harvard Historical Monograph XL (Cambridge, Harvard University Press, 1959), pp. 192–198 and *passim* is the best account of Pinchot's role; but see also Donald C. Swain, *Federal Conservation Policy, 1921–1933,* University of California Publications in History, vol. 76 (Berkeley and Los Angeles, University of California Press, 1963), pp. 124–126; Edith Jane Hadley, "The Crusade of John Muir and His Friends for Conservation of Parks and Forests and Salvation of Beauty of the Wilderness, 1888–1914," in her *John Muir's Views of Nature and Their Consequences* (Ph.D. dissertation, University of Wisconsin, 1956), pp. 503–745; Roderick Nash, "The American Wilderness in Historical Perspective," *Forest History,* VI (Winter, 1963), pp. 8–10; John Ise, *op. cit.,* pp. 86–87; and for view of contemporary participant, Robert U. Johnson, *Remembered Yesterdays* (Boston, Little, Brown and Co., 1923), pp. 307–308. The best manuscript sources for the development of this break between the preservationists and the utilitarians are the *Gifford Pinchot Papers,* Library of Congress, and the *J. Horace McFarland Papers,* Harrisburg, Pa. The Sierra Club Archives also contain much correspondence from McFarland, as well as copies of Pinchot letters, characterizing the dispute.

[47] Robert Shankland, *Steve Mather of the National Parks* (New York, Knopf, 1951), p. 51.

[48] Muir, Martinez, to Johnson, New York, September 2, 1907, *The Johnson Papers,* box 7, folder no. 458.

[49] Sierra Club, *Minutes of the Board of Directors,* August 30, 1907, SCA.

Many conservationists must have been bewildered by the stand of Pinchot and Roosevelt, but "no real inconsistencies were involved," notes Elmo Richardson in *The Politics of Conservation;* he adds, "Federal officials were determined to base their policies on the pragmatic concept of multiple use of resources, and they did not wish to abandon the advantageous support of populous areas," including California, merely for the sake of the preservation principle.[46] The Hetch Hetchy controversy alienated Muir from Pinchot and severed relations between the preservationists and the utilitarian conservationists. So bitter did this split become that Muir was purposely eliminated from the invitation list for the Governors' Conference of 1908, a group which was to meet in May at the call of the President to discuss the conservation of natural resources.[47]

From 1905, then, Muir, both as an individual and through the Sierra Club, did what he could to stir interest in the plight of Hetch Hetchy. A letter to Johnson, dated September 2, 1907, is typical of the Muir sentiment: "This Yosemite fight promises to be the worst ever. Try to prevent the Secretary [of the Interior] from making sudden decision which our enemies are trying for. Have got the Sierra Club at work. You try to arouse the Appalachian Mountaineering Club. Am writing the President and Garfield."[48]

Muir's reference to having the Sierra Club "at work," referred to the meeting of the board of directors, August 30, 1907, which authorized the appointment of a committee to report "on the Welfare and Improvement of the Yosemite National Park."[49] Joseph N. LeConte, William F. Badè, Edward Parsons, and William Colby were appointed to the committee with Muir sitting as chairman, ex officio. Within three weeks the report was ready and sent by the Directors to Secretary Garfield. This was the first official statement of the Club's position, although Muir and the other committee members had personally voiced their feelings and had done their best to motivate other organizations in the United States—particularly the Mazamas, the Appalachian Club, the Saturday Walking Club (Chicago), and the American Civic Association. Most of the resolution of the Sierra Club is presented in full because it is typical of the arguments expressed by the "nature lovers," as the pro-park people were labeled by the opposition:

Whereas the Yosemite National Park was created by an Act of Congress October 8, 1890, [*sic*] in order that the unrivaled aggregation of scenic features of this great natural wonderland should be preserved in pure wildness for all time for the benefit of the entire nation; and

. . .Whereas, Hetch Hetchy Valley, far from being a "common meadow," "a minor feature" as claimed by applicants, is a counterpart of Yosemite and a great and wonderful feature of the Park, and next to Yosemite in beauty, grandeur, and importance;

Whereas, the floor of the Hetch Hetchy, like that of Yosemite is a beautiful landscape park diversified by magnificent groves, gardens, and flowery meadows in charming combinations especially adapted for pleasure-camping; and

Whereas, this wonderful Valley is the focus of pleasure-travel in the surrounding area of the Park, and all the trails from both the South and the North lead into and through this magnificent campground, and though now accessible only by trails, it is visited by large numbers of campers and travelers every summer, and after a wagon-road has been made into it, and its wonders become better known, it will be visited by countless thousands of admiring travelers from all parts of the world;

Whereas, if dammed and submerged one hundred and seventy-five feet deep, as proposed, Hetch Hetchy would be rendered utterly inaccessible for travel since no road could be built around the borders of the reservoir without tunneling through solid granite cliffs; and

Whereas, these campgrounds would be destroyed and access to other important places to the north and south of the Valley interfered with, and the High Sierra gateway to the sublime Tuolumne Canyon leading up to the grand Central Campground of the Upper Tuolumne Valley would be completely blocked and closed; and

Whereas, no greater damage could be done to the great National Park, excepting the damming of Yosemite itself; and

Whereas, all of the arguments advanced in favor of making Hetch Hetchy into a reservoir could be made to apply with equal force to the case of making Yosemite into a reservoir, except that the cost of a dam in the latter case would be greater;

Whereas, the proponents of the San Francisco water scheme desire the use of Hetch Hetchy, not because water as pure and abundant cannot be obtained elsewhere, but because, as they themselves admit, the cost would be less; and

Whereas, we do not believe that the vital interests of the nation at large should be sacrificed and so important a part of its National Park destroyed to save a few dollars for local interests;

Therefore, be it

Resolved, That we are opposed to the use of Hetch Hetchy Valley as a reservoir site, and devoutly pray that the application of the San Francisco Board of Supervisors to the Honorable Secretary of the Interior may be denied.[50]

The men who composed this resolution, all members of the board of directors, had a majority, but not a unanimous board opinion behind them. One member of the board, Warren Olney, in whose office the Club had formed fifteen years earlier, actively supported the San Francisco position. This difference on the board was reflected in the membership itself, many members in the Bay Area tending to disagree, some rather violently, with the views of the majority of directors. In November 1907 five Directors addressed this letter to Club members:

Dear Friend:

Enclosed you will find a description of Hetch Hetchy Valley, and a brief discussion of the immediate danger which threatens it now.

If you are like minded with us, we ask you (and others whom you may

[50] *SCB*, VI (June, 1908), pp. 264–265.

persuade) to kindly address a personal letter, in your own words, essentially as follows:

"To the President, or to the Secretary of the Interior, or to both:

"As a lover of the Yosemite National Park, I most devoutly protest against the use of one of its most important and beautiful features, the Hetch Hetchy Valley, as a reservoir. An abundance of water can be had elsewhere to supply San Francisco."

Thanking you in advance for your attention to this request,

> We are,
> Yours truly,
> John Muir
> Joseph N. LeConte
> Wm. F. Badè
> E. T. Parsons
> Wm. E. Colby[51]

One San Francisco attorney wrote Colby: "I most earnestly protest against the Sierra Club being used as a cat's paw to pull chestnuts from the fire for the Spring Valley Water Company, or for the grafters who have taken up the Sierra's water rights with the object of selling their rights to San Francisco. . . . I regret exceedingly that I have not taken up this matter before, so that it could be laid before your Committee, and probably have tended to avoid further misguided efforts on your part."[52]

Reactions such as this from a small but vocal minority led Colby to direct a formal letter to the editor of the *Sierra Club Bulletin* (McAllister) explaining the attitude of the Committee: "Since there are other adequate sources of water supply available for San Francisco, it is only just to the nation at large, which is vitally interested in preserving the wonders of the Yosemite National Park, that their destruction or alteration should be avoided if it is possible to do so, as it most certainly is when the question resolves itself into one of mere expense."[53]

No open break occurred for several more months, but the differences voiced at directors' meetings and informally along the trail on local walks gradually caused the opposing camps to solidify their views. According to Colby, Muir was greatly downcast by this threat to the effective leadership of the Club in what promised to be its most severe trial. When Muir announced his intention not only to resign the presidency (which he had held from the first) but also his personal membership, Colby persuaded him that the whole campaign would collapse without him, and then, elaborating on a suggestion by Boston attorney Edmund A. Whitman, Colby proposed the formation of a separate organization to take the brunt of attacks, one which could go on the offensive against the city with a united front.[54] Muir immediately recognized the value of this idea and enthusiastically acceded.

[51] Copy of statement, November 1, 1907. Author copy.

[52] H. L. Atkinson, San Francisco, to Colby, Berkeley, December 19, 1907, SCA.

[53] Colby to Editor, *SCB*, VI (June, 1908), p. 268.

[54] Author interview with Colby, June 5, 1963. See also Edmund A. Whitman, Boston, to Colby, San Francisco, March 6, 1909 and April 27, 1909, SCA.

By April 1909 Colby had created, apparently largely out of his own head, the Society for the Preservation of National Parks. Its purposes were stated on the letterhead: "To preserve from destructive invasion our National Parks—Nature's Wonderlands. To enlist the support and coöperation of all organizations and individuals in such preservation and to publish and circulate information to accomplish these objects."[55] An interesting memorandum in Colby's handwriting indicates that at first he thought of calling it the *California* Society, but decided to emphasize its national character, naming it, instead, "California Branch." This suggested that leadership was not based in San Francisco; as we shall see, there was ample justification for use of the term "Branch."

The officers of the new organization were not so much elected as they were chosen. Muir was president. William F. Badè, a professor at Pacific Theological Seminary (now Pacific School of Religion), served as vice president. Other officers were George Edwards, Berkeley, and Rachel Vrooman Colby, who occupied a position in the Society similar to her husband's in the Sierra Club. Among the directors were Joseph N. LeConte, Edward T. Parsons, and Willoughby Rodman, who were also members of the Sierra Club board.[56] To further emphasize the national character of the group, an Advisory Council was established consisting of various men who consented to the use of their names and who, at one stage or another during the campaign, actively supported the position of the Society. Thus, we find on the letterhead: Allen Chamberlain, Appalachian Mountain Club (Boston); Asahel Curtis, Mountaineers (Seattle); Henry E. Gregory, American Scenic and Historic Preservation Society (New York); Robert Underwood Johnson, soon after to be appointed editor of *Century Magazine* (New York); Miss Harriet Monroe, a Chicago poet active in literary circles and the founder of *Poetry* magazine; J. Horace McFarland, president of the American Civic Association (Harrisburg and Washington, D.C.); John W. Noble, a St. Louis attorney and former Secretary of the Interior; Alden Sampson, a member of the University Club (New York); C. H. Sholes, Mazamas (Portland); and Edmund Whitman, Appalachian Mountain Club.

Offices of the Society were shared with the Sierra Club in 302 Mills Building. Colby himself, unable to take an open part in the new Society because of his employment in the law firm of Judge Curtis H. Lindley, one of the leading proponents of the Hetch Hetchy water supply for San Francisco, nevertheless was the guiding figure in its formation and was its real workhorse. In April 1909, shortly after the new society was organized, Colby warned Pinchot: "Let me assure you that we have only begun

[55] The Sierra Club Archives still contain a quantity of blank letterheads.

[56] Rodman, a Los Angeles banker, succeeded Warren Olney when the latter was defeated for election in April, 1909, because of his active support of San Francisco.

98

our fight, and we are not going to rest until we have established the principle 'that our National Parks shall be held forever inviolate,' and until we have demonstrated to the satisfaction of every one, including yourself, that the American people stand for that principle. We are going to keep up the good fight without fear or favor, 'if it shall take until doomsday.' "[57]

VI

As we have seen, on May 11, 1908, Secretary of Interior Garfield reversed his predecessor's decision and granted San Francisco reservoir sites and rights of way at Lake Eleanor and Hetch Hetchy, saying, "Domestic use, . . . especially for a municipal supply, is the highest use to which water and available storage basins . . . can be put. . . . The next great use of water and water resources is irrigation."[58]

Although Garfield "appreciated" the feelings of the scenic protestants, he was convinced "that 'the public interest' [would] be much better conserved by granting the permit." He wrote:

Hetch Hetchy Valley is great and beautiful in its natural and scenic effects. If it were also unique, sentiment for its preservation in an absolutely natural state would be far greater. In the mere vicinity, however, much more accessible to the public and more wonderful and beautiful, is the Yosemite Valley itself. Furthermore, the reservoir will not destroy Hetch Hetchy. . . . The prime change will be that, instead of a beautiful but somewhat unusable "meadow" floor, the valley will be a lake of rare beauty.[59]

Garfield then set forth the advantages "to the public":

. . . The City . . . and probably other cities on San Francisco Bay would have one of the finest and purest water supplies in the world; the irrigable land in the Tuolumne and San Joaquin Valleys would be helped out by the use of the excess stored water and by using the electrical power not needed by the City for municipal purposes, to pump subterranean water for the irrigation of additional areas, the City would have a cheap and bountiful supply of electric energy for pumping its water supply and lighting the City and its municipal buildings; the public would have a highway at its disposal to reach this beautiful region of the Park heretofore practically inaccessible; this road would be built and maintained by the City without expense to the Government or the general public; the City has options on land held in private ownership within the Yosemite National Park, and would purchase this land and make it available to the public for camping purposes; the settlers and entrymen who acquired this land naturally chose the finest localities, and at present have power to exclude the public from the best camping places; and further the City in protecting its water supply would furnish to the public a patrol to save this part of the park from destructive and disfiguring forest fires.[60]

The Secretary said that he did not "need to pass upon the claim that [the Tuolumne supply was] the only practicable and

[57] Colby, San Francisco, to Gifford Pinchot, Washington, D.C., April 28, 1909, copy, SCA.

[58] "Decision of the Secretary of the Interior Department, Washington, D.C., Granting the City and County of San Francisco, Subject to Certain Conditions, Reservoir Sites and Rights of Way at Lake Eleanor and Hetch Hetchy Valley in the Yosemite National Park," May 11, 1908, reprinted in *Reports on the Water Supply of San Francisco, California, 1900 to 1908, Inclusive* (San Francisco, Board of Supervisors, 1908), p. 219.

[59] *Loc. cit.*

[60] *Ibid.*, pp. 219–220.

99

reasonable source [since it was] sufficient that after careful and competent study the officials of the City" insisted that this was the case.

The only solace to preservationists in Garfield's apparent knuckling under to the city's arguments was that the permit imposed certain conditions. The most important of these was the requirement that the Lake Eleanor site be perfected to its full capacity before "beginning the development of the Hetch Hetchy site" and that improvements were not to take place until proven need existed.

On May 12, 1908 the day following release of Garfield's statement, the Secretary wrote William Colby: "It must be remembered that the duty imposed upon the Secretary of the Interior in acting on grants of this kind prevents him from considering merely the preservation of the park in its natural state, but he must, as well, consider what use will give the greatest benefit to the greatest number."[61]

To Garfield, it was clear, "the greatest benefit" was the unlimited source of pure water that the Tuolumne offered "to the greatest number," the people of the growing urban community on the shores of San Francisco Bay.

On May 16, Representative Kahn introduced House Joint Resolution no. 184 for the purpose of exchanging lands between the city and the federal government. However, the House Committee did not begin hearings on the Resolution until December 16, 1908.[62]

Upon the secretary's favorable decision, two things were of immediate concern for the city: One was to file again on the rights that Phelan had originally declared nearly seven years earlier, and the other was to call a special election to determine if the voters agreed with the proposition to acquire lands and water rights at Lake Eleanor and Hetch Hetchy and to incur a bonded debt of $600,000 for this purpose. The preservationist cause reached a low ebb when the results of the city election, November 12, 1908, tabulated a 6 to 1 count in favor of the Tuolumne supply and nearly the same vote for the bonds.[63] The indefatigable McFarland, of the American Civic Association, discouraged for once, wrote Colby, "I find myself without a plan of campaign."[64] And Chamberlain of the Appalachian Club scornfully alluded to the "crazy people out there."[65]

The Secretary's decision did not cause the Sierra Club, or more accurately the majority of its directors, to waver in their determination to save Hetch Hetchy. After the introduction of Representative Kahn's Resolution and before the hearings on it, Colby suggested to Robert Underwood Johnson that the Club issue an illustrated pamphlet containing portions of Muir's ar-

[61] Garfield, Washington, D.C., to Colby, San Francisco, May 12, 1908, copy, *Francis Farquhar Papers*, Bancroft Library.

[62] *Congressional Record*, 60th Cong., 1st Sess. vol. 42, pt. 7 (May 16, 1908), p. 6440.

[63] *San Francisco Municipal Reports*, 1908–1909, p. 1417.

[64] McFarland, Harrisburg, to Colby, San Francisco, November 24, 1908, SCA.

[65] Allen Chamberlain, Boston, to Colby, San Francisco, November 25, 1908, SCA.

ticles on the Hetch Hetchy and statement of the situation, distributing it to Congressmen and other influential persons. In his letter, Colby left no doubt that he considered the resolution a dangerous one, which, ". . . if allowed to pass, will have a strong tendency to perfect the grant. Without an Act of Congress, the grant is dependent upon the discretion of the Secretary, and a succeeding Secretary may, for cause, revoke the grant."[66]

On the question of land exchanges, Colby said: "Muir and I are familiar with all of the lands which San Francisco proposes to exchange for the vacant land on the floor of the Valley. Manson has represented, and Pinchot in his public statement, has endorsed this representation, stating that these lands are fine camping grounds and very desirable additions to the Park, and are not now open to the camping public. The entire statement . . . is without foundation. These lands are mainly made up of small mountain meadows, situated around the rim of Hetch Hetchy, and a few miles distant. They are not desirable camping places when you take into consideration the great attractions in the National Park, and are, only in one or two instances, suitable stopping places for parties intending to visit the Hetch Hetchy. . . . The land on the floor of the Hetch Hetchy, which the city seeks to secure in exchange, is worth a thousand times more than the land to be given up."[67]

The House Committee hearings on H. J. Resolution no. 184, begun in December 1908, have been described by Taylor, in his account of Hetch Hetchy as the first concerted effort of the "nature lovers."[68] However, much of the groundwork for coöperation between the Eastern conservation groups and the Sierra Club had been laid by Colby, Parsons, Chamberlain, and McFarland. At the first session of the hearings Marsden Manson, Supervisor A. P. Giannini, and Secretary Garfield appeared before the Committee on Public Lands to testify in favor of the city; no one appeared for the opposition, although Robert Underwood Johnson spoke with three members of the Committee a couple of days after the hearings, showed them twenty LeConte photographs of the valley, and submitted a brief, letters, and articles.[69] The Sierra Club sent a long telegram signed by four members of the board of directors.[70] Allen Chamberlain sent his views to the Chairman. Other letters were sent to the Committee and a reprint of Muir's description of the Hetch Hetchy originally published in *Century Magazine*. After two days an adjournment was called until January 9, 1909, when the Committee met for hearings on a companion measure, House Joint Resolution no. 223.

The holiday interval allowed both camps an opportunity to organize more formal statements and to send representatives.

[66] Colby, San Francisco, to Johnson, New York, August 17, 1908, *Johnson Papers*, box 3, folder no. 137.
[67] *Loc. cit.*
[68] Taylor, *op. cit.*, pp. 92–93.
[69] Johnson, New York, to John Muir, December 22, 1908, SCA.
[70] *San Francisco and the Hetch Hetchy Reservoir*, Hearings on H. J. Resolution 184, U.S. House Public Lands Committee, 60th Cong., 1st Sess. (Washington, G.P.O. 1909), p. 42. Johnson's brief is on pp. 35–38.

101

San Francisco, which had expected the resolution to pass without a struggle, called for reinforcement of its delegation in Washington. A committee of five was sent including Warren Olney—still officially a director of the Sierra Club. The "save Hetch Hetchy" advocates among the Sierra Club directors had also been active during this lull in the storm. The suggestion that Colby had made to Johnson in the summer of 1908 now was embodied in a pamphlet variously headlined in different editions: "Save the Hetch Hetchy Valley," "Prevent the Destruction of the Yosemite Park," and "Let all the People Speak and Prevent the Destruction of the Yosemite National Park." I do not know whether other editions were prepared, but at least two of them carried a cover letter signed by John Muir and dated (apparently erroneously) January 12, 1908, rather than 1909.[71] How many of these pamphlets were printed also is not known, although they were received by many congressmen, members of the General Federation of Women's Clubs, and other influential persons.

Secretary Garfield's reaction upon receipt of one of the Muir pamphlets was particularly extreme. He sent an open letter to Muir, widely publicized in the press, publicly denouncing the stand of the preservationists and suggesting that Muir could not have signed the statements with his consent as they contained "flagrant misstatements of fact."[72] Muir, in a printed reply to Garfield, called attention to the views of former Secretary Hitchcock and J. Horace McFarland, closing: "The more I study your decision of May 11, 1908 . . . the greater seems the mistake you have made in allowing the city to destroy any part of the Park on any pretext whatever."[73] Muir made no further attempt to justify the circular's contents or to refute the implication that his name had appeared among the signers without his permission. As a matter of fact, the pamphlet had been written by Colby and E. T. Parsons, and although in substance it had been approved by Muir, he had not seen it at the time it was mailed. Colby, Parsons, and Badè jumped to Muir's defense. Their letters to Garfield dealt more directly with the "flagrant misstatements," and took the officer to task for his being "misled by over-zealous partisans."[74]

There is no question but that the wide distribution of the Muir pamphlet resulted in several hundred letters and telegrams to the House Committee on Public Lands asking that San Francisco's case be set aside.[75] These occupy more than 195 pages in the printed hearings. At the hearings in January, attorney Edmund Whitman was asked by the Sierra Club to represent "some of the members," as he put it, although he testified on behalf of the Appalachian Mountain Club as well. His argu-

[71] Copies in Sierra Club Archives, *Farquhar Papers*, *Johnson Papers*, and *McFarland Papers*, Harrisburg, Pa.

[72] *San Francisco Call*, January 26, 1909, p. 14.

[73] Muir to Garfield, Washington, D.C., n.d. (printed letter), *Johnson Papers*, box 13, folder no. 873.

[74] Colby, San Francisco, to Garfield, Washington, D.C., February 2, 1909, copy, *Johnson Papers*, box 3, folder no. 138; Parsons, San Francisco, to Garfield, Washington, D.C., February 5, 1909, Sierra Club Archives; and Badè, to Garfield, Washington, D.C., January 30, 1909, *Johnson Papers*, box 2, folder no. 43. Garfield's angry reply to Colby clearly shows his irritation with the preservationists: ". . . I am very pleased to hear that John Muir did not see the circular which was issued over his name. . . . From further statements in your letter it is evident that you are so ill advised of the facts which have been presented in numerous hearings on the Hetch Hetchy question and the provisions of the permit, that it is useless to further continue the correspondence" (Garfield, Washington, D.C., to Colby, San Francisco, February 9, 1909, *Farquhar Papers*).

[75] The *San Francisco Call*, January 3, 1909, printed a news story to the effect that a "few members of the Sierra Club" sent letters to Congressmen S. C. Smith and W. F. Englebright. The majority of letters came, however, from non-Californians.

ments require twenty-one pages of the printed hearing, not including a short brief that he submitted later to answer the question of what other water supplies beside the Tuolumne would be available to San Francisco.[76] Badè, who was in the East during the hearing, planned to be in Washington, but was detained in Harrisburg and had to wire Chairman Mondell that Alden Sampson would speak for the Sierra Club in his place. Thus, there were no Californians to testify; it must be remembered that the round trip between the Pacific coast and Washington was then a journey of as many days as today's jet flight is of hours. Also Colby felt assured that the Club was well represented at the hearings by Whitman, Sampson, and (in the Senate hearings held later in the month) by Harriet Monroe, who was sent by contributions collected by Stephen Mather and other fellow members of the Saturday Walking Club and the Chicago Geographical Society.[77] Warren Olney made a statement for the San Francisco case at the Senate hearings, as he had at the House hearings.

The preservationists won round one. The House Committee was hopelessly split in its judgment, releasing a majority and two minority reports.[78] The Senate Committee decided not to report at all and withdrew its resolution.

Harriet Monroe, who had been "moved by Mr. Muir's telegrams" to appear at the hearings, wrote a significant letter of impressions to Colby and Parsons: "It seemed to me that the fight, so far as the U.S. government is concerned, is between us and San Francisco. The Spring Valley Water Co. was ably represented, but I doubt if their plea influenced the Senators much. . . . I think their feeling was that the Co. should get out, that the city should control their own water supply and should have Sierra water if she wanted it."[79]

Miss Monroe had a number of ideas for future campaigns. She proposed that the Sierra Club send an engineer into the upper Tuolumne basin to report on the possibility of using some of the high-country lakes outside the park for San Francisco water (a suggestion that had been made by Sampson in the hearings). If it should prove possible to use these waters without damage to scenic value, she felt the Club should then advocate, not oppose, this use for San Francisco. She believed also that the Club should drop from its arguments the idea that the use of Hetch Hetchy as a source of drinking water would compel the closing of the entire watershed to protect the purity of the water. Ex-Mayor Phelan had repudiated this idea in his testimony before the Committee, and Monroe concurred in his opinion. She said the preservationists had two really good arguments and should concentrate all attention on these: (a) the extraordinary beauty of the valley

[76] San Francisco and the Hetch Hetchy Reservoir, Hearings on H. J. Res. no. 223, U.S. House Public Lands Committee, 60th Cong., 1st Sess. (Washington, G.P.O., 1909), pp. 5–26, 66.

[77] Hetch Hetchy Reservoir Site, Hearings on S. R. 123, U.S. Senate Committee on Public Lands, 60th Cong., 1st Sess. (Washington, G.P.O., 1909), pp. 22–29, 30–33. S. Mather, Chicago, to Colby, San Francisco, February 8, 1909, SCA.

[78] Granting the Use of Hetch Hetchy to City of San Francisco, U.S. 60th Cong., 2nd Sess., H. Report 2085 (1909).

[79] Harriet Monroe, Chicago, to William Colby and Edward Parsons, San Francisco, March 2, 1909, copy, Farquhar Papers.

and (b) the bad precedent of invading a national park for private purposes. "We must show that the issues involved are deeper and less temporary" than the immediate damming of Hetch Hetchy for a future water supply. She ended: "You of the Sierra Club may differ from these views, but at least they come from one who listened carefully to both hearings, and watched the effects of the arguments on the Committee. I must say that I was somewhat astonished that no Sierra Club, California, man was there; for no amount of letters and telegrams are a tenth part as impressive as personal appearances and the spoken word.

"Next winter you ought to have some one on hand, if possible, to meet every move in the game. And please permit me one trifling suggestion. If you had heard certain emotional remarks, as I did, you would advise all Sierrans to send no special delivery letters of protest or telegrams so timed as to arrive at night."[80]

The most important suggestion made by Monroe was that the Club drop the argument about the closing of the upper Tuolumne watershed. (There is evidence that continual emphasis on this argument alienated congressmen in the 1913 hearings who felt that the preservationists were indulging in unsound propaganda. Colby's brief on Hetch Hetchy, prepared for the Sierra Club in 1912, modified the sanitation argument substantially.

Whitman reported to Colby, too. His impression was that the chance of the bill's getting through at all was "daily becoming less." The "new 'bunch' have done San Francisco more harm than good," he wrote. Since the printed hearings would not include his brief, Whitman had a thousand copies prepared for distribution to Congressmen, the Appalachian Club taking half and half going to the Sierra Club.[81]

Some idea of the out-of-pocket funds needed on short notice for a campaign such as the preservationists waged during the hearings is possible from Badè's activities. He sent telegrams amounting to $111.85, one to each member of Congress, and apparently was authorized to sign them in Muir's name—at least, his remark that Muir "must be getting any number of letters as a result" implies this.[82] The money that Badè spent was later reimbursed from funds collected by Colby from various concerned members in the Sierra Club; Colby, Parsons, and particularly Muir, often utilized personal resources in such emergencies.[83]

San Francisco accepted the 1909 Congressional defeat grimly. The Board of Supervisors determined to ask for a municipal bond election to begin work on Lake Eleanor. Garfield, of course, granted the city the right to cut timber and trails, make surveys, build conduits and roads, all under the terms of the 1908 permit.

[80] Monroe, *op. cit.*
[81] Whitman, to Colby, San Francisco, February 12, 1909, SCA.
[82] Badè to Colby, February 14, 1909, SCA.
[83] Colby, San Francisco, to Sampson, New York, March 20, 1909, copy, SCA.

VII

In March 1909 a new administration took office in Washington. President Taft appointed a Seattle attorney, Richard Ballinger, as Secretary of the Interior, replacing Garfield. There was a flurry of excitement as the preservationists hurried letters back and forth across the continent and to their associates in the Northwest (the Mountaineers and Mazamas), attempting to learn what they could about the new official. Was this the time for a concerted push for revocation of the Garfield permit? Johnson, Whitman, and Badè thought so and McFarland agreed.[84] He wrote Colby that he thought the campaign ". . . ought to be carefully organized, so as to reach the whole country and have them center on the Secretary, showing the sentiment of the people. It ought not to be a sending of petitions, which do not count, but instead of letters. As a central feature there should be presented the shortest and most clearly set forth statement of the actual conditions, giving the other side fairly, that can be prepared."[85]

He elaborated on these ideas in a letter to Alden Sampson with copies to Badè and Allen Chamberlain—giving some insight into the preservationists' methods in achieving cooperation among the various organizations concerned with the preservation of Hetch Hetchy.

. . . I suggest that we at once get ready for a straightforward, well-organized campaign to have the grant revoked formally. This might be done by uniting all the organizations interested, including the Sierra Club, the Appalachian Mountain Club and the American Civic Association, and by having a uniform plea, based upon the clearest, simplest and least objurgatory statement that can be framed, sent to Secretary Ballinger, showing the sentiment of the country. This plea should not take up the question of water supply for San Francisco any more than to say that the fight brought out the fact that there were other sources of water-supply. We can not properly go into the Spring Valley Company's politics or foster its interests; that is a matter to be fought out locally. What we can do and must do . . . is to plan for a dignified but persistent onslaught on Secretary Ballinger, definitely asking him to revoke the permit . . . for the reason that the people do not want it granted.

. . . I have great faith in a flood of personal letters, written by men of parts, giving their own views as to the value of scenery.

If the proper press effort is made, travel should be directed this summer to the Hetch Hetchy, photographs should be made, the beauties of the place described, and in a rather comprehensive way the value of the Hetch Hetchy from the scenic standpoint should be made known to the people who own it.

The statement sent out to provoke this effort should be accompanied by short, terse, interesting data respecting the Hetch Hetchy Valley and San Francisco's attempt . . . in such a shape as to make it good newspaper stuff. . . . with the growing interest in scenic preservation I believe we could unquestionably arouse the country to protest most efficiently.

[84] Johnson, New York, to Muir, Martinez, February 22, 1909; Badè to Colby, San Francisco, February 25, 1909; Whitman, Boston, to Colby, San Francisco, March 6, 1909; McFarland, Harrisburg, to Colby, San Francisco, March 3, 1909, SCA.
[85] McFarland, Harrisburg, to Colby, San Francisco, March 3, 1909, SCA.

As I look at it, a date should be set about which the protest should be made most effective, not with the idea that it would be confined only to that date, but that the cumulative effect of many people doing the same thing at the same time would occur.

The American Civic Association will reach something over 2500 members, and through these members can more than double that number. If the Appalachian Mountain Club and the Sierra Club can muster an equal number together, that would make something over seven or eight thousand separate persons who could be reached, of whom at least 50%, if I may judge by our experience, would respond. It is possible that the American Scenic and Historic Preservation Society might add its membership. It is also possible, if there is an organized effort, to interest the General Federation of Women's Clubs. Suppose, for instance, that some one who had been in the Hetch Hetchy, like Miss Harriet Monroe, and who could talk as she can talk, was to go to the next meeting of the General Federation and there to talk as she talked before the Senate Committee, it would mean that five or six thousand women from all over the country would be "on the job."

. . .

I am hopeful that this letter, reaching those who have been most efficient and active, will provoke a response, which might possibly lead to a conference and an agreement as to just what to do, how to do it, when to do it, and how to finance it.[86]

A short time later McFarland offered the offices of the American Civic Association in Washington as a clearinghouse and headquarters for the various societies' representatives.

Colby was alert to McFarland's suggestions, as he was to the tactics of the opposition. Having noted that San Francisco's request of land exchanges was to be again introduced in Congress, he wrote Sampson in New York: "I assume that it can not be acted upon at this special session. . . . In this event we will have to plan for a powerful campaign next fall and immediately prior to the next Congress, so as to bring all possible influence to bear in annihilating the proposition. Unless there is some strong assurance that Ballinger would consider favorably a reopening of the case, and would revoke the grant on a strong showing from all parts of the country that the people did not want the Hetch Hetchy to be thus given away, I would hesitate to make the attempt. Failure to secure revocation by Ballinger would only strengthen the enemy. I think we might do better in Congress. . . . My idea is that in any event we should work on the next Congress to secure an appropriation to build a road into Hetch Hetchy, making it accessible to campers from the San Joaquin Valley, and to tourists by stage. Of course, if we can see our way clear to force the issue either in Congress or before Ballinger, with any reasonable hope of success, I would strongly favor it."[87]

With the revocation of the grant as their goal, the preservationists entered the fray on the offensive. First in line was the

[86] McFarland to Sampson, New York, March 11, 1909, copy, SCA.
[87] Colby, San Francisco, to Sampson, New York, March 20, 1909, copy, SCA.

Appalachian Mountain Club; its petition for revocation went to the new Secretary on April 2, 1909.[88] It was followed shortly by a longer petition from Muir and George Edwards, in their capacities as officers of the newly formed Society for the Preservation of National Parks. The Society based its reasons for revocation on the following points: The Department of the Interior exceeded its jurisdiction because the Garfield permit violated the Act of October 1, 1890 establishing Yosemite National Park; it did not take into account the fundamental question of other water supplies but simply accepted the city's word; no necessity for granting the destructive permit was shown; there were other sources of supply that the petitioner was ready to show; the rights of "ninety millions of citizens" were not given adequate hearing; Hitchcock ruled twice against the city application making the whole question *res judicata*; a reservoir would "utterly destroy the Valley as a place of resort" and make necessary, as a sanitary precaution, "the withdrawal of the finest half of the" Park.

The Society requested that several steps be taken to assist the Secretary's review of the permit: that a new opinion be secured from the Attorney General of the United States as to its validity; that the Secretary hold additional hearings so more evidence could be presented; that if a hearing were ordered in San Francisco, "all persons and associations possessing available sources of water supply be invited to present evidence indicating such availability, and the terms on which they may be acquired by [San Francisco]"; that any sentiment of the people that Hetch Hetchy should be sacrificed be expressly determined through further legislation by Congress; and—perhaps most important of all—that a board of competent, disinterested engineers be appointed to represent the United States, to consider evidence, to make independent investigation, and to render an opinion "as to the practical and economic necessity of the use of Hetch Hetchy Valley."[89]

Ballinger told Muir that because bills were pending in Congress for the exchange of lands to effectuate the grant and because the permit was revocable, the question was one only Congress could settle.[90]

In this same spring (1909) the Sierra Club prepared for its ninth high trip. "We are taking the Club Outing . . . into the Yosemite National Park, and spending the concluding week in Hetch Hetchy," Colby informed Sampson, "in order to have the opportunity of getting as many photographs of the place as possible, and educating our members to look at the matter from our view-point."[91] Colby sent invitations to key people in Congress and the administration urging them to come as guests of the

[88] Appalachian Mountain Club, Boston, to Richard A. Ballinger, Washington, D.C., April 2, 1909, copy, SCA. Whitman and R. B. Lawrence, Recording Secretary, signed the petition.

[89] Society for the Preservation of National Parks, San Francisco, to Richard A. Ballinger, Washington, D.C., April 20, 1909, copy, SCA.

[90] Ballinger, Washington, D.C., to Muir, San Francisco, April 28, 1909, copy, *Farquhar Papers*.

[91] Colby, San Francisco, to Sampson, New York, March 20, 1909, copy, SCA.

Club.[92] He particularly hoped that Pinchot and Secretary Ballinger would accept the invitation, but although both wrote letters thanking him, neither was able to accept.[93] (Ballinger, in October of 1909, following President Taft's tour of Yosemite Valley with John Muir and at the President's suggestion, accompanied the naturalist into Hetch Hetchy. Undoubtedly these personal inspection tours influenced both Ballinger and Taft in supporting proposed park legislation and intervening on behalf of the preservationists. Pinchot never did see Hetch Hetchy Valley, although he was familiar with Yosemite and nearby forest areas.) The Outing proved so popular that fifty applications were turned down, and nearly two hundred people started the trip from Yosemite Valley.[94]

VIII

In November 1909 Colby and Parsons hastily put together another pamphlet directed at first "to the American public," and in subsequent editions "to the members of Congress." On October 30 Muir had written Johnson that Colby was calling for copy;[95] by November 20 the campaign material was in press, and a few days later Colby had proof sheets out to McFarland, Allen Chamberlain, and others.[96] Sierra Club colleagues in the East were enthusiastic about the new pamphlet, although a few offered suggestions for improvement.[97]

Colby made certain that the pamphlet was widely distributed to Congressmen, and administration leaders, women's clubs, coöperating organizations, and the press.[98] "[The pamphlet is a] very effective 'big gun,'" Colby wrote McFarland, "We have sent it to the editors of all the newspapers of the country and have most of the Federated Women's Clubs hard at work. We are looking forward anxiously to receiving [the membership list of the American Civic Association] so that we may mail a pamphlet to each one."[99] He was exultant that McFarland was so pleased, and in reply to the criticism McFarland had made of its excessive length, he wrote: "It was the result of months of careful thought and several days of intense labor as we were crystallizing it into final shape. I agree with you that it would have been more effective in many ways if it could have been made shorter, but we have been criticised in the past on the ground that we did not present our arguments fully enough nor give complete enough data, so we felt it was safer to have too much rather than too little."[100]

Colby summed up the feelings of preservationists as Christmas week approached: "This is a great fight and is accom-

[92] Colby, San Francisco, to Pinchot, Washington, D.C., April 28 1909, copy, SCA.

[93] Pinchot, Washington, D.C. to Colby, May 4, 1909; and Ballinger, Washington, D.C., to Colby, San Francisco, May 22 1909, copies, Farquhar Papers.

[94] "Report of Outing Committee, 1909 Outing," SCB, VI (January, 1910), p. 189.

[95] Muir to Robert U. Johnson October 30, 1909, Johnson Papers, box 7, folder no. 465.

[96] Colby, San Francisco, to W. F. Badè, London, November 20, 1909; Colby to E. A Whitman, Boston, November 20, 1909; Colby to Allen Chamberlain, November 20, 1909, copies. SCA.

[97] Harriet Monroe told Colby that she thought it "put the issue clearly and briefly and [met] every essential point. I don't see how it can fail to convince people, and enlist a great many to work for the cause" (Monroe, Chicago, to Colby, San Francisco, November 28, 1909, copy, Farquhar Papers). Chamberlain, who called the paper "tip-top" himself, wrote Colby that Herbert Gleason, the photographer from Boston who accompanied the summer high trip to Hetch Hetchy, urged a headline on the front cover emphasizing "A National Issue" (Chamberlain, Boston, to Colby, San Francisco, November 23 and December 1, 1909, SCA). McFarland wrote "I am full of admiration at the magnificent fight the people of the Sierra Club are putting up in this matter. I could wish, however, that the pamphlet was only half as big, and boiled down so that one could jam it into a man easier" (McFarland, Harrisburg, to Colby, San Francisco, December 7, 1909, SCA).

[98] For example, Colby asked Walter Fisher, Secretary of the Conservation League of America, for his support (Colby, San Francisco, to Fisher, Chicago, December 2, 1909, copy, Johnson Papers, box 3, folder no. 141). A few days later he wrote Johnson asking him to distribute copies (Colby, San Francisco, to Johnson, New York, December 8,

plishing worlds of good by educating the people of this country to an appreciation of the importance of their national possessions in the way of natural scenery. It has also accomplished splendid results in bringing our various clubs together."[101]

Close at home, however, the new pamphlet was not so warmly received. The morning *Call* of December 11, 1909, carried a long article headlined "Enemies Harming the City": "The persistent and vicious opposition that has been directed at San Francisco in connection with the city's attempt to gain a Sierra water supply has taken fresh root within the city itself and a far reaching campaign against the acquisition of Sierra water rights is now being directed by an organization maintaining its headquarters in San Francisco. The Sierra Club, always aligned with the interests opposed to the city on the water question, is at present lending itself and its influence to an attack designed to do the city incalculable harm. From its headquarters in San Francisco there is going out over the country a flood of literature. . . . Tens of thousands of pamphlets addressed 'to the members of Congress' bearing the signature of J. Muir, President of the Sierra Club, and containing a mass of misleading comment and criticisms, are being sent broadcast by the Sierra Club. Few of the pamphlets have been sent out to San Franciscans, and the newspapers of the city have not been favored with copies."[102]

This outburst in the *Call* prompted Marsden Manson, still a member of the Club, to write Warren Olney suggesting that a communication be sent to the newspaper signed by those Club members who favored the San Francisco position, thus showing the public that only a faction of the Club "is the author of vicious attacks upon the acquisition . . . of the Tuolumne or Hetch Hetchy supply."[103] Manson added that as far as he was aware no meeting of the Club had been called at which this important question could be discussed and "the decision of its members or a majority thereof shown in favor of the proposition."[104] Evidently Manson and Olney did organize some kind of protest, or, at least, let the *Call* know that the Club was not unanimous in backing the action of its directors. On the next three days the *Call* referred to the split within the Club's membership in the following terms: "Leaders in the Sierra Club have taken emphatic exception to any attempt to commit the organization to a policy antagonistic to the City. . . . A movement was inaugurated yesterday by which the forces favoring the city may unite and call for a poll of the Club. It is strongly hinted that a majority of the members stand ready to repudiate any action or movement that may be regarded as hostile to the interests of the city."[105]

1909, copy, *Johnson Papers*, box 3, folder no. 142).

[99] Colby, San Francisco, to McFarland, Harrisburg, December 9, 1909, copy, *Johnson Papers*, box 3, folder no. 143.

[100] Colby, San Francisco, to McFarland, Harrisburg, December 17, 1909, copy, SCA.

[101] *Loc. cit.*

[102] *San Francisco Call*, December 11, 1909, pp. 9–10.

[103] Manson, San Francisco, to Olney, San Francisco, December 11, 1909, *Manson Papers*, C-B-416, Bancroft Library, University of California, Berkeley.

[104] *Loc. cit.*

[105] *San Francisco Call*, December 12, 1909, pp. 17–18.

The *Call* noted that officers of the Club were quoted as saying that no action had been taken in the name of the Club, but rather that the literature had been distributed in the name of the Society for the Preservation of National Parks. The newspaper pointed out, however, that the local membership of this group was recruited from among those in authority in the Sierra Club. The article concluded with a list of the members who were protesting the Club's actions: Warren Olney, Professor Alexander McAdie, William Beatty, former governor George Pardee, J. N. Pomeroy, Harold French, and J. H. Cutter.[106]

On December 13 the *Call* published an interview with James S. Hutchinson, a lawyer living in Berkeley and a charter member of the Club, in which he stated that the directors had acted arbitrarily in opposing the city, in enlisting the support of other conservation groups, and in using the prestige of the Club, if not its name, for their purposes. The interview continued: "This agitation concerning Hetch Hetchy started in the Sierra Club two years ago. . . . It has been a burning question in the Club since, and it was the reason for the defeat of Warren Olney as director last April. Olney had favored utilizing Hetch Hetchy as a water site for San Francisco, and the consequence was that the members who are opposing the city's plans caused his defeat. Edward Houghton and other members of the Club thought then of placing in the field a ticket composed of men who were not opposed to the project; for lack of time, they did not. All the directors elected were opposed to Hetch Hetchy as a water source. . . . I intend to confer with Warren Olney, Sr., and Warren Olney, Jr., and Houghton as to a method of forcing the agitation to an issue in the Club . . . and if we find a majority of the Club members with us we shall force the directors to a showdown or resign and organize a new club."[107]

The Monday, December 14, *Call* reported on the local Sierra Club walk to Sutro Forest and Lake Honda; its interest in the hike centered around the lively discussion that took place between members with opposing views on Hetch Hetchy. On this particular trip Manson and Harold French supported the city's side and Clay Gooding, a local attorney, supported Muir and the preservation of Hetch Hetchy. A decision was made on this local walk to call a general meeting of the Club in January and settle the issue. It was reported that the members who were opposed to Muir felt "he had been falsely informed by others who have used his reputation and kindly sentiments as a medium for their political squabbles."[108] Apparently the reporter for the *Call*, whose identity is not disclosed, misrepresented French's statement, for in the next day's *Call* he found it necessary to say that French did not mean to criticize Muir.[109]

[106] *Loc. cit.*

[107] *San Francisco Call*, December 13, 1909, p. 12. The new directors, meeting on May 1, 1909, were Muir, McAdie, Davidson, LeConte, Parsons, Dudley, Badè, Rodman, and Colby. (Sierra Club. *Minutes of the Board of Directors*, May 1, 1909.) In fairness to Hutchinson it should be stated that he not only continued his membership in the Club, but also served as editor of the *Bulletin* in 1925.

[108] *San Francisco Call*, December 14, 1909, p. 5.

[109] *San Francisco Call*, December 15, 1909, p. 7.

The sudden newspaper publicity focused on the Club started tempers rising, and Colby, in a letter to Allen Chamberlain, expressed himself emphatically: "The news that Muir had issued another pamphlet exploded like a bombshell here in San Francisco, where the enemy were resting on the assurance that they had bought peace from the Spring Valley, but they found out to their surprise that that did not include peace from us. . . . In excess of zeal, Manson et al. are stirring up a very wordy dissension in the Sierra Club among the small minority who live in and about San Francisco, and who are selfish enough to put the City before the nation. They are making a lot of noise in San Francisco where the Dailies print everything they say with copious additions and ignore and distort anything we might say. We will probably call a vote of the Club on the question and settle it once and for all."[110]

On December 18 the Board of Directors, per Colby, addressed an open letter to the membership:

Recently certain members of the Club have been quoted in the columns of the San Francisco press as taking exception to the stand of most of the Directors of the Club against the use of Hetch Hetchy Valley as a reservoir site for a San Francisco water supply. The attitude of a majority of the Board composing a committee was published in the January, 1908, issue of the Sierra Club Bulletin . . . , and if any considerable element in the Club had taken exception to the stand then taken by those directors, it would have been a very simple matter under the Constitution and By-Laws of the Club to have made such exception known. This committee report was afterward unanimously adopted at a Board meeting.

While these Directors have felt morally certain that they were supported in their views by a great majority of the Club, nevertheless, in view of the doubts recently expressed, it is only fair that the entire membership of the Club be given an opportunity to vote on this important question.

In order to correct certain erroneous ideas which have obtained circulation through the newspapers, *it should be thoroughly understood that the Directors referred to have never opposed the acquisition by San Francisco of the Lake Eleanor and Cherry River portion of the Tuolumne system,* and what they do object to is the determination, years in advance of any possible necessity, that so important a part of the Yosemite National Park as the Hetch Hetchy Valley should be definitely segregated and set aside for such use in the future, without further impartial investigation.[111]

Accompanying the communication from the Board was a ballot printed on a single sheet of paper and consisting of two statements:

1. I desire that the Hetch Hetchy Valley should remain intact and unaltered as a part of Yosemite National Park and oppose its use as a reservoir for a water supply for San Francisco, unless an impartial federal commission shall determine that it is absolutely necessary for such use.

2. I favor the use of Hetch Hetchy Valley as a reservoir for a future water supply for San Francisco and I favor a present dedication by Congress of the right to such use without further investigation.

[110] Colby, San Francisco, to Chamberlain, Boston, December 17, 1909, copy, *Johnson Papers,* box 3, folder no. 139.

[111] Board of Directors, Sierra Club, to membership, December 18, 1909, *Johnson Papers,* box 13, folder no. 873.

Members were to vote in person from 1 to 4, Saturday, January 29, at the Club headquarters in San Francisco, or to mail their ballots. In a letter to fellow Board member, Willoughby Rodman, Colby further explained the situation: "A few of the disgruntled members of the Club, including the gentleman [Warren Olney] who was not elected when you were, saw fit to get into the local press and even what they said we believe to have been largely misquoted by the local press, . . . However, the present ballot is rapidly coming in and will undoubtedly settle the question as to where the Club stands definitely. The Directors feel quite positive that the very moderate and reasonable stand taken in statement No. 1 will appeal to and be the expression of a very large majority of the Club membership."[112]

With the battle lines clearly drawn for the first time, each side outlined its arguments pro and con in printed broadsides for membership distribution. Warren Olney's seven-page printed letter, mailed in Club envelopes, went out to the membership just before Christmas Day. It was followed on December 31, 1909, by Colby's printed reply. And about the same time, Manson joined the propagandists with a long "Statement of San Francisco's Side of the Hetch Hetchy Matter" addressed to "members of the Sierra Club." The Directors countered with a reprint of E. T. Parsons' discussion of the Hetch Hetchy question before the Commonwealth Club, and included material which that Club did not print in its *Transactions*. Finally, on January 27, 1910, just prior to the closing date for ballots, Colby augmented Parsons' debate with Manson through his own printed letter.[113]

Olney's letter perhaps typifies the opposition of the Club minority. He summarized the arguments for using Hetch Hetchy: that a lake would enhance the beauty of the valley; that inasmuch as there had been no public demand for roads or trails into the valley, such as had existed in Yosemite for several decades, there could not be much interest in preserving the natural floor of the Hetch Hetchy. He agreed that other water supplies existed, but at greatly increased cost to the city. Even if San Francisco did vote to purchase the Spring Valley Water works, this could only offer an adequate supply for the present. The Garfield permit asked that Lake Eleanor be developed first; it would be only after full development of this source, which would take many years, that Hetch Hetchy would be touched, and "Most of you can probably feel secure that the right to camp in Hetch Hetchy and enjoy its scenery untouched will not be taken away in your time."[114]

The most carefully reasoned part of Olney's statement, and the most devastating blow to the arguments of the preserva-

[112] Colby, San Francisco, to Rodman, Los Angeles, December 27, 1909, copy, SCA.
[113] The Olney statement (December 22, 1909) and Colby's replies to Olney (December 31, 1909) and Manson (January 27, 1910) are in the Sierra Club Archives; copies are also available in some of the Bancroft collections. The Manson statement (December 30, 1909) and the Parsons reprint, *A Discussion of the Hetch Hetchy Question; A National Issue* (San Francisco, January 1, 1910, 16 p.) are in the *Farquhar Papers*. There is also a partial transcription of the Parsons paper in the Commonwealth Club of California *Transactions*, November, 1909.
[114] Warren Olney, San Francisco, to membership, Sierra Club, December 22, 1909, printed letter, p. 4, *Johnson Papers*, box 13, folder no. 873.

Hetch Hetchy—the Promise

As to my attitude regarding the proposed use of Hetch Hetchy by the city of San Francisco . . . I am fully persuaded that . . . the injury . . . by substituting a lake for the present swampy floor of the valley . . . is altogether unimportant compared with the benefits to be derived from its use as a reservoir.

Gifford Pinchot (1913)

These temple destroyers, devotees of ravaging commercialism seem to have a perfect contempt for Nature, and instead of lifting their eyes to the God of the Mountains, lift them to the Almighty Dollar.

John Muir (1912)

The retouched photographs are from the report by John R. Freeman to the city of San Francisco, published in 1912; part of the fifty-six-word title of the book reads:

On the Proposed Use of a Portion

—OF THE—

HETCH HETCHY, ELEANOR AND CHERRY VALLEYS

WITHIN AND NEAR TO THE
BOUNDARIES OF THE

STANISLAUS U. S. NATIONAL FOREST RESERVE AND THE YOSEMITE NATIONAL PARK

J. N. LeConte

This is the story of two yosemites. One was the Hetch Hetchy Valley
hardly anyone knew. It was one of the most beautiful valleys in the world.
Handsome cliffs and waterfalls in a charming setting. Trees to frame the
vistas, meadows to look at and to look from, natural beauty under foot and
to walk by—a setting with open space, living space, that a million people might
see and enjoy every year. It was very much like the Yosemite Valley the world
knows today, just a few miles to the south.

The other yosemite is Hetch Hetchy Valley today, now that the setting
has gone.

Hetch Hetchy was a remarkable storage vessel, with a fine damsite
where the walls crowded together. It was dammed to enable Mocassin Creek
powerhouse, in the Sierra foothills, to generate some kilowatts for San
Francisco—at the cost of the nation's scenery. They said the dam would be
"easily covered by grasses and vines."

John Muir, the Sierra Club, and other conservation groups fought hard
against this destructive park invasion. San Francisco argued that without this
water it would wither; it must have this cheap power; there were no good
alternatives; and the dam would enhance the beauty of the place and make it
more accessible. "The greatest good for the greatest number." Teeming San
Francisco against the few people who had yet visited Yosemite.

—and the Result

PHOTOGRAPHS BY PHILIP HYDE

Fifty years ago San Francisco won. This once-beautiful valley, part of a national park, was flooded.

Philip Hyde took these pictures May 13, 1955. The reservoir was down 180 feet, but 60 feet higher than it had been May 1. In June it would probably fill, then start right back down again, for it is a fluctuating reservoir as most power and storage reservoirs must be. Its zone of ups and downs, between high water and low, is a region of desolation. Nothing permanent can grow in it.

This zone is ugly enough at the dam. At the head of the reservoir it is worse. There this much drawdown means two miles of desolation.

We walked a mile up into it. Although it was still early in the season, 1600 people came into Yosemite Valley that same day. Two came to Hetch Hetchy—and we didn't come for pleasure. Who would?

What you see here is what you see at most fluctuating reservoirs and what no one should see in a park. Stumps where the basin was cleared, stumps and more stumps, exposed and reëxposed until silt finally buries them. The stream—it was one of the most beautiful in the Sierra—is silted in. Tuolumne Falls is covered. The banks are silted. The flat living space is silted, and as soon as the surface is dry enough, it is on the move—a dust bowl, from the silt that sloughed off the canyonsides when the reservoir was full. The river brings still more each year, and wind-blown scum collects in the eddies of what was a sparkling river.

They had circulated touched-up pictures of an artist's conception of a pretty lake, always brim-full. San Francisco's mayor wrote, "The scene will be enhanced by the effect of the lake, reflecting all above it and about it, in itself a great and attractive natural object." Secretary of the Interior James Garfield testified: "In weighing the two sides of the question, I thought that it should be resolved in favor of San Francisco, because this use of the valley would not destroy it as one of the most beautiful spots in the West. It would simply change the floor of the valley from a meadow to a beautiful lake."

Congressman Englebright added: "As . . . a lake, it will be one of great beauty; there will be fine fishing in it, and boating, and so on, which would make the lake an improvement to the park.". . .

There were alternate sites. The day of atomic power *could* have arrived
with Hetch Hetchy still beautiful. But the Secretary of the Interior accepted
the city's claim. He had made a "careful, competent study" and no other
way would do. . . .

The alternatives, which would have harmed no precious scenery, remain
unused. And for the million people who come to Yosemite Valley each year
to enjoy it, perhaps a thousand approach Hetch Hetchy—to turn away from
its tragic drabness. Why should they stay? To pack in and camp here? To let
the children play in the meadows? To fish in this stream? To breathe the clean
mountain air? Could this ever have been beautiful?

Above the waterline is a clue to what beauty could have remained.
Colorful lichens, miniature gardens of mosses and ferns—these bring life to
the rocks and rills. Near the promontory where a summer home was built for
city officials, well above the fluctuation zone that dominates every broad vista,
is a pitifully small flat area—too small for camping and almost as
unattractive as the dead zone. On a nearby slope along a dead-end trail we
can find remnants of the former beauty of the place. A temporary stream
runs a few feet through this isolated garden and drops into a desolate zone
of rock, sand, and stumps. A patch or two of grass remains above the high
water line, but there will never be grass enough nor vines enough to conceal
the dam. We found that even this little bit of grass was spoiled by the
high-water debris and the monotonous view.

Across the valley the main falls are still there, shining in the springtime. But where is the setting? Where is the pulsing heartland of this place? It is gone. It is gone beyond the recall of our civilization—thanks to the dam where plaques praise the men who took so much from so many for all our time.

We know from the men who saw Hetch Hetchy before it was destroyed that Yosemite Valley is its nearest counterpart. Hetch Hetchy cliffs were like Yosemite's—free of the bleach and water stains, unspoiled, set in forests, forests where you can walk by the shaded streams.

Yosemite tells what a setting means everywhere you look. Here you can see what the trees which are now stumps ought still to be doing for Hetch Hetchy—providing a place to stroll, to relax, to listen, to see clear water glide over clean rocks, to catch the sun sparkle, to breathe fragrant air, to rest where the river pauses, to feel renewed, to know the beauty of natural things.

Yosemite cannot meet today's recreation needs, let alone tomorrow's. The future will find abundant power outside the parks—parks for which there are no alternatives. So many of the parks are already overcrowded—certainly Yosemite is. And Hetch Hetchy could have given to millions, for ages, much of what Yosemite gives. Its waters could have remained an inspiration in their beautiful natural setting and then be put to practical use downstream—just as Yosemite's river is.

The cliffs, the meadows, the groves, the streamside, the whole setting—what do they mean to man? Something that you can neither measure in dollars nor replace with dollars. Hetch Hetchy's setting is irretrievably lost to all of us and to all generations. It need not have been.

In 1916 Congress put up a sign to prevent any more tragedies like this one. It was the National Park Act, which says to park exploiters, "Do not enter." We'll do well to remember Hetch Hetchy, where once was too often.

William E. Colby wrote the Sierra Club membership on the last day of 1909: "I predict that long before Hetch Hetchy would possibly be needed for a water supply for San Francisco, the travel thither will have become so great and its needs as a campground, particularly in relation to the surrounding park, so urgent, as to preclude the possibility of its use as a reservoir. What I am opposed to is the determination right now that the Hetch Hetchy shall be flooded fifty years from now. I feel that the decision ought properly to be reserved for those who live fifty years hence. We surely can trust that their decision will be a wiser one than any we can make for them."

{Text adapted from the Sierra Club film, "Two Yosemites," by David Brower, produced in 1955 to show the ominous parallel between what has happened in Yosemite and what was then threatened in Dinosaur National Monument, where the Bureau of Reclamation was promoting two unnecessary dams with the same discredited arguments. The Bureau, at this writing, is promoting a far more serious destructive action in Grand Canyon, again with the concurrence of the Secretary of the Interior.}

tionists, was his attack on the idea that use of the entire Tuolumne watershed, or 500 square miles of the Park, would be restricted for reasons of sanitation if the Hetch Hetchy were taken as a public water supply. J. Horace McFarland had said, "Nothing is better established in modern sanitary science than that the watershed of any domestic water supply must be jealously guarded and kept free from human occupancy at all times if that water supply is to result in other than the dissemination of disease and the bringing about of untimely death," and his views seem to have been convincing to preservationists.[115] Olney attacked this view and supported his contention with reference to the many resorts and recreational uses of Lake Katrine, the public water supply of Glasgow, Scotland.

Olney's printed letter closed with a comment about the hearings on Senate Resolution no. 123, which he had attended the previous winter in Washington as a part of the San Francisco delegation, "I became convinced at the time . . . that it was not the Sierra Club, or its directors, or any of their co-adjutators [sic] from the East that influenced the legislators. They undoubtedly furnished arguments that were used by these legislators, but it was the Spring Valley Water Works and the sympathy of all other interests that prevented San Francisco getting all it asked for. . . . Is it not to the interest of the Club to act in moderation and with due regard for the good of all who are so situated as to be able to make use of the waters of a river? Will it not work irreparable injury if the public loses confidence in the sound judgment of lovers of the mountains?"[116]

It was not his original intention, said Colby in his letter of rebuttal, to engage in an open discussion, but certain statements in Olney's letter could not be allowed to pass unchallenged: "Mr. Olney's entire argument is based on a misconception of our stand on the Hetch Hetchy question. His statement that the 'right to camp in Hetch Hetchy and enjoy its scenery untouched will not be taken away in your time,' is entirely aside from the real question at issue. Does Mr. Olney think that you and I are so selfish that we would stand in the way of San Francisco's proposed use of Hetch Hetchy because our personal pleasure would be jeopardized? The fact is that travel to the National Park is increasing so rapidly that fifty years from now no one can conceive of the multitude that will throng to it for rest and recreation. . . . I predict that long before Hetch Hetchy could possibly be needed for a water supply for San Francisco, the travel thither will have become so great and its need as a campground, particularly in relation to the surrounding park, so urgent, as to preclude the possibility of its use as a reservoir. What I am opposed to is the determination right now that the Hetch

[115] Quoted in *Let Everyone Help to Save the Famous Hetch Hetchy Valley and Stop the Commercial Destruction which Threatens Our National Parks* (San Francisco, December, 1909), p. 8.

[116] Olney, *op. cit.*, p. 7.

113

Hetchy shall be flooded fifty years from now. I feel that the decision ought properly to be reserved for those who live fifty years hence. We surely can trust that their decision will be a wiser one than any we can make for them. . . . Mr. Olney feels apprehensive lest the Sierra Club should lose some of its prestige of which it has in the past been justly proud. Let me assure him as well as all the other members of the Club that they need have no fear on this score. Never before has the Club been so widely known or so influential as it is today. Not only is this due to an increasing membership and an improved financial condition, but it is also due to closer affiliations with other clubs and with the best and most influential people of the whole country. More than all else, it should be borne in mind that the Sierra Club will not lack for prestige while John Muir is its president."[117]

Colby reminded the members of the Club that it was Muir himself who suggested to President Roosevelt the possibility of using Lake Eleanor and the Cherry River as a water supply for San Francisco. This seems to be a clear indication that Muir was not unsympathetic to the needs of San Francisco and that he was willing to give up parts of "his" mountain domain, though not at the risk of destruction of a national park, for this purpose. Colby urged the appointment of a federal commission to show cause why the Hetch Hetchy must be taken; that he was willing to abide by the decision of such a commission. A barb was then thrown at the "despoilers" of the Club: "There are individuals in the Club (and I do not intend to include Mr. Olney in this category) who, if they could not bend it to their purposes, would gladly disrupt it, were that possible. I know that such petty feeling is confined to but few, and I feel certain that all the others will do their share in adding to the prestige and power of the Club."[118]

The Sierra Club found itself facing a critical decision. By forcing the organization to an official position and committing it to the historical principle for which it had been established—"to enlist the support and cooperation of the people and the Government in preserving the forests and other natural features of the Sierra Nevada"—the Board of Directors knew that they might be endangering the growth and financial support of the Club as a whole. The fires of dissension, which had been smouldering for nearly two years, now threatened, with the public display of this dissension, to split the Club. The showdown was to come on January 29, when the judges of election tabulated the Hetch Hetchy ballots. Willoughby Rodman, a director and member of the Los Angeles chapter of the Club, was not worried by the prospect of such a Club split; he wrote Colby: "If any members find it impossible to continue in the Club on account of the

[117] Colby, San Francisco, to membership, December 31, 1909, *Johnson Papers*, box 13, folder no. 873.
[118] *Loc. cit.*

114

Board's action, or if the conduct of any members is such as to render their presence undesirable, all one can do is to let them go in peace. Their loss would not destroy the Club, or materially impair its usefulness. While we should regret a decreased membership, we can get along with those we have left. But I do not anticipate a material loss, and I believe this is your idea. I am sure the entire state outside San Francisco is back of the Board."[119]

Response to the Sierra Club ballot was almost immediate—and sometimes critical of the framers of the statements. Guido Marx, a professor of machine design at Stanford University and a consultant to the city, vigorously protested. He suggested that the questions should have been simply stated and mailed without a "leading" circular.[120] Redwood City Attorney, George C. Ross, expressed his belief that the attitude of the Board "has injured the club" and the sooner it "gets in line to assist San Francisco . . . the better it will be for the interest of the club."[121] The most damaging response, however, came from Manson, who had an open letter to the Club membership printed and widely distributed. Said Manson, "Both of these propositions are speciously arranged, and neither presents the question in its true light." He objected to the reference in proposition 1 to "an impartial federal commission" determining the fate of Hetch Hetchy; this decision, in Manson's opinion, had already been made by the Right of Way Act of February 15, 1901, and by the Garfield grant of 1908.[122] Manson asserted that "no dedication of Congress whatever is needed, nor is asked for." Colby, in his reply to Manson, addressed to the membership, wanted to know what "Mr. Manson . . . was doing in Washington before the Public Lands Committee of Congress . . . and why he caused to be introduced in Congress the bills, whose passage he spent several months of his valuable time in urging, and also why, when he failed to secure the passage of the legislation he desired, bills of similar import were introduced . . . and now are pending there. If such legislation were unnecessary," said Colby, "Mr. Manson made much ado about nothing."[123]

When all the ballots were tabulated by the judges the final count stood overwhelmingly in favor of the directors' position, 589 in favor of retaining Hetch Hetchy in its natural state, 161 in favor of allowing San Francisco to take the valley for water storage. As might be expected, the vote tended to split along geographic lines—most of the pro-San Francisco votes coming from members in the Bay Area. Wrote Herbert Gleason, "It certainly has cleared the air over 302 Mills Building."[124]

In the six weeks or so of campaigning prior to voting, the militant minority used every device open to them to convince

[119] Rodman, Los Angeles, to Colby, San Francisco, December 28, 1909, *Farquhar Papers.*

[120] Marx, Stanford, to Colby, December 30, 1909, *Farquhar Papers.*

[121] Ross, Redwood City, to Colby, San Francisco, December 30, 1909, SCA.

[122] "A Statement of San Francisco's Side of the Hetch Hetchy Matter," an open letter from Manson to the Club membership, December 30, 1909, in *Pamphlets on Hetch Hetchy*, Bancroft Library, University of California, Berkeley.

[123] "A Reply to Mr. Manson's Statement," Colby, San Francisco, to the membership, January 27, 1910, SCA.

[124] Gleason, Boston, to Colby, San Francisco, February 4, 1910, *Farquhar Papers.*

115

their fellow members that the city's case was valid. In addition to the various opposition statements described above, they invoked Article XVII of the revised By-Laws, adopted April 29, 1905, which provided that thirty or more members could petition the directors for a special meeting. The necessary signatures were obtained on four separate petitions dated January 8, 1910, and submitted to Colby, as Secretary, before January 17.[125] The petitions requested that a meeting be called by the directors for Saturday, January 22, to consider "any and all matters concerning a water supply for San Francisco and the attitude of the Club and its members toward the City . . . in its efforts to obtain such a supply." Colby was out of town when the petitions were submitted and the Board could not be convened on such short notice; the meeting was thus delayed until after the ballot count.[126]

Postponement of the meeting to Friday evening, February 18, gave Muir and Colby time to send invitations to Bay Area members, hoping thereby to offset the numbers that the minority group might attract to the meeting because of their initiative. One college boy replied that the "Soph Hop" prevented his attendance, but a number of others responded favorably.[127] Colby also devised a proxy vote to offset what was likely to be a "packed" house in favor of San Francisco. This read in part: ". . . It is manifestly impossible for more than a small proportion of the members to be present to consider the matters that may be taken up at that meeting. In order that you may be represented at such a meeting, if you so desire, I enclose you a proxy which should be signed, dated, and mailed to me in enclosed envelope at once."[128]

Colby assured the members that the securing of proxies in his name was with the entire approval of Muir, Parsons, LeConte, Rodman, and other directors. The proxy itself read: "I hereby constitute and appoint Wm. E. Colby, my proxy with full power of substitution, to represent me at any and all meetings of members of the Sierra Club which may be held within six months from date, and for me and in my name and stead, to vote at any and all such meetings, and I hereby grant to my said proxy and to any person substituted by him hereunder, all the powers that I would possess if personally present at such meetings."[129] Apparently several of these proxies were returned to the Club for use in the February 18 meeting, one man sending his to Muir because "Colby is personally unknown to me."[130]

The Assembly Room of the Merchants' Exchange Building was the scene of a lively debate that Friday night. Saturday's *Call* carried a short account of the meeting in which it was charged that the directors had not represented the issues fairly in

[125] SCA. The petitions were signed by the following members: Charles D. Marx, Guido H. Marx, T. P. Andrews, J. K. Moffitt, William A. Magee, William Denman, F. E. Magee, Frank Adams, Louis Bartlett, Paul Elder, C. A. Murdock, Frank P. Medina, James S. Hutchinson, George H. Evans, P. A. Sinsheimer, B. R. Banning, Marsden Manson, Curtis H. Lindley, Henry Eickhoff, Warren Olney, Jr., Philip K. Brown, F. H. Dam, C. P. Coles, J. D. Jamison, Max S. Cohn, Harold French, William Kent, and John N. Pomeroy.

[126] Colby, San Francisco, to Manson, San Francisco, January 16, 1910, SCA.

[127] James Boyd, Jr., Berkeley, to "Dear Friend" [Muir], February 13, 1910, and Warren Gregory, San Francisco, to Colby, San Francisco, February 10, 1910, SCA.

[128] Notice of Proxy "to the members of the Sierra Club," January 29, 1910, SCA.

[129] *Loc. cit.*

[130] C. H. Ames, Secretary of the D. C. Heath Co., New York, to Muir, San Francisco, February 16, 1910, SCA.

116

the *Bulletin*. A resolution was offered by James K. Moffitt censuring the directors and this threw the gathering into such a turmoil that Chairman McAdie "was compelled at times to request the speakers to refrain from personalities."[131] Marsden Manson spoke for the city, supported by Moffitt and Professor Josiah Keep of Mills College. Professors William C. Morgan of Berkeley and E. C. Franklin of Stanford and attorneys William Gorrill and Clay Gooding argued the case for preservation. Director Edward Parsons, on business in Seattle, sent Colby a letter to be read at the meeting with the encouragement: "STAND UP TO THEM. I'd give something considerable to be present and add my VOICE to the discussion. Hope you have our friends organized and lined up to hold fast."[132]

The meeting became such a "hopeless tangle" that Moffitt finally withdrew his resolution; then Cleaveland Forbes of the preservationists started the row all over again by resolving the endorsement of the Board's actions. In the end nothing was accomplished except the sharpening of tongues and the loss of tempers. The *Call* asserted that Muir had packed the meeting with pro-park members, and indeed he had, as he humorously described a few days after the meeting: "I managed to get about 80 of our Club members out to dinner at the Poodle Dog restaurant. The long flowery table flanked with merry mountaineers looked something like a Sierra canyon so they called it, the Muir Gorge. After dinner we marched to the meeting, every face radiant, and entered the hall in a triumphant rush, fairly overwhelming the poor astonished Hetchy dammers. Next morning, the *Call* reported that I had packed the meeting, though forsooth I had only packed seventy-seven stomachs."[133]

The minority faction in the Club never again raised its collective voice in opposition to the policies of the board regarding Hetch Hetchy. Some fifty members resigned in protest, but many members stayed on "because they thought they could do us more harm by saying they were members and were in favor of the Hetch Hetchy."[134]

[131] *San Francisco Call,* February 19, 1909, p. 10.

[132] Parsons, Seattle, to Colby, San Francisco, February 16, 1910, SCA.

[133] Muir, Martinez, to Professor and Mrs. Vernon Kellogg, Palo Alto, February 23, 1910, SCA.

[134] Colby, Big Sur, California, to author, Oakland, November 18, 1956, Author copy.

5

HETCH HETCHY
Lesson in Politics

*"From any one of these sources the
water is sufficient in quantity and is,
or can be made, suitable in quality,
while the engineering difficulties are
not insurmountable. The determining
factor is principally one of cost;"*
—*Army Engineers' Report
February 19, 1913*

WITH THE Sierra Club firmly committed to Hetch Hetchy's preservation, Muir and his allies could resume their battle more cheerfully. Even before the Club vote in January 1910, Colby was optimistic about Hetch Hetchy's prospects. Before the January 10 city bond election on the purchase of the Spring Valley Water Company and the assumption of a debt of $45,000,000 to begin work on the Lake Eleanor project, he wrote to Gleason: "The city will do nothing until that vote has been taken, and I am credibly informed that even if the Lake Eleanor bond proposition should carry, they will attempt to do nothing with Congress, but rely solely on the Garfield permit. This information comes from those very high in authority, and I have no reason to doubt it, but it may be thrown out to lull us into inactivity. If this should turn out to be correct, and the city decides to do nothing, it will then be important for us to determine whether the time is opportune for us to take any positive action or not. We have laid the foundation for a tremendous campaign, and it would seem that the time was ripe to take some affirmative action, but this is a matter that requires most careful deliberation. The enemy evidently are convinced that they have no chance to do anything this session of Congress."[1]

The Sierra Club had strong and very effective support from two Eastern preservation groups. There never was any doubt as to the American Civic Association's role under the leadership of McFarland. The Appalachian Mountain Club, however, was another question. Although its chief attorney member, Edmund Whitman, had reported in April 1909 that the Club was "solid" in its support of the Sierra Club, by the end of 1909—just as it appeared that the Western organizations would need all the help they could get—the Appalachian Mountain Club began to waver. Its officers evidently were seriously swayed by Garfield, Pinchot, and Frederick Newell, Director of the U.S. Reclamation Service. Allen Chamberlain and Whitman kept Colby informed of the Club's internal controversy which prevented its giving wholehearted support. By February 1910, Whitman had become so disgusted with the actions of the A.M.C.'s Council that he had proposed the formation of a New England branch of the Society for the Preservation of National Parks; Chamberlain,

[1] Colby, San Francisco, to Gleason, Boston, December 27, 1909, copy, *Johnson Papers*, box 3, folder no. 145.

however, opposed it on the ground that the Appalachian Club ought to do the work. Whitman had agreed. With Gleason preaching Hetch Hetchy to the A.M.C. and the Sierra Club vote overwhelmingly on the side of preservation, Chamberlain and Whitman urged Colby to have the Sierra Club Directors send a formal letter to the A.M.C. Council "outlining a plan of campaign and requesting their active co-operation."[2] This is precisely what the Sierra Club did, only to have Corresponding Secretary of the A.M.C., Harry Tyler, send the disappointing news that the Council, although agreeing to submit a "soft" resolution supporting Hetch Hetchy's preservation, had decided not to send an official representative to a subsequent hearing.[3] Whitman's ire was raised. Together with Chamberlain and other members dedicated to preservation, this group forced a special meeting of the A.M.C. on April 27, 1910. Ex-President Tyler, who Whitman claimed had defected to the opposition, evidently was disturbed by the commotion raised by Whitman and Chamberlain; he rushed a telegram to Colby on the eve of the special meeting inquiring if it was more important "for your cause that we send delegates or that we avoid public controversy."[4] Colby quickly wired, "Strong delegation very important; we hope Appalachian Club will assist."[5] But neither the "ballot" that Whitman and Chamberlain had mailed to A.M.C. members asking their approval for sending a delegate to a future hearing nor the meeting of April 27 proved conclusive. Chamberlain reported to Colby that the A.M.C. Council's action was sustained by just seven votes out of 150. Five days later, Whitman announced the forming of the New England Branch of the Society for the Preservation of National Parks.[6]

II

We have traced the factionalism that smouldered among Sierra Club members for many months from early 1907 to late 1909 finally ending in an official ballot count of four to one in favor of the directors' policies. We have seen also how the Society for the Preservation of National Parks began as a "California Branch" and, later, following the wavering of the Appalachian Mountain Club, added a New England Branch. But what of the tactics of the cooperating preservationists? What sort of campaign were they planning to influence the new Secretary of the Interior, Richard A. Ballinger, whom President-elect Taft had personally chosen to replace James A. Garfield?

As we have seen, Ballinger's first utterances, in April 1909, concerning Hetch Hetchy were cautious and not designed to give

[2] Whitman, Boston, to Colby, San Francisco, February 17, 1910, Sierra Club Archives. The controversy in the A.M.C. can be followed through the following letters: Whitman to Colby, April 27, 1909, November 10 and 11, 1909, December 28, 1909, March 15, 1910, and April 15, 1910; Chamberlain to Colby, November 13, 1909, November 23, 1909, and January 7, 1910; Colby to Tyler, copies, December 15, 1909, and April 19, 1910, all SCA. See also Chamberlain to Colby, February 18, 1910, *Farquhar Papers*.

[3] Tyler, Boston, to Colby, San Francisco, April 7, 1910, SCA.

[4] Tyler, Boston, telegram to Colby, San Francisco, April 26, 1910, SCA.

[5] Colby, San Francisco, telegram to Tyler, Boston, April 27, 1910, copy, SCA.

[6] Chamberlain, Boston, to Colby, San Francisco, April 28, 1910, and Whitman, Boston, to Colby, May 2, 1910, SCA.

the preservationists much hope. He felt that Congress must be approached if any changes or revocation of the Garfield permit were to be allowed.

With this in mind, then, McFarland, in May, wrote to Colby outlining his ideas, having already discussed them with William F. Badè, the Sierra Club's representative, then on his way to Europe for a year's sabbatical study. McFarland hoped that a bill could be introduced in Congress repealing the proviso in the original Yosemite act relating to water rights. "Let us go back to the source of their power and . . . restore the Yosemite fully to the public domain."[7] He felt it "most inadvisable to get after" Ballinger, as Badè later reported, because he might resent "being importuned."[8] Badè's estimation of the Secretary, at this point, was that he was a "poor ally."

Colby's reactions to Ballinger were practical and action oriented. On letterhead of the Society, he prepared a one-page sheet headlined, "The Present Status of the Fight for the Preservation of Yosemite National Park and Hetch Hetchy Valley." This he sent to key persons in various women's clubs. To Mrs. F. W. Gerard, Chairman of the Forestry Committee, General Federation of Women's Clubs, he wrote: "I am glad you have written requesting information concerning our plan of campaign for the future. There is not much that we can do at present except to quietly work on any and all members of Congress, especially of the Public Lands Committee. Our most effective work can be done with the members of these Committees, and if you can get the women of the locality where these senators and representatives come from to interest themselves in aiding us, it will be of the greatest possible assistance. We are planning to get out another pamphlet . . . which will be distributed this Fall, just before the next session of Congress. . . . We . . . will start a tremendous campaign of publicity in November and continue it into the session of Congress which meets in December. Prior to that time we will inform you as to our exact plan of campaign."

Colby reminded Mrs. Gerard that petitions of the women's clubs would be most effective if they were withheld until December, but he urged the women to "get them in shape and ready to release upon receiving word."[9]

In a second communication to Mrs. Gerard, Colby asked her assistance in distributing at least one of the new Muir pamphlets, to be published in the fall, to each of the women's clubs affiliated with the General Federation. He hoped to mail out at least 50,000 copies.[10]

Although there was a brief flurry of excitement in August when a San Francisco newspaper falsely published a report that

[7] McFarland, Harrisburg, to Colby, San Francisco, May 25, 1909, SCA.

[8] Badè, New York, to Colby, San Francisco, May 18, 1909, SCA.

[9] Colby, San Francisco, to Gerard, South Norwalk, Conn., copy, May 25, 1909, SCA.

[10] Colby, San Francisco, to Gerard, South Norwalk, Conn., copy, June 30, 1909, SCA.

an Interior Department official had publicly sanctioned the cutting of timber on the Hetch Hetchy dam site, preparations went quickly ahead for the winter Congressional session.[11] Taking a cue from McFarland, Colby proposed that the preservationists (1) "work for an appropriation of $25,000" to build a road into Hetch Hetchy Valley, (2) "play for time and try and impress Congress with the dangerous proposition of determining now, fifty years in advance, the necessity for using Hetch Hetchy," (3) urge Congress to appoint an impartial commission "consisting of engineers, including sanitary experts, and perhaps including National Park experts (if creatures of this character exist), to pass on the necessity for using Hetch Hetchy, and the effect of such use on the Park," and (4) lobby for a general bill to safeguard the National Parks.[12] Copies of this letter were sent to McFarland and Allen Chamberlain.

Some time during the fall months of 1909 the directors of the Society for the Preservation of National Parks reached a compromise—one that foreshadows a general political expedient the Club found useful in the years ahead: when it is not possible to achieve all that is desired, choose the most important objective and let smaller or lesser goals go. The Society now made this choice; with Muir's general consent, Colby suggested to McFarland that the preservationists should support the granting of Lake Eleanor, Cherry River, and the Poopenaut Valley to San Francisco (thus allowing an invasion of a relatively minor section of the National Park); and he recommended further that the city be allowed to acquire the public lands necessary to utilize these reservoir sites "only on condition that [the city] exchange to the government the lands which it now owns in Hetch Hetchy."[13] This idea was later officially transmitted to the Chairman of the House Committee on Public Lands.[14]

In a letter to Secretary Ballinger dated December 23, 1909, McFarland reiterated Colby's idea of an "impartial commission," but failed to mention the compromise that the Sierra Club's Secretary had written him about earlier in the month.[15] Perhaps McFarland felt it unnecessary to push the compromise when he conjectured, correctly as it turned out, that the Secretary would look favorably on the wishes of the preservationists without invoking concessions. Two days after Christmas, McFarland notified Colby he had received a personal letter from Ballinger confirming his feelings "which he does not put in words but which plainly appears between the lines."[16]

With San Francisco officials unwilling to press for Congressional action on their bills, which they knew would be doomed to defeat, and with Colby and Whitman anxious to activate the

[11] The news dispatch in the *San Francisco Chronicle*, August 13, 1909, started quite a chain reaction. Colby immediately wrote to Ballinger asking him to resist any encroachment on the Valley that would tend to commit the use of Hetch Hetchy prior to Congressional determination. He also sent letters to Whitman and Mrs. Gerard, requesting that they activate their members in writing the Secretary and President Taft. Along with the letters went a printed sheet on the Society letterhead, signed by George Edwards, with the note: "Editors of newspapers are urged to write editorials and print news to assist in informing the public." There must have been some embarrassment in the Sierra Club office when Assistant Attorney General of the U.S., Oscar Lawler, sent a denial of the *Chronicle* report to the Society headquarters. This episode perhaps shows the trigger-happy but alert state of the Sierra Club directors; nothing escaped the eye of its secretary. (Colby, San Francisco, to Ballinger, August 13, 1909; Colby to Whitman, Boston, copy, August 14, 1909; Colby to Gerard, South Norwalk, Conn., copy, August 21, 1909, SCA. Also Lawler, Washington, D.C., to Society for the Preservation of the National Parks, San Francisco, August 18, 1909; and George Edwards' form letter, copies, SCA.)

[12] Colby, San Francisco, to Whitman, Boston, September 13, 1909, copy, SCA.

[13] Colby, San Francisco, to McFarland, Harrisburg, December 9, 1909, copy, SCA.

[14] Muir, Martinez, to F. W. Mondell, Washington, D.C., January 11, 1910, copy, SCA.

[15] McFarland, Harrisburg, to Ballinger, Washington, D.C., December 23, 1909, copy, SCA.

[16] McFarland, Harrisburg, to Colby, San Francisco, December 27, 1909, SCA.

publicity campaign they had carefully planned, McFarland, whose close Washington connections made him an invaluable ally, had a difficult time holding the others in line. He appealed to Colby not to exert pressure on the administration: "If I was an advocate of the San Francisco Hetch Hetchy grab, and knew what I now know, I should feel somewhat discouraged. If I was William E. Colby, and E. T. Parsons, and particularly if I was John Muir, I would try to read through the lines of this letter and between them, and see that there is strong hope that the right will triumph."[17]

The same kind of warning came after he reported his personal interview with Ballinger and George Otis Smith, Director, U.S. Geological Survey: "I am prohibited by Mr. Ballinger's confidence from telling you just what he is going to do, but I can say that the situation is pleasing, and that before long you are likely to hear something which will make your San Francisco friends sit up and take notice. The Secretary and the President are in hearty accord on the program, . . . I would like to have you avoid by all manner of means making any statement which could get out in advance, as it would 'queer' the whole business."[18]

McFarland was obviously gratified by what he learned in the Secretary's office and elated by the results that the Sierra Club, the Society, and the A.M.C. had achieved—"Mr. Ballinger . . . handed me a tabulated list of the letters he had been receiving for more than a month"; but he was also disturbed that the Secretary might be upset by overzealousness on the part of the "nature lovers."[19]

Late in February 1910 a real break in the long Hetch Hetchy controversy suddenly illuminated McFarland's somewhat mysterious statements. Secretary Ballinger, who the previous October had accompanied Muir into Hetch Hetchy and later instructed officers of the U.S. Geological Survey and the Bureau of Reclamation to investigate and report upon other sources of water supply for San Francisco, wrote to the Mayor and Board of Supervisors asking them to show cause why the Hetch Hetchy reservoir site should not be eliminated from the Garfield permit.[20] The city was requested to submit its proof of need on or before May 1, 1910. One Sierra Club member wrote to congratulate Colby, remarking that "Secretary Ballinger's document sounded so much like Sierra Club literature that you couldn't tell the difference with your eyes shut!"[21]

This was a high point for the preservationists. It appeared that the fight was won and that nothing—not even the hearing in May—could stem the tide of victory.

Not a moment was lost in the preparations. Colby asked

[17] McFarland, Harrisburg, to Colby, San Francisco, February 4, 1910, SCA.

[18] McFarland, Harrisburg, to Colby, San Francisco, February 17, 1910, SCA.

[19] McFarland, Harrisburg, to Colby, San Francisco, February 21, 1910, SCA.

[20] Ballinger, Washington, D.C., to the Mayor and Board of Supervisors, San Francisco, February 25, 1910, reprinted in the *Proceedings before the Secretary of the Interior in Re Use of Hetch Hetchy Reservoir Site in the Yosemite National Park by the City of San Francisco* (Washington, 1910), p. 6. President Taft suggested to his Secretary of Interior that Muir be his guide on the trip to Hetch Hetchy with George Otis Smith. Muir readily agreed and "caused wild alarm among the dam promoters," but "had a very satisfactory trip with Ballinger. . . . The reasons appeared later in the fact that throughout the Taft administration the dam promoters pushed their cause in vain" (Wolfe, *Son of the Wilderness; the Life of John Muir*; New York, Knopf, 1945; pp. 324–325). Colby gives the credit to Robert Underwood Johnson who knew Taft well. (See Colby's letter to McFarland, March 16, 1910, copy, SCA.)

[21] E. L. Bickford, Napa, to Colby, San Francisco, March 1, 1910, SCA.

123

Whitman to speak for the Club and the Society, suggesting to him points that ought to be covered in the hearing.[22] He asked McFarland to handle the sanitary aspect of the watershed problem.[23] William F. Badè, in London, cabled Colby that he would reluctantly give up three weeks of his research in the British Museum if his appearance before Ballinger would aid the cause. An elated Colby quickly offered to pay Badè's passage across the Atlantic.[24]

Toward the end of April a strenuous effort was made to obtain the services of a recognized engineer to assist the Sierra Club's case in Washington. Professor Joseph N. LeConte and Colby met with Charles Gilman Hyde in his Berkeley campus office. Hyde agreed to help, but only on certain conditions, and two weeks later he had gracefully backed out of his commitment, probably, as Colby hinted in a letter to John Muir, because it would be "detrimental to the University."[25] The vigorous attitude of Hyde's university chief, President Benjamin Ide Wheeler, strongly in favor of Hetch Hetchy's use by San Francisco, perhaps proved too difficult an obstacle for Hyde's loyalty to his institution; but, more than this, he genuinely felt that there was insufficient time to prove that other feasible sources of supply were available. He suggested to Colby in his letter of refusal that the best interests of the Club would be served by making its fight purely on ethical and esthetic grounds.[26]

The day following Hyde's negative decision, Colby wired Whitman that the Society would guarantee $500 if a Boston expert could be found. Whitman was unsuccessful in this, and at the last moment, Philip E. Harroun, a Berkeley engineer, made the trip to Washington, charging the Society $1,050 for his services.[27]

Colby completed the Sierra Club's brief and mailed copies to Secretary Ballinger and E. A. Whitman late in April. To Whitman, he expressed his regret that he had not had more time to present the case, but added that he hoped the Boston attorney would "be our champion on the legal questions."[28] To McFarland, who also received a copy of the brief, he advised a meeting of the various conservation representatives immediately prior to the hearings. He warned: ". . . we should be very brief and to the point in presenting our arguments. Each representative should be limited strictly in time and be requested to cover but that particular phase of the subject that has been assigned."[29]

But Whitman's testimony should be an exception to the rule of brevity, said Colby, "for he is to discuss the legal problems and other sources, which are the two vital points now before the Secretary, and he should have full swing in that line."[30]

[22] Colby, San Francisco, to Whitman, Boston, March 3, 1910, SCA.

[23] Colby, San Francisco, to McFarland, Harrisburg, March 3, 1910, SCA.

[24] Badè, London, to Colby, San Francisco, March 22, 1910, and Colby to Badè, April 19, 1910, copy, SCA. Badè, although in Europe on sabbatical leave from the Pacific Theological Seminary, managed to be amazingly active in the Hetch Hetchy controversy as Vice President of the Society and a Sierra Club director; he lost no opportunity to propagandize for the cause. He stopped at several cities en route to New York to consult with various organization representatives, lectured on the *Finland* while crossing the Atlantic, spent a weekend with Mrs. Theodore Roosevelt at her sister's villa on the Riviera, had special Society stationery printed at his own expense with which to discuss Hetch Hetchy problems with his correspondents (see Badè to Colby, November 2, 1909), and, upon his return to New York in June, 1910, he wrote editorials for *The Independent*, a New York review.

[25] Hyde insisted on complete impartiality in the investigations and urged the appointment of a commission of engineers whose findings the "Sierra Club and their friends would loyally abide by" if the Tuolumne development should turn out "to be the most logical, satisfactory, safe, and economical" (Hyde, Berkeley, to Colby, San Francisco, April 25, 1910, SCA); Colby, San Francisco, to Muir, Los Angeles, May 16, 1910, SCA.

[26] Hyde, Berkeley, to Colby, San Francisco, May 6, 1910.

[27] Colby, San Francisco, to Whitman, night letter, May 7, 1910, copy, SCA, and Harroun, Berkeley, to Colby, San Francisco, June 9, 1910, SCA. The statement submitted by Harroun included $500 for contracted time, $250 for an extra five days' services, and $300 for living and travel expenses. This bill was partially defrayed by Muir and a $150 contribution from the Eastern Branch of the Society for the Preservation of National Parks.

The hearings were scheduled for the morning of May 18. Badè arrived in Washington from London two days before this, only to discover to his dismay that the hearings were postponed a week to allow time for the newly appointed Advisory Board of Army Engineers to assemble in the Capital. This delay upset the timetable of the preservationists. When the hearings actually convened on May 25, Robert Underwood Johnson could not be present, but the Sierra Club had allies in Whitman of the Appalachian Mountain Club, J. Horace McFarland and Richard B. Watrous of the American Civic Association, and Henry E. Gregory of the American Scenic and Historic Preservation Society, not to mention, of course, engineer Harroun.

To present San Francisco's side of the controversy some of the top political leaders of the Bay Area appeared: Patrick H. McCarthy, mayor of San Francisco, Percy V. Long, attorney for the city, and Beverly Hodghead, mayor of Berkeley, speaking for the East Bay cities. Technical evidence was given by Professor Charles D. Marx, Stanford University, and Marsden Manson.

A third group to give testimony was the Spring Valley Water Company, represented by Alexander Britton, attorney, and Herman Schussler, consulting engineer for the Company.

San Francisco argued at the morning session that the government was not keeping faith with the original Garfield grant of May 11, 1908. This permit had imposed certain restrictions which the city had tried to abide by. Money and much effort had been expended to secure title to all lands within the Hetch Hetchy Valley held in private ownership. The city had also obtained certain private lands outside the Hetch Hetchy to make an exchange with the government for the remaining lands in the Valley held in the public domain. These conditions had been met, said the city's representatives; why should the Secretary of the Interior now ask the city to show cause why the Hetch Hetchy should not be removed from the 1908 grant? The tactical maneuvering of San Francisco was to gain time; the city was willing to argue that it had not had time to collect the necessary hydrologic data to show that the Hetch Hetchy was a necessary and integral part of the total scheme.

The preservationists, with Whitman in the lead, argued that San Francisco had had plenty of time to gather information, but had simply failed to do so. Technical evidence was presented before the Advisory Board of Army Engineers in the afternoon. Harroun stated that even under the most unfavorable conditions 175,000,000 gallons a day could be assured the Bay cities, all of which could come from Lake Eleanor and adjacent watersheds without invading Hetch Hetchy; if additional supplies

[28] Colby, San Francisco, to Whitman, Boston, April 28, 1910, copy, SCA.
[29] Colby, San Francisco, to McFarland, Harrisburg, Pa., May 6, 1910, copy, SCA.
[30] *Loc. cit.*

should be needed in the distant future, San Francisco could obtain them from rivers to the north of the Tuolumne.

The day after the hearing, the Army Engineers recommended to the Secretary of the Interior:

(a) that San Francisco be granted sufficient time to submit data about all available sources of supply in such form as the Secretary will be able to decide whether the Bay Area cities could secure water in the future, at reasonable cost, from sources other than the Tuolumne.

(b) that the city should furnish a description of the methods to be used in developing the Tuolumne supply, engineering works to be constructed in Yosemite, water power to be developed, and the ownership and potential use to be made of this power.

(c) that data showing the extent of damage to the scenic features of Yosemite should be submitted together with what restrictions the city would consider essential upon the upper watersheds of the Tuolumne in preserving a pure water supply.[31]

The hearings of May 25, 1910 proved disappointing to the preservationists. They had come to Washington in high hopes that San Francisco's need for Hetch Hetchy would be disproven, and the reservoir site thus eliminated from the Garfield permit. They gained only one concession—an independent investigative commission. San Francisco gained a far more subtle ally—time. And time, as it turned out, was to prove the undoing of the best laid plans of the preservationists.

Secretary Ballinger concurred in the Advisory Board's recommendations; he granted San Francisco until June 1, 1911, to submit the data required by the Board. Ballinger's successor, Walter A. Fisher, later granted the city additional time, first to December 1, 1911, then to March 1, 1912, to June 12, 1912, and finally to November 1912.

III

With Secretary Ballinger's decision, the entire Hetch Hetchy case seemed suddenly to depend upon showing that other water supplies existed, or—from the city's viewpoint—were insufficient for San Francisco's needs. At the May hearings, San Francisco had depended upon the advice of consulting engineer, John R. Freeman, who was now contracted to do an exhaustive investigation by the city. The Sierra Club, following its statements published earlier in the Muir pamphlets, urged the Advisory Board of Army Engineers to consider the Eel River, filtration of Sacramento River water, or the addition of the Stanislaus River system to the Lake Eleanor–Cherry River project as alternatives to Hetch Hetchy.[32]

A few months before the new deadline for the presentation of

[31] "Exhibit A—Reports of Advisory Board of Army Engineers," in *Proceedings before the Secretary of the Interior in Re Use of Hetch Hetchy Reservoir Site in the Yosemite National Park by the City of San Francisco* (Washington, D.C., G.P.O., 1910), p. 68.

[32] Colby, San Francisco, to Wadsworth, San Francisco, November 18, 1910, SCA. Wadsworth, a local engineer, was employed as a consultant to the U.S. Advisory Board of Army Engineers.

126

evidence, a change in Secretaries of Interior created new excitement among the preservationists. Colby hurried a telegram to Watrous of the American Civic Association urging him to see the new Secretary, Walter A. Fisher, to attempt to offset any advantages that the city's attorney might be seeking from him;[33] in addition, he sent letters to Fisher and Muir that same day.[34] Fisher himself scotched the rumors that San Francisco's attorney was attempting to secure his approval for introduction of a Congressional bill that would, in effect, perfect the city's permit.[35] Watrous also reported his conversation with Fisher in which the Secretary advised against the introduction of such a bill.[36] Apparently San Francisco's intent was to gain the advantage by having a bill in Congress but not pressing for its passage until after the conclusion of the Secretary's hearing. In anticipation of a *favorable* hearing, the city could then urge immediate action on the bill in Congress, fixing by law the rights that it had previously been granted by Garfield.[37]

If Watrous' letter was not sufficient warning that San Francisco had determined to go to Congress, the introduction of H.R. 7275 in the first session of the 62nd Congress less than a month later should have been forewarning enough that the real fight would come in the halls of Congress and that such a step by the city would, in effect, reduce the Secretary's hearing on the Advisory Board's recommendations to *pro forma* status. H. R. 7275 was the first of several bills introduced by Congressman Raker—whose name was to become very familiar to the preservationists.

IV

Walter L. Fisher, the new Secretary of the Interior in the Taft administration, was a man the commodity conservationists could count on. As an officer in the National Conservation Association he had gained the confidence of Pinchot.[38] Yet he was on friendly terms with the preservationists. He was a personal friend of Stephen T. Mather, later to become the first head of the National Park Service, and was familiar with the arguments pro and con regarding Hetch Hetchy.

The postponement of the Secretary's hearing to the end of 1911 (and finally to 1912) was in part to give Fisher an opportunity to acquaint himself personally with the Hetch Hetchy situation. He was a man who wanted a first-hand look at the scene of the controversy. Toward the end of the summer (1911) he had that opportunity. It was arranged for the Secretary to come West on official business. As they had at the time of Bal-

[33] Colby, San Francisco, to Watrous, Washington, D.C., March 28, 1911, copy, SCA.

[34] Colby, San Francisco, to Fisher, Washington, D.C., March 28, 1911, and Colby, to Muir, Los Angeles, March 28, 1911, copies, SCA.

[35] Fisher, Washington, D.C., to Colby, San Francisco, April 10, 1911, SCA.

[36] Watrous, Washington, D.C., to Colby, San Francisco, April 17, 1911, SCA.

[37] *Loc. cit.*

[38] Richardson, *op. cit.*, p. 135.

127

linger's visit to Hetch Hetchy, the preservationists did an excellent job of placing one of their men in the Secretary's party. This time it was J. Horace McFarland instead of John Muir.

Colby had urged McFarland for three or four years to come to the Coast to accompany the Sierra Club high trips. The Secretary's excursion seemed the perfect opportunity to combine a business trip McFarland planned to Yellowstone National Park with the "cause" in California. He wired Colby asking the Sierra Club to assist him in his train passage,[39] which was arranged, and on Saturday afternoon, September 16, he arrived in San Francisco where he was entertained by the Colbys, Parsons, and Badès. On Tuesday morning at El Portal he joined the Secretary's party—consisting of Fisher's personal secretary, a representative of the Reclamation Service, a reporter for *Leslie's Weekly*, Robert Marshall of the U.S. Geological Survey, and Marsden Manson, San Francisco's city engineer.

The very full report that McFarland gave Colby on this Yosemite trip, although obviously biased, reveals the temper of the meeting and accurately assesses the position of the Secretary, as attested by his subsequent refusal to approve San Francisco's claim for Hetch Hetchy. After describing the exceedingly rough horseback trip into the Valley, McFarland characterizes the city's engineer: "Mr. Manson managed . . . to talk to the Secretary about the lake scheme, in a rather private way. Observing this, and remembering Mr. Manson's usual prolixity of words and his disposition to pass beyond the strict limits of the truth, I concluded, and Marshall coincided, that we would let him use all the opportunities of the sort he could find. Around the camp-fire a little later, the Secretary started the issue, and we had a stiff argument back and forth for over an hour. At that time, through Mr. Manson's propositions, the Secretary was convinced, first, that the Yosemite as a whole was deficient in water and in camping places; second, that the lake would increase the beauty of the place and furnish desirable water; and third, that reliance could be placed on the offer of the city of San Francisco to build a road and to permit access to the watershed. . . . This evening session closed in what Marshall and I considered a draw, with the Secretary thoroughly unsettled as to the accuracy of Mr. Manson's views, but not at all convinced as to ours. You must remember that this was before he had seen the valley, except with eyes and throat full of dust . . . , and after an unreasonably rough and arduous trip, followed by a wretched meal. . . . The next day we went across the valley and up the Lake Eleanor trail. . . . We therefore had the fierce and again dusty climb out of the valley on the west side, Mr. Manson keeping his animated lecture bureau going all the time, but not getting

[39] McFarland, Yellowstone N.P., to Colby, San Francisco, telegram, September 12, 1911, SCA. The ultimate cost to the Club was $170.53.

128

Requiem for Hetch Hetchy Valley

where so many might have come to know the days and nights and the seasons through the ages. Other sources of power and water were at hand and still are. A few men knew it then; all know it now. But the primeval forest and meadow and stream, serene or jubilant, will not be known again. This is yesterday's valley.

Meadow at the foot of the trail.

First view into Hetch Hetchy from Surprise Point.

Kolana Rock from the Lower Valley.

View up Hetch Hetchy from above the Rock Pool.

Meadows in the Upper Valley.

Oak groves in the Upper Valley.

Falls in Rancheria Creek.

Tuolumne River above Fall.

Slide at Rancheria Pool.

General view of the Upper Meadow and Kolana Rock.

Oak groves in the Upper Valley.

Fall in the Main Tuolumne at head of the Valley.

Gorge at extreme lower end, south side.

The river in the Upper Valley.

close to the Secretary. He did have, however, a most excellent dinner ready for us at the camp of his engineer, a little beyond the Army camp on the shores of Lake Eleanor, and this was thoroughly enjoyed. We then went to see the dam site, and the absurdity of the Lake Eleanor dam proposition was thoroughly borne in upon all of us. Mr. Marshall called attention to the fatuous idea of constructing an 1,800-foot-wide dam, 200 feet high, for the small amount of water which could be impounded in Lake Eleanor. I taxed Mr. Manson at once with not intending to use the Lake Eleanor supply unless he could get Hetch Hetchy, and he admitted this was his intention."[40]

The turning point in the Secretary's feelings about the valley apparently came after the party had returned to their Hetch Hetchy campsite. While McFarland, Manson, and others were refreshing themselves with a swim in the Tuolumne River, Fisher walked some six miles "up and around the edge of the Valley," also taking a bath in the river, and returned to camp much relaxed and evidently impressed with what he had seen. But, in McFarland's opinion, the most significant exchange of ideas occurred on the return trip to Crane Flat. "Marshall had very aptly provided a trap, into which Mr. Manson jumped, by suggesting to him that if he would ask him (Marshall) in the presence of the Secretary for the use of the Poopenaut Valley, which could readily be dammed, it might be possible to increase the storage space without difficulty. Mr. Manson did so ask, bringing out his desire to get more storage capacity and more streams and valleys, whereupon the secretary turned to him with great severity and said, 'What other valleys in the Yosemite, Mr. Manson, is it the idea of the city of San Francisco to absorb?' The silence that ensued was thick and heavy!"

Another point on which McFarland had a chance to inform the Secretary was the lack of available camping sites for large numbers of persons and, conversely, the wealth of mountain lakes in the park. McFarland describes this as follows: "Fifteen or twenty minutes of this sort of colloquy, in which the Secretary from time to time freely participated, and in which Mr. Manson also managed to get his foot several times, completely changed the idea the Secretary had had with respect to the availability of the Yosemite as a camping-ground. By the time we reached Crane Flat I felt that we had done the utmost possible with the Secretary and that the condition was very much better than before. In fact, it seemed to both Mr. Marshall and myself that Mr. Manson's stock was at a low ebb. We believe that Mr. Manson has in no sense made good. It may be the Secretary will resolve to simply hold San Francisco down to the Garfield permit, in which case San Francisco cannot go on. It is conclusively

[40] McFarland, Harrisburg, Pa., to Colby, San Francisco, September 28, 1911, SCA.

129

shown that absolutely no work has been done on the ground except surveying. I drew the statement out from Mr. Manson, so that all heard it, that I had understood progress had been made and money spent. He outlined several times the moneys spent for land, but received no sympathy on that account, the Secretary, on the contrary, several times very decidedly making known his feeling that there should be no private ownerships of any sort within the bounds of a national park."[41]

McFarland, always ready with campaign suggestions, closed his long letter to Colby with a plea for from fifteen to twenty-five photographs "showing various places within the watershed of the Hetch Hetchy in which or at which the Sierra Club has camped, so that the beauty and the abundance of water involved may be realized." Colby heartily agreed to this plan, adding a few thoughts of his own: "I wonder what you think of the idea of my writing to various staunch supporters of the Hetch Hetchy proposition, who have visited this region in the Park and upon whom we can rely to write something interesting and intelligent giving their views as to the value of that portion of the Park lying north and east of the Hetch Hetchy, for camping and pleasure resort. I could probably get over a hundred who would do this and some of the letters would be mighty effective indeed. They would all be persons of intelligence and writing from personal knowledge."[42]

Colby also asked McFarland to formulate in his mind the best plan of bringing public opinion to bear upon Fisher. It is clear that Colby hoped McFarland would authorize another letter-writing campaign similar to the effective one that made such "a tremendous impression on Ballinger."[43] The cautious President of the American Civic Association felt it wise, however, to postpone letters to the Secretary until the report of the Advisory Board was available.[44]

V

For the preservationists, the twenty-eight months between Ballinger's hearing in May 1910 and Fisher's in late November 1912 were months of anxiety. With limited resources of money and manpower, the various preservationist groups found themselves engaged in a holding action on Hetch Hetchy while trying at the same time to gain support for other, equally important, objectives. The Sierra Club was particularly concerned about insufficient federal appropriations for the improvement of Yosemite National Park. The Club was also committed to the addition of the Kings Canyon and other superlative high country

[41] *Loc. cit.*
[42] Colby, San Francisco, to McFarland, Harrisburg, October 11, 1911, copy, SCA.
[43] *Loc. cit.*
[44] McFarland, Harrisburg, to Colby, San Francisco, November 13, 1911, SCA.

areas to Sequoia National Park, additions which for the first time seemed a practical reality with a bill by Senator Flint in Congress (S. 10895, introduced February 27, 1911). The American Civic Association, on its part, was spearheading the campaign to obtain a separate federal agency to administer America's national parks. In the fall of 1911 the Association had put much energy and time into a national conference, held in Washington, publicizing the parks—and in this endeavor it had had the almost unqualified support of the Taft administration.

Yet the holding action on Hetch Hetchy was a vigorous one. With San Francisco firmly determined to acquire the Valley, its city engineer, Marsden Manson—who had planned the 1908 water supply scheme with Lake Eleanor and Cherry Creek as the nucleus of the system (in accordance with the Garfield permit), halted further consideration of other supplies. Whether he actually suppressed his assistant engineer's report favorable to the Mokelumne River may never be known (see pp. 157 ff.), but, in any case, Manson and other city officials moved boldly to comply with the Ballinger order.[45] The first step was to hire a consulting engineer of national repute. John R. Freeman of Providence, Rhode Island, filled this role eminently. He had previously been consulting engineer for Boston and New York and was well versed in the water problems of large metropolitan communities. In a letter to Chamberlain, some months before Freeman's report was publicly released, Colby correctly reported on his recommendations, chief among which was that San Francisco should secure its claim to Hetch Hetchy.[46]

With the engineering aspects in good hands, City Attorney Percy V. Long could concentrate on certain legal problems that the city faced. In response to an inquiry from Secretary Fisher addressed to Manson, Long listed six subjects he desired to introduce before the Secretary as further evidence favorable to the city's case, stating: "The cities of Oakland, Berkeley, and Alameda are vitally interested in the pending order to show cause and the future use of the Hetch Hetchy Valley and a number of their citizens desire to submit evidence."[47] Long suggested that "a saving of time" might be effected if the evidence could be taken before a *local* federal official appointed by the Secretary.

Fisher sent copies of Long's letter to Colby, Muir, McFarland, Whitman, and Alden Sampson, asking how the preservationists would feel about conducting a hearing *in* San Francisco.[48] Colby's reaction was immediate and vigorous against the suggestion. After conferring with E. T. Parsons, William F. Badè, and others in the Club and in the Society, he wrote Fisher that "it would be extremely unfortunate to hold a public hearing

[45] In this connection, see Allen Chamberlain, Boston, to Colby, San Francisco, January 10, 1912; Colby, San Francisco, to Chamberlain, Boston, January 16, 1912; E. T. Parsons, San Francisco, to Robert U. Johnson, New York; Allen Chamberlain and E. A. Whitman, Boston, July 15, 1912, and Taggart Aston, San Francisco, to Editor, *San Francisco Chronicle*, copy, July 12, 1913, SCA. The Archives also contain a nearly illegible copy of the Bartel report.

[46] Colby, San Francisco, to Chamberlain, Boston, January 16, 1912, copy, SCA. The letter reads in part: "I am reliably informed that Freeman . . . admits that the Spring Valley holdings can be developed to supply San Francisco for a great many years to come, and this is the only economic and sane course to pursue to acquire the Spring Valley properties. He admits that the Hetch Hetchy system will not be required . . . for a great many years to come. However he has taken such an interest in San Francisco and has such confidence in her future, believing that some day she will even rival New York, that he feels that there is nothing too good to give to San Francisco in the way of preparation for the future, and he feels that the Hetch Hetchy water supply is one of the best supplies that can be preserved for the future, because of the fact that it is inside of a National Park, and he feels that this should be dedicated to San Francisco to use in time of need in the more or less distant future. He therefore urges and advises the city to clinch its hold on Hetch Hetchy."

[47] Percy V. Long, San Francisco, to Fisher, January 20, 1912, copy, SCA.

[48] Fisher, Washington, D.C., to Colby, San Francisco, February 1, 1912, SCA.

131

of any nature in San Francisco." Colby's letter illuminates the difficulties faced by the militant minority in San Francisco: "The local prejudice with reference to this question is so intense that it has passed far beyond the bounds of reason. The public generally through the newspapers have been led to believe that the Hetch Hetchy affords the only source of pure water available for San Francisco, and that if secured it will practically be a gift from the government. There are people in San Francisco who literally believe that as soon as the Hetch Hetchy system shall be acquired, that pure snow water from the mountains will be piped *free* into their residences. This has resulted through constant and exaggerated reiteration by all of the local newspapers of the advantages to be derived from the acquisition of this source of supply, and a wilful suppression of any facts to the contrary. Any opponent of the plan is regarded as an enemy of the city and in league with the Spring Valley Water Company. For a local man to appear at such a hearing would be to offer himself as a sacrifice, for he would become the object of ridicule and abuse by the local papers. The sentiment in favor of the preservation of our wonderful National Parks finds no favor whatsoever when opposed to the claim of an urgent municipal necessity. We have been termed 'hoggish and mushy esthetes,' 'sickly sentimentalists,' and had scores of equally flattering adjectives applied to us in editorials by leading San Francisco dailies. Mr. Muir, even, who is one of the noblest men it has ever been my fortune to meet, has come in for a share of this unreasoning abuse. That any one can honestly and unselfishly advocate the preservation of the Hetch Hetchy Valley, the advocates of this plan are utterly incapable of appreciating and because we oppose them, we are classed as allies of the Spring Valley and get part of the opprobrium which is aimed at that corporation by reason of its misdoings in years past. . . .

"We could accomplish little that would be of value at such a hearing, since practically all of the questions submitted for consideration require expert knowledge which is not at our command. To make any effective showing we would have to employ experts at considerable expense. This we can not afford to do. We are all persons of small means and we have made considerable sacrifice in the past in raising funds to carry on our campaign and in sending M. Philip Harroun, C. E. to Washington in 1910, and it is no longer possible for us to carry a financial burden which is a matter of interest to the nation at large, no matter how much we might wish to do so. The city has employed experts and skilled attorneys at an expense of thousands of dollars because it has a personal advantage to be gained. All of us who have opposed this matter for these years are business men of small means with no possible personal advantage to be gained from a favorable outcome. The sacrifice of time and money has been serious for all of us. The fight has been a most unequal one from this standpoint.

"We have felt all along, Mr. Secretary, that this was no ordinary contest, such as usually arises when two individuals each desire a grant of the same rights. The City of San Francisco is asking for very valuable rights which interfere in a very serious way with the enjoyment of a most wonderful property dedicated by Congress to the American people for their enjoyment and welfare. In opposing this, we are asking for nothing for ourselves and derive no personal benefit from a decision in favor of the interests of the nation. It is the nation's duty to see that these rights are protected and not ours. We took up the unequal burden when we saw that it was being neglected by the nation, but since the appointment of the Board of Army Engineers we have felt that this administration was endeavoring to assume its just share in the determination of this question. We are still ready to aid when we can, but can not carry on an unequal contest against an interest like the City of San Francisco, backed up as it is by practically unlimited power and financial resource. Could we offer anything of substantial value at such a hearing, we would gladly appear, but this does not seem possible in view of the expert character of the evidence in question.

"A hearing of the nature suggested would only tend to create still greater bitterness between us and our opponents, and would serve no useful purpose. They would gladly welcome such an unfair contest because of the opportunity it would afford for local newspaper publicity and local intimidation of witnesses."[49]

Colby, however, saw the reasonableness of the city's position in asking to present evidence and he suggested to Fisher that the city might file affidavits and that then the preservationists might be given the opportunity of replying if they so desired. To the formal letter he appended a personal note, explaining that he was employed by Judge Curtis H. Lindley, counsel to the city on Hetch Hetchy; he noted further that the Judge was fully aware of his position and only requested that he not force his opposition into too great prominence locally.

After receiving copies of this letter to Fisher, Colby's Eastern colleagues, who at first had agreed to a San Francisco hearing provided California preservationists would appear, expressed their objections to the Secretary. Fisher acquiesced in their desires and no hearing was held in San Francisco. In May Fisher informed Colby that another postponement had been granted to the city and sent him a copy of his letter to Mayor James Rolph,

[49] Colby, San Francisco, to Walter L. Fisher, Washington, February 13, 1912, copy, SCA.

133

Jr. San Francisco was given a series of dates by which certain data were required, and on August first the remaining data "necessary to completion" of the city's case were to be filed. The comprehensive plans for the development of Hetch Hetchy were to be in printed form so that copies could be made available to all the "objectors," who were to be given until October first to reply to the city's documents. The Secretary's hearing was to be held late in November.[50]

However, on September 6, George Gove, Assistant to Secretary Fisher, wrote the "objectors" that San Francisco's delay in complying with the Secretary's orders made it necessary to give the preservationists until November first to reply to the documents. The Freeman report was enclosed with the advice that copies of all supporting documents and analyses of other water supplies were available at the United States Customs House in San Francisco and in Washington.[51]

There were some interesting reactions from the preservationists. Robert Underwood Johnson was "appalled by the enormity of the Freeman document."[52] Edmund Whitman remarked that it "looks as though the City might be entirely willing to have the Garfield permit revoked so as to throw the whole matter over into the next administration,"[53] and he warned that the preservationists must be ready for such a move. McFarland thought the final showdown had arrived "in so far as this administration is concerned."[54] He mentioned the meeting of the American Civic Association in November as a "rallying point from which the strongest possible protest should be made to the Secretary." He hoped the Army Engineers would "stand with us, but if not we must at any rate make our statement a strong one from the standpoint of those who love the national parks and the natural scenery of the United States." McFarland urged Colby or some other San Franciscan to be at the November hearing. Harriet Monroe, who was personally acquainted with Fisher, felt that he would decide the matter fairly and according "to his convictions on its merits," but she asked Colby to send her a brief statement to forward to Fisher if he felt this necessary.[55]

VI

By mid-October Colby had prepared the Sierra Club's reply to Freeman and mailed a preliminary draft to George Otis Smith, Director, U.S. Geological Survey, together with a copy of the Freeman report.[56] Copies of the final brief were later mailed to Fisher, Robert Underwood Johnson, J. Horace McFarland, and Edmund Whitman.

[50] Fisher, Washington, D.C., to Mayor James Rolph, Jr., San Francisco, May 28, 1912, copy, SCA.
[51] George Gove, Washington, D.C., to Whitman, Boston, September 6, 1912, copy, SCA.
[52] Johnson, New York, to Colby, San Francisco, September 11, 1912, SCA.
[53] Whitman, Boston, to Colby, San Francisco, September 11, 1912, SCA.
[54] McFarland, Harrisburg, Pa., to Colby, San Francisco, September 11, 1912, SCA.
[55] Monroe, Chicago, to Colby, San Francisco, September 17, 1912, SCA.
[56] Colby, San Francisco, to Smith, Washington, D.C., October 17, 1912, copy, SCA.

Colby's brief, the "splendid and efficient document," which McFarland said could not successfully be combatted, is undoubtedly one of the finest statements made by the preservationists. It represents most of the arguments used by the "solitude lovers" for the preservation of Hetch Hetchy and is a testimony to the unselfish devotion of citizens who could foresee the importance of these national wild areas to future populations. The brief is a hard-hitting legal answer to Freeman, whose 401-page report, *The Hetch Hetchy Water Supply for San Francisco,* so boldly assumed the invasion of a national park and questioned the adequacy of any water supply other than Hetch Hetchy. Perhaps the greatest importance of this document is in its pertinence to current conservation battles; the arguments it refutes are those persistently used by commercial interests seeking to invade reserved areas and they must be countered again and again and again. It is for this reason that the Sierra Club brief on Hetch Hetchy is so fully quoted here.

As an illustration of "what can be done for any cause which has practically unlimited means at its disposal for the purchase of talent," the Freeman report is "a remarkable document," began the Sierra Club brief.

There is little doubt but that Mr. Freeman with his recognized engineering ability could have made out an equally good case for any one of the dozen alternative sources available for San Francisco, by suppressing all of the unfavorable features and enlarging on the favorable ones. This is the result of paid advocacy the world over. Unfortunately for the presentation of the engineering features of our cause, we have no paid experts of nation wide reputation to champion it, and while some of our worthy opponents are strongly inclined to the belief that our campaign "is presumably financed in part at least by those who have a source of their own to sell," their inference is without foundation. We have no funds at our disposal beyond the meager contributions which a few of us have given to meet essential expenditures. Our opponents have all through this contest shown that they utterly fail to appreciate our motives which are solely to save for the people of this nation and for future generations, a great national playground already dedicated to their use but which is in grave danger of being seriously mutilated. This unfair burden of fighting the people's cause has been thrust upon us. We earnestly contend that it should be assumed by the government and we have good reason to believe that with the appointment of the Hon. Board of Army Engineers and with the earnest attention which has been given to the proper disposition of this question by the Hon. Secretary of the Interior, that the interests of the nation in one of its greatest National Parks will be adequately safe-guarded.

The attitude of the City of San Francisco in this matter puts one strongly in mind of the fable of the Arab and his camel. As a most generous concession granted with extreme reluctance and in the belief that it was an imperative necessity, the Roosevelt administration made the great mistake (so we feel) of giving the city a foothold in the Yosemite National Park, but it was expressly understood that the terms of the Garfield Permit were to be rigidly complied with and the use of Hetch-Hetchy Valley postponed to as remote a date as possible. Having once got its head inside it now boldly pushes itself in and if its latest demands are granted will practically control one of the most important portions of the National Park. Sweeping aside and ignoring the stipulations entered into by a former Board of Supervisors, and upon which the Garfield Permit was contingent, the City now boldly demands as a matter of right the Hetch-Hetchy Valley itself. If this change of front can take place in these few years what is going to be the limit of these demands and what assurance has the federal government that there will be any limit to the demands of the city in the future? Each succeeding city administration can abandon and violate the stipulations entered into by preceding administrations if this precedent is sanctioned. So in other matters, such as scenic roads etc. so freely promised as a bait invented to catch the gullible, the city can later repudiate all obligation to construct as easily as to repudiate stipulations already entered into between itself and the federal government.

A careful analysis of this report will disclose that it is singularly biased in its presentation of facts and that few opportunities have been lost to advance statements which tend to make the contentions of those who would preserve Hetch-Hetchy appear in as unfavorable a light as possible. As will be pointed out in greater detail hereinafter items of cost of alternative projects are greatly exaggerated or items of cost of the Hetch-Hetchy project immensely underestimated; danger of contamination of these alternative supplies are emphasized while the danger of contamination resulting from increased use of a public park are minimized; a single case of "walking typhoid" when occurring on another project becomes a serious menace (see p. 343 of the report) but in the case of the Hetch-Hetchy project, where thousands may walk and camp, there is no cause for alarm.

To illustrate with examples:

On p. 57 it is stated that nearly all of the scenery of any special interest in the Hetch-Hetchy is comprised within one mile. Any unbiased person who has visited the Valley and travelled up the seven miles extending from the lower end of the Valley to the upper end of Little Hetch-Hetchy, all of which it is proposed to flood, will realize how grossly inaccurate this statement is.

On p. 60 a broad meadow is referred to as being a desirable camp site. Lieut. Co. H. C. Benson, former Superintendent of the Park, has informed one of the writers that camping at this spot except very early in the season is impossible because of absence of water, and this statement coincides with our knowledge of conditions.

On p. 148, the expense of visiting Hetch-Hetchy is greatly exaggerated to the personal knowledge of the writers, who know of many parties who have made the trip for from $10. up to $50. each, and at the latter figure any one can visit the Valley comfortably.

On pp. 59 and 149, other camping sites are referred to as being available if the extensive Hetch-Hetchy camp grounds are flooded. The writers of this brief are familiar with all of the meadows for miles around the Valley and they can state without reservation that such suggestions are merely thrown out in the endeavor to minimize the result of flooding the Hetch-Hetchy camp grounds. Practically no campers ever voluntarily resort to the meadows referred to or would do so in the opinion of the writers who have for years been familiar with all phases of mountain and tourist travel. These meadows are not situated on the natural lines of travel and do not possess the advantages of meadows more favorably situated elsewhere and would in no sense atone for the wiping out and destruction of the broad camp grounds on the floor of the Hetch-Hetchy Valley.

On p. 152, it is stated that "for every acre of ground that the city desires to obtain from the United States, it offers in exchange lands intrinsically just as good or better etc." This statement is not warranted by the facts. Who would exchange an acre of ground on the floor of Hetch-Hetchy or Little Hetch-Hetchy for one at Hog Ranch? There is no comparison in intrinsic value. One is a piece of ordinary meadow land like thousands of others in the mountains while the other is on the floor of one of the most beautiful Valleys in the world. The Yosemite National Park would never have been created to preserve Hog Ranch. One of the specific purposes for the creation of the Park was the preservation of Hetch-Hetchy Valley as John Muir and R. U. Johnson, who were largely instrumental in creating it, can testify. The Yosemite Valley at that time needed no preservation as it was then a State Park.[57]

The brief mentions the persistent misrepresentation of the preservationists' motives.

We have heretofore called . . . attention to this fact, but it seems to have no effect. In several places in the city's report, more or less derogatory reference is made to "solitude lovers" and the question advanced as to whether a mere handful of those shall be allowed to selfishly stand in the way of a great city's needs and progress.

We shall be patient in our attempt to reiterate our stand in this matter.

In 1889 some of our public-spirited citizens had foresight enough to call the attention of Congress to the remarkable scenery embraced in the territory now occupied by the Yosemite National Park. As a result, Congress formally dedicated this wonderful tract of land as a national playground. It is idle for the city to argue that it was not intended to create a National Park, for the act is identical in language with the act of a few days previous creating the "Sequoia National Park" and the Yosemite Park act was worded so as to add another tract to the "Sequoia National Park" which had evidently been overlooked, further establishing the identical character of the two acts. Subsequent acts of Congress and appropriations refer to the "Yosemite National Park" . . .

Because of this reservation it has been impossible for any one to obtain a foothold in the Park and secure the right to flood the floor of Hetch-Hetchy Valley. Now comes the City of San Francisco and in one fell stroke attempts to undo the labor and foresight of those who aided in the creation of the Park, and by reason of which the Valley has been preserved from private occupation all these intervening years. The "solitude lovers" created the condition which now makes it possible for the City to demand the priceless gift. And the only reason that the City can advance in undoing the work of all these years is not that it can not obtain water elsewhere but it will be *cheaper. Cheaper!* Why? Because it is obtained at the expense of the nation and as the result of a great national sacrifice.

But to come to the position taken by the so-called "solitude lovers." We are not selfish enough to let our personal wishes stand in the way of the needs of a great city. There is not one of those contending for the preservation of Hetch-Hetchy Valley, who would not willingly relinquish in favor of San Francisco any future personal pleasure he might hope to gain through visiting the Valley.

The sole reason that we are opposing the use of the Valley is because of the great future of the Yosemite National Park and the growing need for the preservation of its wonders intact.

The Alps were practically unfrequented at the commencement of the 19th century and now its visitors are counted by millions. What shall be said of the future of our Park which John Muir, Stewart Edward White and other world

[57] *Brief of Sierra Club in Opposition to Grant of Hetch-Hetchy Valley to San Francisco for a Water Supply* (San Francisco, n.d.), pp. 1–5 and ff. All quotations from pp. 135–145 are from this brief.

137

travellers declare presents attractions in scenery and climate unrivalled the world around. The City of San Francisco is looking into the future for the needs of her water supply and yet would deny us the right to also look ahead into the centuries to come. It is not what the present generation shall say regarding the damming of Hetch-Hetchy, for on that theory many of the great wonders of the world would have perished, but the true test is what will the generation to come and the ones after that say. It is their need and their use of the Park which we seek to protect. Hetch-Hetchy dammed now can not be returned to its present state of native beauty if the needs of the nation 50 or 100 years from now should require this to be done.

The City has argued at length that the travel to the Hetch-Hetchy Valley is at present quite limited. On this theory most of our National wonders could at some time or other have been given away or destroyed. What we contend is that 50 or 100 years from now the need of the Nation for Hetch-Hetchy Valley and the extensive camp and hotel sites on its floor will be greater than the need of San Francisco for its use as a reservoir site, especially when it can secure all the water it can use elsewhere. Measured by the standard the city attempts to apply, the Yosemite National Park would never have been created. The travel to this Park at the time of its creation in 1890, outside of Yosemite Valley, which was not made a part of the National Park until 15 years later, amounted to practically nothing. The Yosemite National Park was created for the future and the wisdom of this foresight is being demonstrated each year. If the travel to the watershed of Hetch-Hetchy Valley is allowed to increase normally, it will amount to thousands in a comparatively few years.

To turn Hetch-Hetchy into a reservoir will mean a stronger and stronger attempt on the part of the City to stifle travel to this region for the presence of thousands there can not help but become a serious menace to a domestic water supply.

Since the Freeman report made so much of the beauty of a lake in place of the Valley floor, the Sierra Club brief emphasized that the real significance of Hetch Hetchy was the charm and value of the flat camping area.

. . . On this floor many thousands in future will camp and enjoy its sylvan beauty and from these headquarters visit the neighboring features of the Park. It is one of the three great foci of the Park and in the opinion of qualified experts has charms and features not elsewhere found.

. . . Mr. F. E. Matthes of the United States Geological Survey, in a monograph on the origin of the Yosemite and Hetch-Hetchy Valleys, describes them as follows: "Within this area (Yosemite National Park) lie scores of lofty peaks and noble mountains, as well as many beautiful valleys and profound canyons; among others, the Hetch-Hetchy Valley and the Tuolumne Canyon, each scarcely less wonderful than the Yosemite Valley itself. . . . The Merced, occupying with its drainage basin the southern half of the tract, gives the park its most admired feature, the Yosemite Valley; the Tuolumne, embracing with its tributaries the northern half, produces the somewhat smaller yet scarcely less remarkable Hetch-Hetchy Valley. . . . These two valleys, though in many respects resembling the glacial canyons of the High Sierra, nevertheless possess a distinctive, if not exceptional, character that places them in a category by themselves. They may be described as deep-hewn, clean-cut moats bordered by precipitous rock walls that sharply trench across the surface of the uplands and spring abrupt from broad, level, grassy floors. Waterfalls and cascades of great height and beauty leap down into both chasms from the hanging valleys of the upland, and the cliffs themselves are sculptured into a variety of bold and picturesque forms, such as are scarcely known elsewhere."

. . .

On pages 6 and 10 of Mr. Freeman's report are pictures fanciful in their import and misleading in their intended significance. They are an invention to catch the uninformed. Mirror effects on lakes in the Sierra Nevada occur only for a few minutes on a still morning just before sunrise and again, but less frequently just after sunset. The phenomenon is well understood and has been made the subject of an interesting study by Mr. F. E. Matthes of the U.S. Geological Survey. It occurs only at the diurnal turning of the breeze which continues all day and destroys all possibility of reflection on the Sierra lakes. This will be especially true in the Hetch-Hetchy Valley where the wind will be continually blowing either up or down the gorge. The reproductions of photographs of foreign lakes and reservoirs in Mr. Freeman's report show no such reflections. . . .

In this entire presentation by Mr. Freeman he has ignored that part of the Hetch-Hetchy Valley above the big pool, commonly called the Little Hetch-Hetchy. While narrow, it has beautiful wooded margins along both sides of the river, from which rise strikingly impressive cliffs, and a trail at present extends several miles above the Pool. While Mr. Freeman promises us a road along the south side of the river his own plans (page 11) show all this margin, necessarily destroyed as to natural growth and beauty, uncovered and exposed at time of low water in the reservoir when it will inevitably be a fetid and slimy exposure to the pleasure seekers along the road which "for psychological reasons" has been promised by Mr. Freeman, but which on a later page (160r) has been estimated as more expensive than first thought and so is promised only in part at present.

The persistent mosquito rumors were laid to rest by the brief:

In their endeavors to belittle the significance of the Hetch-Hetchy Valley the zealous advocates of the city have slandered it by calling it "swampy" and a "mosquito meadow." There is no more certain indication of a losing cause than a resort by its proponents to misrepresentation and we are surprised to find these erroneous statements repeated in Mr. Freeman's report on page 56 and in other places.

The Merced River is so high in flood-time that annually a large portion of the floor of the Yosemite Valley is converted into a temporary lake. In their brief season, the mosquitoes in the Bridal Veil Meadows at the lower end of the Yosemite Valley will match the Hetch-Hetchy cohorts. Such arguments would be equally applicable to damming Yosemite itself. Only the lower third of the Hetch-Hetchy Valley is subject to temporary flooding, and the mosquitoes there last but a short time each season. The loose sandy soil soon dries out naturally and the beautiful floral growth of the lower meadows follows such as no permanent "swamp" would ever produce. A clearing out of the boulder-choked outlet at the lower end of the valley would perfect its drainage for all time.

The upper two-thirds of the Valley is a high landscape garden, beautified by exquisite groves of mighty oaks and carpeted with flowers and ferns. As is the case with the Yosemite, a system of drainage and a liberal use of petroleum will eradicate the mosquitoes. The advocates of this water system say that the Hetch-Hetchy is inaccessible and can only be visited three months in the year. This is a poor reason for destroying it when it can be made easily accessible with the expenditure of a few thousand dollars and can eventually be kept open to the public throughout the year, as is the case now in Yosemite. These arguments would have been equally applicable to the Yosemite a few years ago.

The Sierra Club felt less competent to tackle the several engineering problems discussed by Freeman, but did make it plain that "even to the layman" several discrepancies were obvious. It seemed curious, for example, that every item of expense mentioned in connection with the Sacramento River project should appear as expensive as possible when substantially identical items of cost in the Hetch Hetchy project were figured at a lower rate.

In connection with water power, the brief noted that the Freeman report

very sagaciously keeps power in the background, except that it is estimated that the city can eventually develop 200,000 horse power from this source, "an amount greater than is developed today at any one hydraulic power house outside of Niagara," and that this "power privilege will be a most valuable asset of the Tuolumne water supply system." Why give away this tremendous asset in addition to the water if it is not needed for pumping? Evidently it is more than water that the city is after.

. . .

Why not reserve this power for sale and the proceeds be devoted to improving the Park? If the Park is to be mutilated as the city plans, why is it not a just proceeding for the government to reserve some measure of the spoils which admittedly are not an essential part of the city's plan to secure pure water?

The brief filed by the city demonstrates what we have contended all these years was the fact—that ample water of good quality can be obtained for its needs from many other sources. In the early part of this contest this fact was strenuously denied by the Hetch-Hetchy advocates, and many persons were led to believe that Hetch-Hetchy was the only adequate supply of pure water available for San Francisco. The question resolves itself into one of comparative cost and we contend that the Federal Government can better afford to make an outright gift to the city of any possible increased cost, if it should prove that an alternative system would mean increased cost.

That it would be necessary to cut off of the entire Tuolumne watershed for sanitary precautions, as pictured in sketch maps reproduced by the Society for the Preservation of National Parks, has been mentioned earlier as one of the preservationists' extravagant claims and one that did not aid their cause during the Congressional hearings on the Raker bill. In this brief, however, Colby's comments on sanitation are much more conservative and appear to place Freeman in a somewhat untenable position:

. . .

1. The discussion of the sanitary rules needed to render the water supply hygienically safe, proceeds upon an entirely mistaken assumption regarding the kind of use to which campers and tourists are now putting the park. This is shown for instance by the contradictory statements on pages 55 and 34, where in one case bathing is to be prohibited, and in the other it is stated that "no limit

which does not now exist need be placed on the use of the park for camping purposes."

It is assumed that the use of Yosemite National Park is analogous to that of some city park where people view the scenery from the roadway and live at hotels or fixed camps. This is clearly impossible where people must and do move their own camping outfits over an area comprising many hundreds of square miles. Fixed camps are susceptible of sanitary supervision. But hundreds of people moving independently from point to point, carrying their own outfits and camping at a new site every night, are not susceptible of sanitary supervision. Yet, to put a check upon them is to deprive them of the best recreational use to which the Park is now being put. Steep slopes, impervious soils, and frozen ground greatly increase the danger of pollution that arises from such promiscuous camping. To such conditions the argument presented by picture and paragraph in the City's report has no application, because in the examples cited people either do not live and camp on the area, or else live at certain fixed places where extraordinary measures have been taken to guard against pollution, and where the public is under strict police supervision.

As will be clearly shown further on, the sanitary rule of all the protected watersheds cited as analogous cases by Mr. Freeman prohibit camping on the edge of streams and reservoirs, and bathing or washing in the same. But as any one knows who has camped at all in the Sierra Nevada, proximity of a camp to flowing water is so necessary for the comfort both of man and of beast that an outing in the park would lose all its charms without it. For example, of the two hundred and more persons who annually visit the park regions as part of the Sierra Club outing alone, few miss the luxury of a regular daily bath in the waters which Mr. Freeman gratuitously assumes would have no attraction by reason of their coldness, but in which bathing will have to be forbidden. Does any one suppose that the many hundreds of people who go camping for four weeks at a time in the Tuolumne Canyon and upper watershed carry along tubs, or postpone their baths for that period? The forbidding of bathing in the Tuolumne and its tributaries means practically no bathing within an area of about 450 sq. miles containing most of the finest scenery in the park. This alone is a serious impairment of the use of that area as a recreation ground.

2. It seems incredible that an engineer should minimize the need of sanitary safeguards to the extent to which it is done in this report. On pages 32–52 an appeal is made to all the laxities of sanitary control which could be used to "prove the utter absurdity of the statement . . . that the use of the Hetch-Hetchy as an impounding reservoir . . . would exclude from its watershed tourists and campers, now or in the future, or *lessen the pleasure to be found within the limits of the Yosemite reservation*" (p. 52). The underlined part of the statement has already been disproved under paragraph (1) in the matter of one very large item of pleasure which will have to be eliminated, although on Mr. Freeman's reasoning it is not altogether clear why. If, as he says, "Any pathogenic germs die in a month or two at the most" in a storage reservoir like Hetch-Hetchy, pollution from bathing would be removed as effectively as the danger of chance pollutions arising from the presence of campers in the watershed.

But apparently Mr. Freeman does not himself believe in the laxities of sanitary control he advocates in the case of Hetch-Hetchy, for on page 343 he urges as an objection to the McCloud River source that "a single case of 'walking typhoid' on the shores of the river might become a serious element of danger" unless a large storage reservoir or a filtration system were established. (N.B. Surely the McCloud water can be delivered, as he says the Hetch-Hetchy

141

water will be, "into storage reservoirs at Crystal Springs or Lake Chabot, or a projected San Antonio reservoir," p. 344.) Then he cites the case of "*a lake* which serves as the source of water supply to a certain city." Although the lumbermen near the lake, he writes, "are all concentrated in two camps and closely watched, it is found difficult to maintain full and efficient sanitary precautions." Now Hetch-Hetchy will not even be a storage reservoir in the sense in which a lake is, for a large river is flowing through it constantly. One expert to whom we stated this difficulty said it would be necessary to lead the surplus flow of the Tuolumne through the reservoir by a channel on the side. Any one who has seen Hetch-Hetchy knows that such a thing is impossible.

In the light of these facts and of Mr. Freeman's expressed fears where they could be used to disparage a rival source of supply, what are we to think of his statement that "camping more than a mile upstream from the head of the reservoir (Hetch-Hetchy) can do no possible harm?" (p. 36.) Again on page 60 he wants to have campers excluded from the Poopenaut Valley until the twelve miles of aqueduct tunnel have been built from the dam to the intake. A reservoir through which a master stream like the Tuolumne flows will set up currents that will render pollution above the dam almost as dangerous as below. We do not want the city engineers to defer the *discovery* of this fact until it can no longer hurt their case.

On page 33 of the Report, Mr. Freeman makes the statement that those who have urged the difficulty of a joint use of the Tuolumne watershed for park and water supply purposes "set up a fanciful standard of their own . . . far more rigorous than is in force for drinking-water supplies of Boston, New York, Los Angeles, Seattle, Portland (Oregon), Portland (Maine), Glasgow, Manchester, Birmingham, or so far as is known now, any city in the world either with or without filtration works."

This statement is in part totally *erroneous,* in part *misleading,* and in part carries approval of a *high typhoid rate as satisfactory.*

ERRONEOUS.

Portland, Oregon. The City of Portland, Oregon, which derives its water supply from Bull Run Lake absolutely prohibits all residence camping, or sojourning on any part of the 222 square miles of the Bull Run Timber Reserve. To make this still more drastic, the City caused to be passed by Congress an Act providing $500 fine for any one who shall be caught trespassing on the Reserve. What Mr. Freeman means by his reference to the control of this watershed among others as an illustration of what will satisfy both the City of San Francisco and future visitors to the Tuolumne watershed, we must leave to him for explanation. . . .

It will be observed *that nine years after* the Bull Run Reserve was established as a water supply for the city of Portland it was found desirable to have Congress pass a law excluding "the public from the reserve and fining each trespasser not to exceed $500.00." No permission is ever given to "visit or camp." If the city should acquire the right to use Hetch-Hetchy will she wait nine years before demanding the exclusion of the public?

Seattle. The city of Seattle derives its supply from the Cedar River watershed. Mr. Freeman refers to the control of this watershed as an illustration that tourists and campers need expect no interference in the Tuolumne watershed. But the . . . city is "allowing no habitation or industrial camp to exist in the watershed of any kind or character excepting those doing municipal work and one or two camps which under the condemnation award were allowed to finish logging certain lands." While the latter continue every workman before he is engaged is examined for typhoid and required to submit to typhoid immunization by a physician representing the City's Health Department. The watershed now "is almost free from human life other than above," and the purpose is to keep it so. Tourists and campers, of course, are neither wanted nor permitted, for, under ordinance No. 27534 . . . , it is declared "unlawful for any person or persons to camp, picnic, loiter, trespass, fish, or otherwise be within the Cedar River watershed." Mr. Freeman's assurance that prospective users of the Tuolumne watershed of the Yosemite National Park need not fear anything more rigorous than that is certainly not lacking in grim humor, although his argument may be said to have committed suicide. . . .

A good deal is made of the soft-water argument used by Freeman. The brief cites recent German research to indicate that calcium salts are essential in the proper hygiene of the body,

but the advocates of Hetch Hetchy declare that lime is "conspicuously absent" in its water; that it has the remarkable softness of "twenty parts per million" (p. 153). In the light of Emmerich and Loew's experiments that ought to decide the case in favor of Sacramento water, or some other water less soft, unless it is desired to bring reinforcement to a considerable list of diseases.

. . .

Freeman had placed considerable emphasis on the saving of soap bills for Bay Area residents receiving Hetch Hetchy water, but this the brief attacks as "heedless commercialism."

Perhaps the most prophetic and in many ways the strongest arguments by the Sierra Club were those concerning increased future travel and the use of Yosemite for winter sports and enjoyment:

The statement frequently made in the report to the effect that the Hetch-Hetchy Valley and the Tuolumne watershed are accessible only three or four months in the year has an important bearing upon the question of sanitation. The purpose on the one hand is to palliate the damage inflicted upon the public uses of the Park, and on the other to minimize the need of safeguards against pollution. We wish to point out as emphatically as we can the entire falseness of these assumptions.

A. Questions of sanitation will have to be considered in the light of the enormously increased numbers of people who will visit this region in years to come. Our opponents claim recognition for the virtuous necessity of providing against municipal needs that may arise in a distant future, but do not compare these putative future needs with the equally enlarged recreational needs of a greater California and a greater nation. They very illogically compare their inflated population with the few people who, they say, now visit the Valley. As a matter of fact, from thirteen to fifteen thousand persons have annually visited the Park during the last few years, and a very large number of these have gone into the Tuolumne watershed. These constantly increasing numbers of visitors will reach the figure of a hundred thousand annually before San Francisco has a population of a million. Many thousands of these will visit the Tuolumne watershed. The recreational needs of these persons, as well as the effect of their visits upon the hygiene of the water supply, will have to be considered now. A project is on hand for the rehabilitation of the Tioga Road for automobile use. If the money can be raised to put the Big Oak Flat and the Tioga Roads in good

143

order it takes little imagination to figure out what countless thousands will visit Hetch-Hetchy Valley as a side excursion and then pass out over the Tioga Road.

. . .

B. But the biggest element in the problem has received no consideration at all in the report. So far as altitude and climatic conditions are concerned, Yosemite and Hetch-Hetchy are in the same class, the advantages being rather in favor of Hetch-Hetchy as a winter resort. The difficulties which at present confine tourist travel in Hetch-Hetchy to the summer months are not rigors of altitude or climate, but the exigencies of travel and accommodation. As soon as a good road is built to Hetch-Hetchy (not by the City, but by the Federal Government) and transportation facilities are provided, hotels will spring up and the tide of tourist travel, attracted both by the sublime beauty of the Valley and the wonders of the canyon above, will turn to Hetch-Hetchy *both in winter and in summer.*

The direction which the recreational use of parks in winter is now taking is best indicated by what is taking place in Switzerland. One of the writers recently spent the months of December and January in the Alps and visited a considerable number of winter resorts ranging from four to seven thousand feet above sea level. All these places were crowded with tourists and the hotels were over filled. They came from all parts of Europe and the British Islands to attend the winter sports and to enjoy the scenery of the Alps in winter.

If any one thinks that the cold and altitude will keep people out of the Yosemite, Hetch-Hetchy and the Tuolumne Meadows in winter he only needs to be reminded that the Swiss-Alpine winter resorts now annually visited by many thousands lie in a latitude ten degrees farther north than Yosemite National Park, and as regards altitude and scenery it is difficult to conceive of places that offer greater attractions for winter sports than Yosemite, Hetch-Hetchy and the Tuolumne Meadows. Only one not conversant with the facts would contend that climatic conditions forbid their use for winter recreations. We can testify from personal experience that the climatic advantages are decidedly in favor of our so-called "High Sierra" and that the Tuolumne Meadows as regards its adaptation to winter sports, its spaciousness, its magnificent entourage of peaks and forests, its strategic situation with regard to Hetch-Hetchy, Yosemite, and the Mono Lake country, is unrivalled by any Alpine valley of Switzerland.

For many persons the climate of California, from the Sacramento Valley southward, demands for its complete salubriousness the stimulus of ready access to snow altitudes. Therefore the number of those who in summer visit the National Park for the scenery, will in winter be increased by those who go for their health, for the sports, and for the novelty of those winter scenes that never visit a sea-level Californian among his ever-blooming roses.

Judging by the trend of out-door sports in other parts of the world, this winter use of the Park will in the near future reinforce the summer use as surely as morning succeeds night. Even the present rate of increase in winter visitors indicates that from thirty to fifty thousand people will knock at the portals of Yosemite National Park in the winter of 1930 if facilities of access are provided. Long before these populations arrive on whose behalf San Francisco desires to drown Hetch-Hetchy, Yosemite Valley will be entirely inadequate to the task of caring for winter visitors, let alone those who come in summer. Hetch-Hetchy is the only other valley in the Park that ranks with Yosemite in point of availability for hotel sites; it is the only one comparable to Yosemite for the sublimity of its scenery. It is the indispensable entrance and exit to the Grand Canyon of the Tuolumne, next to the Canyon of the Colorado, the most wonderful gorge in America.

From both valleys the overflow of travel will go to the Tuolumne Meadows, the great future Mecca of winter sports. When its snows have been trodden by thousands as they now are on the lofty ski-fields of Switzerland, and the spring thaws carry all manner of unavoidable pollution into the flood waters of the Tuolumne, will San Francisco accept the situation with its probable typhoid epidemics, or try to restrict the use of the watershed?

If it proposes to do the latter, then it is proper to point out that the Park was dedicated as a playground for the people of the United States and not as a washbowl and soap-saving institution for San Francisco, who can get abundant, better, and more readily protectable water elsewhere.

Further, reference to Switzerland's enormous profits from tourist travel shows that an economic factor is involved here of such proportion that it will ultimately knock San Francisco's soap and power profits into a cocked hat. The nation would save the outlay several times over in the future if it were to buy a water supply for San Francisco and keep Hetch-Hetchy.

It is serious enough to propose to destroy a uniquely beautiful valley with its fauna, sylva, and flora to make an artificial lake in a park that abounds in beautiful natural ones; but it aggravates the situation immeasurably to take away at the same time a valley imperatively needed in the near future for the accommodation of winter as well as summer visitors; to obstruct the natural highway through the Tuolumne Canyon up to the Tuolumne Meadows; and to expose the use of the whole watershed to the unending annoyance of a sanitary control under which both the consumer and the recreation-seeker are bound to suffer.

That the necessity for future increasing irksome restrictions is recognized and anticipated by the city's experts is shown on page 55 of Mr. Freeman's report: "It is further assumed that the superintendent of the Park would make from time to time such *special regulations* respecting sewage from steamers upon the lake, sewage of hotels, and *any other matters* that might develop, *not covered by present rules,* as were reasonably necessary, *and as were suggested and requested by* the proper *authorities of the City of San Francisco.*"

This is a matter so subversive of public interest and provocative of endless strife for the future that only a clearly demonstrated public necessity could excuse it.

The Sierra Club's brief ended with a plea for the revocation of that portion of the Garfield permit granting the use of Hetch Hetchy and was signed by William F. Badè, Joseph N. LeConte, and E. T. Parsons. John Muir and William E. Colby placed their signatures in "attest," but it is clearly the work of attorney Colby.

VII

The hearing before Secretary Fisher began on Monday, November 25, 1912, and lasted six full days. San Francisco,[58] the Spring Valley Water Company, the irrigationists, and the preservationists were all represented in Washington. On hand for the preservationists were J. Horace McFarland and Richard Watrous of the American Civic Association; Stephen Mather,

[58] In addition to John Freeman, his assistants, and M. M. O'Shaughnessy, City Engineer who had replaced Manson in September, San Francisco was represented by its Mayor, James Rolph, Jr.; Supervisor Alexander T. Vogelsang, Chairman of the Public Utilities Committee; Percy V. Long, City Attorney; and John S. Dunnigan, Clerk of the Board of Supervisors. For a San Francisco view of these hearings, see M. M. O'Shaughnessy, *Hetch Hetchy; Its Origin and History* (San Francisco, 1934), pp. 40–44.

145

Chicago Geographical Society; Edmund Whitman, Appalachian Mountain Club; William F. Badè, Sierra Club; Warren Gregory, American Scenic and Historic Preservation Society; Alden Sampson, and Robert Underwood Johnson.

Monday night the preservationists gathered at the Army and Navy Club in Washington for dinner with Colonel Forsyth, Acting Superintendent of Yosemite, Robert Marshall of the U.S. Geological Survey, and others.[59] Apparently strategy for the hearings was discussed and the part each of the representatives would play was assigned. According to Badè the strategy worked well; "We balled up Freeman and others badly," he wired to Colby.[60] Toward the end of the week, however, the preservationists were less confident. Badè wired, "Hard to tell outcome, may grant Hetch Hetchy with severe restrictions, reported city will try Congress."[61] Badè wrote more fully two days later: "We have been nearly dead each day with fatigue during these strenuous hearings. There has not been much to do for us except to 'be on the job' and nag the other side with tough questions. In this respect our battery of *nine* men on the Secretary's left was a *power*, and even as a silent assertion of the public's interest, of tremendous value and influence. On one occasion which McFarland called 'dramatic,' I read from Hazen's [engineering assistant to Freeman] own book an opinion directly the opposite of the testimony he had just given and read into the record also other expert testimony. I think we discredited him pretty thoroughly. Johnson (R. U.) did not help us much. . . . Freeman got several awful 'jawings' from the Secretary for his lack of candor and his desire to dismiss all other sources with a wave of the hand. But he has proved an extremely able Devil's advocate. Nevertheless, the balance hangs in our favor, I think. Should he give H. H. it will be under conditions that will make it worthless to them. Phelan, Rolph, and Freeman, with their pockets full of Great Western and other electric stock, nearly had heart failure when the Secretary announced that he would not give the city any power rights except on condition of immediate development. I once got Freeman into awful trouble by insisting on an explanation of the difference in cost of pipe as shown in our brief. The Army Engineers said they had for weeks tried to get Freeman to equalize his estimates on the same unit basis—but without avail. The Secretary practically served notice on the city that their failures along these lines was presumptive evidence against them. . . . The city is to be given about two months to revise estimates and furnish additional information. The Secretary thinks he has the right to grant a permit under the present act [Right-of-Way Act of 1901] but thinks it is a very bad one and urges its repeal."[62]

[59] Sampson, Washington, D.C., to Colby, San Francisco, telegram, November 25, 1912, SCA.

[60] Badè, Washington, D.C., to Colby, Berkeley, telegram, November 25–26, 1912, SCA.

[61] Badè, Washington, D.C., to Colby, Berkeley, telegram, November 27, 1912, SCA.

[62] Badè Washington, D.C., to Colby, San Francisco, November 29, 1912, SCA.

At one point, toward the end of the hearings, the Sierra Club's 1909 ballot was brought up when J. H. Cutter, a member of the minority faction in the Club, sent a telegram to Washington informing the Secretary that some members of the Club were firmly supporting the city. The telegram was read at the hearing and picked up by one of the wire services, which transmitted this news to the San Francisco papers. According to Ernest J. Mott, a San Francisco attorney and member of the minority in the Club, the *Examiner* immediately dug up the 1909–1910 stories and approached several minority members for statements, which the paper then wired to Washington.[63] When Secretary Fisher read the Sierra Club ballot of 1909 he was severely critical of the wording—so critical that Colby found it necessary to write him a letter of explanation.[64]

The Fisher hearing was inconclusive. San Francisco was given additional time in which to file further evidence and correct certain estimates in the data previously submitted. Although the Secretary seemed to be leaning toward a restrictive grant of Hetch Hetchy to the city, the preservationists were hopeful that the Army Engineers final report would show that other sources of supply could be substituted for Hetch Hetchy. Still, there was sufficient doubt that McFarland sent Fisher a twenty-page letter in which he proposed certain "safeguards to the public interest" should the government deem it "advisable to grant the permit in the changed form insisted upon in the Freeman report."[65] These "safeguards" included (a) construction of adequate roads, trails, and campgrounds; (b) adequate sanitary patrol of the Tuolumne watershed at the expense of San Francisco; (c) avoidance, so far as possible, of any destruction of the natural features of the Hetch Hetchy Valley other than flooding by the reservoir; (d) retention of power rights entirely by the government, or, if permitted to the city, only on condition that they be developed within a reasonably short time . . . and that all power so developed bear a substantial surcharge . . . for the uses and development of what is left of the Yosemite National Park; and (e) a carefully worded stipulation that when a certain number of campers and hikers begin to use the Tuolumne watershed filtration of the water will begin as a part of the costs of development of Hetch Hetchy to San Francisco.

It is not possible to be certain at this distance from the controversy that these stipulations for a mitigated invasion helped the preservation cause; they may well have weakened it by implying that the preservationists were not sincerely devoted to their argument in behalf of the principle that national parks should not be invaded at all for utilitarian purposes. If McFarland's proposal, coming from one of the leaders of the defense, was construed to

[63] Mott, San Francisco, to Colby, San Francisco, December 20, 1912, SCA. Mott had written to Colby on December 13, 1912, inquiring if there was any truth in the rumor that the directors intended to ask for the resignation of the minority members of the Club. Colby replied on December 14 that the directors had no such intention, but were considering mailing a statement to the membership explaining the attitude of the majority. Mott, in effect, gives Colby a vote of confidence in remarking: "I think you have done exactly right in financing the majority's action from personal contributions. I have often been asked whether the Board of Directors was spending Club money for this purpose, and I have unhesitatingly answered that I knew better because I knew the men back of the idea, and that they were all sincere fellows, willing to back up their opinions by personal contributions."

[64] Colby, San Francisco, to Fisher, Washington, D.C., December 6, 1912, copy, SCA. Fisher confessed to Colby on December 16 that his letter did not remove the impression of unfairness in the wording of the ballot when he read it the first time, but admitted that "at no time" did he have any doubt that "the majority of the members of the Sierra Club would be opposed to permitting the City of San Francisco to use the Hetch Hetchy as a water reservoir unless the practical necessity for so doing was clearly demonstrated."

[65] McFarland, Washington, D.C., to Fisher, Washington, D.C., December 11, 1912, copy, SCA.

be an admission of weakness and of likely defeat and a concomitant move to get the best of a bad bargain, then the preservationists' position was indeed weakened by what might otherwise have appeared to be a moderate and sagacious posture.

The moderate and sagacious position of McFarland during the hearings and, indeed, throughout the Hetch Hetchy campaign was of inestimable value to the Sierra Club, a fact that Colby particularly appreciated. Something of McFarland's attitude is shown in this communication with Colby: "Recent correspondence with the Secretary [Fisher] seems to indicate a reasonable confidence by him in those of us who are moderate in our statements and are as willing to admit an advantage to the other fellow as we are to insist upon one for ourselves. This was made notably apparent during the hearings, when under pressure our good friend Robert Underwood Johnson took an absolutely indefensible position and stuck to it, thereby losing all influence with the Secretary, while under similar conditions, although it was a seeming disadvantage, it seemed best to me to state my frank conviction, even though it was at the moment seemingly favorable to San Francisco."[66]

McFarland was remarkably free of the emotional bias that occasionally led some of the preservationists into exaggerated statements or unsound arguments. He believed firmly that Hetch Hetchy was a test case for the preservationists and that its successful conclusion depended upon an enlightened and factual presentation at all times.

VIII

By the middle of January San Francisco had completed its additional findings and transmitted them to Washington.[67] On February 19, 1913, the long-awaited Army Engineers' report was released. The hopeful expectation of the preservationists that this report would, once and for all, settle the most vexing problem of Hetch Hetchy was soon dissipated. The Report obviously favored Hetch Hetchy, but it did leave a small loophole and around this point the preservationists immediately rallied. The Engineers had said: ". . . there are several sources of supply which could be obtained and used . . . to supplement the nearby supplies as the necessity develops. From any one of these sources the water is sufficient in quantity and is, or can be made, suitable in quality, while the engineering difficulties are not insurmountable. The determining factor is principally one of cost; . . . the project proposed by the City of San Francisco

[66] McFarland, Harrisburg, to Colby, San Francisco, December 28, 1912, SCA.

[67] See O'Shaughnessy's letter to Secretary Fisher, January 18, 1913, reproduced in O'Shaughnessy's *Hetch Hetchy; Its Origin and History*, pp. 42–44.

. . . is about $20,000,000 cheaper than any other feasible project for furnishing an adequate supply."[68]

The preservationists were quick to seize upon this; what price tag could be placed on a remote mountain valley preserved in its natural state?

Far from acquiescing in the Board's recommendations, McFarland sent Fisher a six-page letter which is masterly in its praise for the engineers and at the same time jolting to their logic: "Before you grant this permit, I venture to suggest that you consider the relation of its granting . . . to the whole subject of National Parks . . . The recommendation of these capable Army Engineers may be assumed, with accuracy I believe, to be a purely economic recommendation, based entirely upon factors of cost, although, rather surprisingly, 'sentiment' appears in one case, where, in the first of the conclusions, the Board says, 'the determining factor is principally one of cost. In some cases, however, such as the Sacramento, *sentiment* must be taken into consideration.' . . . throughout this report the Engineers have looked upon the Hetch Hetchy Valley . . . apparently on precisely the same basis that they have looked upon any other and every other source of water presented or known to them. That is, they have not discussed, except in respect to sanitation, in respect to the location of roads for scenic viewing, and in respect to the comparison of scenic value between the Hetch Hetchy and the Yosemite Valleys, the relation of such a grant to Yosemite National Park. With the minor exceptions above noted, the able discussion of the Advisory Board is exactly the same in respect to the portion of the Yosemite National Park to be given up as if it applied to some other part of the national domain not specifically set aside as a park. For this reason I respectfully present to you that nothing has yet appeared to warrant the granting of the permit asked for by the city of San Francisco, even as modified by the suggestions of the Advisory Board of Army Engineers. The final, primary and unique *necessity* of the city to use the Hetch Hetchy Valley has not been shown. It has not been shown that there is no other alternative source of water supply practically available."[69]

McFarland suggested that since costs of the project would be spread over several generations, other factors might intervene "to make other sources equally or quite as cheap as the Hetch Hetchy source." He alluded to the sentiment of distaste expressed by San Franciscans at the possibility of drinking filtered water from a supposedly impure Sacramento River, and proposed that this argument should be dismissed by the Secretary as "a temporary feeling . . . due to lack of knowledge."

McFarland also referred to the original act to set aside Yosem-

[68] U.S. Advisory Board of Army Engineers, *Hetch Hetchy Valley; Report . . . to the Secretary of the Interior on Investigations Relative to Sources of Water Supply for San Francisco and Bay Communities* (Washington, D.C., 1913), p. 50.

[69] McFarland, Harrisburg, to Fisher, Washington, D.C., February 25, 1913, copy, SCA.

149

ite as well as subsequent acts including the notorious Right-of-Way Act of 1901. In connection with the latter, he urged the Secretary ". . . to note that the modifying act under which and only under which access to the park may be had for the establishment of the works required to create a municipal water supply cannot in this case be properly construed favorably if its construction is assumed to largely decrease the utility of the park *as a park* under its original setting aside by Congress."[70]

Edmund Whitman, the A.M.C. president, had noted that San Francisco specifically requested the Poopenaut Valley in addition to Hetch Hetchy, and this elicited the following statement from McFarland: "Either we are to have National Parks or we are not to have National Parks. It is inconceivable that we can have National Parks which are at the demand of any municipality as water sheds for a water supply, to their distinct disadvantage for the purpose of parks, except in cases of unique and primary necessity, such as has not been shown in this case."[71]

Colby received a copy of McFarland's letter and this further assessment of the Army Engineers' report: ". . . the Engineers practically recommend that the Hetch Hetchy permit be granted. They do not do so with any enthusiasm. They show that San Francisco can get water elsewhere, and they are quite plain in indicating the inaccuracy of the Freeman report and the unfairness of the comparative figures. I think it is a fair, straightforward, honest, and capable report. It does not discuss the value of parks, or, except in three instances, relate a National Park to this watershed at all. It treats the Yosemite just as a report on the Los Angeles supply might have been considered to treat any part of the public domain."[72]

In McFarland's opinion Fisher "would be in a strong position if he refused to grant the permit on the higher ground of the value of parks."

Secretary Fisher was faced with a dilemma, but a choice had to be made. Three days before stepping down from his office, the out-going Secretary of the Interior wrote to the Mayor and Board of Supervisors of San Francisco in these words: "If it were clear that I should issue to the City of San Francisco a permit of the general character it requests, it would have been and would now be absolutely impossible within the time available to embody the details of such a permit in a properly considered document. This is a matter of the greatest regret to me as I had hoped to be able at least to draft a permit embodying the provisions which, in my judgment, should be contained in any permit for the use of the Hetch Hetchy Valley as a reservoir site by the city of San Francisco and the communities around San Francisco Bay. The importance of doing this, however, is much reduced by

[70] *Loc. cit.*
[71] *Loc. cit.*
[72] McFarland, Harrisburg, to Colby, San Francisco, February 26, 1913, SCA.

the fact that I have reached the conclusion that a permit for this purpose should not be issued by the Secretary of the Interior under the existing law. This conclusion . . . is based upon the fact that the only statutory authority under which such a permit could be issued is the act of February 15, 1901."[73]

Fisher did not believe the act of February 15, 1901, gave him clear authorization to grant the permit desired by San Francisco when the principal determining factor in the Advisory Board report in favor of Hetch Hetchy over other sources of water supply was one of cost. The Secretary concluded, therefore, that the Ballinger order to show cause should continue in effect until the city could apply to Congress for action.[74]

[73] *Water Supply, City of San Francisco,* letter from Secretary Fisher to the Mayor and Supervisors of San Francisco, March 1, 1913 (Washington, D.C., 1913), pp. 5–6.
[74] *Ibid.,* p. 9.

6

HETCH HETCHY
The End

*". . . Nothing that we can do on the side
of justice can be wholly lost . . ."*
—*John Muir*

I

THE "great victory" thus won by the preservationists was a sober one and was so received by Colby, who realized that the real test now lay immediately ahead. A new Congress and a new administration took over the national government on March 4, 1913—the first Democratic administration in the twentieth century. President Wilson appointed as his new Secretary of the Interior Franklin K. Lane, the man who had been City Attorney in San Francisco at the time of Mayor Phelan's first Hetch Hetchy filings. There could be no doubt where the new Secretary's sympathies would lie.

San Francisco was quick to test the Secretary; less than a week after Lane's accession to office, Percy Long, the incumbent City Attorney, called on him in Washington. The meeting is reported by Richard Watrous, the American Civic Association's secretary, who was present at the express invitation of Lane. It was made absolutely clear that the new Secretary's position was in favor of San Francisco and that he would support the city in Congress. To Watrous, the value of the meeting was in showing "where one is 'at.' " "We are up against a staunch advocate of San Francisco's," he reported to Colby, "and that means a prodigious fight to get Congress to decline the permit."[1] Watrous pointed out to Colby that the American Civic Association was so involved in its fights to preserve Niagara Falls and to secure the creation of a Bureau of National Parks that it would be forced to leave the "engineering" of the Hetch Hetchy campaign to the Sierra Club. He assured Colby, however, that he would keep him advised of anything that developed and wire him if necessary. McFarland later confirmed Watrous' analysis of the situation.[2]

Colby, of course, was disturbed by McFarland's and Watrous' letters to him, yet deeply grateful to the American Civic Association for its important work.[3] In a long communication to McFarland he set forth his concerns and plans for the future Hetch Hetchy campaign:

I am somewhat at a loss to know just what we should do in this Hetch Hetchy matter. It would seem that with the favorable recommendation of the Secretary, that the weight of the administration would be behind such a grant, and to a certain extent this is reinforced by Secretary Fisher's decision. Most of the

[1] Watrous, Washington, D.C., to Colby, San Francisco, March 10, 1913, SCA. Badè had alerted McFarland by wire that Long was going to seek approval of the permit from Lane. This information was relayed by McFarland to his colleague, Watrous, in the Washington office of the A.C.A., and thus the "invitation" from Lane when Watrous questioned him about Long's visit. See also Watrous, Washington, D.C., to McFarland, Harrisburg, March 10, 1913, original in SCA.

[2] McFarland, Harrisburg, to Colby, San Francisco, March 11, 1913, SCA.

[3] Colby, San Francisco, to McFarland, Harrisburg, April 2, 1913, copy, SCA.

fighting ground left us is that the Army Engineer's report shows that San Francisco can for a few millions additional obtain an adequate water supply, and the question resolves itself into whether the nation wants to create such an important precedent in the way of breaking down our National Parks. It appears to me and also to Mr. Parsons, and I am sure that Mr. Muir is of the same mind, though I have not seen him since Secretary Fisher's decision, that we should issue a final pamphlet somewhat similar to the earlier Muir pamphlet, containing a statement of the case to date, backed up by quotations and containing a few good illustrations of Hetch-Hetchy Valley. The front page would be occupied by an open letter from Mr. Muir, appealing to the American public to aid in preventing this precedent from being established, and the pamphlet itself would suggest that those interested write to their Congressmen to prevent it. In my opinion, the pamphlet should also contain a carefully veiled argument to the effect that if by any possibility (without admitting that it is possible) that Congress should make such a grant that it should be hedged about with mighty restrictive conditions. And futhermore that if $45,000,000 worth of water power is to be given the city outright, that it should make some adequate annual return out of this to be devoted to the improvement of that portion of the Park which will be injured by the grant. It would seem to me that common equity would compel such a return. If Congressmen get appeals from all parts of the country along this line, it would seem to me that it is going to accomplish a great deal of real good, even though we may not be able to block the grant. In talking this over with Mr. Parsons and Dr. Badè, it seemed best that such a pamphlet be published in the East, for any such publication in this vicinity would come to the ears of the supervisors without delay, and they would be prepared to backfire. We ought to delay the information of our plans as long as possible until we are ready to strike the effective blow. The agitation will undoubtedly be for the general benefit of our Parks. . . . My idea is to send out to every name appearing in Who's Who, also to send to every member of the Appalachian Club and other clubs that might seem desirable. The number issued would of course depend largely upon our means, but we will be able to raise quite a little money among ourselves, because I purposely insisted upon going to as little expense as possible in preparing our case before Secretary Fisher. Some of our co-workers here thought we ought to have issued a pamphlet at that time in order to try and influence Secretary Fisher. I felt that we could accomplish little in that direction and my judgment has been justified to a great extent by the outcome. I am sure that we can raise several hundred dollars for the purpose of paying for printing, postage, etc. Mr. Parsons has himself personally drawn his check for $200 in my favor. . . . I know Mr. Muir will contribute liberally. I will be able to give something and there are other friends of ours who are loyal club members who are able to contribute liberally. I hope that this will be our final "Big Gun" in this Hetch-Hetchy fight, but it seems to me that it is worth while to fire it at an opportune moment.[4]

Calling the Army Engineers' report "a severe blow," Colby nevertheless felt the fight had been worth while "in its general effect in educating the public."

We have not as yet lost by any means, especially when the views of the American public are still to be counted on as a factor, and they are very much more liable to be adequately affected by Congressional action. Many of the findings in the Engineers' report are a source of considerable satisfaction to us, and make it appear that our statements made in the beginning of this fight when

[4] Colby, San Francisco, to McFarland, Harrisburg, March 14, 1913, copy, SCA.

154

we were much less informed, are so remarkably supported. For example, we stated that San Francisco was asking for practically $50,000,000 worth of water power, and the Army Engineers say that the amount that can be derived from this source can readily be capitalized at $45,000,000. They also seem to agree on the question of filtration, which they state will be demanded by all communities before the end of the century, and also support us in our contention that the city should be compelled to filter rather than to exclude the public from the water shed. For your own information, I will state that the Army Engineers themselves estimate that the Sacramento River project discounted to 1914 will only cost $13,000,000 more than the Hetch-Hetchy project. This is for an ultimate supply that will be satisfactory in the year 2000. They also state in their report that the experts think it possible that San Francisco may have to filter the Hetch-Hetchy supply in fifty or more years. If this is the case the capitalized cost of such filtration should properly be added to the cost of the Hetch-Hetchy Project, figures as adequate for the year 2000. While the expense of this discounted to 1914 will materially reduce the capitalization necessary fifty years from now, it will go a long way toward cutting down the difference of $13,000,000 between it and the Sacramento River Project. . . .[5]

To the city of San Francisco, Fisher's ruling was only passing irritation. Confident that Lane, Wilson, and the new Congress would support their project, Mayor James Rolph, Jr., and the Board of Supervisors authorized John S. Dunnigan's trip to Washington to assist in the framing of a proper bill.[6] He was followed later by O'Shaughnessy and by City Attorney Long, for the second time. As previously noted, Representative Raker, in whose district Hetch Hetchy lay, had introduced a bill two years previously to accomplish what the city now asked him to do again. On April 7, 1913, he brought into the House H. R. 112, the first of five bills; it was not until August 1 that a satisfactory bill was found, one that would please a majority of the Public Lands Committee, the city, and the administration.[7]

It is not our purpose to detail here the legislative history of the Raker bills or to review the lengthy discussions that took place in Committee or on the floor of Congress. Florence Monroy has thoroughly analyzed the Raker bills.[8] Debate in the House and Senate fills over 380 pages in the *Congressional Record*. Our concern is with what the Sierra Club, its leaders, and allies were doing to stem the tide of events now that the final showdown had come.

John Muir, as President of the Society for the Preservation of National Parks, wired his 1889 Yosemite companion, Robert Underwood Johnson, on June 17: "Hetch Hetchy situation critical. City trying to rush bill through Congress speciously urging imperative necessity which does not exist. Send strong wires, letters to Public Lands Committee, House, requesting delay until regular session."[9]

Another urgent telegram followed on June 25, as well as

[5] *Loc. cit.*

[6] O'Shaughnessy, *op. cit.*, p. 45.

[7] Other bills introduced were: H. R. 4319 (April 25); H. R. 6281 (June 23), the first one upon which hearings were held; H. R. 7207 (August 1), the bill which finally passed the House; and H. R. 7297 by Representative Mondell. See *Congressional Record*, 63rd Cong., 1st Sess., vol. 50 (1913), pp. 82, 497, 2143, 2545, and 3023.

[8] Monroy, *op. cit.*, especially Chapter III. See also reference to unpublished dissertations in the "Bibliographical Note."

[9] Muir, San Francisco, to Johnson, New York, June 17, 1913, *Johnson Papers*, box 7, folder no. 476.

wires to other friends. To Professor Henry Fairfield Osborn of the American Museum of Natural History he said: "San Francisco schemers making desperate efforts to rush bill through Congress under the plea dire necessity giving Hetch Hetchy Valley fee simple enabling to dam and destroy at leisure. They have long been scheming in dusk and din of tariff clouds. House Public Lands Committee have unanimously agreed to devote six hours tomorrow to department heads in developing elementary principles of bill, succeeding six hours to its proponents and following six hours to opponents. Hearing expected to continue until fate of valley is fixed. Nevertheless we hope salvation. You know the President and am sure you will strike hard."[10]

Johnson and Osborn were both active in writing letters to Congress, and to the *New York Times* and other papers. That Muir was cheered by their work and that he still saw victory for the preservationists is indicated by his letter to Johnson during the House hearings: "We all send you many thanks for your brave Hetch Hetchy work. In all our fights on park matters you have been and are our main stay and leader. Do not allow yourself to be handicapped by lack of a stenographer. We will gladly furnish all the money you want. Send the bills to me. . . . Be of good cheer. Nothing that we can do on the side of justice can be wholly lost. . . . Don't fret, all will turn out for the best in the long run."[11]

As this letter and others from Muir and Colby indicate, the Society for the Preservation of National Parks, California Branch, was largely responsible for the funds that were expended by the Johnson group in the East, at least until the formation of the National Committee for the Preservation of Yosemite Park. As a matter of fact, much of the money came from three members of the Sierra Club—Muir, Colby, and Parsons.[12]

The preservationists had little time to act when word came that the House would hold hearings on the third Raker bill, introduced only two days previously, but the quick action of Muir, Badè, and others in requesting letters and wires to the House Public Lands Committee evidently resulted in a certain uneasiness among the Committee members. At one point during the hearing the Chairman wondered who had inspired telegrams from Texas, Maine, Illinois, and New York "all worded alike, all asking that this be put over until December, without any reason therefor."[13] City Attorney Long, who was present at this session, was asked if he knew who sent the wires and implied that he did but would keep his views to himself. Edmund Whitman, the only representative for the preservationists at the House hearings, rebuked Long and set the record straight by reminding

[10] Muir, San Francisco, to Osborn, New York, June 24, 1913, copy, SCA.
[11] Muir, San Francisco, to Johnson, July, 1913, *Johnson Papers*, box 7, folder no. 478.
[12] See the following Muir letters to Johnson in the *Johnson Papers:* August 8, 1913 (box 3, folder no. 146); October 1, 1913 (box 7, folder no. 483); October 16, 1913 (box 7, folder no. 485); October 28, 1913 (box 7, folder no. 488); and November 3, 1913 (box 7, folder no. 491). See also the Colby letter to Johnson, September 8, 1913 (box 7, folder no. 1072), and Edward Parsons to Johnson, November 15, 1913 (box 8, folder no. 1126).
[13] *Hetch Hetchy Dam Site,* Hearing . . . on H. R. 6281, U.S. House committee on the Public Lands, 63rd Cong., 1st Sess. (Washington, D.C., 1913), p. 129. Badè's telegram to Edward Taylor of the Committee is reproduced on p. 128 of the hearings.

the Committee that "a body of gentlemen . . . have for ten years constantly fought this project from the highest motives, the leader of them being John Muir."[14] Whitman testified nearly four hours before the Committee, to no avail since "most of the members had firmly made up their minds in advance," as his friend, G. Frederick Schwartz, later wrote Colby.[15] San Francisco's gallery of administration supporters included the secretaries of Agriculture and Interior; the Chief Forester, Henry Graves; the directors of the Geological Survey and the Reclamation Service; and Gifford Pinchot. A star witness was William Denman, a San Francisco judge and charter member of the Sierra Club, who had once accompanied a Colby-led high trip through the Hetch Hetchy. His testimony that the action of the Sierra Club was not in "perfect candor" and that the Club was not united on the preservation of Hetch Hetchy tended to neutralize the Club's influence during the hearings.[16]

II

An odd event now occurred—an event which might have resulted in a successful conclusion of the Hetch Hetchy hearings for the preservationists. On the fourth day of the House hearings, Chairman Scott Ferris received a wire from a Mr. Eugene J. Sullivan who signed himself "President, Sierra Blue Lakes Water and Power Company."[17] In the telegram he claimed that city officials were deceiving the committee as they had already deceived the Advisory Board and engineer Freeman. He asked time to complete his data and submit proof of his allegation. Subsequently Sullivan came to Washington after the Committee agreed to postpone its deliberations over the July 4th holiday and testified that his company, with rights on the Mokelumne River, could easily supply San Francisco with all the water it needed. However, Sullivan so conducted himself before the committee that he was embarrassed and quite discredited in the end. His consulting engineer, a Mr. Taggart Aston, who had provided much of the data used by Sullivan, disassociated himself from his former employer and "acting as a disinterested public citizen" made available to E. T. Parsons his file of data and his knowledge about a "suppressed" report. The report referred to was the Bartel-Manson report on the Mokelumne River (see p. 131), which gave much higher estimates of daily runoff figures than those used by the Army Engineers' consultant and which also contained the statement that this source was "sufficient to meet the demands of the region around the Bay of

[14] *Ibid.,* p. 170.
[15] Schwartz, Brookline, Mass., to Colby, San Francisco, July 19, 1913, SCA.
[16] *Hetch Hetchy Dam Site, op. cit.,* p. 242.
[17] *Ibid.,* p. 179.

San Francisco when reinforced with a full development of Lake Eleanor."[18]

Aston, upon discovery of this report, which he describes in his letter to the Senate Committee, wrote to H. H. Wadsworth, consulting engineer to the Advisory Board, asking him if he had ever seen or heard of the Bartel report. Wadsworth replied that this report did not appear among the list of those supplied by the city officials, although he had talked to Bartel, Manson's assistant, and secured from him "considerable data" and "deductions therefrom." It was on the basis of this evidence that Aston attempted to get the Congressional committees to reopen the case.

On July 15, 1913, Edward Parsons mailed photographic copies of the "suppressed" report and Aston correspondence to Robert Underwood Johnson, Allen Chamberlain, and Edmund Whitman along with the following observation: "I have gone through this correspondence carefully, and have seen the originals of the replies received by Mr. Aston from Washington and from Mr. Wadsworth, which are correctly copied in the copies attached hereto. . . . The reports embodied in the Freeman presentation of the City's case, and mentioned in the report of the Army Board prepared by Mr. Wadsworth, made no mention of this Bartel-Manson report or its findings, but were based on a report made by Mr. Grunsky. It seems that this entire data should be furnished to some Senator, possibly the Honorable Reed Smoot, who has declared himself against the passage of this bill, as it would undoubtedly give him powerful ammunition not only in preventing the passage of the bill but in demanding a complete investigation as to the character of the evidence furnished to the Army Board, from which alone they were able to draw their conclusions, and this for the reason that if their conclusions are founded on incomplete and erroneous evidence, it follows that not only their conclusions but the dictum of public officials who have based their views on those conclusions should be discounted and that our public officials and both Senate and House of Representatives should have the entire truth of this matter before final action. I believe, with this data in hand to show, that such papers as the Transcript, the Springfield Republican, the New York Tribune and Post would make a pretty full exposition and demand pretty forcibly an investigation of these charges so apparently significant and so evidently made in good faith by Mr. Aston."[19]

Parsons' letter to his Eastern friends produced immediate results in the public press. Chamberlain wrote at the end of July that the *Boston Transcript* had used his story on the "suppressed" report.[20] But, although many newspapers—among them the *New York Times, Philadelphia Inquirer, Seattle Post*

[18] Taggart Aston, San Francisco to George E. Chamberlain, Chairman, Senate Public Lands Committee, Washington, D.C., July 16, 1913, copy, SCA.

[19] Parsons, San Francisco, to Johnson, New York, Chamberlain and Whitman, Boston, July 15, 1913, copy, SCA.

[20] Chamberlain, Lakeport, N.H., to Parsons, San Francisco, July 29, 1913, SCA. See *Boston Transcript,* July 26, 1913, for story and editorial.

158

Intelligencer—were eager to hit the Wilson administration and support the preservationists (often for reasons of their own), the tactics did not work on the House Committee. Scott Ferris wrote to Parsons that the hearings were closed on July 7 and that the Committee was considering the various features of the bill, "with a view to coming to some final determination."[21] He advised Parsons to correspond with the Senate Committee.

Less than a month later the House passed the Hetch Hetchy bill by 183 to 43.[22] Although the preservationists had a number of friends on the floor of Congress, among them Representative Halver Steenerson of Minnesota, H. R. 7207 had become an "administration bill" and was endorsed by California's House delegation. This proved too powerful a combination to defeat. Parsons, who later complimented Steenerson on his "enlightened attitude" and the "staunch fight" he put up "for the people who own the parks," commented on California's representatives: "I have . . . noted in this debate with much regret, the inaccuracies as to facts of statements made by our own Representatives. . . . I will not attempt to assign any reasons for the attitude taken by our Representatives. However the statements made by Mr. Church and similar statements made by others of our Representatives must of course be founded on lack of information, or else are intentional misstatements of the truth."[23]

The leaders of the Sierra Club were not discouraged, however. Muir wrote Johnson a few days after the House passage, "we have to strike hard and very fast until the close of the special session."[24] And strike hard they did. Both the California and Eastern branches of the Society issued leaflets and circulars for broadcast distribution to newspapers and influential individuals. These were printed in large lots of 5,000 to 20,000 and were designed to be easily used by editorial writers or for fillers.[25] As Parsons said to Colby, ". . . I believe that counting on the public is the only thing at the present time, and I fully believe that we ought to send out the general pamphlet to the public, at least to most of Who is Who."[26]

"Circular no. 7" of the Society for the Preservation of National Parks is typical of those sent out by the California Branch. A sample letter and a list of senators decorates its cover page. Inside pages are devoted to a sketch map of the Yosemite Park showing how "more than one-half the entire national park would be destroyed as a public playground"—an allusion to the closing off of the upper watersheds from the public in order to maintain a pure water supply below—to discussions of the various arguments against the flooding of Hetch Hetchy and a description of the valley by Muir.

This propaganda was distributed very widely. On September

[21] Ferris, Washington, D. C., to Parsons, San Francisco, July 30, 1913, SCA.

[22] *Congressional Record*, 63rd Cong., 2nd Sess., vol. 50, pt. 5 (September 3, 1913), p. 4151. 194 did not vote and 9 answered "present."

[23] Parsons, San Francisco, to Steenerson, Washington, D.C., September 29, 1913, copy, SCA.

[24] Muir, Martinez, to Johnson, New York, September 12, 1913, *Johnson Papers*, box 7, folder no. 480.

[25] Parsons, Seattle, to Colby, San Francisco, August 1, 1913, *Johnson Papers*, box 8, folder no. 1102.

[26] *Loc. cit.* See also Whitman, Boston, to Colby, San Francisco, August 11, 1913, SCA, in which he states the Eastern branch sent out pamphlet to every member of Congress and to about 1,000 newspapers throughout the United States. The pamphlet was titled, "The Truth about Hetch Hetchy."

14 Muir wired Johnson that 500 new circulars had been sent out and that 5,000 would soon be ready.[27] The following day he sent Johnson a hundred of the 1909 pamphlets and informed his New York friend that he could have as many more as he needed.[28] The evidence is fairly conclusive that the Society, composed as we have seen of those Sierra Club members dedicated to Hetch Hetchy's preservation, carried the brunt of the battle and that most of the Club members played only a small part—an occasional financial contribution or a letter to a Congressman. Two letters from Muir indicate that, in his opinion, the Sierra Club was not helping enough. In response to urging from Johnson that he get the societies to work, Muir replied in a note with a "confidential" written across the top of the page: "I hope to get more Californian help soon. Have just discovered that both Col [by] and P[arsons] have carefully concealed all our circulars from California—not even sending copies to our Sierra Club members, fearing, I suppose the S.F. press and damage to their business and profession. This is natural and perhaps reasonable enough. Mr. C's. employer [Judge Curtis Lindley] is or has been the city's leading lawyer in H.H. affairs and Mrs. C. is President of the Alameda County Women's Club, and, of course, keeps quiet. . . . Of course, I'll do what I can without open assistance of our Club members who may be dimly on our side."[29]

In the light of what we know of both Colby's and Parsons' untiring efforts and personal sacrifices on behalf of Hetch Hetchy's preservation, Muir's letter is difficult to understand. Perhaps his coworkers' pessimism, when all the facts seemed to point to bitter defeat, annoyed the usually optimistic Muir. Perhaps he was concerned because more Club members did not share the burden of the strenuous campaign—at least not with the same eagerness as the inner circle of comrades. Certainly the reports that Watrous and Johnson sent to Muir on the Senate Public Lands Committee hearing would be enough to discourage the most sanguine. Watrous wrote the day after the hearing:

Mr. [Robert Underwood] Johnson has just been into the American Civic Association on his way to make some calls, including one at the White House, where he has an engagement to see the President. . . . He says he is tired with the strain of work he has been doing for a week, and particularly of yesterday. . . .

I wired to Mr. [E. T.] Parsons that we went into the fight knowing exactly what the outcome would be, but that we made our fight. I say that we knew, and I believe that all of us felt as soon as the Committee meeting was opened, that it was only a formality that they were opening to us to present a case, and that when the vote came it would be a vote practically unanimous, if not unanimous, in favor of ordering the bill passed on to the Senate with their approval.

[27] Muir, Martinez, to Johnson, New York, September 14, 1913, *Johnson Papers,* box 7, folder no. 1073.

[28] Muir, Martinez, to Johnson, New York, September 15, 1913, *Johnson Papers,* box 7, folder no. 481.

[29] Muir, Martinez, to Johnson, New York, September 25, 1913, *Johnson Papers,* box 7, folder no. 482.

They had, in the Senate Committee, been placing their reliance for information on the hearings before the House, and when the question arose as to how extended the hearing might be yesterday, some of the Senators said that they would object to the introduction of new evidence, papers, pictures, etc., and they objected to having a stenographic report made. We were told that we might present arguments, and with that understanding, and a certain allowance of time, the hearings started in.

Mr. Johnson introduced as the first speaker, Mr. Herbert Parsons [a member of the Public Lands Committee during the 1909 hearings] who made an admirable address and confined his talk particularly to making it clear that to transform the floor of the Hetch Hetchy into a lake, would not contribute to the beauty of the Yosemite Park. He said that there were plenty of lakes there; rock bound lakes, and he showed pictures of them, and that there would be no new feature introduced by making a lake in the Hetch Hetchy. It was one of the best statements on that particular point that I have heard. Then, Mr. Whitman made his statement, and he was asked a good many questions. He is completely informed, and always makes a strong showing. Then, it was time to adjourn for luncheon. After we started in, Mr. Johnson asked that I be allowed a few minutes, and I made a short statement, reading to the Committee a letter that Mr. McFarland had addressed to me with the request that it be read. I have made copies of the statement that he wanted read, and am giving you one herewith. You will agree that it is an excellent and very practical statement, I am sure.

Then, Mr. Johnson came on and he made his talk, referring to the public opinion that has been developed and to the newspaper editorials from all parts of the country. The committee was rather inclined to ask a good many questions of Mr. Johnson, and asked a good many in particular about the man Sullivan, who has been quoted. I was sorry that any reference to him was made, because he proved before the House Committee, at least, to be unprepared to substantiate the first statement he had made, and I rather regretted that he should have been made to appear as an authority we were quoting at all in any of the work we have been doing. So far as we have been concerned I have paid no attention to him. That completed our four talks. One of the irrigation men from Modesto made a long talk and said that the giving of the water to San Francisco would put them out of business, but of course so far as he was concerned, it was simply a question of which should have the water, San Francisco or the irrigation people. Personally, I would rather see it go to the irrigation interests. But the Committee was then ready to take a vote, and being anxious to do so, as it was getting to be six o'clock, the motion was made that the bill as it came from the House be approved for passage, and it was unanimously carried.

There was just a quorum present in the morning, although they were not there during the entire day, but it was a working quorum, as I understand it, particularly as one member at least had given the Chairman his proxy. Senator Smoot was not there; in fact, there was no one on the Committee to lend a voice in favor of our stand, or of the stand of the people who want the Hetch Hetchy preserved. It is very apparent that it has been made a bill that is to go through, and as we see it, there is only one way that it can be prevented, and that is by finding some one powerful man who has the power to say that it shall not pass. Who that man is we don't know, and I don't suppose you know.

It is, of course, very disappointing to see things proceed as they have, but it seems to be San Francisco's day, and my own feeling is that the bill will be passed by the Senate, and I rather imagine that it will be signed by the President. Of course it marks a step backwards in our National Parks development, but the friends of the Hetch Hetchy have worked loyally and done their best. Who could do more? I could wish that there might have been a presentation of our side of the case before the House Committee, where the matter was thrashed out more fully, although my feeling is that from the start, it has been intended that it should go through, and that it would go through whether or no.[30]

The burden of proof before the Senate Committee on Public Lands fell to Johnson, Whitman, Watrous, and Herbert Parsons—all Easterners. Johnson's report of how the preservationists were received is revealing: "Of course we were discouraged by the action of the Senate Committee . . . but I have not given up the fight. I am starting it on another line. Senator Norris of Nebraska said he had received 'hundreds of letters' from constitutents asking him to save the Valley. So I presume others have. Before I left Washington I had a hurried interview with the President. All he said was that he understood only a portion of the Valley was to be taken (one of their lies!). I then left with him about 60 or 70 clippings on our side asking him to have his Secretary tell him the tone and temper of them and telling him they were almost all strongly against the scheme."[31]

Johnson's autobiography, published ten years after the event, refers to the fact that the Senate Committee was unwilling to give the preservationists an official hearing and objected to a stenographic report. According to Johnson, he obtained permission to have it reported "on my own personal account and consented to share the expense" with the opponents. "When the report of my testimony came to me it was so extremely bad that I protested to the stenographers against it. I was glad it was a private and not an official record. One may judge of my astonishment, when the debate in the Senate in December took place, to find that the Committee had *officially* issued this record of the hearing, and moreover, without giving me an opportunity to correct the glaring errors in my testimony, some of which represented me as saying diametrically the opposite of what I had said!"[32]

Johnson was not happy about paying $90 for the stenographic report and hoped that Muir was collecting contributions for "the cause" through the Society's circulars, although he thought he would be able to arrange "to relieve you of part of my Washington expenses."[33]

The Senate questioning of Johnson in regard to Sullivan obviously upset the *Century* editor. He complained to Muir that he had not been sufficiently warned about the man, and ended, "Oh, for *one Senator* who is thoroughly with us."[34] The prestige of the nature lovers had indeed reached a low ebb in 1913, in the 63rd Congress, compared to the relative esteem they had ac-

[30] Richard Watrous, Washington, D.C., to Muir, Martinez, September 25, 1913, SCA.

[31] Johnson, New York, to Muir, Martinez, September 26, 1913, SCA.

[32] Robert Underwood Johnson, in his *Remembered Yesterdays*, pp. 311–312. The Senate hearing was published and is available in the *Johnson Papers*, box 12, folder no. 851.

[33] Johnson, New York, to Muir, Martinez, September 26, 1913, SCA.

[34] *Loc. cit.*

quired in their first Congressional appearance of 1908 and 1909.

III

After the disheartening experiences in the Congressional committees, the preservationists rallied for the "last stand" on the floor of the Senate. Johnson reported to Muir that he had a plan. He realized the political dilemma that President Wilson must face if the Hetch Hetchy bill were presented for his signature. He hoped he could reach Wilson's close advisers who would convince him that it would be political suicide for the bill to be passed and to reach his desk for signature. "If he signs it, he will do so in the face of the opposition of the press and the public," wrote Johnson, "If he doesn't, he must face opposition in California, and of course they will use this to the utmost."[35] It would be to Wilson's advantage, therefore, to see that the bill was defeated or, at least, held over to the second session.

In addition to attempting to enlist the aid of Wilson's advisers Johnson was prepared to do more. In October he met with several of his New York friends, and out of this meeting, apparently at the suggestion of Henry Fairfield Osborn, was born the National Committee for the Preservation of Yosemite National Park.[36] Johnson became its chairman and Edward Hagaman Hall, Secretary of the American Scenic and Historic Preservation Society, its secretary and treasurer. An intensive campaign for financial support and membership succeeded in enlisting the names of many prominent people throughout the United States.[37] E. T. Parsons, the Secretary of the Society for the Preservation of National Parks, in San Francisco, assisted the new national committee by sending the last 2,000 copies of its circular to Hall with the advice that 2,000 copies of a new edition would soon be forthcoming.[38] Parsons also coöperated with the new committee by sending out letters to persons "on the Coast who have co-operated so far with us in this field."[39] Five days later Parsons was able to mail copies of the newly revised Hetch Hetchy pamphlet "on the fast express train" to Hall's New York office. He also enclosed a list of nominations for membership in the National Committee. Parsons was full of optimism. "We continually hear of encouraging things from many directions and I feel sure that the great work you are planning to do with your National Committee, and your great meeting of protest, can not fail to have very great weight in the final outcome of the matter."[40]

There may have been many reasons for Johnson's conviction

[35] Loc. cit.
[36] Johnson, New York, to Hall, New York, October 20, 1913, copy, Johnson Papers, box 1, folder no. 11.
[37] Membership lists may be found in the Johnson Papers, box 6, folder no. 500.
[38] Parsons, San Francisco, to Hall, New York, October 18, 1913, copy, SCA.
[39] Loc. cit.
[40] Parsons, San Francisco, to Hall, New York, October 23, 1913, copy, SCA.

that he should take the leadership of the new National Committee. He was, of course, familiar with the reasons for setting aside the Yosemite National Park in the first place, and also his warm friendship and admiration for John Muir doubtless inspired him to action. He may have felt further that the difficult position of the Sierra Club in the campaign, with a minority group that still resisted any effort to commit the Club fully, weakened any bargaining power it might have had in conducting and coördinating a last-ditch national publicity program.

Whatever the reasons, it was the National Committee, according to Muir, that inspired the Sierra Club to renewed efforts on behalf of the Valley's preservation. In the middle of October, Muir announced to Johnson, "Our Sierra Club thoroughly awakened at last."[41] And by the end of the month he enthusiastically reported to Johnson: "We held a Sierra Club meeting last Saturday, passed resolutions and fanned each other to a fierce white Hetch Hetchy heat. I particularly urged that we must get everybody to write to Senators and the President, keeping their letters flying all next month thick as storm snowflakes."[42]

The National Committee, following the lead of the Society for the Preservation of National Parks, issued two bulletins in October and November and circulated them widely.[43] But the Eastern preservationists were upset, as they had been at earlier Congressional meetings, because no Western representatives were in New York to participate in the planned protest meeting. Johnson, particularly, was sensitive about this and wired Muir early in November asking William F. Badè to be present. When he received no reply from Muir he addressed a letter to him on November 15; the letter shows how intense Johnson felt about the campaign: "I have the greatest difficulty in getting a reply to my telegrams to you. . . . I telegraphed to Parsons November 6, and have this morning a reply from him, saying that you have not communicated with him. I am very sorry for this because we need Badè badly. Do keep in touch with each other. You have no idea how absorbed I am in this fight. We are trying hard to raise money and to make a noise. We shall have sent out nearly ten thousand circulars within the present fortnight and are still at work. Our second bulletin will be a broadside. I dislike to take the time to write you details, which ought to be given to the canvass. . . . It is absurd for us to be carrying on the campaign without the help of a Californian here. Having said the above, may I express my fear that my message to you was intercepted or purposely delayed. I believe the enemy is not above doing tricks of this kind. Please let me know when you got my message of November 4."[44]

Parsons later cleared up this temporary lapse in communi-

[41] Muir, Martinez, to Johnson, New York, October 16, 1913, *Johnson Papers*, box 7, folder no. 485.

[42] Muir, Martinez, to Johnson, New York, October 27, 1913, *Johnson Papers*, box 7, folder no. 487.

[43] *Bulletin no. 1* is reprinted in the *Congressional Record*, 63rd Cong., 1st Sess., vol. 50, pt. 6 (November 10, 1913), pp. 5875–5876. There are copies of both *Bulletins* in the *Johnson Papers* and *Farquhar Papers*.

[44] Johnson, New York, to Muir, Martinez, November 7, 1913, copy, *Johnson Papers*, box 1, folder no. 16.

cation, but unfortunately Badè was not able to be in New York because of teaching commitments in Berkeley.[45]

IV

In December, Senate floor debate raged to a climax and finally at midnight on December 6, the preservationists went down to defeat, 43 to 25. Richard Watrous, Secretary of the American Civic Association, provides valuable insight into attitudes and actions during these last days in a post-mortem letter written to his chief.

. . .

During the month of November much work was kept up by the Sierra Club, by the newly organized National Committee under the direction of Robert Underwood Johnson and by our office in getting out circular matter and good news articles. I think I told you that one of the good uses we made of our new mailing list was to get out hurriedly copies of an admirable address by Congressman Towner on the subject. I found out that five thousand copies of this speech could be obtained at quite a low price and I asked the cooperation of the Sierra Club and the Scenic Society of New York with us to have that number printed. It had appeared in the [*Congressional*] *Record* of November 20th and we were able to have them delivered to us by November 27th. They went out in the franked envelopes of Representative Towner.

The real fight came on with the beginning of the regular session, December 1st. It had been growing on me right along that really little impression was being made on the Senators from the *Scenic* standpoint. That, however, is not due to the fact that a most determined fight was not being made to create that kind of an impression. It was wonderful the amount of stuff that was sent out. But, of course, the senators are loaded down with printed matter all the time and they have been a very tired lot of men at the best. Then, too, I could not forget at all the feeling that the matter had an administration stamp on it, at least so far as receiving the approval of the Democratic House caucus which meant also the Democratic Senate, and with the o.k. of such men as Underwood whose interest was secured by Secretary Lane. I wrote San Francisco and New York that my feeling was if the vote were taken on the issue as between scenic beauty and San Francisco, San Francisco would win easily. We could not avoid it and I am sure you would have felt as I felt if you had been here on the ground and could have seen the situation.

The appearance, however, at a late day, of a new group of irrigationists did put a different aspect on the situation. If they had been on the ground earlier and had had time to present the case to the House and Senate hearings, I think no action would have been taken. You remember, I wrote you in June that there had been some kind of an agreement between the Irrigationists and San Francisco, whereby the San Francisco people had promised the Turlock-Modesto people an amount of water which *at that time* the representatives accepted and thereupon they ceased their opposition. It developed during the month following that those representatives entered into an arrangement which did not meet with the approval of the great body of the irrigationists and when they woke up to the situation it was with the determination to fight harder than ever to save the water for their use. Thus, it was that their fight during the big week in

[45] Parsons, Berkeley, to Johnson, New York, November 15, 1913, *Johnson Papers*, box 8, folder no. 1126. Parsons explained that after he had received Johnson's telegram he had discussed it with Muir and that Muir had said he would wire when he got home that night. Parsons later learned that Muir had forgotten to wire Johnson, but he did nothing further about it because by that time Johnson had been informed by letter. (Parsons, Berkeley, to Johnson, New York, December 31, 1913, *Johnson Papers,* box 8, folder no. 588.)

December was an important phase of the matter. I did not feel that we could turn in and work directly with them along those lines, because our fight has been sharply outlined from the beginning as, namely, a fight for the preservation of the Hetch Hetchy valley on the principle that as a great scenic wonder it should be preserved and as a part of the National park it should be kept free from commercial spoliation. Of course, we could watch with great approval and satisfaction any dent they could make in the enemies' lines, and they did make a dent, although, as the vote showed, not nearly deep enough to prevent the passage of the bill, because in the vote practically all the Democrats voted for it and a few Republicans.[46]

McFarland had been seriously ill during the late summer and fall of 1913 and not able to take as active a part in the Hetch Hetchy campaign as he wished. However, Watrous, in Washington, wrote McFarland that the value of their organization was in keeping "the others advised as to just what was going on." In his opinion, ". . . if our San Francisco friends, and also the New York and Boston ones, could have been more adequately represented at the hearing before the House in June and July the matter might not have gotten such headway. Although when you get down to it, it was an almost impossible proposition they had to beat, with the line up of support beginning with Secretary Lane and enforced with the support of Secretary Houston, Forester Graves, and other Bureau heads with the practical endorsement of the Democratic Caucus which allowed that it might be considered and with the backing of such big leaders as Underwood. . . . Of course I felt during November, that while we ought to give all attention possible to [Hetch Hetchy], we could not afford to let it overlap our other work. . . . We can all have the satisfaction of knowing that we have made a vigorous fight and along fine, high lines."[47]

Watrous singled out a "miserable statement" in *Harper's Weekly*, asking McFarland if he had seen it, and noting that it described the "zealous" friends of scenery as "consciously or unconsciously . . . being used by interested individuals and corporations in the fight against San Francisco." Norman Hapgood, first as editor of *Collier's* and later of *Harper's Weekly*, continued to exploit the Gifford Pinchot line as Watrous noted in this letter. Watrous closes, "While it is not pleasant to lose out or to give up the fight, is not the present situation one in which we must look things in the face and say the 'end has come,' at least on this particular fight? . . . I guess you know that I have been as zealous as anyone in the fight and so far as you and I are concerned we have overworked in the matter, possibly to our own weariness and at some sacrifice to the other interests of the Association."[48]

McFarland, in forwarding Watrous' letter to Colby, expressed the "forlorn hope" that Watrous might gain a "five-

[46] Watrous, Washington, D.C., to McFarland, Harrisburg, Pa., December 15, 1913, original in SCA.
[47] *Loc. cit.*
[48] *Loc. cit.*

minute interview" with the President: "We believe [the President] will sign the bill because the truth has not reached him. We believe that Pinchot is the responsible man and that the wonderfully efficient promotion of the San Francisco schemers has created the clamor. . . . One thing is certain: If we are beaten we are beaten after a fight against tremendous odds."[49]

The thirteen days between the passage of the Raker bill by the Senate and President Wilson's signature were days of great anxiety for Muir and Johnson as "it had been credibly reported that President Wilson would veto the bill. . . ."[50] But on the day following McFarland's "forlorn hope" letter to Colby, Wilson—although recognizing the justice in the arguments of the preservationists—could not ignore the dictates of his party and his officials in the cabinet. In a very real sense he was committed to signing the bill and this he did on December 19, 1913.

McFarland told Colby that "at least President Wilson's message . . . freed us from the slanders of the San Francisco promoters." Once again he placed the blame on his ex-friend, Pinchot: "It seems quite evident that he and the Forest Service were the final determining causes. . . . It has been a good fight, and you and your friends in San Francisco and in California have surely done nobly in the public interest. I wish we could have done more in the east; yet I have had the feeling from the moment that Mr. Lane was put into the cabinet that we were absolutely lost, because the San Francisco people had operated so cunningly as to get political influence at the right spot. It is pretty hard to go to the President and say anything in direct criticism of one of his cabinet officers."[51]

Harold Bradley, who was many years later to be President of the Sierra Club, summed up the preservationists' position, as a young professor at the University of Wisconsin, in a letter to Norman Hapgood. "What we sentimentalists . . . desired and fought for was a fuller examination of conditions, a more exact collection of data and estimates, not only on the sources shown by the Army Board to be adequate, but on those which have been suggested in addition. What we inexact dreamers have demanded is a really adequate canvass of facts obtainable at some pains and expense and time so that a final judgment of the case might represent a proper weighing of the economic value of playground areas over against the economic value of their conversion into municipal assets. . . . We have preferred not to establish a precedent which will inevitably be used against the integrity of our already scant Park areas. You on the other hand—you men of cold analytical temperament, trained to be exact and study exact conditions, unemotional, knowing just what you are

[49] McFarland, Harrisburg, Pa., to Colby, San Francisco, December 18, 1913, SCA.

[50] Johnson, *Remembered Yesterdays*, p. 313.

[51] McFarland, Harrisburg, Pa., to Colby, San Francisco, December 20, 1913, SCA.

doing—you desire to turn over the Park areas on the advice of a few prominent men, like Pinchot, and to do it as expeditiously as possible. It is not necessary for you to check up on the facts—these men are persuaded that it is all right; isn't that enough? Why investigate further? Why look over the facts? Why even subject the statements of these men to analysis? That would be sentimental; it would indicate that you easily went up in the air; 'it would suggest that you did not know what you were doing. How indeed shall we explain the fact that a fierce agitation all over the country is kept up against a measure which has had the support of Gifford Pinchot.' Why it's only a crowd of sentimentalists up in the air. Pinchot himself will say so.''[52]

"Muir was greatly cast down," Johnson reported, "but he was also relieved" that the end had come. To his friend, Vernon Kellogg, at Stanford University, Muir wrote: "As to the loss of the Sierra Park Valley it's hard to bear. The destruction of the charming groves and gardens, the finest in all California, goes to my heart. But in spite of Satan & Co. some sort of compensation must surely come out of this dark damn-dam-damnation.''[53]

And to another friend he wrote, "I'm glad the fight for the Tuolumne Yosemite is finished. . . . Am now writing on Alaska. A fine change from faithless politics to crystal ice and snow.''[54]

To his daughter, Helen, Muir wrote that he was "somewhat run down for want of exercise, and exhausting work and worry.''[55] Actually he was seriously ill with an infected right lung. On Christmas Eve, 1914, Muir died, and the Sierra Club lost the guiding hand of the man who had been its president for the first twenty-two years. If the loss of Hetch Hetchy did not kill Muir (as he had once suggested to Helen it would), it may well have hastened the end for the "Grand Old Tramp" of the Sierra.

v

The Sierra Club learned important lessons from its Hetch Hetchy experience. Its younger leaders—men like William Colby, William Badè, and Joseph N. LeConte—came out of the campaign much wiser politically than they had entered it. They had all participated actively, if sometimes behind the scenes, in local and national efforts to stem San Francisco's invasion of a national park and they were thoroughly familiar with the requirements of political maneuvering. The campaign proved to the Sierra Club and to the preservationists generally that there was need for greater coördination in preserving the wilderness

[52] Harold Bradley, Madison, Wis., to Norman Hapgood, New York, December 7, 1913, copy, SCA.

[53] Muir, Martinez, to Kellogg, Palo Alto, December 27, 1913, Colby Papers, Bancroft Library, University of California, Berkeley.

[54] Johnson, Remembered Yesterdays, p. 313.

[55] Quoted in Wolfe, op. cit., p. 341.

and natural scenic areas of America. There was need, too, for national as well as local organization and initiative.

Most important of all, the importance and influence of the Sierra Club in conservation matters was firmly established by the Hetch Hetchy controversy and was to lead to advisory and policy-making roles in future decisions involving the public domain—particularly under the leadership of the first director of the National Park Service, Stephen T. Mather, who had become a Sierra Club member in 1904. The Hetch Hetchy campaign established permanently the ideals for which the Club was originally established. The majority of its directors and two-thirds of its members never wavered from that policy, and in so doing, they strengthened the ideologies that have served to elevate the Sierra Club to nationwide prominence with more than 27,000 members in the 1960's.

Appendix A

Agreement of Association

We, the undersigned, hereby associate ourselves together for the purpose of forming a Corporation under the laws of the State of California, to be known as the Sierra Club. Said Corporation shall not be for the purpose of pecuniary profit, but shall be for the purpose of exploring, enjoying and rendering accessible the mountain regions of the Pacific Coast, and to enlist the support and co-operation of the people and the government in preserving the forests and other features of the Sierra Nevada Mountains, and for such other purposes as may be set forth in the Articles of Incorporation to be formed. The principal place of business of Said Corporation shall be at the City and County of San Francisco, State of California.

Dated at San Francisco, California, June 4th, 1892. Here follows the list of Charter Members.*

Alvord, William   Bank of California, San Francisco
Anderson, Prof. M. B.   Stanford University, Palo Alto
Armes, William D.   University of California, Berkeley
Babcock, William   306 California St., San Francisco
Bailey, Charles A.   20 Montgomery St., San Francisco
Bartlett, L. de F.   1233 Charles St., Alameda
Bayley, George B.   210 Davis St., San Francisco
Beatty, Hon. William H.   305 Larkin St., San Francisco
Behr, H. C.   1212 Jackson St., San Francisco
Behr, H. H.   California Academy of Sciences, San Francisco
Belcher, W. C.   Palace Hotel, San Francisco
Belding, L.   Stockton
Bentley, William R.   Seattle, Washington

Berry, T. B.   120 Sutter St., San Francisco
Bioletti, F. T.   University of California, Berkeley
Blake, E. T.   University of California, Berkeley
Blum, Max   217 Sansome St., San Francisco
Blum, Sanford   University of California, Berkeley
Boalt, John H.   Stock Exchange Building, San Francisco
Booth, Franklin   University of California, Berkeley
Bradley, Prof. C. B.   University of California, Berkeley
Branner, Prof. John C.   Stanford University, Palo Alto
Brandegree, T. S.   California Academy of Sciences, San Francisco
Brooks, Elisha   1725 Sutter St., San Francisco
Bryant, Walter E.   California Academy of Sciences, San Francisco
Bucknall, Dr. G. J.   Sutter St. and Grant Ave., San Francisco
Buelow, Dr. F. von   Eleventh and Mission Sts., San Francisco
Bunker, Dr. R. E.   802 Kearny St., San Francisco
Bunnell, James S.   New Montgomery and Mission Sts., San Francisco

Campbell, D. Y.   119 Bush St., San Francisco
Campbell, Eliza C.   1120 Twelfth St., Oakland
Carrigan, William L.   17–19 Beale St., San Francisco
Carroll, A. W. de la Cour   Lone Pine, Inyo County
Chambers, Samuel A.   Berkeley
Chapman, R. H.   U.S. Geological Survey, Berkeley
Chesnut, V. K.   University of California, Berkeley
Clark, Galen   Yosemite
Coleman, William T.   2516 Fillmore St., San Francisco
Christy, Prof. S. B.   University of California, Berkeley
Crocker, C. F.   Fourth and Townsend Sts., San Francisco
Curtis, Marvin   2024 Pine St., San Francisco

Davidson, Prof. Geo. U.S. Coast and Geodetic Survey, Appraisers' Building, San Francisco

Davis, Hon. Horace 41 First St., San Francisco

Davis, Dr. H. C. 131 Post St., San Francisco

Deering, F. P. 14 Sansome St., San Francisco

Denman, Will 2101 Webster St., San Francisco

D'Evelyn, Frederick W. 219 Geary St., San Francisco

Dingley, Charles L., Jr. 29 Stuart St., San Francisco

Doe, J. S. 46 Market St., San Francisco

Donohoe, J. A. Montgomery and Sacramento Sts., San Francisco

Douglas, T. B. 120 McAllister St., San Francisco

Douty, F. S. Fourth and Townsend Sts., San Francisco

Drew, E. R. 472 Twenty-fourth St., Oakland

Dwyer, J. J. 8 Montgomery St., San Francisco

Dyer, H. P. Lehi, Utah

Eckley, John A. Port Costa

Eckley, J. H. Post Costa

Eddy, H. H. University of California, Berkeley

Edwards, Prof. George C. University of California, Berkeley

Emeric, H. F. 621 Sansome St., San Francisco, California

Flagg, Prof. Isaac University of California, Berkeley

Foley, D. J. Turlock

Freeman, A. C. 609 Clay St., San Francisco

Gallaher, F. M. Santa Barbara

Gompertz, Miss Helen Berkeley

Goodman, T. H. Fourth and Townsend Sts., San Francisco

Greene, Prof. E. L. University of California, Berkeley

Gregory, Warren 206 Sansome St., San Francisco

Griffin, Prof. James O. Stanford University, Palo Alto

Hall, Wm. Hamm Mercantile Library Building, Golden Gate and Van Ness Avenues, San Francisco

Hallidie, A. S. 9 Fremont St., San Francisco

Harker, Charles G. 1909 Pine St., San Francisco

Harkness, Dr. H. W. California Academy of Sciences, San Francisco

Harrison, Hon. Ralph C. Larkin and McAllister Sts., San Francisco

HasBrouck, J. 609 Clay St., San Francisco

Haskell, Prof. M. W. University of California, Berkeley

Haymond, Edgar 101 Sansome St., San Francisco

Henry, W. H. 1221 Harrison St., Oakland

Heron, James New Montgomery and Mission Sts., San Francisco

Hesse, Prof. F. G. University of California, Berkeley

Hittell, Miss Katharine 808 Turk St., San Francisco

Hoffman, Dr. C. von 1014 Sutter St., San Francisco

Holder, Charles F. 1101 Pine St., San Francisco

Hooker, C. G. 917 Bush St., San Francisco

Hopkins, Timothy 19–20 Chronicle Building, San Francisco

Howard, Prof. George E. Stanford University, Palo Alto

Howard, John L. 132 Market St., San Francisco

Howard, Shafter 1206 Alice St., Oakland

Hurd, N. H. 328 Montgomery St., San Francisco

Hutchings, J. M. 112 St. Ann's Building, San Francisco

Hutchinson, James S. 1910 Howard St., San Francisco

Hutchinson, Joseph 130 Sansome St., San Francisco

Janin, Louis 211 Sansome St., San Francisco

Jenkins, Prof. Oliver P. Stanford University, Palo Alto

Jepson, W. L., Jr. University of California, Berkeley

Johnson, Willard D. U.S. Geological Survey, Berkeley

Jordan, Pres. D. S. Stanford University, Palo Alto

Keeler, Chas. A. California Academy of Sciences, San Francisco

Keep, Prof. Josiah Mills P.O., Alameda County

Keith, William 115 Kearny St., San Francisco

Kelly, Allan Occidental Hotel, San Francisco

Kerr, Mark Brickell 402 Front St., San Francisco

Kip, Lawrence 175–6 Crocker Building, San Francisco

Knox, Thomas R. 310 Pine St., San Francisco

Kower, Prof. Hermann University of California, Berkeley

Lawson, Prof. A. C. University of California, Berkeley

LeConte, Prof. Joseph University of California, Berkeley

Le Conte, Joseph N. University of California, Berkeley
Lemmon, Prof. J. G. 1015 Clay St., Oakland
Libby, Dorville 1 Flood Building, San Francisco
Loughridge, Prof. R. H. University of California, Berkeley
Lukens, Ed. G. 18 California St., San Francisco

MacEwan, P. A. California Academy of Sciences, San Francisco
MacNeil, H. L. Los Angeles
Magee, Thomas 20 Montgomery St., San Francisco
Marten, Dr. Arthur 903 Sutter St., San Francisco
Marx, Prof. Charles D. Stanford University, Palo Alto
McAllister, Elliott 328 Montgomery St., San Francisco
McChesney, Prof. J. B. 1364 Franklin St., Oakland
McKee, R. H. U.S. Geological Survey, Berkeley
McKisick, L. D. 319 Pine St., San Francisco
McLean, Rev. J. K. 520 Thirteenth St., Oakland
McLean, Dr. John T. Alameda
Mills, D. O. Mills Building, New York, N.Y.
Mills, Mrs. C. T. Mills College
Mills, James E. Copperopolis
Molera, E. J. 40 California St., San Francisco
Mosebach, F. C. 322 Montgomery St., San Francisco
Muir, John Martinez
Muir, Miss Wanda Martinez
Murdock, Charles A. 532 Clay Street, San Francisco
Myrick, M. H. 14 Sansome St., San Francisco

Naphtaly, Joseph 428 California St., San Francisco
Nash, H. C. Fourth and Townsend Sts., San Francisco
Nolte, William F. 110 Golden Gate Ave., San Francisco

O'Brien, Thomas V. 402 Montgomery St., San Francisco
Olney, Warren 101 Sansome St., San Francisco
Olney, Warren, Jr. 101 Sansome St., San Francisco
Oulton, George Hotel Richlieu, San Francisco

Page, Charles 316 California St., San Francisco
Palache, Charles University of California, Berkeley

Perkins, Hon. George C. 10 Market St., San Francisco
Pheby, Frederick S. 1275 Alice St., Oakland
Pheby, Thomas, Jr. 1275 Alice St., Oakland
Platt, H. G. 402 Montgomery St., San Francisco
Powell, H. A. 207 Sansome St., San Francisco
Price, R. M. University of California, Berkeley
Price, W. W. Stanford University, Palo Alto

Rankin, George A. 142 Sansome St., San Francisco
Regensburger, Dr. A. E. Stanford University, Palo Alto
Reinstein, J. B. 217 Sansome St., San Francisco
Richardson, Prof. George M. University of California, Berkeley
Richter, Dr. C. Max 614 Geary St., San Francisco
Rixford, G. P. 137 Montgomery St., San Francisco
Robinson, C. D. 506 Battery St., San Francisco
Rochemont, H. S. de 415 Montgomery St., San Francisco

Sanderson, George H. 122 Market St., San Francisco
Sanford, Prof. Fernando Stanford University, Palo Alto
Senger, Prof. J. H. University of California, Berkeley
Shinn, Charles H. University of California, Berkeley
Shortridge, Samuel M. Palace Hotel, San Francisco
Smith, Prof. E. E. Stanford University, Palo Alto
Smith, N. T. Fourth and Townsend Sts., San Francisco
Smith, W. C. 1173 Market St., Oakland
Solomons, Theodore 1707 Scott St., San Francisco
Sutro, Adolph Sutro Heights, San Francisco
Sutton, James University of California, Berkeley
Swift, Charles J. 216 Bush St., San Francisco

Taylor, Edward R. 207 Sansome St., San Francisco
Thayer, I. E. 204 Front St., San Francisco
Thayer, Dr. O. V. 218 Post St., San Francisco
Thomas, William 206 Sansome St., San Francisco
Tompkins, Gilbert Souther Farm, San Leandro

Van Dyke, E. C. University of California, Berkeley
Van Ness, T. C. 53 Nevada Block, San Francisco

Vecchi, Dr. Paolo de   610 Market St., San Francisco

Westervelt, Miss Bessie   206 Sansome St., San Francisco

Wheeler, Harold   Crocker Building, San Francisco

Wieland, Charles S.   1500 Larkin St., San Francisco

Wilkinson, Prof. C. T.   Institute for the Deaf, Dumb, and the Blind, Berkeley

Williams, George N.   4 Sutter St., San Francisco

Wright, Selden S.   71 Nevada Block, San Francisco

Appendix B

Articles of Incorporation

Know all men by these presents:

That we, the undersigned, a majority of whom are citizens and residents of the State of California, have this day voluntarily associated ourselves together for the purpose of forming a Corporation under the laws of the State of California. *And we hereby certify as follows, to wit:*

I.

That the name of said Corporation shall be the Sierra Club.

II.

That the said Association is made, and the said Corporation is formed, not for pecuniary profit.

III.

That the purposes for which this Corporation is formed are as follows, to wit: To explore, enjoy and render accessible the mountain regions of the Pacific Coast; to publish authentic information concerning them; to enlist the support and co-operation of the people and the government in preserving the forests and other natural features of the Sierra Nevada Mountains; to take, acquire, purchase, hold, sell and convey real and personal property, and to mortgage or pledge the same for the purpose of securing any indebtedness which the Corporation may incur, and to make and enter into any and all obligations, contracts, and agreements concerning or relating to the business or affairs of the Corporation, or the management of its property.

IV.

That the place where the principal business of said Corporation is to be transacted is the City and County of San Francisco, State of California.

V.

That the term for which said Corporation is to exist is fifty years from and after the date of its incorporation.

VI.

That the number of Directors or Trustees of said Corporation shall be nine (9), and that the names and residences of the Directors or Trustees who are appointed for the first year, to serve until the election and qualification of their successors, are as follows, to wit:

John Muir, Martinez, Cal.

Warren Olney, Oakland, Cal.

J. H. Senger, San Francisco, Cal.

Wm. D. Armes, Oakland, Cal.

David S. Jordan, Palo Alto, Cal.

R. M. Price, Berkeley, Cal.

Mark Brickell Kerr, Golden Gate, Alameda Co., Cal.

Willard D. Johnson, Berkeley, Cal.

John C. Branner, Palo Alto, Cal.

VII.

That the said Corporation has, and shall have, no capital stock. *And we further certify and declare:*

That the above-named Directors of the Corporation were duly elected Directors thereof by the members of said Corporation, at an election for Directors held at 101 Sansome Street, in the City and County of San Francisco, State of California, at eleven A.M., on this 4th day of June, 1892, and that a majority of the members of said Association and Corporation were present and voted at said election, and that at such election each of the said Directors received the votes of a majority of the members of the Corporation present at such election; as more fully appears from the certificate of the two Tellers of Election hereunto annexed and hereby referred to and made a part hereof.

In witness thereof, we have hereunto set our hands and seals this 4th day of June, A.D. 1892.

W. H. Beatty,	James O. Griffin,
Ralph C. Harrison,	Willard D. Johnson,
George C. Perkins,	Josiah Keep,
G. B. Bayley,	Hermann Kower,
John C. Branner,	Hubert P. Dyer,

W. H. Henry,	Charles A. Bailey,
L. deF. Bartlett,	C. D. Robinson
W. L. Jepson, Jr.,	C. B. Bradley,
Warren Olney,	Fred S. Pheby,
John Muir,	Charles G. Harker,
J. H. Senger,	R. M. Price,
William D. Armes,	Will Denman,
Mark Brickell Kerr,	Warren Gregory,
Dorville Libby,	

The certificate of the Secretary of State of the State of California was issued June 17th, 1892.

Appendix C

By-Laws
of
THE SIERRA CLUB
(Adopted June 4th, 1892)

The members of the Sierra Club, at a meeting this day held at 101 Sansome street, in the City and County of San Francisco, State of California, have adopted the following as the By-Laws of said Club:

ARTICLE I.
Government.

Section 1. The government and management of the Club shall be confided to nine of its members, to be known as the Board of Directors, from whom shall be elected a President, a First Vice-President, a Second Vice-President, a Secretary, a Treasurer and Corresponding Secretary.

Section 2. The Directors shall enter upon their term of office on the first Tuesday after their election, and shall hold office for one year and until their successors are elected and have qualified.

Sec. 3. The President, Vice-Presidents, Secretary, Corresponding Secretary and Treasurer shall be elected by the Board of Directors for the term of one year from the commencement of their office as Directors, and until their successors shall have been elected and qualified.

Sec. 4. If a vacancy shall occur in the office of President, Vice-Presidents, Secretary, Corresponding Secretary, or Treasurer, such vacancy shall be filled by the Board of Directors by the election of one of its own number; and in the event of a vacancy occurring in the office of Director, the Board shall elect a member from the Club at large to fill the same. The Di-

rectors shall likewise have the power to elect from the members of the Club at large a Director in the place of any one of their number who shall be absent from any three consecutive regular meetings of the Board of Directors. The officer or officers so elected shall hold office until the next annual meeting of the Club, and until the election and qualification of their successors.

ARTICLE II.
President.

Section 1. It shall be the duty of the President to preside at all the meetings of the Club and of the Directors; to see that the By-Laws and such rules and regulations as may be adopted by the Directors are rigidly enforced, and to report to the Board of Directors any infraction of the same; to call such meetings as are herein provided to be called by him; to have a general supervision over all the affairs of the Club; and at the annual meeting to make a report of the accounts and general concerns of the Club during the previous year.

Sec. 2. He shall be ex-officio a member of all the Standing Committees, which committees shall be nominated by him at the commencement of his term of office, and shall be presented to the Board of Directors for confirmation.

Sec. 3. The President and Secretary shall sign all checks, contracts, bonds, and other instruments in writing, which may have been first approved by the Board of Directors.

Sec. 4. The President shall have the casting vote at all meetings of the Club.

ARTICLE III.
Vice-Presidents.

Section 1. During the absence or disability of the President, the First Vice-President shall perform the duties and exercise the powers of the President. And during the absence or disability of both the President and First Vice-President, the Second Vice-President shall perform the duties and exercise the powers of the President.

Sec. 2. If both the President and the two Vice-Presidents shall be absent from any meeting of the Club, the Secretary shall call the meeting to order, and an acting President shall be elected by the meeting.

ARTICLE IV.
Secretary.

Section 1. The Secretary shall keep an exact record of the proceedings of the Club and of the Board of Directors; he shall have general charge of the books and accounts of the Club.

ARTICLE V.
Treasurer.

Section 1. It shall be the duty of the Treasurer to receive all moneys belonging to the Club, and to disburse the same, under the direction of the Board of Directors, upon checks or orders signed by the President and Secretary. He shall deposit the same, in the name of the Club, with the bank or banks designated by the Board of Directors. He shall submit a statement of his accounts at each monthly meeting of the Board of Directors, with proper vouchers, and settle the same whenever required.

Sec. 2. The funds of the Club shall not be loaned to any member.

ARTICLE VI.
Corresponding Secretary.

Section 1. It shall be the duty of the Corresponding Secretary to keep up communication, on behalf of the Club, with similar clubs in Europe and America. He shall make a report to the Club at its annual meeting of all matters of interest of which he has acquired knowledge through his correspondence with other clubs.

ARTICLE VII.
Standing Committees.

Section 1. The Standing Committees, to be appointed by the President, shall each consist of three members of the Board of Directors (except the Admission Committee, which shall consist of thirteen members, who shall be appointed from members outside the Board of Directors), and shall be as follows, viz: an Auditing Committee, a Committee on Publications and Communications, and an Admission Committee.

Sec. 2. It shall be the duty of the Auditing Committee to examine and audit all accounts and bills as often as the same shall be necessary. Before any accounts or bills shall be paid they must have been first approved by the chairman of the Auditing Committee.

Sec. 3. The Committee on Publications and Communications shall select such papers and documents as in their judgment will be of interest to the Club, to be read at its meetings and for publication.

Sec. 4. The Committee on Admissions shall consist of thirteen members, a majority of whom shall constitute a quorum. All candidates for admission to this Club shall have their names presented to the Secretary, who shall immediately refer the same to the Committee on Admissions, and said committee shall take action thereon as soon as possible thereafter. A majority of the committee shall constitute a quorum. The candidates for membership shall be voted for by ballot, and two adverse ballots shall be sufficient to prevent the admission of such person as a member.

Sec. 5. The committees mentioned in this Article shall be subject to the supervising power of the President, and to the authority of the Board of Directors. Placards containing a list of the Standing Committees, and of the persons composing the same, shall be placed in the office of the Club. All vacancies in the Standing Committees shall be filled by the President, and be submitted for confirmation to the Board of Directors.

Sec. 6. The members of said committees shall hold office for the term of one year from their appointment, unless otherwise ordered by the Board of Directors.

ARTICLE VIII.
Nomination of Officers.

Section 1. The Board of Directors shall, at least two weeks previous to the annual election, appoint from the members of the Club at large a committee of five, who shall submit a ticket of candidates to serve as Directors for the ensuing year; provided, however, that any five members of the Club may propose to the committee any member for Director. Such proposals shall be in writing, and every name so proposed shall be placed by the committee on every ticket, with nothing to distinguish it from the committee's nominations.

Sec. 2. All the names of nominees shall be posted in the office of the Club at least forty-eight hours prior to the opening of the election; and all of said tickets shall be printed under the direction of the Secretary, and at the expense of the Club.

ARTICLE IX.
Election of Officers.

Section 1. The annual election for Directors shall be held on the last Saturday of April in each year, and the voting shall be by ballot. No notice of such election, by advertisement or otherwise, shall be necessary.

Sec. 2. The polls shall be open at one o'clock P.M., and shall be kept open until six o'clock P.M., on the day of election. A plurality of votes shall elect.

Sec. 3. The Board of Directors shall appoint three Judges of Election from the members of the Club at large to supervise said election, at least one of whom shall be present the whole time the polls are open. The Judges of Election shall count the votes and report to the President in writing the number of votes cast for each candidate, and the names of those elected to serve as Directors; and the President shall thereupon notify in writing the members elected.

ARTICLE X.
Removal from Office.

Section 1. Any Director or member of the Committee on Admissions, or other officer of the Club, may be removed from office for good cause shown, by an affirmative vote of not less than three-fourths of the members present at a special meeting of the Club convoked for that purpose.

ARTICLE XI.
Meetings of the Club.

Section 1. The Club shall hold an annual meeting on the last Saturday of April of each year, at its office, at the hour of two o'clock in the afternoon. Special meetings may be called by order of the Directors. The Board shall, at the written request of fifteen members, call a special meeting of the Club. The Club shall also hold a general meeting on the last Saturday of October of each year, at the hour of two P.M.

Sec. 2. At any meeting of the Club twenty members shall constitute a quorum for the transaction of business, but a smaller number than a quorum may, in the absence of a quorum, continue and adjourn any meeting from time to time until a quorum shall be present, and until the business of the meeting shall have been accomplished.

Sec. 3. No notice of the annual meeting in April or of the general meeting in October need be given to render the proceedings taken thereat valid, but it shall be the duty of the Secretary to give notice by mail to each member of such meeting at least one week before the day fixed therefor. Notices of special meetings shall be given by the Secretary by written notice, specifying the time of the meeting and the object for which the same is called, at least five days prior to the day of meeting.

ARTICLE XII.
Meetings of the Board of Directors.

Section 1. The Board of Directors shall fix definite times for the regular meetings. Special meetings of the Board shall be held when called by the President. Notice of each special meeting shall be given by the Secretary by written notices, specifying the time of the meeting, at least one day prior thereto.

Sec. 2. A majority of the Directors shall be necessary and sufficient to constitute a quorum, and to form a Board for the transaction of business.

ARTICLE XIII.
Admission Fees and Dues.

Section 1. The admission fee shall be five dollars.

Sec. 2. The annual dues for all members residing in the city and county of San Francisco, and in the counties of Alameda, Solano, Napa, Sonoma, San Mateo, Santa Clara, Contra Costa and Marin, except undergraduates of colleges, shall be five dollars: for all other members and for undergraduates of colleges the annual dues shall be one dollar. Any member may commute his annual dues by the payment of fifty dollars. Such payment shall constitute the member paying it a life member, and exonerate him from the payment of all further annual dues.

Sec. 3. Any person may become an Honorary Member of the Club by a two-thirds vote of the members present at either the annual meeting in April or the general meeting in October. The vote shall be taken by ballot.

ARTICLE XIV.
Payments.

Section 1. The annual dues shall be payable in advance, at the Secretary's office, on the last Saturday of April of each year. If the payment of such dues be not made at that time, written notice of the delinquency shall thereupon be given by the Secretary to the delinquent member.

Sec. 2. If any such delinquent member shall not pay the amount of his delinquent dues within one month after the notice of delinquency has been given, as by Section 1 hereof provided, such member may thereupon be suspended or dismissed from the Club; but the Board of Directors, on good cause shown, may restore to membership any member who may have been suspended or dismissed for such default.

ARTICLE XV.
Resignation of Members.

Section 1. All resignations must be made in writing, addressed to the Board of Directors.

Sec. 2. No resignation of membership shall be accepted or shall take effect until all indebtedness to the Club shall have been paid by the resigning member.

APPENDIX D

SIGN THIS

To the Honorable, the Legislature of the State of California:

We respectfully petition your honorable body to oppose any movement for the purpose of receding the Yosemite Valley to the Federal Government.

The Yosemite Valley is California's greatest pride. It should be cared for by California in a manner reflecting glory upon the State.

There is no legitimate reason for placing the management of this marvel of natural scenic beauty in the hands of the Federal Government,

NAME ....

ADDRESS ....

Sign this, cut it out and mail it to the Yosemite Editor, Examiner Office, San Francisco

EL CAPITAN.

RECESSION PETITION. On December 18, 1904, the *San Francisco Examiner* first published a petition urging public expression against the recession of the Valley to the federal government. Later, the *Examiner* dramatically introduced its petition, containing several thousand names, in the course of debates in the California Legislature. (California State Library, Sacramento.)

DOES THIS BEAUTIFUL LAKE RUIN THIS BEAUTIFUL VALLEY

THE REAL FACTS ABOUT HETCH HETCHY

"THE REAL FACTS ABOUT HETCH HETCHY." On December 2, 1913, the day the
Senate voted on the Hetch Hetchy bill {the Raker bill} a special edition of the San
Francisco Examiner, propounding the benefits of the dam, was placed on every
Senator's desk. (*Hetch Hetchy* by Ray W. Taylor; San Francisco, 1926.)

179

MAY 2, 1908

TO THE PRESIDENT OF THE UNITED STATES AND THE GOVERNORS
OF THE STATES ASSEMBLED IN CONFERENCE.

Greeting: We, the undersigned, Directors and Officers of the Sierra Club, have been gratified to learn of the Conference of Governors called at the White House for the purpose of considering the Conservation of Natural Resources. Acting upon the conviction that this is a matter of utmost public concern, we wish to record, in connection with this Conference, our strong sense of the paramount value of scenic beauty among our natural resources. The moral and physical welfare of a nation is not dependent alone upon bread and water. Comprehending these primary necessities is the deeper need for recreation and that which satisfies also the esthetic sense. The establishment of gardens and parks is the immemorial expression of an ever present human desire. Our country has a wealth of natural beauty which is far beyond the power of human hands to create or restore, but not beyond their power to destroy. It is an untaxed heritage that may be had for the lifting one's eyes; whose influence upon the life of the nation, physically, morally, mentally, is inestimable, and whose preservation is the greatest service that one generation can render to another. Nor are we unmindful of the incalculable economic value of our scenic resources. Consular reports indicate that the stream of tourists attracted to Europe by its scenic, no less than its mural, beauty is worth $550,000,000 annually. America affords the newest, and in many respects the finest, of the world's natural pleasure-grounds. Tourists of wealth and fashion, as well as mountain climbers and lovers of outdoor life from all over the world are flocking in constantly increasing numbers to the Cordilleran system of mountains on our Western Coast. Even from a purely economic point of view it would be extremely unwise to administer our scenic resources in such a way that comparatively private gain results in universal public loss. In taking this stand we express the sentiment of our membership of more than a thousand persons, who have subscribed not only to the purposes of the Sierra Club, "to explore, enjoy, and render accessible the mountain regions of the Pacific Coast; to publish authentic information concerning them; to enlist the support and co-operation of the people and the Government in preserving the forests and other natural features of the Sierra Nevada Mountains," but who follow with intelligent and appreciative interest every effort to secure to our and coming generations the benefit of our scenic resources.

Respectfully yours,

JOHN MUIR,	GEO. DAVIDSON,
A. G. MCADIE,	W. R. DUDLEY,
J. N. LE CONTE,	WARREN OLNEY.
WM. E. COLBY,	E. T. PARSONS,
WM. F. BADÈ,	
	Board of Directors.

SIERRA CLUB LETTER to the President and Governors assembled for the Conference on Conservation of Natural Resources. Although Muir was excluded from the conference, the Sierra Club was hopeful that scenic resources might be considered along with commodity resources.

RESULT OF SPECIAL ELECTION ON HETCH-HETCHY QUESTION

To the Directors of the Sierra Club.

Gentlemen: We, the undersigned, judges of the special election of the Sierra Club on the Hetch-Hetchy question report as follows: That we have carefully canvassed the ballots cast at said election and find that a total of 759 ballots were regularly voted.

The two propositions printed on the ballot received the number of votes set opposite each respective proposition, as follows:—

1. I desire that the Hetch-Hetchy Valley shall remain intact and unaltered as a part of the Yosemite National Park and oppose its use as a reservoir for a water supply for San Francisco, **589** unless an impartial federal commission shall determine that it is absolutely necessary for such use.

2. I favor the use of Hetch-Hetchy Valley as a reservoir for a future water supply for San Francisco and I favor a present dedication by Congress **161** of the right to such use without further investigation.

In addition there were qualified ballots for Proposition No. 1 2
Qualified ballots for Proposition No. 2 4
Rejected ballots as invalid 3
                                    ———
                    Total as above   759

> J. H. Cutter,
> N. L. Taggard,
> Tallulah Le Conte,
> Mary Randall,
> William H. Gorrill,
> *Judges of Special Election.*

San Francisco, Cal., January 29, 1910.

A SPECIAL Sierra Club election on the Hetch Hetchy question, held January 29, 1910, settled the dispute over the club's stand.

SOCIETY FOR THE PRESERVATION OF NATIONAL PARKS

California Branch, 402 Mills Building, San Francisco

VIEWS OF JAMES BRYCE.

The Rt. Hon. James Bryce, until recently British Ambassador to the United States has for years been keenly interested in the preservation of Hetch Hetchy. In his address before the American Civic Association, on "National Parks—The Need of the Future," he said:

"The world seems likely to last a long, long time, and we ought to make provision for the future.

"The population of the world goes on constantly increasing and nowhere increasing so fast as in North America.

"A taste for natural beauty is increasing, and, as we hope, will go on increasing.

"*The places of scenic beauty do not increase, but, on the contrary, are in danger of being reduced in number and diminished in quantity,* and the danger is always increasing with the accumulation of wealth, owing to the desire of private persons to appropriate these places. There is no better service we can render to the masses of the people than to set about and preserve for them wide spaces of fine scenery for their delight.

"From these propositions I draw the conclusion that it is necessary to save what we have got, and to extend the policy which you have wisely adopted, by acquiring and preserving still further areas for the perpetual enjoyment of the people."

CIRCULAR NUMBER SEVEN

The Press of the whole country has heartily responded to the call for aid in this fight. If the good work is continued and all public spirited citizens urge their congressmen and the president to prevent this destructive measure from becoming a law the battle to save the people's parks will surely be won.

Every American citizen who believes that our National Parks are worth while is also urged to write or wire without delay to his Senators in Congress (see list on this page) and request them to put a stop to this commercial destruction which threatens our whole National Park system. Write also to the same effect to President Woodrow Wilson, White House, Washington, D. C.

VIEWS OF HON. JOHN W. NOBLE, FORMER SECRETARY OF THE INTERIOR.

Upon the policy of surrendering the Hetch Hetchy Valley and its surroundings to the use of the city of San Francisco for water supply, allow me to express to you my conviction that such appropriation should not be made.

Permit me also to recall that during the Harrison administration these reservations, in connection with Yosemite Park, were discussed and advanced, with the system then inaugurated of protecting our natural and wonderful scenery and our forests and other resources. It took labor and moral courage to withstand the fierce opposition of local interests to do this.

Among the most important reservations secured were these now asked for a city to be abandoned. It ought not to be done. The city has abundant water supply other than the reservoir to be constructed here, and it is not necessary to give this up.

There is a growing public opinion in favor of a strict *preservation* of what has already been redeemed for national reservations; and an appropriation of this, one of the chief works of John Muir's patriotic foresight, will be deemed a surrender of the national policy and a return to the idea that the nation has nothing that cannot be appropriated to other interests sufficiently persistent in assertion.

HOW TO HELP TO PRESERVE THE HETCH HETCHY VALLEY AND THE YOSEMITE PARK.

1. Write at once to President Woodrow Wilson, White House, Washington, D. C. Do it now. Ask him to oppose this Hetch Hetchy Bill.

2. Write also to the Senators from your State and get as many more as you can, addressing each at "Senate Chamber, Washington, D. C.," requesting them to oppose this Hetch Hetchy Bill.

3. Get as many of your friends as possible to write. Remember! every letter and every protest counts.

4. Interest your newspapers and get them to publish editorials and news items and send copies to your Senators and Representatives.

5. Send the names and addresses of any persons who would be interested in receiving this circular to "Society for the Preservation of National Parks, 402 Mills Building, San Francisco, Cal."

It is particularly urgent that you impress Senators from your State with the importance of *opposing* any bill granting the Hetch Hetchy Valley to San Francisco. See them personally if possible, wire them, write to them and send resolutions to them.

SAMPLE LETTER.

HON...

Senate Chamber, Washington, D. C.

SIR:—Our national parks are already too few in number. We are vitally interested in preserving intact those now existing. We earnestly protest against the destruction of any of the wonderful scenery of the Yosemite National Park and urge you to oppose any bill which will permit San Francisco to use Hetch Hetchy as a municipal water tank. Strengthen our park laws instead of allowing them to be overriden.   Very truly,

....

(Write letters similar to the foregoing in your own language and in accordance with your own ideas).

Clubs which wish to aid us pass resolutions somewhat as follows:

WHEREAS: The Hetch Hetchy Valley is one of the grandest and most important features of the great Yosemite National Park belonging to the ninety millions of people composing the American public;

WHEREAS: This valley is threatened with destruction by those seeking a water supply for San Francisco and the use of the park by the public would thereby be seriously restricted;

WHEREAS: The precedent thus established would destroy the integrity of our whole national park system;

WHEREAS: The need for great public playgrounds is becoming vastly greater instead of diminishing;

WHEREAS: Eminent engineers report that this proposed invasion of a national wonderland is wholly unnecessary and that San Francisco can get an abundance of pure water elsewhere;

Now Therefore be it Resolved: That we are earnestly opposed to such a needless local use of a priceless national possession in which the entire citizenship is interested, and we petition the President and urge all Senators and Representatives to defeat any bill which proposes to confirm any such invasion; and that a copy of this resolution be sent to the President and our Representatives in Congress.

List of Senators. Address each Senate Chamber, Washington, D. C.

EDITORS are respectfully requested to write brief editorials and news items informing the public and calling on them to write to their Congressmen and Senators and protest.

CLUBS should send copies of resolutions they may adopt to President Wilson, and the Senators and Representatives from their State.

FUNDS ARE NEEDED to carry on this fight. Those who would like to render pecuniary assistance may send their contributions to Mrs. R. V. Colby, Treasurer of The Society for the Preservation of National Parks, 402 Mills Building, San Francisco, Cal.

Kindly read carefully, act promptly, and hand this pamphlet to a friend in order that it may keep working.

CIRCULAR NUMBER SEVEN, "Society for the Preservation of National Parks." As a result of William Colby's persuading Muir to organize a second conservation group to take the initiative in the Hetch Hetchy campaign, several thousand circulars were distributed to newspaper editors, various organizations, and women's clubs throughout the country.

Sweeping Back the Flood

"Sweeping Back the Flood." Together with all the city's newspapers, the *San Francisco Call* was a persistent advocate of the Hetch Hetchy water supply and attacked any group that opposed this use. (Bancroft Library, University of California, Berkeley.)

THE FOLLOWING TELEGRAM JUST RECEIVED

Sierra Club,   Harrisburg, Pa., February 19, 1911.
   Mills Building, San Francisco, Cal.

Urgent effort on Congress is immediately necessary to continue the existing protection to Niagara Falls. The power companies there located are seeking additional water to increase their present income by $4,000,000 yearly. United States Army Engineers report that the Falls are now unquestionably seriously injured, and that additional diversion would be disasterous. Please arouse the newspapers, also telegraph congressmen favoring the passage of Senate Joint Resolution No. 133.
                              J. HORACE McFARLAND, Pres. American Civic Assn.

We are sending out copy of the above telegram to the members of the Sierra Club and others interested, as it is self-explanatory. The directors urge every member to comply therewith, and to follow their telegrams with letters, or at least write; also interest as many more as possible to do the same, in order that the greatest possible pressure may be brought upon Congress to prevent this imminent destruction of one of the world's most magnificent wonders.
                              BOARD OF DIRECTORS OF SIERRA CLUB,
                                          Per Wm. E. Colby, Secretary.

MEMBERS OF CONGRESS FROM CALIFORNIA.

House of Representatives		Senate Chamber
Hon. W. F. Englebright	Hon. Duncan McKinlay	Hon. Frank P. Flint
" E. A. Hayes	" Jas. McLachlan	" Geo. C. Perkins
" Julius Kahn	" Jas. C. Needham	
" Joseph R. Knowland	" S. C. Smith	*Washington, D. C.*

To the Members of the Sierra Club and all who are interested:

Please write to your Congressmen *at once* urging them to support the following important legislation:

1. *The Creation of a Bureau of National Parks,* for the purpose of concentrating the "supervision, management and control of the several national parks and national monuments, etc." A general scheme of improvement of the parks with the aid of expert assistance is contemplated. This bill will accomplish much for the welfare of all of our national parks.

2. *The addition of the Kings-Kern High Sierra region to the existing Sequoia National Park.*—This region contains the Kings and Kern River Cañons, Tehipite and Paradise Valleys, Golden Trout Creek, and other important scenic points of interest that should be more carefully protected.

This is the short session of Congress and immediate action is imperative. Do your share in the work of the Club, and write to other Congressmen you can influence, and get others to write.   BOARD OF DIRECTORS OF SIERRA CLUB.
                                          Per Wm. E. Colby, *Secretary.*

MEMBERS OF CONGRESS FROM CALIFORNIA.

House of Representatives		Senate Chamber
Hon. W. F. Englebright	Hon. Duncan McKinlay	Hon. Frank P. Flint
" E. A. Hayes	" Jas. McLachlan	" Geo. C. Perkins
" Julius Kahn	" Jas. C. Needham	
" Joseph R. Knowland	" S. C. Smith	*Washington, D. C.*

HELP TO PREPARE YOSEMITE VALLEY FOR 1915

To the Members of the Sierra Club and their Friends:

Here is an opportunity for the members of the Club to aid in its work. The proximity of Yosemite Valley was one of the effective arguments used in securing the 1915 Panama-Pacific Exposition for San Francisco. Yosemite Valley is of world-wide interest and thousands of Exposition visitors will wish to see this famous attraction. A great many improvements are needed to properly prepare the Valley for these crowds. Yellowstone Park has recently had over $1,000,000 spent on a splendid road system and other necessary improvements. The Yosemite Park needs the same expenditure and Congress should appropriate $250,000 each year for the next four years so that the Valley and vicinity may be ready for 1915. It should not be forgotten that improvements made therefrom would remain a permanent asset of the nation. Congress has made no general appropriation for the Exposition and can well afford to help California to prepare for the Exposition in this way. The State Legislature at the request of the Club passed a joint resolution asking Congress for this appropriation.

We count on your influence to aid in this effort to secure what Yosemite and the State are entitled to. Please write a brief letter without delay to each of the Congressmen from California named below, and to other Congressmen you can influence, asking that they do all they can to secure such an appropriation; and get as many of your friends as possible to do the same. Every letter counts. Also get the substance of this in your local paper if possible.

Thanking you for your co-operation in this matter, we remain.
                              Very sincerely yours,
                              BOARD OF DIRECTORS OF SIERRA CLUB,
                                          Per Wm. E. Colby, *Secretary.*

MEMBERS IN CONGRESS FROM CALIFORNIA.

Hon. Geo. C. Perkins.	Hon. E. A. Hayes.	Hon. J. C. Needham.
Hon. John D. Works.	Hon. Julius Kahn.	Hon. John E. Raker.
Senate Chamber,	Hon. Wm. Kent.	Hon. S. C. Smith.
Washington, D. C.	Hon. Jos. R. Knowland.	Hon. Wm. D. Stephens.

House of Representatives,
Washington, D. C.

Campaign postcards. Typical of cards sent out by the Sierra Club whenever a preservation issue demanded action by members.

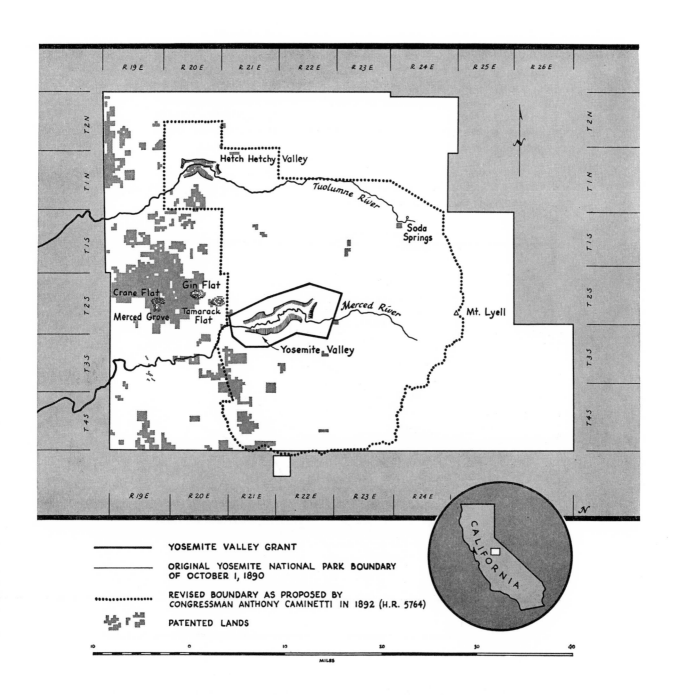

PROPOSED REDUCTION OF YOSEMITE

NATIONAL PARK, 1892

1 · HAYSHED (1883)
2 · SLAUGHTER HOUSE (1883)
3 · LEIDIG'S HOTEL (DESTROYED IN 1888)
4 · CHAPEL (1886)
5 · GEORGE FISKE'S STUDIO AND RESIDENCE (1886)
6 · GALEN CLARK'S RESIDENCE
7 · LOWER HOUSE (BLACK'S HOTEL, DESTROYED IN 1888; COOK, MANAGER)
8 · COFFMAN AND KENNEY STABLES (1886)
9 · COSMOPOLITAN BOARD WALK (1886)

10 · MRS. GLYNN'S POND
11 · COSMOPOLITAN SALOON
12 · SENTINEL HOTEL
13 · SINNING COTTAGE
14 · HUTCHINGS CABIN
15 · SAW MILL
16 · CEMETERY
17 · HARRIS CAMP GROUNDS SITE OF PRESENT AHWAHN
18 · STONEMAN HOUSE (1887 - 1896)
19 · J. C. LAMON ORCHARD

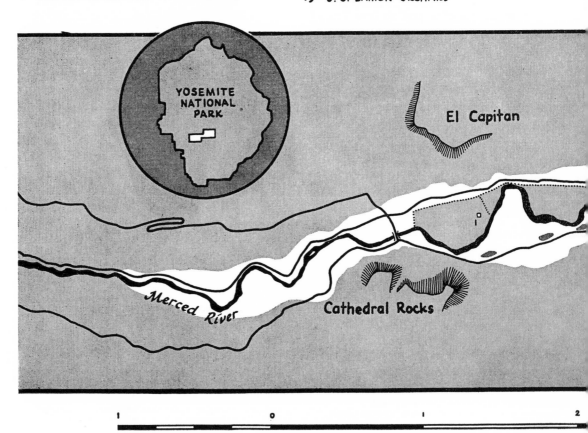

YOSEMITE
NATIONAL
PARK

El Capitan

Merced River

Cathedral Rocks

1   0   1   2

CULTIVATED FIELDS, FENCES, AND AREAS

YOSEMITE VALLEY,

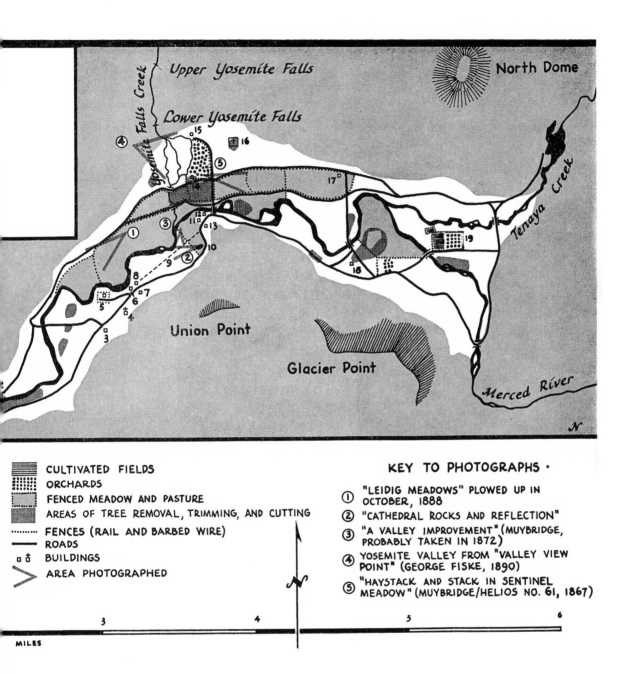

Upper Yosemite Falls

North Dome

Lower Yosemite Falls

Yosemite Falls Creek

Tenaya Creek

15

16

④

⑤

17

14

12
11   13

③

①

②   10

9

8

7

6

5

4

3

19

18

Union Point

Glacier Point

Merced River

N

CULTIVATED FIELDS
ORCHARDS
FENCED MEADOW AND PASTURE
AREAS OF TREE REMOVAL, TRIMMING, AND CUTTING
FENCES (RAIL AND BARBED WIRE)
ROADS
BUILDINGS
AREA PHOTOGRAPHED

KEY TO PHOTOGRAPHS ·

① "LEIDIG MEADOWS" PLOWED UP IN OCTOBER, 1888
② "CATHEDRAL ROCKS AND REFLECTION"
③ "A VALLEY IMPROVEMENT" (MUYBRIDGE, PROBABLY TAKEN IN 1872)
④ YOSEMITE VALLEY FROM "VALLEY VIEW POINT" (GEORGE FISKE, 1890)
⑤ "HAYSTACK AND STACK IN SENTINEL MEADOW" (MUYBRIDGE/HELIOS NO. 61, 1867)

N

3   4   5   6

MILES

OF EXCESSIVE LANDSCAPE MANAGEMENT,

1883-1890

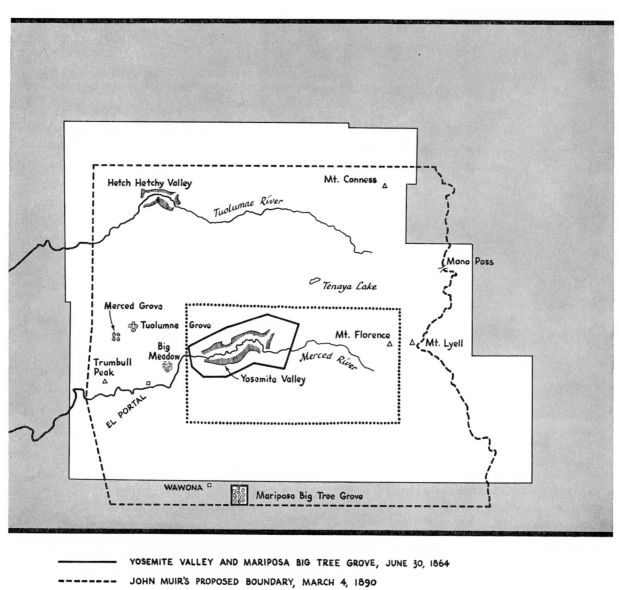

YOSEMITE VALLEY AND MARIPOSA BIG TREE GROVE, JUNE 30, 1864
JOHN MUIR'S PROPOSED BOUNDARY, MARCH 4, 1890
WILLIAM VANDEVER'S PROPOSED BOUNDARY, MARCH 18, 1890 (H.R. 8350)
BOUNDARY ESTABLISHED BY FEDERAL STATUTE, OCTOBER 1, 1890

A CENTURY OF BOUNDARY PROPOSALS AND

NATIONAL PARK

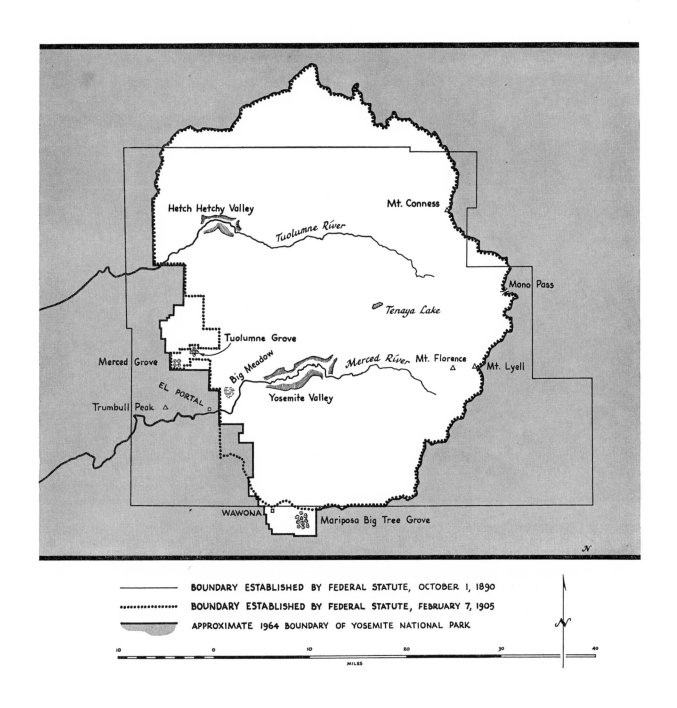

Map legend:

——————— BOUNDARY ESTABLISHED BY FEDERAL STATUTE, OCTOBER 1, 1890

••••••••••••••••• BOUNDARY ESTABLISHED BY FEDERAL STATUTE, FEBRUARY 7, 1905

APPROXIMATE 1964 BOUNDARY OF YOSEMITE NATIONAL PARK

```
10          0          10          20          30          40
                              MILES
```

CHANGES, YOSEMITE VALLEY GRANT AND

1864-1964)

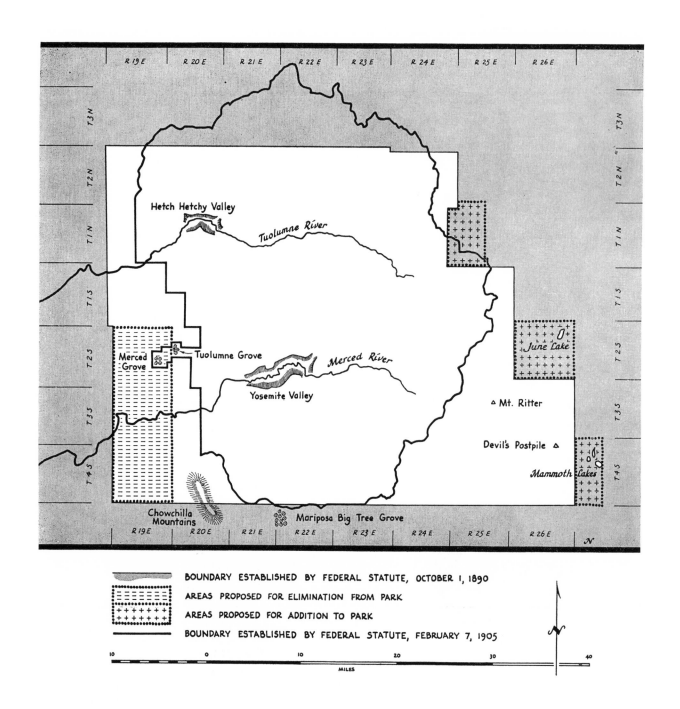

R 19 E | R 20 E | R 21 E | R 22 E | R 23 E | R 24 E | R 25 E | R 26 E

Hetch Hetchy Valley

Tuolumne River

Merced Grove

Tuolumne Grove

Merced River

Yosemite Valley

△ Mt. Ritter

Devil's Postpile △

June Lake

Mammoth Lakes

Chowchilla Mountains

Mariposa Big Tree Grove

BOUNDARY ESTABLISHED BY FEDERAL STATUTE, OCTOBER 1, 1890

AREAS PROPOSED FOR ELIMINATION FROM PARK

AREAS PROPOSED FOR ADDITION TO PARK

BOUNDARY ESTABLISHED BY FEDERAL STATUTE, FEBRUARY 7, 1905

10   0   10   20   30   40
MILES

SIERRA CLUB BOUNDARY PROPOSALS TO
YOSEMITE PARK COMMISSION, 1904

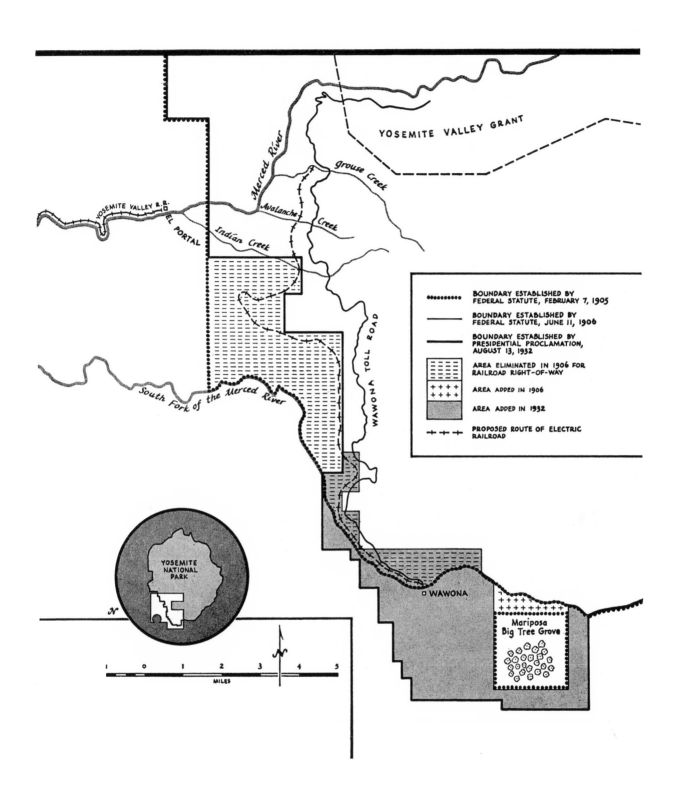

YOSEMITE VALLEY GRANT

YOSEMITE VALLEY R.R.

EL PORTAL

Merced River

Grouse Creek

Avalanche Creek

Indian Creek

South Fork of the Merced River

WAWONA TOLL ROAD

□ WAWONA

Mariposa
Big Tree Grove

BOUNDARY ESTABLISHED BY
FEDERAL STATUTE, FEBRUARY 7, 1905

BOUNDARY ESTABLISHED BY
FEDERAL STATUTE, JUNE 11, 1906

BOUNDARY ESTABLISHED BY
PRESIDENTIAL PROCLAMATION,
AUGUST 13, 1932

AREA ELIMINATED IN 1906 FOR
RAILROAD RIGHT-OF-WAY

AREA ADDED IN 1906

AREA ADDED IN 1932

PROPOSED ROUTE OF ELECTRIC
RAILROAD

YOSEMITE
NATIONAL
PARK

N

1   0   1   2   3   4   5
MILES

N

BOUNDARY CHANGES IN THE
SOUTHWEST CORNER OF THE PARK

SOURCES OF WATER SUPPLY
FOR SAN FRANCISCO, 1912

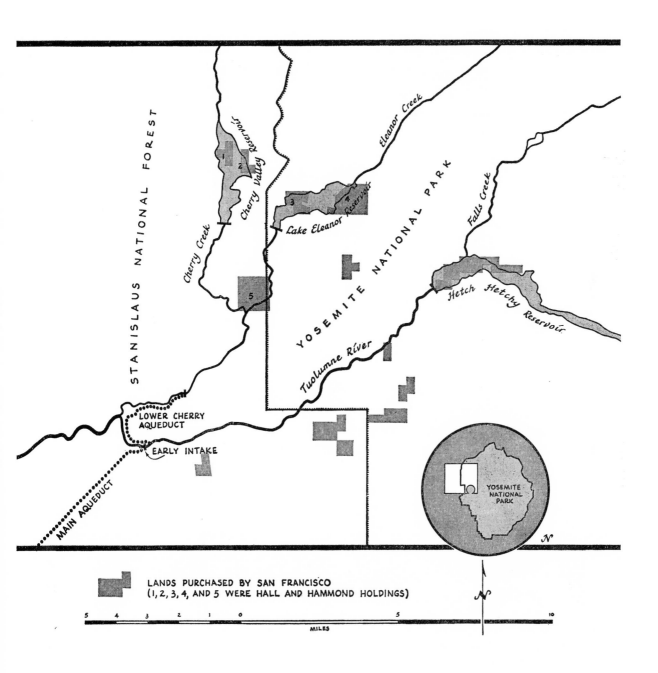

RELATIVE POSITIONS OF HETCH HETCHY,
LAKE ELEANOR, AND CHERRY CREEK RESERVOIRS

Original Sierra Club seal
(1892–1894).

Sierra Club seal of today.

Sierra Club seal as
adapted for publication.

BIBLIOGRAPHICAL NOTE

A simple listing of significant titles in the history of American conservation would run to perhaps half the length of this book. An annotated bibliography would surely run much longer, and a comprehensive guide to such materials would be a separate book in its own right. The scholar who invades this subject area soon becomes aware of the vast amount of primary documents through which he must sift; this led me to undertake a corollary project to *John Muir and the Sierra Club* with the working title, "Scenic Resources and Conservation: A Guide to the Literature." When completed, I hope that this guide, patterned after Paul Wasserman's *Information for Administrators* (Ithaca, N. Y., 1956) or J. Richard Blanchard's and Harald Ostvold's *The Literature of Agricultural Research* (Berkeley and Los Angeles, 1958), may open new insights into the field of resource management for the policy-maker and the conservation historian.

The present "Bibliographical Note" is a very modest reference to a few of the principal sources used in writing this book. These sources comprise primarily letters, pamphlets, books, and articles by the people who participated in the events. Official government publications, both executive and legislative, were essential in establishing the authenticity of those activities sketchily or obliquely referred to in personal correspondence. Newspapers form a special source for the California Legislature investigation of the Yosemite Commissioners and for the details of recession of the Valley because of the peculiar role played by the *San Francisco Examiner* in both these events.

The Sierra Club Archives were the major source for the Hetch Hetchy chapters, but were less important for the earlier chapters since all records of the Club were destroyed in the earthquake and fire of 1906. Correspondence of Secretary Colby and other officers of the Club with preservationists in similar organizations, the President and his cabinet officers, and congressmen form the main bulk of the Club Archives. There are comparatively few Muir letters; these are to be found principally in three manuscript collections, *Muir Papers* at the American Academy of Arts and Letters (New York) and the Bancroft Library, University of California (Berkeley) and in the *Robert Underwood Johnson Papers,* also Bancroft Library. Some of the most important letters have been published, in full or in part, by William F. Badè, *The Life and Letters of John Muir* (2 vols.; Boston, 1923) and by the Club in "The Creation of Yosemite National Park," *SCB* (October, 1944), 49–60. Available in the Club Archives are numerous copies of campaign literature issued by the Club, the Society for the Preservation of National Parks, and the National Committee for the Pres-

195

ervation of Yosemite National Park. Many of these may be found in other manuscript sources, too, particularly the *J. Horace McFarland Papers,* Pennsylvania Historical and Museum Commission, Harrisburg; the *Francis P. Farquhar* and *R. U. Johnson Papers,* Bancroft Library, University of California; and some of the Record Groups at the National Archives listed below. Copies of the Sierra Club briefs, various statements prepared as memorials to Congress or the President, many newspaper clippings, and a few maps complete sources in the Club Archives.

The *Sierra Club Bulletins* are the major printed source for the history of the Club, particularly the summary by charter member Joseph N. LeConte, "The Sierra Club," *SCB* (January 1917), 135–145. More valuable than the feature articles, for the purposes of this story, are such regular special columns as the "Secretary's Report," "Notes and Correspondence," "Report of the Outing Committee," and, in the earliest numbers, "Proceedings of the Sierra Club," and William Dudley's "Forestry Notes." Other important printed Sierra Club sources are its *Circulars,* an unnumbered and a numbered series; miscellaneous publications, such as the late 1890 maps of the central Sierra preceding the federal topographic sheets; and Minutes of the Board of Directors after April 1906, which are frustratingly concise.

Aside from the Sierra Club Archives, the two most important sources of manuscript material are the Bancroft Library and the National Archives. At Bancroft, the *R. U. Johnson Papers,* a major repository of letters reporting the activities of the preservationists and describing the break between the utilitarian conservationists and the "nature lovers," was the basis for much of this book, but other important papers used were: *Francis P. Farquhar Papers,* especially strong on campaign literature and documents related to the national parks; *William E. Colby Papers,* which contain copies of early Muir letters related to the Club; *Marsden Manson Correspondence and Papers; Governor Pardee Papers; John Muir Papers;* and the *Sierra Club Records,* which mostly post-date the period of this book.

No book or article with any pretense to scholarship in this subject could be written without a visit to the National Archives and Records Service, Washington, D.C. Here a vast array of official and unofficial documents, memoranda, letters, and brochures are available of which the most valuable for this book are: Record Group no. 79, Records of the National Park Service, including the manuscript reports of the military Acting Superintendents and their agents many years before the establishment of the Service in 1916; Record Group no. 48, Records of the Department of Interior, Correspondence of the Office of the Secretary; Record Group no. 49, Records of the General Land Office; and Record Group no. 95, Records of U.S. Forest Service with its wealth of Hetch Hetchy items clearly reflecting the intense interest of its chief in the controversy.

A number of other, widely scattered, manuscript sources were utilized, somewhat tangentially: *John P. Irish Papers,* Stanford University; *Walter L. Huber Papers,* Water Resources Center Archives, University of California; *Theodore P. Lukens Papers,* Huntington Library (San Marino); *Enos Mills Collection,* Western History Division, Denver Public Library; *Appalachian Mountain Club Historical Records* (Boston); *J. Horace McFarland Papers* mentioned earlier; and at the Manuscripts Division, Library of Congress, the *Frederick Law Olmsted Papers, Theodore Roosevelt Papers,* and *Gifford Pinchot Pa-*

pers. Sources not used for this book, but certainly essential for the *definitive* study of Hetch Hetchy (which this account does not pretend to be) are listed by Samuel P. Hays and Roderick Nash in their studies given below.

Letters and other unpublished materials not intended for distribution or general accessibility, frequently reveal the participants' motives more clearly than do printed sources. Nevertheless, printed materials are also invaluable; these are extensive and published in a wide range of nineteenth- and twentieth-century journals, such as *American Forestry, American Journal of Science and Arts, American Naturalist, Appalachia, Atlantic Monthly, Century Magazine, Collier's Weekly; Forest and Stream, Forester, Harper's Monthly, Independent, Out West, Outlook, Overland Monthly, Scribner's Monthly, Sunset,* and *World's Work.*

Monographs by participants are also essential sources—the works of John Muir, for example, and especially *The Yosemite* (New York, 1912). A nearly complete bibliography of the naturalist's writings may be found in Jennie Elliot Doran, "A Bibliography of John Muir," *SCB* (January, 1916), 41–54, and in C. B. Bradley, "A Reference List of John Muir's Newspaper Articles," *SCB* (January, 1916), 55–59. Robert Underwood Johnson's autobiography, *Remembered Yesterdays* (Boston, 1923), is a disappointing source, partly because it was written many years after the Yosemite events and partly because Johnson tends to exaggerate the importance of his role while failing to give sufficient background data. Highly important, although often disappointing also, are strongly biased works, no matter which side of the controversy they support, such as M. M. O'Shaughnessy's *Hetch Hetchy: Its Origin and History* (San Francisco, 1934). Still other reports by participants, such as Frederick Law Olmsted's "lost" document prepared for the California Legislature, "The Yosemite Valley and the Mariposa Big Tree Grove," *Landscape Architecture* (October, 1952), 12–25, and his *Governmental Preservation of Natural Scenery* (Brookline, Mass., 1891), are excellent statements of principles that can and should be currently applied.

The numerous official executive and legislative documents defy general characterization in a note as brief as this one. Many issues of the *Congressional Globe* and *Congressional Record* were consulted. Congressional committee hearings are essential sources for the Hetch Hetchy chapters; complete listings of these may be found in the Nash dissertation listed below and in my "The History of the Sierra Club," unpublished Master's thesis, University of California, Berkeley, 1957. In addition to various House and Senate reports—particularly those accompanying hearings—there are special reports useful for background and as verification of materials in manuscript sources, such as *Report of the Yosemite Park Commission,* Senate Document no. 34, 58th. Congress, 3rd Session (Washington, D.C., 1904) and *Reservation of Certain Lands in California,* Senate Document no. 48, 55th. Congress, 3rd Session (Washington, D.C., 1898). The most valuable executive documents are the *Annual Reports* of the Interior Department and the Acting Superintendents of Yosemite National Park; also some special reports such as U.S. Department of the Interior, *Proceedings Before the Secretary of the Interior in Re Use of Hetch Hetchy Reservoir Site in the Yosemite National Park by the City of San Francisco* (Washington, D.C., 1910) and the U.S. Advisory Board of Army Engineers, *Hetch Hetchy Valley Report . . . to the Secretary of the Interior on Investigations Relative to Sources of Water Supply for San Francisco and Bay*

Communities (Washington, D.C., 1913). Among the many California Assembly and Senate documents used none proved more interesting than the Legislative investigation of the State Commissioners in the official proceedings. The Commissioners' archival material is unfortunately most incomplete—particularly the all-important "Letter Books." However, some of the *Minute Books* and reports of officers are helpful in establishing dates and an outline of activities. Complete sets of the Commissioners' *Biennial Reports* are difficult to find in libraries; however, Legislative sets of the reports may be found in the *Appendices to the Journals of the Senate and Assembly.* Municipal reports used included legal briefs and engineering documents prepared by city attorneys Franklin K. Lane and Percy V. Long and city engineers C. E. Grunsky, Marsden Manson, and M. M. O'Shaughnessy, but the most important document is John R. Freeman, *The Hetch Hetchy Water Supply for San Francisco* (San Francisco, 1912).

Many excellent secondary sources aided my understanding of the background for this book. One of the most important of these is George E. Mowry, *The Era of Theodore Roosevelt and the Birth of Modern America, 1900–1912* (New York, 1962). The same author has also written *California Progressives* (Berkeley and Los Angeles, 1951) which should be compared with Carey McWilliams, *California; the Great Exception* (New York, 1949). The latter two works touch on Southern Pacific domination in California politics; other useful studies on the railroad are: Stuart Daggett, *Chapters on the History of the Southern Pacific* (New York, 1922); Oscar Lewis, *The Big Four; The Story of Huntington, Stanford, Hopkins, and Crocker, and of the Central Pacific* (New York, 1938); and the sympathetic Neill C. Wilson and Frank J. Taylor, *Southern Pacific: The Roaring Story of a Fighting Railroad* (New York, 1952).

Two books by John Ise are indispensable in understanding resource policy concerning forests and national parks: *The United States Forest Policy* (New Haven, 1924) and *Our National Park Policy; a Critical History* (Baltimore, 1961). For California, a somewhat comparable study is C. Raymond Clar, *California Government and Forestry from Spanish Days until the Creation of the Department of Natural Resources in 1927* (Sacramento, 1959).

The best general discussion of conservation in the Progressive Era with emphasis on the dispute between the utilitarians and preservationists is Samuel P. Hays, *Conservation and the Gospel of Efficiency; the Progressive Movement, 1890–1920* (Cambridge, Mass., 1959). Approximately the same time span from more local viewpoints is covered by Elmo Richardson, *The Politics of Conservation, Crusades and Controversies, 1897–1913* (Berkeley and Los Angeles, 1962). Less useful, but nevertheless important are: Richard G. Lillard, *The Great Forest* (New York, 1947), Judson King, *The Conservation Fight from Theodore Roosevelt to the Tennessee Valley Authority* (Washington, D.C., 1959), and James B. Trefethen, *Crusade for Wildlife: Highlights in Conservation Progress* (Harrisburg, Pa., 1961). Augmenting these studies are some excellent biographies, such as Linnie Marsh Wolfe, *Son of the Wilderness; the Life of John Muir* (New York, 1945), indispensable because the author had complete access to the *Muir Papers;* Robert Shankland, *Steve Mather of the National Parks* (New York, 1951); and Shirley Sargent, *Galen Clark, Yosemite Guardian* (San Francisco, 1964).

Yosemite is rich in literature as testified by two bibliographies: U.S. National Park Service, *A Bibliography of National Parks and Monuments West of the Mississippi River* (2 vols.; Berkeley, 1941), of which a major section is devoted to Yosemite history; and the well annotated Francis P. Farquhar, *Yosemite, the Big Trees and the High Sierra; a Selective Bibliography* (Berkeley and Los Angeles, 1948). Of all this material, the following two secondary accounts relate the general history of Yosemite: Carl P. Russell, *One Hundred Years in Yosemite: The Story of a Great Park and Its Friends* (Berkeley and Los Angeles, 1947) and Hans Huth, "Yosemite: The Story of an Idea," *SCB* (March, 1948), 47–78.

The article by Huth was forerunner of a landmark work on the American's conception of nature which he published nine years later, *Nature and the American; Three Centuries of Changing Attitudes* (Berkeley and Los Angeles, 1957). This theme has been elaborated upon by some younger scholars in recent dissertations (see below), but two other people have also contributed to the published record. The first to recognize the importance of Yosemite in the park idea was Albert Matthews, "The Word Park in the United States," *Publications of the Colonial Society of Massachusetts,* Transactions, 1902–1904, VIII (Boston, 1906); the most recent statement is Carl P. Russell, "Birth of the National Park Idea," in *Yosemite, Saga of a Century, 1864–1964* (Oakhurst, Calif, 1964). Among published accounts on Hetch Hetchy, is Ray W. Taylor, *Hetch Hetchy; the Story of San Francisco's Struggle to Provide a Water Supply for Her Future Needs* (San Francisco, 1926), an uncritical study; and a short but scholarly article by Elmo Richardson, "The Struggle for the Valley: California's Hetch Hetchy Controversy, 1905–1913," *California Historical Society Quarterly* (September, 1959), 249–258.

Not to be overlooked are the many unpublished dissertations. Two general studies are: Ralph M. Van Brocklin, "The Movement for the Conservation of Natural Resources in the United States Before 1901," Ph.D., University of Michigan, 1952; and Harold T. Pinckett, "Gifford Pinchot and the Early Conservation Movement in the United States," Ph.D., American University, 1953. An unusually fine local study is Lawrence Rakestraw, "A History of Forest Conservation in the Pacific Northwest, 1891–1913," Ph.D., University of Washington, 1955. John Muir and his contribution to wilderness preservation have been dealt with in Edith J. Hadley, "John Muir's Views of Nature and Their Consequences," Ph.D., University of Wisconsin, 1956, and, more recently, in Daniel B. Weber, "John Muir: The Function of Wilderness in an Individual Society," Ph.D., University of Minnesota, 1964. Another dissertation that relates Muir (and others) to a history of American thought (in the mold of Hans Huth) is the outstanding study by Roderick W. Nash, "Wilderness and the American Mind," Ph.D., University of Wisconsin, 1965. His chapter on Hetch Hetchy supplements my account in discussing the Congressional debates. (Nash has also published the best brief description of "The American Wilderness in Historical Perspective," *Forest History,* Winter, 1963, 2–13.) Finally, two more specialized studies help the historian to understand wilderness policy as applied by state and federal government: James P. Gilligan, "The Development of Policy and Administration of Forest Service Primitive and Wilderness Areas in the Western United States," Ph.D., University of Michigan, 1953; and Roger C. Thompson, "The Doctrine of Wilderness: A Study of the Policy and Politics of the Adirondack Preserve-Park," Ph.D., College of Forestry, University of New York, Syracuse, 1962.

For the Yosemite, several unpublished theses exist. The best of these, and

199

really an excellent discussion of the administrative aspects of Hetch Hetchy, is Florence R. Monroy, "Water and Power in San Francisco Since 1900; A Study in Municipal Government," M.A., University of California, 1944. Also good for its chapter on Olmsted's Yosemite role is Diane K. McGuire, "Frederick Law Olmsted in California; An Analysis of His Contributions to Landscape Architecture and City Planning," M.S., University of California, 1954. Much less useful because they are insufficiently documented are Edith G. Kettlewell, "Yosemite: The Discovery of Yosemite Valley and the Creation and Realignment of Yosemite National Park," M.A., University of California, 1930; and Suzette Dornberger, "The Struggle for Hetch Hetchy, 1900–1913," M.A., University of California, 1935.

If this "bibliographical note" seems insufficient, I can only comment that the literature is immense and that the note in the back of the Samuel P. Hays volume and the bibliographies in some of the dissertations above listed will open additional doors into this rich area of investigation.

INDEX

Numbers followed by an asterisk refer to plates

ACKNOWLEDGMENTS

Numerals refer to half-tone plates

1 *Sierra Club Bulletin,* Vol. 10;

2 Ansel Adams;

3 and 4 *Illustrated History of the University of California* by William C. Jones (Berkeley, 1901);

5 *Sierra Club Handbook;*

6 *Sierra Club Bulletin,* Vol. 25;

7 *Illustrated History of the University of California* by William C. Jones;

8 Archives, Stanford University Library;

9, 10 and 11 California Historical Society, San Francisco;

12 Bancroft Library, University of California, Berkeley;

13 and 14 California Historical Society, San Francisco;

15 Elliott McAllister, Jr., San Francisco;

16 *Flora of the Santa Cruz Mountains of California: A Manual of the Vascular Plants* by John Hunter (Stanford University Press);

17 Sutters Fort, Sacramento, California State Park System;

18 California State Library, Sacramento (portrait by William Shew);

19 California Historical Society, San Francisco;

20 Hans Huth, Carmel, California;

21 California Historical Society, San Francisco;

22 National Park Service, Yosemite;

23 California State Library; Sacramento;

24 California Historical Society; San Francisco;

25 Sierra Club Archives;

26 *Sierra Club Bulletin,* Vol. 29;

27 Richard Pitman, Oakland, California (Muybridge/Helios no. 61);

28 William Hood, Los Angeles, California (no. 148–11);

29 and 30 Richard Pitman, Oakland (Muybridge no. 1506 and 1507);

31 Bancroft Library, University of California, Berkeley;

32 William Hood, Los Angeles, California;

33, 34 and 35 *Century Magazine,* Vol. 40;

36 Ventura Pioneer Museum and County Historical Society, Ventura, California;

37 and 38 National Park Service, Yosemite;

39 California State Library, Sacramento (Print by Paul Frenzeny from *Harper's Weekly,* Nov. 30, 1878);

40 California State Library, Sacramento;

41 and 42 National Park Service, Yosemite;

43 William E. Colby, Big Sur, California;

44 and 45 Ansel Adams;

46 *Sierra Club Handbook;*

47 California State Library, Sacramento;

48 *Logging Operations in the Yosemite National Park* by Willard G. Van Name (1926)

49 Hank Johnston, Long Beach, California;

50 California Historical Society, San Francisco;

51 California State Library, Sacramento;

52 Bancroft Library, University of California, Berkeley;

53 *Hetch Hetchy* by Ray W. Taylor (San Francisco, 1926);

54 Bancroft Library, University of California, Berkeley;

55 *Hetch Hetchy* by Ray W. Taylor (San Francisco, 1926);

56 National Park Service, Yosemite;

57 Sierra Club Archives;

58 National Park Service, Yosemite;

59 *Remembered Yesterdays* by Robert U. Johnson (Boston, 1923); 1923);

60 Modern Poetry Collection, University of Chicago;

61 Sierra Club Archives;

62 Mrs. William F. Badè, San Diego, California;

63 and 64 Bancroft Library, University of California, Berkeley;

APPENDIX

All maps were drawn by Keith Newsom. Unless otherwise indicated, the remaining material is from the Sierra Club Archives.

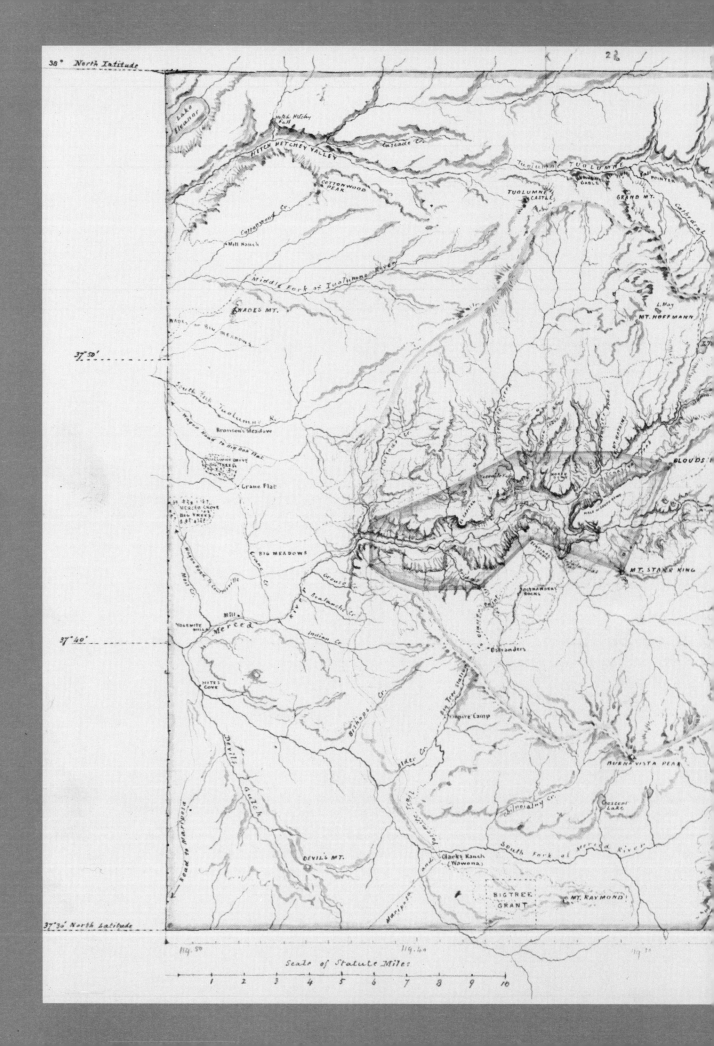